D0833867

27 JAN 2009

12/09
6/12

Please renew/return this item by the last date shown.

So that your telephone call is charged at local rate, please call the numbers as set out below:

	From Area codes 01923 or 020:	From the rest of Herts:
Renewals:	01923 471373	01438 737373
Enquiries:	01923 471333	01438 737333
Textphone:	01923 471599	01438 737599

L32   www.hertsdirect.org/librarycatalogue

Alport

Alport

A study in loyalty

Mark Garnett

© Mark Garnett, 1999
Foreword © Kenneth Clarke, 1999

First published in 1999 by Acumen

Acumen Publishing Limited
17 Fairfax Road
Teddington
TW11 9DJ

ISBN: 1-902683-00-5

British Library Cataloguing-in-Publication Data
A catalogue record for this book is available
from the British Library.

Designed and typeset in Bembo
by Kate Williams, Abergavenny.
Printed and bound by Biddles Ltd., Guildford and King's Lynn.

For Carole, Hattie and Mary

"It goes back to your old point, with which I heartily agree,
that it is character that really matters"
Lord Alport to Rab Butler, 31 October 1961

Contents

Acknowledgements

Many people have helped with the writing of this book, and acknowledging their kindness is a great source of pleasure. The following were kind enough to reply to my questions, either in interviews or in writing: Edward and Anne Alport; Joyce Brooks; Lady Butler; Lord Callaghan; Lord Carr; Mary Fairhead; Roger Gale MP; Lord Harris of High Cross; Lord Holderness (Richard Wood); the late Sir David Hunt; Lady Macleod; Conor Cruise O'Brien; Pamela Powell; Lord Renton; Baroness Thatcher; and the late Sir Patrick Wall.

Throughout the research for this book librarians were extremely helpful. In particular I would like to express my thanks to Jill Davidson at the Bodleian, Rita Hills at Essex County Newspapers, and John Smith at Trinity College, Cambridge. At times Nigel Cochrane and Robert Butler must have cursed the fact that Lord Alport decided to lodge his papers at the Albert Sloman Library, University of Essex, before appointing an official biographer; nevertheless they tolerated my repeated intrusions with remarkable good humour, and given his other tasks I am amazed at the skill with which Robert Butler has managed to catalogue Lord Alport's papers.

Chapters (or parts of chapters) were read by Roger Barltrop, Lord Denham; Sir Charles Fletcher-Cooke; my parents, Allan and Betty Garnett; Brian Harrison; Chris Holmes; Hattie Llewellyn-Davies; Alexandra and Ezio Rocca; John and Monica Royle; Sir David Scott; Carole and Ian Taylor; and Charles Wilson. Ian Gilmour and Rob Shepherd submitted themselves to the whole manuscript. In addition to reading the book as it progressed, my editor Steven Gerrard deployed his usual happy mixture of threat and encouragement to prevent me from subjecting the finished product to endless revision. I am most grateful for the numerous suggestions that resulted from the careful reading which the book received from all of the above; any errors of fact or judgement in the text are my responsibility.

I have attempted to acknowledge my debt to the late Lord Alport in the introduction.

Mark Garnett
November 1998

Foreword

by Rt Hon Kenneth Clarke MP

Cub Alport was one of the select group whose work ensured that the Conservatives of my generation could declare their faith with pride. In the late 1950s university students such as myself rarely heard the tired old allegation that we were supporters of a "stupid party". The illustrious names of Butler, Macleod, Maudling and Powell acted as our shield, and although the full extent of Cub's contribution was less well known to us at the time we all knew that he belonged in that company. We were rather proud that four of these Conservative thinkers belonged to our own university of Cambridge, and that Cub, like Butler, had served as President of the Union.

Thanks to Mark Garnett's painstaking research we can now appreciate that the intellectual revival of the Conservative Party after 1945 owed as much to Cub as to anyone else, with the obvious exception of his mentor Rab Butler. Even before the Second World War he was working against the notion that Conservatives were uncaring, publishing a pamphlet (*A National Faith*) which laid down the main lines of postwar policy. After his wartime service in Africa he co-founded the Conservative Political Centre and saw through the press many tracts which developed his idea of a party that put the national interest above class prejudice of any kind. Elected to Parliament in 1950, he was the key figure in the creation of the "One Nation" group that symbolised and cemented the new image in the party of Winston Churchill and Harold Macmillan.

Ironically, Cub was far more interested in the British Common-wealth and Empire than in the social affairs which won attention for the work of "One Nation", but he was seen as one of the most prom-ising members of the great 1950 Tory vintage. Had he played his cards with the required skill his national reputation would have rivalled that of my personal hero, Iain Macleod. But unlike Macleod Cub was not interested in card-play. For him politics was purely a matter of high principle. This outlook probably helped to delay his advancement, and ultimately persuaded him to leave the Macmillan Government. But it can hardly be said that it caused his career to end in failure, because his efforts helped to ensure that the Conservative Party iden-tified itself with his principles for much of the postwar period and he remained an eloquent advocate until shortly before his death. In the present unsettled state of British politics it is impossible to tell what his ultimate legacy will be.

Cub certainly considered himself to have been a lucky man, and his good fortune continued when, less than a year before his death, the plan of this book was hatched with its author. The finished product – which Cub read with delight in his last weeks – provides an intimate portrait of a remarkable human being. Cub's warts are pencilled in with great affection, but there is no attempt to disguise them. I sup-pose that most people will regard serious politicians as eccentric by definition. It appears that Cub's main foible was a sense of pride which sometimes toppled into pomposity but his consistent desire to leave the world better than he found it meant that his friends could easily forgive any lapses of this kind. In everything he did – above all, perhaps, in the romances that are presented in this book with great relish – Cub emerges as a man of solid integrity.

Author and subject obviously agreed on most political matters, yet above all this is a critical study and Cub's mistakes are recounted with engaging candour. During his time as British High Commissioner in the Federation of Rhodesia and Nyasaland he might be excused for quarrelling with almost everyone he dealt with. Probably the mistake here lay with Harold Macmillan and Duncan Sandys, who were looking for a politician on the spot to deal with the growing tension in the Central African Federation but needed a plausible communicator rather than a man whose idealism for this constitutional experiment was widely known. Having appointed him they ought to have made the most of his talents, and without endorsing some of the present author's strictures it is disappointing to learn from this book that on occasion he was not kept fully informed of the government's intentions. Mark Garnett believes that Cub was growing tired of his ministerial duties in the House of Commons, and put himself forward for the post because he wanted to contribute something to the cause of partnership between Britain and its overseas territories. Whether his views were realistic on this subject is quite another matter: all that emerges with certainty is that he did his best in an impossible situation.

We discover that Cub was treated unfairly when contrary to a public promise Macmillan failed to offer him a new government position on his return from Rhodesia. But Cub had known the risks when he left the government – and had taken a peerage against Macmillan's advice. He felt no grievance against Macmillan or his successor Alec Home, and continued to speak very highly of them up to his death. His subsequent actions were inspired not so much by resentment as by a swelling sense of frustration at his self-imposed exclusion from decision-making. This surely explains his inability to regard the struggles of the Heath Government with a benevolent eye and his later emergence as a determined opponent of almost every reform proposed by the Conservatives under Margaret Thatcher. In criticising Edward Heath he sometimes spoke as if Britain was as easy to govern as it had been in the 1950s – as if his own desire for a sense of national unity was shared by the overwhelming majority. But if it existed at all at that time, this sense of unity was deeply submerged, and Heath could not have worked harder to bring it back to the surface.

Cub clearly felt during 1970–74 that he had a duty to speak up for the "One Nation" approach, and the fact that Heath had been a recruit to the group he instigated made Cub more determined to say exactly what he thought whenever the government's decisions fell short of his ideal. A personal element was also present in his attitude to Margaret Thatcher: after all, the Prime Minister had been a Young Conservative in his Colchester constituency. Even before Mrs Thatcher became leader Cub had burned his boats by questioning in public her suitability for the post as if she were still the inexperienced enthusiast he had met in the late 1940s. Every politician must differ from the party leadership at some time in his or her career, but an immediate declaration of all-out war against a new regime before it has had the chance to provoke hostility seems a little hot-headed. Once the Conservatives returned to office in 1979 Cub might have lent some assistance to those who broadly shared his views by saving his efforts for those occasions when he could hope for the greatest effect. Instead, his random fire caused no casualties in what he evidently came to regard as the enemy ranks. Always personally courageous, he laughed off the unprecedented removal of the party whip in the Lords. But I think that he was quite mistaken in thinking that he could best fight for his principles by constant repetition of those hard things which younger politicians were too inhibited to declare. For all his faith in coalitions, he had forgotten the extent to which major political parties are coalitions in themselves. The climate of opinion within a party cannot be fixed forever – as Cub himself knew very well, given his belief that the approach of Butler and Macleod was jettisoned after 1970. At times the odds against a change might seem daunting, and Cub's outspoken pronouncements suggest that he had lost all hope for the future of his party.

In giving his biography the sub-title "A Study in Loyalty", Dr Garnett has focused attention on one of the most important and complex of political questions. Clearly Cub's career can be explained through his loyalty to the ideals which he formed in the 1930s. Apart from loyalty to one's principles and party, the other thought-provoking element of this book is the question of loyalty to friends. As Garnett shows, political differences proved too much for the strong sense of comradeship that was generated within the original "One Nation" group. Cub even fell out with his oldest and dearest friend, Rab Butler, when by a strange twist they were brought to serve in the same field of African politics. There can be few books that better illustrate the extent to which, for some people, politics is capable of making and breaking relationships. It also shows how during the course of a long political career the same people crop up again and again in one's affairs for the most unexpected reasons.

Since the serious setback of the 1997 general election several excellent books on Conservative Party history have been published. This biography must be counted among them: after all, Cub was involved in the politics of his party for more than sixty years. Some people think that a phenomenon can only be understood when its history is over, and the appearance of all this work on the Conservative Party has coincided with a sudden rush of experts ready to produce its death certificate. But, as this readable and perceptive biography shows, we have been here before, and the recovery after 1945 was almost as dramatic as the previous decline. So long as dedicated and able people like Cub Alport continue to join and work for the party we will be sure to have updated histories into the distant future.

Introduction

The original purpose of this book was to tell the story of the Conservative "One Nation" group of MPs from the viewpoint of one of its founder members. The group has played an important role in the politics of Britain during the second half of the twentieth century – originally as a kind of "think tank" within the Conservative Party, then as a pool of talent for Conservative ministries, and, in recent years, as the source of a slogan for the Conservatives and the Labour Party. "Cub" Alport never became as famous as other founder members, who included Edward Heath, Enoch Powell, Iain Macleod, Robert Carr and Angus Maude. But unlike the obscure members – Richard Fort, Gilbert Longden and Sir John Rodgers – his name generally cropped up in published studies of the period, and his archive of over fifty boxes (which include the early minutes of "One Nation") promised to reveal new insights into the group and its times.

The original members did not know when they set up "One Nation" that a group of Conservatives would still be meeting under that name at the end of the century; they would have been amazed (or aghast) back in 1950 to learn that within fifty years a Labour leader would try to win votes by posing as a "One Nation" politician. Most of them were ambitious, but they had no idea how famous they would become and not one of them wrote a contemporary account of their early meetings. As a result, the precise details of some events which led to the publication of the *One Nation* pamphlet will continue to be debated. But there can be no doubt that Alport first had the idea for a group, as was natural since he was keen on organising people and had established the Conservative Political Centre soon after the war.

Yet in the context of Alport's career this piece of information seemed to be of marginal importance. His key contribution to policy ideas came immediately before and after the Second World War, when he was the trusted lieutenant of Rab Butler. His short book *A National Faith* (1938) presented Conservatism as a middle course between Communism and *laissez-faire* – a creed around which all classes could unite. The experience of war reinforced rather than changed Alport's existing views; he welcomed the defeat of the Conservative Party in 1945 not because he regarded its existing MPs as incurable right-wing ideologues, but because he thought they could never embrace a truly "National Faith" due to their general ignorance of social problems. Alport was not an intellectual isolated from the rest of his party: after holding the Presidency of the Cambridge Union he had worked for the Conservatives, first as a tutor at Ashridge College then as a key participant in Butler's drive for greater political education. The continuity of his ideas disproves any suggestion that the Conservative Party was transformed from a hard-nosed vehicle for business interests into an organisation which aimed for wider appeal simply because it lost the 1945 election: in truth the party of Butler and Macmillan was gestating before the war.

Despite his interest in domestic policy Alport left "One Nation" in February 1953 because he believed that it paid too little political attention to the empire, which was his greatest pre-occupation. In the end he gave up his parliamentary seat in the hope that he could make a practical contribution in Africa, as Britain's empire was transformed into a commonwealth of independent nations. In addition to the light it sheds on the Conservative Party, the story of Alport's career provides new insights into the last years of Britain's role as a colonial power. As British High Commissioner in the Federation of Rhodesia and Nyasaland he lived a hand-to-mouth existence, as British ministers tried to square their continued feelings of duty towards British subjects overseas with their desire to retain the good opinion of more powerful forces such as the United Nations and the United States. Among those ministers was Rab Butler, and a great friendship was effectively closed by the stressful retreat from empire. At the same time that Britain was casting off its imperial past it was failing to secure a place in the new adventure of European co-operation. Alport's spell in Africa coincided with Britain's first, unsuccessful attempt to join the European Economic Community; when he returned the confident Conservative Party he had left behind had experienced something like a nervous breakdown. His response to the new environment was to work for major constitutional change and to keep his party fixed in the centrist position that he had helped to secure before and after the war. In both of these endeavours he failed, and, despite his years of service to his party, in 1984 he became the first person ever to be deprived of the Conservative whip in the House of Lords.

Alport's career thus involved a great deal more than his intimate involvement in "One Nation", and apart from his contributions to national politics he remained a major figure in his adopted home of East Anglia, while his private life was marked both by tragedy and romance. He revealed everything of relevance to his biographer, making no attempt to direct the research and taking a particular pleasure when the written records uncovered facts and incidents that he had half-forgotten.

At a time when so many politicians retire to spend more time with their memoirs it seemed odd that Alport had never produced an account of his own life. After all he was a gifted author, and half a century of political activity had left him with something more than the usual list of scores to settle. After his return from Africa he wrote a memoir of his time as High Commissioner; *The Sudden Assignment* (1965) was well-written, but it only covered two years and by the time it appeared the phase in the Rhodesian crisis to which it related had been superseded by the events which led up to Ian Smith's illegal declaration of independence. Although Alport was sent out as the representative of Harold Wilson's Labour government in an attempt to pave the way for an agreement with Smith, he never published an account of this experience.

In June 1984 Alport did put together an outline proposal for a book about his career. The book was to be called *The Furniture of One Man's Life*. As Alport explained,

> It would be a conversational book, with communication established directly between the author and his reader. At the start I would invite the latter to my house, take him round it and tell the stories behind some of the things which my house contains. None of them are of great historic or monetary value, but many, indeed, most of them have some connection with political and public affairs and the history of the last thirty years and more. They also have significance for anyone interested in the story of a happy family life, lived within the ambit of an ancient provincial town and against the background of the English countryside.

Alport went on to say that he would write about the personalities he had known, and provide new insights into the great events he had lived through. But the damage, from a publishing point of view, had already been done. Coming from a major public figure the proposal might have been considered by some of the large publishing houses – although the author would still have been encouraged to drop the "conversational" stuff and get on to spilling the beans about his contemporaries. An apparently second-ranking figure like Alport would be asked politely to try elsewhere.

As an autobiographer Alport suffered from two great handicaps. Before the war he had edited a book entitled *Thoughts and Talks*, by the soldier Sir Arnold Wilson. It was a "conversational" work by someone who was fairly well-known without being an international celebrity, and it proved to be successful enough to justify a sequel. If Alport was going to write a memoir he could only think of Wilson's book as his model: but public tastes had changed since 1939.

His second handicap conspired with the first to destroy his chances of publishing an autobiography. From his days as a young tutor at Ashridge he had found it easy to win publishing contracts; as a result, whenever he encountered rejection with his later books he immediately gave up the battle. *The Furniture of One Man's Life* was turned down by the only publisher who ever saw it. The author abandoned his book after a single chapter, having barely managed to furnish a single room.

This was not the first time Alport had failed to persevere with an ambitious project. In 1979 he had worked hard on a biography of his wife's ancestor, the Tudor adventurer Sir Richard Bingham. Instead of a formal proposal he submitted for consideration the first chapter, which included a rationale for his work. To begin his self-justification Alport wrote that "I believe that for many reasons it is worth the effort – and yet I am well aware that I may not be really qualified for the task". Warming to his theme, he admitted that "historic biography should properly be undertaken at the first flush of academic zeal and not in the latter years of a long and active life". The first chapter is highly readable, but the author had talked himself down so successfully that the book was rejected. Again Alport refused to make another attempt, and the book began and ended with brave Sir Richard halfway through his first campaign.

Fortunately Alport was so interested in his own life that he did put together a memoir on the lines of *Thoughts and Talks*; but he had been disappointed too often and he compiled this hundred-page manuscript with the intention that it should be placed in his private archive. Alport was incapable of writing dull prose, and the memoir is a delight to read, but (apparently in the belief that he had covered this before) he left out Rhodesia, which had occupied so much of his public life. Rather than offer himself the tribute he had paid to Sir Richard Bingham, he relied on his own memory instead of researching in other archives to fill in the inevitable gaps – and to correct his mistakes.

This unlucky autobiography is the first debt of gratitude which I owe to Lord Alport; an unpublished, under-researched and well-written memoir must be the Holy Grail of all biographers. My second and greater debt is to the generosity he has shown with his time and resources; he has regarded this book as a joint enterprise, and helped in every way he could. In the end it was probably for the best that the record of his life should be written by someone else; the diffidence which has always been his main characteristic would have prevented him from doing justice to his personality which, for all the political events recounted here, is the most important feature of this book.

This introduction was written in August 1998, after the completion of the main text. By that time Lord Alport was already unwell, but only in the following month did his condition cause serious concern. In his last weeks he recounted that he had spent many evenings after the death of his beloved friend Pat Llewellyn-Davies musing on his favourite lines from Tennyson's poem *Crossing the Bar*:

> Twilight and evening bell,
>   And after that the dark:
> And may there be no sadness of farewell,
>   When I embark

When the time came, it proved impossible for some to avoid "the sadness of farewell". But he died peacefully on 28 October; his ashes were interred in the grave at Layer de la Haye that already housed his parents and his wife.

As the book neared completion Cub urged that somewhere should be included Burns' reflections *On a Louse* (with his own addition, which he used to recite with some relish):

> O wad some Power the giftie gie us
> To see ourselves as ithers see us!
> *– and now it has!*

Chapter One

Father and Son

Arthur James McCall Alport died of meningitis in June 1911, only a month after his second birthday. His death was a particularly savage blow to his father, a doctor based in Turffontein, near Johannesburg. Neither his own skill, nor that of a specialist who was called in from town to assist, could save his only child. At the funeral he allowed no one else to touch the tiny coffin.

When describing the incident in an otherwise light-hearted memoir many years later, the father, Dr Cecil Alport, pretended that the bereaved doctor was not himself but a fictitious character named "Dr Curious". "Curious" is suddenly introduced to the reader late in the book as a fellow-student of the author, who married someone from the same town as Alport's wife and emigrated to "a suburb of Johannesburg just about the time that I did".[1] The parallels between the two characters extend to their dreams, notably their shared desire to secure a large fortune through speculation in mining and the Stock Exchange or gambling at the local race-track.

If Cecil Alport had really wanted his readers to think that he and "Curious" were different people, it would have been advisable to think up an alternative title to *The House of Curious* for a book about himself and his family. At first readers might be puzzled about the identity of "Curious", then baffled as to why the author should adopt this disguise at all if he was going to make it so transparent. In fact the flimsy subterfuge was a protection for Cecil Alport's own feelings; the likely reaction of readers was not a consideration. "Dr Curious" was an attempt to distance Cecil from the remembered pain of his son's death. Splitting himself into two characters also offered a better chance to indulge in simultaneous praise and self-criticism during the few pages when "Curious" is on the stage. After the birth of young Curious, for example, Cecil is consulted by the anxious father on how best to treat a recalcitrant child. For the first two weeks of its life the baby had been looked after by a nurse who responded to its cries by picking it up and soothing it. When the nurse leaves, "Mrs Curious" takes the same approach regardless of the hour; within a week both parents are worn out. In his own character, Cecil admonishes Curious to adopt stern measures in the belief that the baby is only crying to manipulate its parents. At the first sign of a new and harsher regime "Mrs Curious" abuses both her husband and Cecil, whom she blames for giving cruel advice; in response to his remark that the child is only "suffering from a predisposition to self will and temper", she agrees that "it does seem a lot like my husband". When the baby begins its next outburst "Dr Curious" reaches the end of his patience and locks the baby in the bathroom; eventually its angry yells subside and it goes to sleep, defeated by superior cunning. A week later "Mrs Curious" thanks Cecil for his advice, acknowledging that he is far wiser than her own husband. Evidently the same approach was taken to the second heir of the "House of Curious"; after reporting the birth of Cuthbert James McCall, the future Lord Alport, on 22 March 1912, Cecil proudly observes that discipline was never a problem with either of his children. The fact that the second product of the marriage arrived nine months after the death of his brother is significant; because of Janet's delicate health child-bearing was a problem, but Cecil believed in the hereditary principle and wanted his line to continue. Thus Lord Alport owed his existence to the death of the elder brother he never met.[2]

"Mrs Curious" was being a little unfair when she spoke of her husband's "self will and temper". Cecil Alport was not free from these, but his was a character in which the usual complexities and contradictions of humanity were greatly magnified. In politics he held what would normally be classed as extreme right-wing views on many subjects, yet his deeply felt sympathy for the poor would later lead him into one of his numerous scrapes. Despite his intense love for Britain, he chose to spend much of his life abroad. A compulsive writer, during his life he produced great masses of poetry which indicate a passion for the rhythms of language rather than profound spiritual yearning. Under cover of the character "Curious" he admitted that his sense of humour was "perverse in the extreme" – what else could one say of someone who wrote a book on the great 1914–18 world conflict with the title *The Lighter Side of the War*? – but although this cost him "numbers of patients and friends", "it gave people a totally wrong impression of the man". His prose style conveys the impression of a down-to-earth personality, yet his career was like a picaresque novel, with more than a faint echo of *Don Quixote*.[3]

Dr Alport's Quixotic streak emerges clearly from his account of his new son's christening. The ill-fated first-born had been baptized in the local church, and Cecil relates that "Curious" was provoked by the mass of strangers who turned up into vowing that the ceremony would be held at his own house if he ever had another child. When the time came he could not find a clergyman of the English Church of South Africa who was willing to officiate at the Alports' home, whereupon "Curious" threatened to christen little Cuthbert himself – in a garden bird-bath. This was too much for Cuthbert's mother, and after some enquiries the parents found a volunteer in the Reverend Leake, a member of the rival (and "low") Church of England in South Africa. His church was some distance away, but the Alports were regular attenders after he agreed to perform the christening in the drawing-room at "The House of Curious".[4]

In later life Cecil poured some of his demonic energy into a search for his ancestors. He traced the Alports back to a seventeenth-century Warden of the London Skinners' Company, a Royalist who prudently returned to his native Staffordshire after the execution of Charles I. Certainly the Alports had strong links with the Midlands; one was a merchant of Stourbridge in Worcestershire, who died in 1792. The family eventually moved to Essex, which provided the background for more than half of Lord Alport's life. Lord Alport's grandfather Arthur Cuthbert was less inclined to establish solid roots. After attending Durham School he decided to claim a fortune overseas. In February 1863, aged about eighteen, he embarked on the *Fusi-Yama*, a steamship bound for Vancouver. After an eventful four months' voyage the ship reached its destination, whereupon Arthur Alport walked three hundred miles (in eleven days) to a goldfield, William's Creek. Other adventurers prospered, but Arthur's claims yielded very little. By now he had been joined by his elder brother Charles, and together they set up a bakery in Victoria, British Columbia. As Cecil remarked, "they were greatly handicapped in this business by the fact that neither of them had anything but the most rudimentary knowledge of the baking of bread".[5]

The brothers were undeterred by the rapid failure of the bakery. The entrepreneurial virus induced them to buy a cigar shop for £5. They inherited plenty of cigar boxes from the previous owner, but none of them contained any cigars. Enough money was scraped together to buy a box of a single brand; whenever a customer came in these cigars would be recommended as a great improvement on whatever variety was asked for. This ruse succeeded for a time but the Alports were not a race of shopkeepers. After earning some money by whitewashing the town of Nanimo on Vancouver Island, Arthur tried coal-mining, then bought a hotel which also failed. His doctor son later attributed the financial instinct to "the special development of certain areas of the frontal lobes of the brain"; Arthur's frontal lobes were, if anything, over developed, but the lobe of luck was entirely absent. By this time he had been in North America for eight years, and the attractions of a new beginning were increased when his brother Charles was offered a position in a South African business owned by an uncle, Percy John Alport. This was soon followed by a similar offer to himself, which he accepted.[6]

Arthur spent the remainder of his life in the village of Beaufort West, more than three hundred miles from Capetown. He gained little advantage from his blood-relationship with the owner of his firm, working long hours for scant reward, but he resisted the lure of lucrative adventures in the South African Gold Rush. It was time to settle down. In 1878 he married Eleanor Thwaits (or Thwaites), the

4

daughter of a wealthy local farmer who also held the post of Surveyor-General of the Cape. This union produced four children, including Cecil (born in 1880), and another family legend. Eleanor's mother had been a direct descendant of Jan Bantjes, an officer in the Dutch East India Company who had jumped ship in 1755 and settled in Capetown. He had gone to sea against the wishes of his rich father, who retaliated by disinheriting him. Jan was an only child, and his father placed his money in trust for the benefit of any of his descendants who might be alive one hundred years after his death. When in 1894 South African newspapers carried advertisements in accordance with the will the Alports suddenly became very popular along with other representatives of the Bantje family, but they received nothing from a legacy which was even then calculated at over £10 million. Unfortunately Eleanor's father died when it seemed that his daughter would be well provided for from this fund, so he left his own money to the children from his second marriage. Arthur Alport lived long enough to witness this latest piece of financial ill-fortune, but he died, worn out by his search for security, in 1898. On a visit to South Africa in 1951, his son Cecil scattered a boxful of English soil on his grave at Beaufort West.[7]

Arthur's uncle made some amends for his shabby treatment of the father by paying for the son's schooling. Cecil went to South Africa College in Capetown, where by his own account he overworked and took too little exercise. Even so he achieved enough to pursue a medical career which he chose after a year in an office, having rejected law because the unscrupulous conduct of some South African lawyers he met disgusted him. He decided to study in Edinburgh, partly because of the high reputation of the university's medical faculty, but also because his father had taught him to love Britain. In the first few weeks the constant rain forced him to consider a speedy departure, but he was disuaded by an uncle who was on a visit to Scotland. He never regretted his persistence, and easily passed the final examinations despite sneaking away from his revision to watch the Open Championship at St Andrews. In his books Cecil pays regular tributes to the teachers at Edinburgh, in particular to the Professor of Surgery, John Chienne, who hung two pictures on his wall: one of a young chicken scratching for food, the other of a cuckoo waiting to be fed by a wren. The chicken was intended as an inspiration for the students, while the cuckoo stood as a warning to those who demanded spoon-feeding from the lecturers. According to Cecil, Chienne would explain the pictures to his students; then he would go into the wards "and spoon-feed us to the limits of our digestions". When he became a teacher in his turn Cecil displayed copies of the pictures, and had more success than Chienne in living up to their message.[8]

Cecil returned to South Africa as Dr Alport, having missed through his residence in Edinburgh the Boer War which caused such bitter and lasting divisions in his homeland. Before taking his degree he had been offered a partnership in Turffontein by his brother-in-law. Dr Alport soon changed his status in a different way. During his time in Edinburgh he had befriended a trainee nurse, Katherine McCall, who invited the young South African to meet her family at Caitloch House, near Moniaive, Dumfriesshire. Katherine was the eldest of three daughters of a Scottish landowner, whose father had purchased Caitloch after a successful legal career in Edinburgh. When the good-looking Cecil arrived at the isolated family home complications inevitably arose. The second sister, Isobel, promptly fell in love with him, but his preference was for the youngest, nineteen year-old Janet. The latter accepted his proposal of marriage, and in 1907, when he had established himself at Turffontein, she sailed to join him – with Isobel as her self-sacrificing chaperone for the outward voyage. On the ship a fellow-passenger developed a passion for Janet. Years later her son discovered a letter from him containing an unsuccessful request that "your lips must touch mine in tremulous fear" before they parted; he expressed surprise that someone could be lovesick and seasick at the same time. Perhaps Janet preserved the note to remind herself during her years with Cecil that she had once inspired lyrical passion. But there were no more twists in this romantic tragi-comedy, and the marriage came off as planned. Isobel, who drove ambulances in France during the First World War, died unmarried.

The depth of Janet's original feeling for Cecil is beyond dispute; travelling 6000 miles to live among strangers was daunting enough, but she was also asthmatic and allergic to the horses which were more numerous in Johannesburg even than in rural Dumfriesshire. Clearly the young man had been on his best behaviour during the courtship, and disarmed potential opposition from a staunch Liberal family. The evident success of the marriage, which lasted until Cecil's death in

1959, is a testament to Janet's patience. If *The House of Curious* is to be trusted on this point, it was not until Dr Alport set up his brass name-plate in Turffontein that his nature blossomed into real eccentricity. Prior to this point in his book, he poses as an amused spectator of other peoples' foibles; henceforth he is an unstinting reporter of his own. After reading a newspaper report which claimed that victims of the great San Francisco earthquake had starved to death after two or three days, he refused to believe it until he had tried the experiment for himself. For nine days he existed on water only, and records that by the end of the first week he had no desire to eat. He only broke his fast because a neighbour, watching him entering his trap with the assistance of his driver, concluded that he had been drunk and spread her tale. According to Cecil, the driver, "who was in the secret, seemed to think I was a bit mad".[9]

While he was quite prepared to perform strange deeds in the interests of his profession, money lay behind most of Cecil's peculiarities. His work brought him a reasonable income, but he had a strong urge to make a quick fortune. Possibly the stories of Bantje's gold, and a desire to put right the misfortunes which his father had suffered, produced this gambling streak. But in money matters Cecil was as ill-starred as his father had been. Together with a friend he invested in a gold mine which showed such promise that a financial group from Johannesburg offered to purchase it for £40,000 – provided that it continued to produce the same amount of gold over a six month trial period. All went well for four months, then the gold-bearing reef seemed to peter out. Alport remained convinced that further drilling would have struck more gold, but neither he nor his friend had the resources to carry on. If they had been luckier on the turf finance would not have been a problem, but having carefully planned for a *coup* at Auckland Park races and invested the enormous sum of £800 on what inside information suggested was a "good thing", they watched in dismay as the jockey made no attempt to win. Just before the off someone had bribed the trainer with £25 to instruct the jockey to lose; the horse cantered to victory in two races over the next three weeks without carrying a penny of Cecil's money. Cecil was successful enough when he lowered his aim and depended entirely on his own skills; in order to improve his golf game, he offered to play all comers for a box of balls. At first his losses were considerable, but before he left South Africa in 1914 he was handsomely in profit, his handicap was down to four, and he had acquitted himself well in the Transvaal Open Championship. During his residence in Egypt years later, Alport would watch the professionals on the practice ground during that country's Open Championship, and, according to an obiturist, offer his advice "with the same persistent conviction that he brought to the rest of his activities" no matter how eminent the player.[10]

Cecil's characteristics were inherited by his son Cuthbert, albeit in diluted form. He shared his father's interest in windfall riches, but this trait only showed itself in later life when he enjoyed a weekly flutter on the National Lottery. Cecil thought that sweepstakes were "the poor man's hope", but both men were comfortably off and their real motive was the chance to be in a position to exercise their native generosity without ruining themselves. When he left Turffontein Cecil calculated that he was owed around £9000 by his patients, but this knowledge caused far less of a pang than the wealth he could have accumulated through better fortune in his speculations.[11]

Cecil once admitted that Cuthbert had more "balance" than himself; more accurately, the son was better able to restrain his impulsive nature. Many domestic political arguments were avoided because Cuthbert learned to bite his tongue, and sit quietly through his father's regular diatribes. The only occasion when his good temper failed was just before the Second World War, when the family were having lunch at the Roehampton Club. The meal took place after father and son had played a round of golf; the result is not recorded, but one suspects that the younger man had won. During his residence in Edinburgh Cecil had become an ardent admirer of Mary, Queen of Scots; from his reading of history at school Cuthbert had conceived a strong passion for Elizabeth I. Through some misfortune the subject was broached during the meal, and the temperature rose quickly. On Cuthbert's later account Cecil struck the first low blow, by branding Elizabeth "a bloody whore"; his son countered with the opinion that Mary had been a murderess. Cecil rose in his seat, as if preparing to throw a punch; Cuthbert, whose boxing career was more notable and recent, followed suit. Both came to their senses when the waitress arrived, and the two long-dead (and equally dubious) ladies were forgotten for the rest of the meal.[12]

Cuthbert later acknowledged that he had not inherited his father's "splendid memory", but he did recollect something of his brief childhood residence in South Africa. His nanny met a policeman friend in his company; the result was a warning to the child that he would be taken off to jail if he gave any trouble. This frivolous remark had a deep effect on Cuthbert, who was still uneasy in the presence of the police in his mid-eighties. In his third year he recalled being given a dose of milk and castor oil during a thunderstorm. This produced a more predictable long-term antipathy to castor oil – a favourite remedy of his father's, who in the course of his military career in South Africa won the nickname of "The Castor Oil Doctor". Finally, Cuthbert had a memory of slipping into the scuppers of a Union Castle liner, on a voyage which he thought had taken place when he was four years old.[13]

Thanks to Cecil's published account of his experiences during the First World War, this childhood memory can be dated with some precision. In *The Lighter Side of the War* Cecil relates that in September 1915 he sailed for England in the *Durham Castle* with his wife and small child. At the time Cuthbert was three-and-a-half years old. Although this journey is the most likely source of his memory, it was not the first one of the kind which he had undertaken. In the late spring of 1914 Cecil had shipped his family to England, having awarded himself six months of leave from his Turffontein practice. He spent a few months with his wife's relatives in Dumfriesshire, but by July he grew bored of doing nothing while the European powers moved towards conflict, and volunteered his services in the cause of Ulster. This was not his first attempt to participate in war; in 1905 he and a friend had written to ask if they could help the Russians in their struggle with the Japanese. Having been refused, they promptly offered themselves to the other side, with an equal lack of success.[14]

When Cecil made a gesture of this kind he invariably went to the top, and he preserved a letter from the Unionist leader Sir Edward Carson who accepted his services. However, he did not cross to Ireland from Stranraer to keep his rendezvous with Carson. Germany declared war on Britain while he was awaiting his instructions; he immediately volunteered, but being already a captain in the South African Medical Corps he was sent out to his native country, where he took part in the suppression of the rebellion by the Boer

War veteran De Wet before serving with the forces which conquered German South-West Africa. Here he demonstrated that he had inherited his father's physical stamina, covering with his infantry brigade 250 miles in just over three weeks, the final burst of forty-five miles in thirty-six hours being accomplished after almost a week on quarter-rations.[15]

Cecil's family had gone back to South Africa with him; now he volunteered for service in Europe, and sailed there with Cuthbert and the long-suffering Janet. The child remembered his accident on deck; he also became ill on the journey and arrived at Plymouth with severe broncho-pneumonia. According to Cecil, Cuthbert "hovered between life and death" while his anxious parents nursed him at a private hotel in Torquay. Once the boy had recovered Cecil helped with the recruitment and training of a medical unit, which in October 1916 was ordered to the Middle East. At the last minute it was decided that its services would not be required in that theatre, and it was disbanded. Cecil was posted to the Balkans instead, sailing in the same month on a White Star liner, *Britannica*, bound for Salonika. The ship was sunk by enemy action on its next voyage.[16]

During his military career in South Africa Cecil's irascible nature hardly surfaced. Once in the Balkans, however, it was given free rein. On the voyage he had made an enemy of his commanding officer, Colonel A. E. Kidd, by telling him what he should do once they had reached their destination. Finding himself barred from meaningful duties in retribution for his unseasonal advice, he looked around for some suitable land on which to construct a golf course. The most promising area, however, was a marshland which Dr Alport quickly identified as a breeding ground for malaria. Thus began Cecil's private war against the mosquito. Despite the opposition of Colonel Kidd, he organised the draining of the marshes using Bulgarian prisoners of war for most of the heavy spade-work. His original purpose was not completely overlooked, however; on the first day of digging the canal which drained the various stagnant pools, he found time to start work on the tees and greens of his course. After rustling up a couple of clubs and two golf balls, he played in the first match from which Kidd and his partner emerged conveniently victorious on the last green. After an urgent request Janet sent out forty clubs and more balls, on a ship which was promptly torpedoed.[17]

Cecil's golfing exploits were acceptable on a front where physical exercise was encouraged; he later rode at a race-meeting, and looked likely to win the five-furlong sprint for mules until his mount saw some of its fellows and bolted off into the crowd, taking all but one of the other runners with it. Colonel Kidd had already marked Alport down as a trouble-maker, and his crusading approach to the drainage scheme made him unconscious of the bad effect he might be having on the rest of his unit. It certainly made him insensitive to the feelings of his wife, who had taken rooms in London. Eschewing poetic talk about tremulous kisses his letters only refer in passing to either Janet or Cuthbert, then plunge into self-congratulatory accounts of his engineering feats. "The canal is no longer a success – it is a triumph", he crowed. "The Serbs say England must win the war if a Major can work the way I do". No doubt Colonel Kidd was jealous of the canal; possibly Cecil was right to claim that his adversary was soon plotting to get rid of him, so that he could grab the credit for himself. For whatever reason Kidd informed the Director of Medical Services that he "had found [Alport] extremely difficult to get on with", and that disruption was particularly serious in a unit which was isolated from other British personnel. In his view, the only way to curb "the unrest he was causing" was to post the troublesome doctor elsewhere.[18]

Cecil received the fatal message while knee-deep in one of his newly dug trenches. Kidd informed him that he must join a unit in Salonika as soon as possible; typically, Alport asked for a little more time, and drove both himself and his team even harder to finish the main job on the canal. By the end of that day almost all of the stagnant pools – the water hazards of his golf course – were draining off into a nearby lake. The completed canal was more than a mile long; as he told his wife, "I have made a mark on the surface of Macedonia which will last for all time". At least in Salonika he was able to continue another part of his anti-malaria campaign, urging with more force than tact that victims of cerebral malaria were best treated with large intravenous doses of quinine. With no canals to dig, the rest of Cecil's spare time in Macedonia was devoted to the writing of a text-book on the disease, which was published after the war. Just before the conflict ended he was transferred at his own request to France, but after barely a month he was sent home to receive medical treatment himself. This was probably just as well, because while he admired the Serbs for their fighting spirit – and was proud to have met one of the assassins of Archduke Franz Ferdinand – he had no time at all for the French.[19] At least he ended the war with the rank of Major, which he had lost through his move to Salonika.[20]

This was far from being the last of Cecil Alport's collisions with medical colleagues or bureaucrats. It would be easy to say that with a quieter manner he might have achieved more than the undoubted improvement in sanitation he brought about; equally, had he been other than he was the canal might never have been thought of. If the incompetents around him would not recognise his genius, he could appeal to a wider audience; thus he preserved all the letters he sent home as raw material for *The Lighter Side of the War*. This was published in 1935 complete with crawl-on roles for "Bill the lizard" and "Tim the tortoise", who appeared in his letters as entertainment for his only son. Between 1961 and 1963 Cuthbert was confronted with a dilemma in Central Africa which resembled in many respects the situation his father had faced during the war. His response showed that he had learned to avoid Cecil's excesses; nevertheless, there are some uncanny echoes from the Macedonian front. Compared to his father Cuthbert was a volcano in minature, but he was still capable of dramatic eruptions: and if he felt that he had been badly treated he was determined that the world should know of it.

For over a year Cecil remained in Britain, where he passed the examination to qualify as a Member of the Royal College of Physicians (MRCP). Still attached to the Medical Corps, he worked for nine months in Cambridge and for a month in Colchester, the base for much of his son's life. After demobilisation he returned with his family to South Africa, where he found that his practice had been taken over by another doctor (his brother-in-law having died before the war). Before his departure for military service he had been earning £2000 every year from his work, despite his problems with non-payment; now he was offered just £35 for his share of the practice. This insulting price was the most that his supplanter would offer; his son believed that in addition to Cecil's long absence, his British loyalties and origins weakened his bargaining position in an area which was now dominated by the Dutch. He angrily refused the money and transported his family back to England on another White Star liner – the *Ceramic*, which was sunk during the Second World War.[21]

By now it was the summer of 1921, and Cuthbert had passed his
ninth birthday. The question of a school for him was looming, but the
nomadic life was not yet over and he continued to be taught by his
mother while Cecil worked as locum for a series of provincial doctors.
Finally, in October 1921 he was appointed second assistant to Professor Frederick Langmead, Director of the Medical Unit of St Mary's
Hospital, Paddington. After Cecil's death Langmead confessed that he
had been daunted at the prospect of working with someone whose
boat-rocking record was well known, but Alport was happy at St
Mary's, where no-one interfered with his methods of teaching.
Nearly forty years later he died there, after making a final journey
from South Africa in search of treatment for his last illness.[22]

In 1922 Cuthbert was enrolled at Wilkinson's School, on Orme
Square, just off the Bayswater Road. It was said that the boys of the
school inspired part of J. M. Barrie's *Peter Pan*; certainly Barrie was
living round the corner while that book was being written, nearly
twenty years before Cuthbert arrived. His surviving school reports
apparently reflect the lack of formal tuition in his early years; at
Christmas 1924 he languished in eleventh place out of a class of 12,
but two months later he had moved to ninth, and his last report, written in July 1925, placed him seventh. While he was catching up with
his contemporaries in academic matters, he was showing himself as a
leader in other fields; he became captain of cricket, and founded a
debating society. George Wilkinson's message of regret at losing the
boy was presumably a fairly standard summary of a career at the
school, but it seems that Cuthbert was well behaved and hard-
working without showing extraordinary promise. Apart from the
headmaster's good wishes, the youngster took away with him a nickname which never came unstuck. Apparently "Cub", apart from being
a diminutive of Cuthbert, was considered suitable because whenever
he was involved in a fight he was fierce as a young tiger. Perhaps after
one encounter with this creature the other boys decided that they had
better pick on others, so the nickname was not necessarily incompat-
ible with his reputation for good general conduct.

All the evidence suggests that he was a happy boy, particularly
enjoying his regular holidays at his uncle's home ("Auchencheyne",
also in Moniaive) where with his three cousins he divided the
playroom into principalities populated by lead soldiers. As Cub later

recalled, "most of the leading figures of these had names and, to us, distinctive personalities. We made and unmade cabinets. We anticipated the EMU by having a common currency called the "Alla" and comprising different sizes of beads." The principalities played Test Matches against each other, with minature bats and marbles; occasionally their disputes would lead to war, but they also banded together in an (invariably successful) fight against the "barbarian hordes", called "The Sangorians", who "consisted of large numbers of empty cartridge cases collected from the butts at the end of grouse shoots". On the long train journey home to the family's London flat, the boy would try to re-enact some of the conflicts without his fellow-rulers, but "somehow it did not seem quite the same". As an only child, Cub felt very keenly the contrast between these intense bursts of companionship and his normal life; he particularly missed his favourite cousin, Isabel, who remained a close friend until the end of her life.[23]

Cub also spent many hours with the gamekeeper on the estate, Tom MacLeary. While Tom tramped the hills shooting birds and the boy gathered the spent ammunition which filled the ranks of the "Sangorians", the gamekeeper explained his political faith. He was a determined communist, whose approval for the Bolshevik revolution of 1917 was tempered only by the fact that the Russian golden retrievers which served as gun dogs on the estate could no longer be imported into Britain. From MacLeary Cub learned that his father's light-hearted anecdotes about the First World War reflected the outlook of an unusual man; MacLeary had fought with the Cameron Highlanders, and his political views had been shaped in reaction to the conduct of superior officers chosen for their social status rather than their abilities.

Cecil had emerged from his own exposure to wartime incompetence with his political ideas reinforced. He was a staunch admirer of Britain's public schools, and believed that "the British Empire in its conception and its achievements has been the greatest influence for good in the history of the world". He arranged for Cub to proceed to Haileybury College in his fourteenth year. Originally established by the East India Company in 1806 – the great economist Malthus taught there – Haileybury was closed temporarily when the Company was dissolved in the 1850s. When it re-opened as a public school in 1862 it quickly established a reputation for nurturing future servants of the empire. The imperialist ethos was particularly strong during the Boer War, when Clement Attlee was among the pupils. Although he was more interested in public service on the home front, the emotional attachment to empire which Attlee developed at Haileybury was slow to fade; at Oxford he was still a firm believer in "the legend of the White Man's burden and all the rest of the commonplace of imperialist idealism". He always interested himself in Old Haileyburians, even when they were political opponents who were still stirred by the "commonplace" teachings of the school.[24]

Attlee was not a great success at Haileybury, but he was handicapped by his lack of sporting prowess. As at all English public schools games were an important part of the Haileybury curriculum, and the regime was designed to suit "the virile type of boy who could stand up to more or less tough conditions". All in all, the school offered a check-list of ideal features for Cecil Alport, who already harboured dreams of greatness for his surviving son. Years later he explained these ambitions to his future daughter-in-law in a letter which, true to form, conveyed more information about the writer than the ostensible subject. In preparation for his eventual role as Prime Minister of Great Britain, Cecil believed that Cub should become an able debater and a first-rate cricketer. At the beginning of every holiday he was interrogated about his progress as a speaker. During his time at Haileybury his father arranged for him to take speaking lessons, and some records survive of his activities. His tutor, Captain J. F. Finn, was an experienced platform orator who taught his pupils ("a retired Admiral, a sprinkling of asprant political candidates and some elderly ladies . . . intent on improving their technique for opening bazaars") "to stand squarely to the audience with heads erect and feet apart". Gestures were allowed only when emphasising a point; there were to be no nervous jerks or shufflings of feet. The voice should be projected to the back of the hall, and the pitch varied. The speaker should begin with a statement or story which won the attention and sympathy of the audience. "After that he was at liberty to launch out into his main argument, being careful not to try to make more than three points. If he was able to illustrate these from personal experience so much the better. Lastly came his peroration in which he reminded his audience of the general theme he had expounded and ended up with a stirring appeal to their emotions". At sixteen, Cub was by far the youngest member of the strangely assorted class. The lessons continued until he left Haileybury. In January 1931 another specialist informed Dr Alport that while Cub was performing "I noted in particular that he always adopted a very good standing position, that his gestures were appropriate and generally well made . . . he was always quite confident when speaking". While ensuring that his son's speaking manner would be proficient, Cecil was just as keen that the content should be appropriate; this report was sent from the "Anti-socialist and Anti-communist Union", Victoria Street.[25]

This training was one of several masterstrokes which Cecil performed on his son's behalf. Cub was a noted orator from the start of his career in politics, being much better at handling hecklers than his father, whose budding career in South Africa had ended when during a speech at a meeting he jumped from the platform, tore off his jacket and confronted a vociferous opponent (typically, in *The House of Curious* he conceals this incident, choosing instead to relate his heroic actions when a mob attacked the visiting Keir Hardie). Yet Cub could not bring off the "double"; he fell short of the cricketing blue which his father longed for. Despite intensive lessons – his father alleged that he had taken "two hundred" of them, some with Surrey professionals – he never worked his way into the Haileybury First Eleven. According to Cub, he developed a majestic style "but, alas, my bat seldom contacted with the ball". Even so, there was something for Cecil to boast about in later years – an innings of 99 in 90 minutes for Cub's army regiment, the Artists' Rifles. The reported score arouses immediate suspicions; Cecil was even more prone to distortion when talking about his son than he was when recounting his own exploits. It was comforting to imply that Cub's cricketing career had been an instance of "so near, yet so far". In rugby it was not remotely "near"; at an international match in the 1920s Cecil bet a friend in the crowd that his son would one day play for England, but even by his previous standards this was an ill-judged wager.[26]

In boxing Cub certainly did excel, although his father apparently selected his House, Highfield, on the grounds that this was the most suitable for delicate boys. He became captain of the Haileybury team; subsequently he confessed that he had only secured this honour because his opponent in the Lightweight Championship was a good friend who was already captain of cricket, and sportingly let Cub beat him. Whatever the truth of this, under his leadership the school won a four-sided competition against Eton, Bedford and Dulwich. Prior to the encounter the team trained hard for over a month, and Cub remembered being fed steak for breakfast on the big day. The report from a match against Tonbridge School in March 1929 implies that the "tiger cub" was discernible in the ring, if not on the playing fields; in what was considered to have been the best bout, "J. O. Banning beat Alport after a really exciting contest, in which there was plenty of hard hitting, but very little science". The honour of the boxing captaincy – which, according to Cub, also carried the privilege of becoming a prefect – was dearly bought. Cecil informed Cub's fiancée ("But for heaven's sake don't tell him I told you this!") that it put an end to his acting career; although he had become Secretary of the Dramatic Society, a master had objected to the captain of boxing taking any more of the female roles which had come his way because, like his father, he looked younger than his years. Cecil consoled his correspondent with the information that her beloved Cub had been "very good looking before his nose was broken during a fight". Possibly Cub sinned as much as he was sinned against; the Labour MP Geoffrey de Freitas used to enjoy telling visitors to the House of Commons that Cub broke *his* nose during a Haileybury boxing match.[27]

Despite all his distractions and the repeated blows to the head Cub continued at Haileybury the academic progress he had made in his previous school. When he was eighteen his English teacher observed that his essays were "still clumsy and halting. They are the essays of a person who has the greatest difficulty in saying what he means". This was a serious setback for the father, with his visions of a son who would in future stand at the dispatch-box and reel off well constructed arguments at a moment's notice. Before Cub had left Haileybury, however, great improvement in his style was noted. The big problem was languages; although during the war Cecil had anticipated coming home on his next leave to be greeted by a fluent French-speaking son, Cub would never master any tongue but his own. His Haileybury report of 1930 judged that his French was "shocking. His ear seems utterly untrained to the language".[28]

History was far more congenial to him. Cub's interest in the past had already been encouraged by his father who took him round as many London churches as possible. At the age of sixteen he was taken to a service in St Botolph's Church on Bishopsgate. In a small congregation they sat in the front pew, only for Cecil to storm out when he realised that the vicar was using the new 1928 version of the Prayer Book. Cub's favourite teacher at Haileybury was the left-wing historian John Hampden Jackson, newly arrived from Oxford. Jackson "wore his hair long and he had a taste for colourful clothes"; he taught sixteenth-century British history without betraying any bias on that promising period for Marxist speculation. His enthusiasm, rather than his creed, transmitted itself to his young pupil; indeed Cub remained a fervent supporter of the Stuarts, keeping up his membership of the Jacobite White Rose Society until he discovered that it was raising funds for Franco in Spain. Outside his contractual teaching hours Jackson coached Cub for a Cambridge history scholarship. He was often invited to take tea with Jackson and his wife, and was attracted by what he regarded as their Bohemian lifestyle. He heard later that his old tutor had left the school because a group of parents had complained about his political views. In the House of Lords many years later Cub remembered this incident as he opposed educational changes designed to give parents more influence over schools, but in his writings Jackson made no secret of his vehement opposition to the empire, which made him an unlikely member of the Haileybury staff.[29]

Bullying was a problem at Haileybury in Attlee's day, but Cub gave no hint of suffering from it – perhaps promising boxers were exempted. His only surviving letter (undated), addressed to his father, is quite free from childhood anxieties, complaining of nothing more serious than the result of a rugby match against Richmond ("we were beaten by 19-10 they were very good"). He revealed that he had just started "fagging", but would only elaborate to the extent of saying that he "had quite a lot to do". Newcomers were subjected to an initiation ritual, but this was not especially sinister; the victim was made to stand on a chair in the corner of the dining-room and sing a song, which would be greeted either with applause or a hail of cushions, depending on the singer's ability. Cub attempted "Yes, we have no bananas"; he had more cushions thrown at him than anyone else. Unlike Attlee, who was caned for overexuberant celebrations after the relief of Mafeking, Cub seems to have avoided corporal punishment.

In his final year he became Head of Highfield House, and promptly prohibited what he called "this indignity" throughout his jurisdiction. Public school certainly left no scars on him; he was happy to stay on for an extra year in obedience to the wishes of his father who thought that no-one should go to university before they were 19. In his last surviving report, written just before his nineteenth birthday, the Master could only comment "Good in every way".[30]

Despite Jackson's encouragement, Cub did not win his scholarship. Yet this failure was a blessing in disguise. He still went up as his father had planned to study history and law at Pembroke College, which was so pre-occupied with sporting activities that even having participated in the scholarship exam was sufficient to win him repute as an "intellectual". Writing to his parents on his arrival in Cambridge in October 1931 he noted that few other "freshmen" had arrived, which would allow him to settle down to some preparatory work. Yet unlike Enoch Powell, who had entered Trinity College in the previous October, Cub was content to let people think he was an intellectual without taking any pains to deserve the label. He had not come to Cambridge to translate Herodotus; neither, however, did he intend to concentrate on sport. Instead he threw himself into politics.[31]

Cub already thought of himself as a Conservative. He later admitted that there had been a moment when he was tempted by the Labour Party, under the influence of his Haileybury contemporary Geoffrey de Freitas. Another very close friend was Jock Butler, who supported Labour despite being the younger brother of a rising Conservative, Richard Austen ("Rab") Butler. Just over a month before Cub went up to Cambridge Ramsay MacDonald's Labour government had fallen, and the Prime Minister had been persuaded to stay on as head of a national administration while the great majority of his party went into opposition. De Freitas and Butler were thus advocates of a deeply divided party, but Cub could not be accused of rejecting Labour for opportunistic reasons. The outlook was equally uncertain for the Conservatives whose leader, Stanley Baldwin, was just emerging from a series of bruising battles over empire free trade. In March the Conservative candidate, Alfred Duff Cooper, had won a by-election at St George's Westminster in a straight fight with a protectionist candidate supported by the newspaper proprietors,

Beaverbrook and Rothermere. While the main political parties were fighting amongst themselves, unemployment had risen above two million; in September, the month before Cub went to Cambridge, Britain abandoned the gold standard and the navy mutineed at Invergordon. Three days after Cub wrote to his parents about his plans for academic work, Parliament was dissolved in preparation for the general election of 27 October.

This was a little early even for Cub, who was still settling into his new lodgings when the election took place. He was very pleased with the landslide victory for the National Government, which now had an overall majority approaching 500, but the two Cambridge University seats were carried for the government without a contest and he seems to have taken no active part in the election: only graduates of the university had the vote for the seats. Throughout Cub's university career Britain was governed by a coalition – even if this was dominated by the Conservatives, who held 473 seats in the new House of Commons. No doubt this, along with a cooling of partisan feelings which the university magazine *The Granta* noted in an editorial of January 1934, helped to produce in Cub the view that the national interest is far more important than party labels. This outlook brought him some unlikely friendships, and, in later years, a good deal of trouble from his own "side".[32]

Many accounts of Cambridge at this time concentrate on the brilliant and glamorous set which gathered around John Maynard Keynes, whose lectures in the university reflected the thinking behind his *General Theory of Employment, Interest, and Money* (1936). This group, centred on the Cambridge "Apostles", included Victor Rothschild and Richard Llewelyn-Davies, whose future wife Patricia Parry had won a Girton scholarship. These people figured in Cub's future life, but at Cambridge he knew none of them, and although he later read Keynes' work he attended none of the economist's lectures. The lifestyle of the Apostles was not to Cub's taste, and while some historians might assume that everyone at Cambridge in the 1930s was dying to join this circle, there were plenty of other opportunities for intelligent and gregarious students. Cub joined a Pembroke literary society, "The Martlets", and eventually became vice-president; he also co-founded a small dining club called "Dr Oliver's". This was inspired by the memory of a Pembroke man whose firm produced the cheese-biscuits of that name, and members wore waistcoats dyed in the same colour as the delicacy which they honoured.

Although he resolved to keep a diary after visiting Pepys' Library at Magdalene College in February 1932, Cub was presumably too busy to maintain it. One of the few entries in the diary contained a prophetic self-criticism: "I am indeed too prone to taking up a thing and then dropping it". One diary resolution which he did not drop was a declared intention of visiting Germany during the long vacation of 1932. Cub was normally an acute observer on his overseas trips, but though he toured extensively throughout the country with three friends in the late summer he was primarily interested in recording his impressions of the architecture for his parents, rather than commenting on an unemployment rate which was approaching six million, or the outbreaks of disorder in several cities. Most surprisingly, he said little about the Nazi phenomenon, even though in the elections of July 1932 the party won the largest representation in the Reichstag with over 37 per cent of the vote. In Munich the group visited the notorious beer-garden from which Hitler had launched his failed *putsch* in 1924, but only out of idle curiosity.

By far the greatest attraction for Cub at Cambridge was the Union. Unlike Enoch Powell, who never attended a meeting and only joined to please his father, Cub was a regular attender from an early stage. In his second year he acted as a teller against the proposition that the Soviet political system was superior to that of the United States, and he often took the opportunity of speaking after the proposers and seconders. He remembered that he was first put down to speak "on the paper" (i.e. advertised as either the proposer or seconder of a motion) early in his third year. By this time he had moved into his college, and occupied rooms in the court where Pembroke's greatest product, William Pitt the Younger, had lived. A card arrived from the Union President, inviting him to speak first in the debate of 21 November 1933 in favour of the motion "That this House hunts". According to his own self-deprecating account, due to the consciousness "that the mantle of one of Britain's greatest Prime Ministers was about to fall on my shoulders, there followed six days of exhilaration, spiced with painful anxiety". He had no practical experience of hunting; indeed his only attempt to ride a horse, at his uncle's house in Scotland, had ended with a tumble into a bed of roses. At least this meant that Cub's advocacy of hunting was unimpaired by an excess of emotional commitment. It was a successful debut, which the then President, Geoffrey de Frietas, celebrated twenty years later for its "Freudian study of a repressed Bo-peep hunting for her sheep". Jock Butler, following Cub, asserted that "the Hon. Proposer had been doing too much debating lately, and this had affected his reason . . . Could we trust the opinion of such a man? – obviously no".[33]

While contemporary reports tended to dwell on the flippant remarks in most speeches, Cub had evidently gathered from Captain Finn that a few good jokes at the outset will warm up an audience. The Cambridge Union did debate grave issues – Butler gained a majority for his motion "This House hates Hitler" – but on the light-hearted topics which were introduced for variety Cub became known as "one of the most humorous speakers in the Union". On a motion attacking the institution of marriage, he "quoted an advertisement from the Matrimonial Times which sent the House into paroxysms of laughter". With his audience on his side he could more readily establish his serious point – that "It was absurd to discredit the ideal because certain people failed to live up to it".[34]

In June 1934 Cub stood for the Secretaryship of the Union. By this time he had become Vice-president of the Cambridge University Conservative Association (CUCA) – the post of President was not open to undergraduates – and he carefully mobilised his forces for what was a crucial election, since the Secretary almost invariably progressed to the Presidency. Three friends (one of whom was a Haileybury old boy) ran his campaign, though since overt canvassing was illegal he was never quite sure what methods they had employed. According to his father's account, he and Janet visited the candidate in his rooms on the eve of the contest. Cub told them that if his support-ers all turned out he would outpoll his Labour opponent – his friend Jock Butler. The snag was that most of the Conservatives were keen sportsmen, who would be occupied elsewhere on the big day unless it rained. The anecdote is an interesting counter to the view that at Cambridge (as at contemporary Oxford) socialists were in the majority at this time; rather, it implies that the Conservatives were more distracted by outside interests.[35] Cub's father claimed that this perverse ordering of priorities by the Cambridge Conservatives exasperated Cub so much that at the end of his first year he had sworn to copy the recent example of Sir Oswald Mosley, and establish his own party. If this threat was ever made at all it was unlikely to have been a serious one, but Cecil could not resist telling his future daughter-in-law that he had talked Cub out of a disastrous move by pointing out the reverses Mosley's New Party had suffered in 1931.[36]

Cecil was entitled to plume himself on his son's success when the rain came down and he was elected Secretary by eight votes. Without his generosity Cub would not have stood for the position. Being in his final year, he could not reach the Presidency unless he had the chance to stay on at Cambridge after taking his BA. Fortunately Cecil promised to finance this extra stint if he became Secretary. As Cub noted much later, his final year was "a period of uninterrupted pleasure"; he had no need even to pretend to work, having graduated with second class honours in 1934, although theoretically he was now reading for the Bar. He took up residence in a house in Brookside, off the Trumpington Road, where the then socialist (and later Conservative MP) Charles Fletcher Cooke depicted him for *The Granta*, sipping sherry from a stirrup-cup while reading alternately Stephen Spender (rather an "advanced" taste for Cub) and the imperial adventure story *Sanders of the River* (much more predictable). Fletcher Cooke also offered his readers a glimpse of an "upright figure in a brown cardigan", who would "dive into the Blue Boar with a far-away look in his eyes". While the author had his tongue in his cheek for most of the article, his sincerity in judging Cub "an unqualified success" as President can be guessed from the fact that he actually gave reasons for his opinion – notably that Cub had interested himself in "the less visible portions of the society", inspecting the cooking facilities and even drawing up plans for extra ladies' lavatories.[37]

Fletcher Cooke and Cub were good friends, which explains the affectionate references scattered through the former's ebullient reporting of Union debates. After a speech on a motion deploring "The Old School Tie", Fletcher Cooke applauded Cub as "the very best type of Englishman. His sentiment brings tears to the eyes". In an earlier report he claimed that "Alport exudes a halo of Scottish lairdness. And it is not assumed for the occasion . . . . On the squash court he exudes it (*inter alia*) just the same". In February 1935 the friends travelled together for an inter-university debate in Dublin, where they took opposite sides on the proposition that "This House approves of the Totalitarian State". Cub drew the short straw on this occasion, and was forced to speak against his firm principles: the "antis", including Fletcher Cooke, won by 39 to 13. Cub claimed that through his efforts during this trip Fletcher Cooke began to drift away from Labour; years later he asked his friend to stand as a god-parent to his second daughter. This degree of intimacy must be held to excuse Fletcher Cooke's declaration in *The Granta* that President Alport had "infused brightness where there was no brightness before". One remarkable fact which the profile omitted was that Haileybury had now provided three Cambridge Union Presidents over three consecutive years, after Michael Barkway (1933) and de Freitas (1934); since Barkway was a Liberal, the trio represented each of the major parties. This is a reasonable indication that the coalition spirit at Westminster was reflected at other political levels.[38]

Presiding over the Union was not the sole source of excitement for Cub in 1935. At that time Cambridge University sent two representatives to Parliament – an anomaly which presumably escaped the attentions of reformers in the previous century because so many MPs had spent time at England's oldest universities. While Cub was President one of the Cambridge seats fell vacant. He was convinced that one of his history tutors, Kenneth Pickthorn, would be an ideal candidate. Cambridge was not Haileybury, and Pickthorn, an expert on the Tudor period, could display his political allegiances without fear of dismissal; indeed he was President of CUCA. Pickthorn could be regarded as a good advertisement for the old university seats; he was deeply eccentric, but the learning which he had poured into noted books on the reigns of Henry VII and VIII was arguably more valuable to the House of Commons than the army of "hard-faced men" which Stanley Baldwin had deplored on the Conservative side after the First World War. At first Pickthorn hesitated, but Cub flattered him into submission, telling him that it was his duty to stand, and that he might become "the Disraeli of the twentieth century". This unlikely prophecy was the more discreditable to Cub since he already knew his tutor's limitations. Perhaps he was prejudiced in his views by many pleasant evenings in Pickthorn's oak-panelled room in Corpus Christi, "set with the magnificence of the College silver, the officers of the Association gathered to meet a series of distinguished Tory politicians and to enjoy the luxury of political gossip to the

accompaniment of port and cigars". However, the new Disraeli
secured the seat unopposed, and proved adaptable enough to find a
parliamentary berth in a mining area after the abolition of the university constituencies by the postwar Labour government. Hence he was
in the House throughout Cub's eleven-year career as an MP, but they
never held a private conversation. Pickthorn's former student later
explained that "when I met him pacing the long corridors of Westminster I always waited for him to say something. He never did – and
to my shame, neither did I". Their only verbal exchange occurred in
the Chamber, when Cub as Minister of State at the Commonwealth
Relations Office was interrupted by Pickthorn's correction of a
grammatical slip. Cub hoped "that memories of my debt to him for so
many kindnesses so many years before softened my reply to his
intervention", but their lack of intimacy in spite of their previous
connections must be attributed to the older man's peculiarities – and
the bizarre atmosphere of the House.[39]

In July 1935 Cub bade a sad farewell to Cambridge after settling
some debts with the town's tradesmen, including "the grocer opposite
Corpus who had regularly supplied the marmalade, Bourbon biscuits
and coffee". His last few days had been a mixture of joy and regret:

> In company with friends who would soon be scattered, to meet
> only occasionally and perhaps never again, I tried to cram into
> these few brief hours a final taste of all those experiences which
> had become so familiar. We took our punt from the boathouse
> above Silver Street and lay for a long sunny day beneath the
> dreaming willows. We listened to the madrigals sung in the light
> of lanterns under the powdered stars on the Backs at King's. We
> had sumptuous dinners and drank the extra green beer at the
> Festival Bar. We returned to College in the early hours of each
> morning by a route which took us stealthily across the gravel of
> the Master's Lodge and over a high brick wall not yet protected
> by barbed wire or glass.[40]

But at twenty-three Cub had learned to avoid public displays of
emotion; he reserved these bitter-sweet reflections for an autobiographical novel which he began (and soon abandoned) during the war.
At Cambridge he preferred to show to his friends the self-deprecating

side of his nature, as betrayed in this mock-epitaph which survives in his short-lived undergraduate diary:

Poor Cuthbert A has drunken deep
To the brim was filled life's cup.
In mother earth he lies asleep –
The silly little pup!

Despite having found the law component of his degree course "intensely boring" Cub had enrolled at the Middle Temple and taken his preliminary Bar examinations in 1935. He failed in one paper, but "scraped through" overall. However, at best the law had always been regarded by his father as a reliable route into politics, and the Presidency of the Union had opened a promising short-cut. On 25 August he sent a polite but confident note to Major-General Sir Reginald Hoskins, applying for the post of Junior Tutor at the Bonar Law Memorial College, Ashridge, near Berkhamsted in Hertfordshire. It was not until November that his appointment, at a salary of £150 per year, was formally confirmed; he attributed his success to the influence of Kenneth Pickthorn, who had brought the position to his attention, but he must have seemed a strong candidate regardless of patronage. The first few inches of the greasy pole which Cub was set on climbing had been passed without a slip.[41]

Chapter Two

A National Faith

Cub's extra year in Cambridge had clearly paid political dividends, and before the end of 1935 it gave him the opportunity for some more foreign travel. As one of two Cambridge Union representatives he sailed from Southampton for the United States on 23 October. They were leaving for a six-week speaking tour of universities in the East; also on board were two Oxford men, on a similar mission to the western states.

At twenty-three Cub was already a seasoned traveller, and the journal which he managed to keep for much of this trip betrays no special sense of excitement. His father's reaction was quite different. On the pretext of illustrating the contrast between Cub's journey and the voyage to Vancouver undertaken by his own father seventy-two years before, Cecil provides a star-struck account for readers of *The House of Curious*. Admittedly it was relevant to point out that Cub's journey, on the *Berengaria*, had taken only six days compared with the five months endured by Arthur Alport in 1863, but it was less justifiable to allude to the cocktail party which Cub and his fellow students threw for their fellow-passengers in 1935. As Cecil breath-lessly reported, among the guests were "Sir Ronald Lindsay, the British Ambassador to Washington; Aubrey Smith, the cinema star, and other distinguished persons".[1]

In fact Cub's diary records no other revellers "distinguished" enough to be named, and clearly both he and his father were more interested in two guests who were too seasick to turn up – the "two beautiful and famous young ladies from Hollywood, Merle Oberon and Tilly Losch, laid low" as Cecil put it, "by an unchivalrous and angry sea". It was some consolation that Aubrey Smith (a Cambridge man and former English cricket captain) had starred in one of Cub's favourite films, *The Life and Times of a Bengal Lancer*. Cub enjoyed the chance to interrogate the Ambassador, who treated his fellow-guests to some indiscreet remarks about the United States. When Edward Heath embarked on a similar trip as an Oxford representative in 1939 he was given official instructions to avoid political controversy at a time when Britain needed US assistance in the struggle with Germany. Even in 1935 the "special relationship" was under discussion, but the atmosphere was much more relaxed; Lindsay merely warned the delegates that they should not be too "snooty". The Ambassador remarked that the links between the two nations were "psychological rather than political", and to illustrate the point he mentioned the boost to Britain's popularity in the States after the recent Jubilee celebrations for George V. An American guest chipped in with the prediction that the travellers were unlikely "to find so many trollops in the bigger cities as we did in London or Manchester", information which the representatives of Britain's great universities politely acknowledged.[2]

The party was a success, even if it was regularly punctuated by the sound of an elderly lady being sick in the cabin next door. It certainly helped to break any remaining ice between the four travellers. One of the Oxford men was Tony Greenwood, the son of the former Labour Minister of Health and a new addition to Cub's list of socialist friends. Although the teams went their separate ways soon after reaching America the relationship with Greenwood lasted far beyond this trip; indeed Cub and Greenwood regarded themselves as "political twins", whose careers advanced at a similar rate within their respective parties.

Cub's Cambridge partner, John Royle from Peterhouse, had no party affiliation but had been a regular and entertaining speaker in the Union. Richard Kay-Shuttleworth from Oxford, the heir to a peerage, made up the travelling group. As Royle joked many years later, of the four he was the only one not to end up in the House of Lords.[3]

In New York the young orators saw a production of *Porgy and Bess*: Cub told his companions that he had enjoyed it "except for the music".[4] This was the only day for relaxation, and some hard work lay ahead. Over the six-week tour Cub and Royle spoke at twenty-seven venues, "ranging from Yale University to a small negro college in the South". At the University of Michigan, Detroit, they contested the relative merits of the British and American political systems in front of an estimated crowd of 2000; perhaps Cub recalled the occasion at the Cambridge Union three years earlier when he had opposed the view that "This House sees more hope in Moscow than in Detroit". No doubt he still felt the same, but after touring the Detroit slums in a bullet-proof police car he was probably reinforced in his opinion that while America might be superior to the Soviet Union, Britain was better than both. Cub and Royle would have preferred to avoid debating questions which might have offended their hosts but their own suggested topics had been overruled. As a result, throughout the tour they found themselves having to apologise for what they were about to say before demolishing the pretensions of the American constitution.[5]

The team also took part in four radio broadcasts. On the first occasion Cub admitted to feeling "terrified", but "although it was not at all easy to be profound at such a short notice" he felt that his performance had improved by the end of the tour. They were often photographed and interviewed by reporters; on these occasions Cub behaved with street-wise cynicism, noting in his diary that "there is always a great satisfaction in telling lies to those very excellent men. One may be certain that they will always be substituted for bigger and better lies". In fact Cub's diary showed that he was, at least temporarily, acting in the character of "those very excellent men"; discussions about prohibition with his Detroit taxi-driver, and on juvenile delinquincy with a court official in Cleveland, were carefully recorded. Perhaps he was thinking of writing a book, but his reflections were turned into an article on American attitudes towards

Britain for *The London Imp.* This magazine was published by the Junior Imperial League, a youth body attached to the Conservative Party. Even this limited success had some of its lustre removed when the editor asked him to take out "sweeping generalisations" including the claim that only six of the American students he had met were interested in politics; as a final insult his initials were printed wrongly.[6]

The trip was not completely absorbed by work; Cub claimed that during the entire six weeks they were never in bed before midnight, and never up before eight.[7] He remembered ascending the Empire State Building, and seeing the orange groves of Florida. The team also made a foray across the border to Montreal, where the snow emphasised the vast distances of North America. Among the many people they met were Colonel House, close confidant of the late President Woodrow Wilson, and the Justices of the Supreme Court in Washington. In Montreal Cub had a social encounter of a different kind. In a cabaret he met a show-girl, and invited her to his table. He confessed that he "waited in trepidation. My experience of this sort of thing is limited in the extreme. I have only been at one night club in London. Chorus girls have always filled me with suspicion, as the sort of people who spend their spare time in blackmailing young men". If the young lady anticipated any transactions of that kind, she was to be disappointed; indeed all the profit was on Cub's side, because before their brief conversation ended she had given the inquisitive Englishman some useful insights into her life in Montreal. Even so, this was one interview which went unreported in his article. John Royle recorded in his diary that he was charmed by many of the female students they encountered, but the majority seemed to be in love with Anthony Eden.[8]

When Cub visited Germany in 1932 his reflections were those of an intelligent tourist. The records of his American visit show that he was right to envisage a career in politics. He was anxious to learn from everyone he met, and his comments on what he found showed that he was quick to draw general lessons. After reflecting on Roosevelt's New Deal in his article, he claimed that "the internal problems of the United States will never really be solved until the commercialisation of politics is finally suppressed". This was rather naive even in 1936 when the article appeared, but it tallied with the attitudes which he had brought away from Haileybury. "Americans are beginning to realise that service to the community is one of the obligations of every citizen", he wrote, "and though this attitude may not be very widespread as yet, Mr Roosevelt has done a great service in encouraging it". In truth Cub was not very impressed by the Americans he encountered, and his optimism about their devotion to public service was more the product of wishful thinking than of observation. He had good reason for wanting to think well of them; as he put it, "now is a moment when friendship between the two nations should be greatly strengthened, for Anglo–American co-operation would not only be an antidote to war, but would give to Western civilization that element of stability which it so urgently needs". This was impressive work for a twenty-three year old, and the political outlook which informed the article shows that Cub's progressive Conservatism, based on a sense of duty to the whole community, was already formed at least in outline.[9]

On his return from America Cub found that his application to the Bonar Law College had been successful, and he began work in March 1936. His appointment showed that there might not yet be a "wind of change" within the Conservative Party, but a refreshing breeze had certainly sprung up. "Ashridge", as the College was usually known, had been set up after some furious fund-raising by Conservative supporters, notably Stanley Baldwin's close friend Sir John Davidson who was also instrumental in setting up the Conservative Research Department. Previously the home of the Earls of Bridgewater, Ashridge was bought to replace the party's previous educational establishment, the Philip Stott College near Northampton. Significantly the latter had been opened in 1923 – the year after Labour formed its first government. The Conservatives could no longer rely on unthinking loyalty for their votes, and now felt that they were engaged in a "war of ideas" against socialism.

The Philip Stott College had proved unsuitable as a base for the party's new educational drive, and Ashridge was opened by Davidson on 1 July 1929. Major-General Hoskins, who had previously been Principal at Philip Stott, was transferred to the new college. The students, as described by Cub, were scarcely a representative cross-section of British society: they included prospective parliamentary candidates, elderly female activists, agents and organisers, retired army officers "and a number of serious minded girls and young men, for whom a mild interest in politics gave substance to what otherwise was a somewhat idle and frivolous existence". Cub's Cambridge background allowed him to feel comfortable in this *milieu*; nevertheless, he was the son of a gold-prospecting doctor, and in a party which still demanded heavy financial contributions from its MPs it is noteworthy that Hoskins considered him a suitable candidate for a job which was a promising launching-pad for the career of a young and ambitious tutor.[10]

Cub certainly regarded his post as a marvellous opportunity. The lectures he gave provided a further chance to hone his speaking skills, although he would have to be careful in future not to lapse into a slightly pedantic style, as if the MPs in the Commons' chamber were a class at Ashridge. In fact at least two of his later colleagues, Gilbert Longden and Peter Thorneycroft (both of whom were his seniors), attended his lectures; when Thorneycroft became Chancellor of the Exchequer in 1957 his tutor (Cub) was a junior minister, and his tutor's tutor (Pickthorn) had returned to the back-benches after a brief spell as a humble PPS in the Department of Education.

Ashridge also gave Cub the chance to meet many leading party figures, including Baldwin and the former Foreign Secretary Austen Chamberlain. Cub was a great admirer of Baldwin's politics of class concilliation, but his most vivid memory of the visit was that the Prime Minister had a spot of blood on his collar, which reminded him of Cromwell. Chamberlain gave a talk on the non-aggression pact which he had negotiated at Locarno in 1925. Cub thought that Chamberlain, though elegant, was a rather light-weight politician; possibly this later view was coloured by the knowledge that Locarno, which had been hailed as a guarantor of lasting European peace, was already crumbling by the time its author spoke at Ashridge. In addition to political stars of the past and the present, Cub met some who would play a considerable part in the future, including the later Chancellor Kingsley Wood and Duncan Sandys who gave a talk in 1936 on the darkening international situation. The person who impressed Cub the most was the great imperial soldier and administrator, Lord Lugard, then in his late seventies. Perhaps Cub was captivated by a political figure who was also a man of action; more likely, given that the young lecturer was already specializing in imperial affairs, the nature and setting of Lugard's work gave him his greatest appeal.[11]

Given their diverse backgrounds, the students at Ashridge were almost as interesting as the visiting lecturers. Among the "serious-minded young men" was a follower of G. K. Chesterton, who recalled conversations with fellow-students which ranged over Nietzsche, Marx and Jacobitism. On one occasion Cub was delivering a brash survey of the development of native policy in Cape Colony before 1914; when the lecture was over "a little man in the audience got up and said that he was very interested in what Mr Alport had told them about the Cape native legislation, because he had been Secretary of Native Affairs at the time and [had] been responsible for drafting the various Acts. Very gently he corrected one or two of my errors". This kind of coincidence was unlikely to happen very often in future, but it taught Cub to master his subjects as far as possible before airing his views in public. Like most teachers, he had to tackle some subjects which were outside his specialist area; when confronted many years later with a student's notes of a lecture on "Law and the Citizen", delivered in October 1936, he admitted that he had been skating on rather thin ice when dealing with Magna Carta.[12]

Set in a beautiful woodland park, Ashridge was an ideal venue for the beginning of a love affair. The student who took these notes (and at first misspelt her tutor's name "Allport") was the nineteen year-old Rachel Bingham. The daughter of Ralph Bingham, a grandson of the fourth Earl of Lucan and a distinguished soldier, Rachel had been presented as a debutante to George V in the previous year. In a much later newspaper interview, Rachel explained that she was "brought up and educated to become a good wife and mother and to enjoy the social activities of the circle to which I belonged". Yet she had no intention of being merely a decorous parasite in a society which she knew to be deeply divided. She recognised that her position brought obligations; after leaving school her preparations for a life of public service included a fact-finding mission to a South Wales colliery, and her attendance at Ashridge which was known as a breeding-ground for "good citizens". Here the attractive brunette caught the tutor's eye, although Cub jokingly accused her of not paying much attention to his wise words ("in fact I imagine you were flirting with a boyfriend in the row behind"). They kept in touch after Cub left Ashridge in 1937, and were together to watch the coronation procession of George VI in May of that year; Cub, who obtained tickets from a contact in order to impress his former student, drew on memories of this occasion to enliven his first book. Rachel asked Cub to partner her at some social engagements, which were not always comfortable for him since Rachel seemed to know everybody and was constantly being dragged away to meet acquaintances. Cub, by contrast, knew nobody, and would be left "in embarrassed isolation until I took her off to supper". On one occasion a young man in a similar predicament turned to him and said "You're a bit old for this sort of thing, aren't you?". The besotted ex-tutor – only twenty-five at the time – felt deeply chastened, but nevertheless he told his mother at about this time that he intended to marry Rachel. Apart from her physical attractions, Rachel combined an enjoyment of life with a serious appreciation of public issues; to Cub her desire to make herself useful if she could exemplified the paternalistic Conservative tradition at its best. These were solid foundations for a lasting attachment – which was just as well, because they would be severely tested over the next few years.[13]

Meeting Rachel Bingham was the most important example of fortune favouring Cub while he was at Ashridge. His acquaintance with "Rab" Butler could not be described as having arisen through luck; he had kept up his friendship with Butler's younger brother Jock, and it is strange that their paths had not crossed through the normal course of Cub's work at Ashridge. But the circumstances of their first meeting were certainly fortunate for Cub. Early in 1936 his successor as President of the Cambridge Union, Charles Fletcher Cooke, invited him to speak in a debate alongside Rab; Attlee, the new Labour leader, led for the opposition. Given the relationship with his brother Rab was bound to watch Cub closely, but even without this motive he would have been impressed by the ex-President who made one of his best Union performances. Butler at this time was an under-secretary at the India Office, a position of acute political sensitivity during the 1930s; in 1935 he helped to draft and push through the India Act, against Churchill's enraged opposition. Of more immediate relevance for Cub was Rab's growing influence within the party organisation; in 1937 he was given the chairmanship of the Conservative Central Education Committee. Cub was determined to cultivate this connection, and in June 1937 sent Butler a note congratulating him on his next appointment in the Ministry of Labour; his efforts were rewarded in December of that year, when he was offered the post of Assistant Secretary for Political Education at the Conservative Central Office.[14]

Many good things flowed from Cub's association with Ashridge, and even his decision to leave in late 1937 turned out to be well judged. Instead of a useful staging-post, the college might have proved a dead-end had he stayed. During the Second World War the building was requisitioned, and never fully returned to its former role. Finding a job within the Conservative Party was not a formality when the war ended, but things would certainly have been more complicated had he retained his link with Ashridge. The new post brought him to work in Palace Chambers, near the House of Commons, and while Ashridge was not exactly peripheral to party activity he was now much closer to the centre of the political world.

Cub was probably not aware that his appointment was an important move in Rab's campaign to revitalise the party's education wing. In October 1937 the chairman of Ashridge, Sir Geoffrey Ellis, had protested to Butler that his ideas for the education committee would involve "a certain amount of overlapping" in the functions of the two organisations. Ellis tried to draw a distinction between education, which was Ashridge's job, and partisan propaganda, which should be handled by the education committee. His fears for the college were well founded; Butler's insistence that the Education Department should reach out to uncommitted voters through well argued pamphlets and lectures rather than crude propaganda made Ashridge seem redundant. Poaching one of Ashridge's most promising young men was a masterstroke in this campaign; Butler was so anxious to secure Cub's services that he explained his plans in detail over the telephone, and another committee member, Lady Falmouth, pressed Cub to leave the college. Writing to accept the offer on 15 December Cub told Butler that "My conversation with you put the whole matter in a different light . . . it is something in which I would not willingly miss the opportunity of taking a part". Butler scribbled "This is a triumph" on Cub's letter; Lady Falmouth wrote of her delight at Cub's acceptance, and noted that the higher salary they were offering "is worth it to get him". The newspaper correspondent who observed that Cub's appointment meant that "Ashridge is rapidly becoming the Staff

College of the Conservative Party" was revealing more than he knew. To cement his alliance with the Butler family, Cub shared lodgings with Jock off the Tottenham Court Road until the latter's marriage.[15]

After the shock of the 1945 general election it was easy for Conservatives to feel that the party machinery had decayed during the 1930s because of a sense of complacency arising from the crushing victory of 1935. The idea that these were wasted years, followed by a burst of activity after the war, is associated with the impression that Conservative-dominated governments during the 1930s appeased their foreign enemies and met economic crisis with grim-faced inactivity; it is also fostered by the fact that the most glittering Conservative talents of the early postwar period, such as Iain Macleod, Reginald Maudling and Enoch Powell, had little or no contact with the party prior to 1945. Like most historical clichés, this view is at best a partial truth. The defeat of 1945 merely accelerated developments which were already taking place within the Conservative Party; it provided extra impetus for those, like Butler and Cub, who before the war had embarked on the task of "modernising" the organisation and its policies.

The strongest evidence of continuity in the prewar and postwar periods is the new emphasis on political literature. Ashridge could help to ensure that Conservative activists were kept up to date on contemporary issues, but it necessarily catered for a restricted audience. Cub and Butler could make a similar effort through the Conservative Political Circle, which they set up to provide weekly lectures, and through regular conferences to inform and encourage party activists. To attract a wider public Butler planned a series of "cheap, concise, and readable books", which were to be published by Faber & Faber. The first of the series, *A National Faith*, appeared towards the end of 1938. Cub was the author of the tract, although at Rab's suggestion his identity was concealed by the *nom de plume* "A Modern Conservative". Ironically Butler had originally approached Kenneth Pickthorn to write the book.[16]

After the polished essay on America which Cub had written in 1936, he had quickly advanced to more ambitious projects. His father had published *The Lighter Side of the War* back in 1935; Cub had found himself reading it when he should have been studying for his Bar examinations. During his spell at Ashridge he had begun work on a book of his own, a study of imperial constitutional history with the provisional title *An Introduction to British Empire Development*, and a contract was agreed with the publisher Lovat Dickson in March 1937. What Cub had designed as a textbook became the subject of a small controversy. The Right Book Club, which had sprung up in response to the successful left-wing series published by Victor Gollancz, expressed an interest in making Cub's volume its "Book of the Month". But the Conservative Party had forged links with a rival book club, the National Book Association, and Cub came under pressure to change his allegiance. Despite the efforts of Sir Arthur Bryant and Sir John Davidson, he refused to break with the Right Book Club. A compromise was reached, whereby the book (now entitled *Kingdoms in Partnership*) was promoted by both organisations. Cub's stubborn stand paid off; later he recalled that the two deals brought him sales of 28,000 from which he received £158 – more than his original annual salary.[17]

Kingdoms in Partnership is very dated reading for the generations who regard the British Empire as an embarrassing relic of the nineteenth century. Although most of the book is given over to an explanation of past developments, the author is preoccupied with hopes for the future; his writing comes alive in these sections, and one is left with the impression that the historical information has been swotted up and pasted in to provide some basis for the fabric of his vision. For Cub, the commonwealth was an ideal because it had grown organically from an empire which was forged without a design – unlike the League of Nations, which had been the product of abstract thinking. As an association of free nations bound by friendship and a common allegiance to the Crown, the commonwealth might even develop into the League's more effective replacement.

The book was widely reviewed, and inevitably the critics took issue with Cub's optimism. According to the *Manchester Guardian* reviewer, the book could only end on a hopeful note because the author had chosen to leave India and the dependent colonies out of his discussion. This was a telling blow: although E. H. Carr was a little harsh to claim in his review in *The Times* that "one misses any attempt to relate the ideal of the commonwealth with the wider ideal of humanity", Cub had begged serious questions by dealing exclusively with white-dominated nations which had been shaped to varying degrees by exposure to Anglo-Saxon traditions. Ultimately *Kingdoms in Partnership* can only be regarded as an uncritical hymn of praise to the British system of government, but it was a notable achievement for a twenty-five year-old. Indeed, one critic sought grounds for complaint in the book's "polished and over-sophisticated" nature. Cub might have learned from the book's reception that his idealism should be restrained (or better supported by fact) in the future, but he had no reason to worry about his prose-style. Carr was particularly taken by a sentence in the concluding chapter; "The tendency of every institution is to become rigid; and unless the commonwealth is for ever prepared for change, it will be crushed by the pressure of events like a ship in an Arctic ice-pack". Cub was providing a gloss, in an international context, for Edmund Burke's celebrated remark that "A state without the means of some change is without the means of its conservation": but unlike Burke he relished the prospect of change. Fortune could not have thrown a more suitable recruit in Butler's path.[18]

Cub's personal interests were reflected in *A National Faith*, which contained two chapters on the empire. But that tract was written under the shadow of the European controversies that now clearly threatened a new war. As Butler's friend, Cub was better informed than most; in March 1938 Rab was moved from the Ministry of Labour to the Foreign Office, where as Under-Secretary to Viscount Halifax he supported the government's attempts to appease Hitler. Cub was spending regular weekends at Butler's Essex home, Stanstead Hall, during the summer and autumn of 1938. Both Rab and his wife Sydney eagerly read *A National Faith* through its various drafts – Butler even worked on it while attending the League of Nations Assembly at Geneva in September. Foreign developments must have been discussed when they met, but it is unclear how much Butler divulged, and to what degree Cub concurred with the older man's views. One discussion at Stanstead was very clearly recalled by Cub in later years; while they were walking together in the grounds of the house Rab suddenly declared that "what I really need is a spaniel". In an oblique fashion typical of him, he was offering to help Cub's career in return for blind loyalty. Had Butler never spoken these words their relations might well have developed along these lines as the natural product of friendship; after the proposal had been made (especially by means of the canine metaphor) Cub was torn between his obvious need for a powerful patron and his desire to stand on his independent merits.[19]

When Cub heard on the radio that Neville Chamberlain was planning to fly to Munich in September 1938 he exclaimed "Bloody old fool". Yet he knew that Butler considered Chamberlain's action to be exactly "what a sensible, civilised Conservative Prime Minister should do or at any rate attempt". Cub has suggested that Butler's natural preference for negotiation as a means of settling international problems was reinforced by a deep ambivalence about the military life. Prevented from active service himself by a partial paralysis of one hand resulting from a childhood accident, he seemed envious when Cub enlisted; even so, among the many guests whom he met at Stanstead Cub could not remember any soldiers. The only time he saw his friend in military guise was when he attended the enthronement of a Bishop of Chelmsford and watched Rab, as a Deputy Lieutenant of Essex, saunter down the aisle "looking extremely shamefaced and using his sword as a sort of rolled up umbrella".[20]

Given Cub's real views on the Munich negotiations it is ironic that the policy of appeasement should have induced the only awkward passage in *A National Faith*. After discussing the sanctity of treaty obligations he includes a list of those countries which Britain was bound to assist in the event of war; it ends with a lame acknowledgement that this should "probably" include "the new Czechoslovakia". The "probably" was well advised, since on the previous page he had claimed that the failure to maintain sufficient forces to defend allied nations is just as serious a breach of trust as to disregard treaties entirely, and although Britain had guaranteed the new Czech borders it was hardly in a position to honour the promise. His unease on this subject is indicated by an attempt to clarify the position in the pamphlet's only footnote, which trots out the party line on appeasement, congratulating Mr Chamberlain and applauding the "sacrifices" which the Czechs had made "to prevent war". In fact as late as October Butler was wondering "whether it is possible to write a chapter about our attitude to foreign affairs without doing more harm than good", given the uncertain international outlook.[21]

This was not an ideal year to be making clear statements of long-term principle on any subject; the overall impression left by *A National Faith* is one of an author running hard to avoid being overtaken by events. For once Cub had been unlucky; if the pamphlet had appeared in the previous year there would have been no need for the stark contrast between the positive aspects and the sombre note on which it ended. The iminence of war meant that the campaign of political education on behalf of the party could never win anything like the attention which it received when it was renewed after 1945. As a result of the Second World War, the continuity between the ideas expressed in Cub's pamphlet and those associated with the party's postwar "relaunch" have never received adequate recognition.

A National Faith could be interpreted as a clever piece of party propaganda, which tricks the reader into confusing the Conservative Party with Britain, and concluding that the opponents of one are traitors to the other. To match this message, most of the chapters are written with a Baldwinesque lyricism, evoking "the faded colours of merry simple England, full of white-washed cottages and maypoles on the green" to illustrate the national character of "patriotism, personal service, and a real spirit of independence". The reforms of the past are effortlessly absorbed into a Conservative world-view. Democracy, for example, is described as "natural, national, almost axiomatic"; the Conservative Party is not given exclusive credit for its introduction, but the reader would not be able to guess that the thought of working people exercising the right to vote had appalled so recent a leader as Lord Salisbury.[22]

This kind of thing is only to be expected from a tract intended to help Conservatism "justify itself in the eyes of a new democracy". But there are two features of *A National Faith* which make it something more than a propaganda exercise. The first has such a strong bio-graphical relevance that it must have been sincerely meant. The twenty-six year-old author praises the "broad aristocracy" which governed Britain up to the First World War. This "was an aristocracy in the real sense of the word. The majority of its members realised instinctively that their privileges carried with them the duty of public service". Later he returns to the same theme, and goes further: "It may eventually become recognised that the real justification for privilege and wealth is the contribution which the individual makes to the life and advancement of the nation". This implies that those who do not fulfil their obligations should lose their privileges, and Cub does not shirk that conclusion, toying with unworkable ideas for heaping extra taxes on those who neither work for their money nor perform useful services. All this was quite easily said, but Cub had delivered the same message in his reflections on America, then fallen in love with his ideal of civic duty in the shape of Rachel Bingham.[23]

The second reason for reading *A National Faith* as more than a partisan pamphlet is its reformist spirit. Like Butler, Cub was already impatient with the stereotyped Conservatism which grudgingly accepted yesterday's reforms but set its face against those of the present. In passages which clearly anticipate Quintin Hogg's classic *The Case for Conservatism* (1947) he argues that Conservatives should accept the nationalisation of public utilities, opposing state ownership in other cases not as a dogmatic principle, but because on balance it is likely to prove less efficient than private enterprise in raising overall living standards. He traces the growing involvement of the state in economic activity with relish, urging this especially when its purpose is to reduce unemployment; among his positive suggestions here is an extensive programme of re-training, as well as public works. He denies that Conservatives are opposed to the trade unions on principle; they only deplore their influence if it is used to push apart the different classes of Britain. Perhaps most surprising is his advocacy of radical reform for the House of Lords: "It is possible to envisage an Upper House to which the members are elected partly by the peerage itself and partly as representatives of the professions, trade unions, and various other industrial and social bodies". This showed that Cub had been studying the ideas of Harold Macmillan and others who believed in a "corporate" state; but Macmillan was regarded as a rebel, and Cub was smuggling his ideas into an official publication. His thinking had clearly moved on since he had defended the Lords in a Cambridge Union debate of February 1934 – although even then he had quipped that the Upper House "was only needed to correct the grammar and spelling of the very busy House of Commons".[24]

A National Faith, then, looks forward to *One Nation* more than backwards to Baldwin. Appropriately, Disraeli's is the presiding spirit of its pages, and Cub refers to his warning, in the novel *Sybil*, about Britain becoming "Two Nations": the rich and the poor. Now that the Conservative Party had accepted full democracy it could make a reality of Disraeli's message: it could be a truly national party, "unallied with any special interest and concerned for the welfare, not of a single class, but of Britain and the empire as a whole", and capable of building "a national unity upon a basis of fairness and justice". To those who only think of politics as a contest of sound-bites, the latter phrase might ring hollow. But the circumstances in which it was written were very different, and Cub believed that things were moving in the direction which he and Butler both wanted. He remained true to these principles throughout his career, and at some cost to himself.[25]

After completing his pamphlet Cub set off alone on a tour of Italy. Determined to see the country before a new war broke out, he spent the Christmas of 1938 there. It was the second successive winter that he had travelled; in January he had invested his profits from *Kingdoms in Partnership* in a trip to Cairo, where he combined business with pleasure by visiting his parents and giving a talk on behalf of the Conservative Education Department about the special study he had made of political youth movements. At that time Cecil and Janet were embarking on a new life in Egypt. Now a Fellow of the Royal College of Physicians, Cecil had enjoyed fourteen trouble-free years at St Mary's Hospital. His laboratory had been close to that of Alexander Fleming, and he was among the first to inspect the mould which produced penicillin. But he had not lost his taste for adventure, and when in June 1936 Fleming suggested that he might put in for the Chair of Clinical Medicine at Cairo University he readily agreed. He was appointed in October, but the first hint of future trouble came with a delay of six more months before he was asked to take up the post. Cecil sensed that he would soon be breaking lances with his favourite enemy – the bureaucratic mind.[26]

From Italy, Cub sent his parents regular sight-seeing bulletins. In Florence he posted a card of the Pontevecchio, and in Rome he saw the Sistine Chapel before attending an audience with the Pope. However, as in America his journalistic nose was twitching. He was particularly keen to gauge the mood of the Italian public, and was disappointed to meet only one outspoken opponent of Mussolini. His three reports (which for some reason he sent for publication in the *Cornish Times*) show that he was not deluded by apparent friendly feelings towards the British. The first two, written before Neville Chamberlain flew in for talks with the grasping dictator, hint at concessions but conclude hopefully that the Prime Minister's arguments would be backed by sufficient military power to "impress such a realist as Signor Mussolini". However, the third, composed after

Chamberlain's visit, has a darker tone. He sensed an "almost pathetic anxiety of the ordinary Italian for peace", but he had already warned that the Italian public was ignorant of international dealings and could be expected to back the leader who had brought greater prosperity at home. He concluded carefully that although he "might be speaking out of turn – I hope that whatever the cost may be, France and Britain will put an end to the business of blackmail . . . We can't go on living from spring to autumn, always faced with the possibility of war". These were not the words of an appeaser – especially since, when the "possibility of war" turned into a certainty, Cub expected to be in the thick of the fighting. Whether or not Butler thought that he had secured a "spaniel", Cub was already showing that no leash could hold him for long.[27]

Cub had been commissioned into the Artists' Rifles battalion while still at Cambridge, in 1934. This unit, originally founded for volunteers by the Victorian painter Frederick, Lord Leighton, was now used to train future officers for an expanded wartime army. Most of its recruits were young men from the City of London and other professions, who were learning the rudiments of soldiering in their spare time. Others were more experienced; Cub was given a lift to his first training camp in the back of a chauffeur-driven Rolls Royce owned by an Alderman of the City who had fought in the First World War. The training was handicapped by a shortage of equipment – to signify incoming mortar fire they waved blue flags – but at least by 1939 Cub had gained a little knowledge of drill and tactics.

On 2 September 1939 Cub was playing golf at Barton-on-Sea, near Bournemouth, when his game was disturbed by the sight of six destroyers sailing past the Isle of Wight. That Saturday afternoon he caught the train to London, arriving at the Artists' Rifles Headquarters in time to hear Chamberlain's declaration of war after the ultimatum to Germany expired on the Sunday morning. The battalion was marshalled under the arches of Charing Cross station, then proceeded to Dymchurch on the Kent coast via Hythe. The last leg of the journey for the battalion, with all its equipment, was conducted by a train on the famous minature railway; this struck Cub as "a most undignified and unmilitary" procedure.[28]

At Dymchurch Cub was given his first wartime command, of a company of riflemen who had been considered unsuitable for commissioned rank. After a few weeks of listening to their complaints he was sent to Aldershot, where for six months he led another company, including a group of young actors. During this posting he wrote to his parents, proudly explaining that "the very scratch affair with which we started is [now] a going concern". He remarked that he enjoyed "making our barrack-rooms tidy and have become much more methodical myself . . . I feel that I have cured myself of some of the casualness of which I was previously guilty". This was a cunning ruse to impress his father, since Cecil had been a rigid enforcer of tidiness whenever he had charge of his units in the previous war; indeed that was probably the main reason for the friction he had caused. Cub was no doubt more relaxed than his letter would imply; he seems to have escaped with nothing worse than a reputation for eccentricity, earned through his habit of lecturing his company on military history.[29]

Soon after writing his letter Cub was on the move again, this time to the 9th Battalion of the Royal Welch Fusiliers. This was a serious test for his powers of organisation, since the batallion included soldiers who had proved difficult to handle in regular units in France, and the War Office had just decided to replace the previous Welsh officers with a Gordon Highlander and four English company commanders. Cub could not be certain that morale improved very much during his short stay, although the new officers tried to catch the right spirit on St David's Day by eating raw leeks with one foot on the mess-room table. But the experience gave him more intimate contact with the human tragedy of unemployment, since few in his company had been in work before the war. Despite the mixed reputation of the men in the unit, he saw clearly that they would have much to contribute if they were given an opportunity to make something of their lives when peace returned.

As the "phoney war" drew to a close and Britain found itself confronting the Axis powers alone Cub's training at home continued. For six months in 1941 he was on the War Office Staff, before being sent to the 6th War Staff Course at Camberley. His military career seemed to have gone round in a circle since he had been sent to Aldershot more than a year before, but this time he knew that his training would end with a posting abroad. His colleagues on this course included his Cambridge contemporary Enoch Powell, but having formed a low opinion of his fellow-trainees Powell was no more sociable now than he had been as a student. Unlike Powell Cub felt he learned a great deal from Staff College, and having applied for a posting to the Middle East he read everything he could about T. E. Lawrence. As it turned out, Powell was sent to Cairo in October 1941, while Cub had to make do with an appointment as Brigade-Major in the 25th Northern Rhodesia Brigade based at Lusaka.[30]

Before Cub sailed off to war he decided that the time had come to face a different challenge. While at Camberley he had written regularly to Rachel Bingham, although he had hedged his bets by making his letters entertaining rather than romantic. For one moment during this period he came close to blasting his hopes entirely. Rachel's father, who commanded the unit stationed next to Cub's at Camberley, was a compulsive writer of letters to the press, usually on subjects where his thoughts ought to have been concealed. In most cases they remained private through the intervention of his sympathetic Adjutant, who instead of posting them would file them in the waste-paper basket. Perhaps the fact that his reflections never appeared in print convinced Ralph Bingham that writing to the press was a harmless way to exercise his feelings; certainly it did not put him off. Eventually *The Times* did receive a letter, in which Bingham expressed some very impolitic views about the quality of officer recruits from the lower- and middle-classes. It was published, to an understandable storm of protest which almost cost Bingham his career. Cub was one of those who wrote a furious response, but needed no kindly colleague to intervene on his behalf; having made his point, he considered the certain consequences of posting the letter and tore it up instead. This was further evidence of the advantage of "balance" which Cub enjoyed over his father: no doubt Cecil would have dispatched one copy of a blistering note to *The Times* and delivered a second to Bingham by hand. Even so, the incident was a setback to Cub's matrimonial plans, since he had already suspected that Rachel's parents would consider him an unsuitable match on social grounds.

At the end of the Camberley course, reinforced by his new tactical acumen, Cub made a swift advance to Thaxted in Essex where Rachel, now a member of the Womens' Volunteer Service, was looking after a group of evacuee children while spending the evenings reading to the blind vicar, Conrad Noel, who was a well known radical. Cub whisked her off to the Huntingdon races, where he told her of his political ambitions; she acknowledged that he was certain to make a mark for himself. On the drive back to Thaxted he tried to steel himself for the next step, but the miles went by and he cursed his own cowardice. Finally, one mile short of their destination he summoned the courage to ask her to marry him. Later he wondered whether this rash step had been provoked by "the springtime or the war or one might only be in love with love", but he was in deadly earnest – and so did Rachel seem when she refused him. It must have been a difficult final mile.[31]

Nursing his bruises, Cub set off from Liverpool on 2 November 1941 for Africa, in a convoy which also contained a division destined for Singapore. The troops were protected by warships, but they must have felt vulnerable enough when they got news that the British vessels *Repulse* and *The Prince of Wales* had been sunk by Japanese aeroplanes off Malaya, with the loss of 600 men. The Americans had entered the war a few days earlier, but Britain was on the verge of losing both Malaya and Singapore; added to the unpromising state of the European conflict, this was almost its darkest hour. At Durban Cub was transferred to a smaller vessel bound for Mombasa; true to the Alport form-book, this ship was sunk by the Japanese on its return journey. On this leg of his voyage Cub played bridge with three fellow-passengers; one of these, a war correspondent, annoyed Cub by claiming that at the end of the war only Russia and the United States would really count in world affairs. Later he recognised that this newsman was more far-sighted than he; at the time he was furious, and took special pleasure from the money he won in the card-game.

From Mombasa Cub travelled to Nairobi to receive instructions from Lord Francis Scott, the Military Secretary of the Command. Scott, a Kenyan settler who disapproved of pushy newcomers, in-formed him that his original appointment had already been filled. Cub later recalled that he "protested somewhat energetically" against a decision which would set him back to the rank of Captain. His father would no doubt have approved of his outburst, and of its result. Cub was sent to join the 6th King's African Rifles battalion at Marsabit, but retained his promotion to Major. He travelled in the cab of a 3-ton truck, and the journey across the sandy terrain was occasionally hair-raising. Even so, he managed to write a five-verse ballad about the journey (much in the style of his father) with the paper resting on his knee.[32]

Cub's new battalion had just returned to Marsabit, "an oasis in the middle of three deserts", after taking part in the Abyssinian campaign. The other officers were away on leave after their exertions, so he was nominally the senior officer on duty. Despite the circumstances of his birth and his deep interest in imperial affairs Cub's knowledge of Africa was theoretical rather than practical. He took the opportunity of this quiet period to explore the tropical forest around Marsabit and admire the game which was both plentiful and dangerous – a fortnight before Cub's arrival the District Commissioner's residence had been wrecked by a rampaging herd of elephants.[33]

Lord Francis Scott persisted in thinking that Cub was a "difficult character", but after a month at Marsabit he found him a new posting as a Grade II Major (Staff Duties). His new appointment was at the East African Command Headquarters, and his arrival coincided with that of a new Commander-in-Chief, General Sir William Platt. Platt had recently seen action at the battle of Keren, which ended with the surrender of Italian forces in Ethiopia and the restoration of the Emperor Haile Selassie. Soon after his arrival Platt received orders from Winston Churchill to recruit African troops to reinforce the war effort elsewhere, particularly in the Far East. This was a great challenge, since African soldiers had never before been sent to fight outside their own continent. The expansion was Cub's military preoccupation for the next two years, and culminated in the despatch of the 11th East African Division to Burma.

Cub described this period as "the time of my life". It was the closest he had yet come to playing out his childhood games at Moniaive on the adult stage. Although something less than the dictator of a principality he knew that he could ruffle a few feathers without any fear of a check from above. In organising the expansion he had the full backing of General Platt, who gave him the playful nickname of "Brains". Cub was spared the obstructions which had infuriated his father – and his happy position could be traced back to the care which Cecil had taken with his education.[34]

Cub's work, as so often in his career, was of the sort which won no banner headlines but which laid strong foundations for others. As he put it, "I did all the planning of the expansion, issued orders, broadcast for the formation of new units, trespassed ruthlessly on the provinces of the Adjutant and Quartermaster-General's branches and had the satisfaction of watching day by day the East African forces respond to the challenge which the Prime Minister had made to our command". As he became more familiar with Africa he showed special sensitivity to tribal loyalties, ensuring that, as far as possible, their intended roles tallied with their traditional activities. In addition he was responsible for equipping the new units, and ensuring that the right calibre of officers were brought over from the United Kingdom to lead them. Typically his predominant emotion when they were ready to leave for the brutal fighting in Asia was not pride in his organisational skills, but regret that he should be sending men out into danger while himself remaining "in the security and comfort of a rear headquarters".[35]

The various pressures and emotions associated with Cub's role were reflected in his correspondence. Despite the rebuff after the Huntingdon races he occasionally wrote to Rachel. The real importance of his work was much harder to explain than tales of brave deeds in the field. One surviving letter, dating from December 1941, could be taken as an exercise in light irony but is really a sustained piece of self-mockery. On a break in Durban, he wrote that "we gallant boys overseas are having a pretty tough time I can assure you. Take sand: it's so hot when I lie on it after bathing that I get grilled like a lobster". He explained that "when I was coming back to camp the day before yesterday I heard a pounding behind me and the squeal of an elephant – they always squeal before charging – I looked round and there were two huge bull elephants with trunks raised. I stepped aside quite coolly and let them pass – unfortunately the rest of the circus wasn't so interesting". In case Rachel had missed the edge of desperation in this banter, he added a postscript: "Don't forget me entirely please".[36]

Cub's life in Africa did offer him social distractions, including encounters with girls at dances which he reported to Rachel in an attempt to make her jealous. "Out of sight, out of mind" is more often applicable in cases of separation than "absence makes the heart grow fonder", but during the war Cub was the perfect exemplar of the latter outcome. When he wrote from Durban he had little idea of how long he would be away, but as the months turned into years the sense of distance between them increased his despair at the thought of losing any chance he might have of changing her mind. Undated letters, clearly written early in his African career, show that a second, written proposal was no more successful than his first, but he stuck to the task even though letters to and from the UK took so long that intervening events could easily make them irrelevant. In April 1943 Cub twice sent letters to Rachel, both of which include the anguished enquiry "Are you married yet or engaged or nearly engaged?". In the first, he continues "I have laid an even dollar that it will be one of those sailors with the deep blue of the sea in their eyes, slow of speech, with a strong jaw and crisp hair – a deadly type I fear". In spite of his loneliness, Cub still remembered to protect himself from his feelings for Rachel with a touch of levity.[37]

Before Cub wrote again he received a piece of news which made him put away frivolous thoughts of hot sand and circus elephants. A telegram arrived from Jock Butler's wife Hermione, informing him that his friend had been killed in action. As a civil servant in the Home Office Jock had been exempted from service, but having "found a loophole in the regulations" he joined the RAF as a navigator. Almost immediately his plane crashed on take off, and he was killed. Even reports of Cambridge debates in *The Granta* show how deeply loved was Rab's brother, and amidst the grief he felt on Jock's death Cub was able to draw some inspiration. After reporting the news Cub told Rachel that "we were both going to do big things. Now it remains for me to do big things for both of us, although he has already done the greatest thing of all". The circumstances which brought Jock into the conflict gave life to a reflection which can so often sink into a cliché. To Cub he belonged with the noble characters who had sacrificed themselves during the First World War; his career was full confirmation that his own generation could live up to the highest ideals.[38]

Ashamed after Jock's death of his administrative role, Cub tried once more for a Middle East posting, but without success. Instead he was sent, again as a company commander, to the 16th King's African Rifles, stationed at a camp in Yatta thirty miles from Nairobi. For the first time he was in command of African soldiers rather than arranging for them to be sent overseas; the troops were drawn from Kenyan and Ugandan tribes. This period gave Cub his single opportunity of firing a shot at a living target. He took the company on a day and night exercise, during which his Sergeant-Major spotted an old waterbuck about 150 yards away. He pointed to the beast and said "Bwana, nyama". Despite his ineptitude for languages Cub had picked up sufficient Swahili to translate the second word as "meat". According to his own account he instantly knew what was expected; his troops had eaten no meat for several weeks. He borrowed the Sergeant-Major's rifle, "lay down, took careful aim, closed my eyes and fired knowing that my whole reputation depended upon success". The waterbuck obligingly dropped dead, and Cub had earned himself a new nick-name – "Major Smarty-Boots".[39]

Cub was generally very happy in his work with this unit, although there was one unpleasant incident. Platt had been invalided home shortly before Cub's transfer, and his replacement, General Sir Kenneth Anderson, had no experience of colonial troops. Hearing reports of widespread absenteeism, he ordered that the next culprit would be flogged on his return. This decision stood, despite protests, and when the time came it was carried out by the Regimental Sergeant-Major, using the handle of a polo stick, with the battalion drawn up in square formation to witness the punishment. The outcry even affected Anderson, who rescinded the order; Cub believed that he had witnessed the last occasion on which corporal punishment was administered in the British Army. For Cub, long an opponent of the practice, the only comfort was that the victim on this occasion probably suffered little, and enjoyed "the sympathies of all ranks".[40]

After six months with the 16th KAR Cub was asked to move on again, this time to become second in command of the 46th KAR, one of the new battalions which he had helped to establish. This was not an appealing prospect, since the 46th had been earmarked for garrison duty in Ceylon; Cub by this stage of the war wanted either front-line action, or a post more in keeping with his proven organisational skills. He was rescued from this dilemma by a call to East African Command Headquarters, where the Chief-of-Staff, Brigadier Williams, offered him promotion to Lieutenant-Colonel (GSO I), on the strength of his previous success in preparing troops for service overseas. This was not the role which Cub would have chosen for himself, but he acknowledged that it was one which he had performed successfully; he accepted the offer (which, incidentally, brought him to the same military rank as Ralph Bingham). As Cub explained to Rab Butler, his new duties were not exactly free from danger. He travelled 16,000 miles by air and crossed the Indian Ocean twice to visit the East

African forces in Burma and Ceylon (Sri Lanka), visiting the Seychelles and the Maldive Islands for refuelling during his flights. On one of these occasions the Catalina flying boat encountered a typhoon. Cub was sleeping in the rear of the plane at the time, "and when I woke up I suddenly realised that instead of the plane being at 3000 feet it was about 500 feet above a seething and violent sea". For the rest of the journey Cub fluctuated between terror whenever the plane sank even further, and thankful prayers when it climbed. After landing the next morning in the Seychelles he remarked that it had been a rough night; the pilot replied "Yes. I had a hell of a time getting the old bus down to 500 feet because if we had stayed higher in that wind the plane would have disintegrated".[41]

Cub was at Colombo, waiting with General Anderson for a plane back to Africa, when the Commander-in-Chief received a message asking him to send a representative to the War Office for a high-level Staff Duties conference. Although the East African Command was small in comparison to those in Europe and South-East Asia, it was independent and therefore entitled to its own representation. Anderson decided that Cub should go. When they got back to Kenya he caught a flying boat from Mombasa to Khartoum and then to Cairo; over the Nile the pilot took the plane down to 500 feet, but this time to allow his passengers to see the hippopotamus herds. Cecil and Janet had left Cairo by that time, so Cub spent an uncomfortable night at the Shepherd's Hotel. He had brought with him some secret documents, including the order of battle of the East African forces, so he decided to take no risks, trying (with limited success) to sleep with a dog-chain padlocked to his briefcase and attached to his ankle. From Cairo he flew to London via Gibraltar.

Shortly after his visit to England Cub wrote that

When I arrived, the snow was still lying under the hedgerows and in the furrows of the ploughland, and bitter winds were blowing across the bare countryside; but, within a day or two, the weather changed into the faint sunshine which gives the early promise of spring, and I felt, as we all have felt year after year on those occasions, the same uplift of spirit and a sense of returning life. It was perhaps because I saw England at that particular time that everything appeared so reassuring. It appeared symbolic of a promise that in the not-so-far future the dead hand of war would fall away and things which we all love in the English scene would start to reappear.

These words – still marked by the influence of Stanley Baldwin – were written for a broadcast which Cub made on his return to Africa. The speech was designed to remind his listeners that while they guarded the frontiers of the empire everything at home was just as they left it; but for the author of that lyrical tribute to the mother country, a few short weeks had changed life forever.[42]

Chapter Three

"Love and War"

While Cub sailed to Africa in late 1941 Britain was suffering its worst defeats of the war. When he started his return journey the tide had turned. Montgomery's forces had defeated Rommel at the second Battle of El Alamein in November 194~~3~~; the news of this 2 major victory provoked Churchill's famous declaration that, at least, this might be "the end of the beginning". The Prime Minister was still preoccupied with the war effort, but others made planning for peace their priority. The appearance of the Beveridge Report on 1 December, while the country was still celebrating Montgomery's victory, was an unfortunate coincidence for the Conservative Party which was caught off-balance by an overwhelming public welcome. This is not to say that the party had ignored the future entirely; as early as the summer of 1940 the idea was floated of a committee with the limited brief of "collating and presenting to the Prime Minister the views of the Conservative and Unionist Party on post-war problems". By July

1941, when the Post-War Problems Central Committee started its work, Rab Butler had been selected as its chairman.[1]

Butler had kept in regular touch with Cub after the latter's departure for Africa. Cub believed that after Jock's death Rab began to look on him as a surrogate younger brother, but even before the tragedy his friend had written very warmly of future collaboration. In August 1942, for example, he sent to Cub a brief summary of work which had already been done by sub-committees on postwar problems, on youth and education. As Butler put it, "one feels a certain awkwardness in handling these affairs in the present state of the war, but in peace we failed to prepare for war, with the results we have seen. In war we must therefore not fail to prepare for peace". He went on to wish that Cub "could come back and give a hand with all this work. I find it very difficult to go on without able lieutenants". Butler wondered whether Cub might return to take part in army education. Later many Conservatives blamed the dominance of "socialist" army instructors as a primary reason for their election defeat, and in view of this there is some irony in Butler's acknowledgment that Cub would probably consider that his work in Africa was much more important than educating the troops.[2]

In his long letter Rab set out what he regarded as the best guiding principles for the party once peace returned. He believed that "we have to focus the attention of the nation upon . . . the need for fostering the best traits of the national character. The first of these traits is the cultivation of the individual spirit, of enterprise and independance [sic]". He contrasted his own position with that of "the Beveridge school"; "We believe in leading up and not levelling down, in diversity and not in uniformity". He was concerned that the principles enshrined in Beveridge's work would reduce postwar politics to "an auction between the different Parties". The task of Conservatives would be to stress the difference in principle between themselves and their opponents – even, he clearly implied, when these principles led to similar policies.[3] "Thinking aloud" for the benefit of his friend, Butler had identified the problem which would face moderate Conservatives for the rest of the century, and anticipated the position which Cub and his "One Nation" colleagues set out in their famous publication of 1950.[4]

Understandably Cub was anxious to apply some of the new things he had learned in Africa to Britain's postwar position: "I suppose that reform like charity begins at home, but if we don't think out a future for the colonial empire, there won't be any empire to think about". He saw great opportunities for development in Kenya, and confessed that he was tempted to stay out there himself. After Jock's death, however, he turned his thoughts to the domestic political outlook. On 3 February 1943 Rab had told him that "the English Revolution is in being though the manner of its being carried out is not quite clear". The letter fired Cub's imagination and ambition, to the extent that he confessed to feeling "a little swollen headed at the moment". He had just read an article by Churchill's son Randolph, which discussed the revival of "the Tory party". If this party was to be just the same as it was before the war, as Cub took Randolph to mean, he wanted nothing of it.

> I often hoped for a chance in which we could cut all the drift-wood of ideas and interests away and that chance has come . . . Let's be not the Conservative Party but the Constructive Party, the builders, the architects, under God, of a new society. Not led by the nose either by ancient prejudice or modern fashion, by the stubborn Tory or the left intellectual both of whom I have little use for: the latter particularly I despise.

Echoing Rab's letter of October 1942, he declared that

> the wealth of a country is not in its foreign investments or its mines or the fertility of its fields, the antiquity of its institutions, but the spirit, character, industry of its men and women. See that they are sound and everything else will follow. If you know what you want your people to be like then everything else follows – your attitude to health, social development, education, unem-ployment[,] wealth[,] tradition[,] democracy and all the rest . . . I'm going to build good men and women.

Jock's recent death obviously had a part in inspiring these thoughts, and also Cub's resolve that "those of us who had the good fortune to survive, must struggle on to carry it not only to the physical victory but the victory beyond that – over stupidity, self-interest and material-ism".[5]

Cub descended from his rhetorical perch for long enough to promise that he would be willing to come home the next day "if you really want me and you think that I can be of use"; even so, he suggested that "a year more and my apprenticeship will be more or less complete". Having thought the matter over Butler presumably decided that Cub's personal interests lay for the time being in his military career – after all, he had once told Cub that "knowledge of administration" was a vital foundation for a political life – and he took no steps to bring his friend home. Besides, Butler was now more pressed by work than ever. When Cub's letter arrived he was putting together the White Paper which led to the most celebrated legislation of the war – his 1944 Education Act. Had Cub already been at home he would have been very helpful to Butler in this task: when he saw the White Paper he suggested that "some of the ideas in it – or perhaps ideals would be better – have made their appearance in conversations at Stanstead at one time or another". With the principles of the Act settled in his mind, Rab now had to worry about negotiations with the affected interests – notably the churches. Cub lacked the experience for this delicate process. Even so, when Butler next wrote (in October) he told Cub that "I still wish that I had you here . . . Are you quite sure that you would not like me to press for you to come back and take part in the new army education schemes?".[6]

Cub replied that "I was on the point of writing to you to ask your advice and help when your letter arrived". While awaiting news from Butler he had decided that he was now ready to return, and although he was happy to help with army education in the short-term he was set on higher things. He guessed that a general election would not be long delayed after the war ended, and was impatient to get into the House of Commons. He knew that Butler thought it was a mistake to go in too early, but felt that his African experiences had prepared him sufficiently; more important, "for the first time I think that I might have enough money to stand for the House if the opportunity arose". Butler, he felt, would have little difficulty in arranging his return, since "the tendency out here is towards contraction".[7]

Cub, in short, felt the pull of Westminster more strongly than ever before, and he implied that the counter-attractions of Africa were growing weaker. Butler must have been surprised that this letter was swiftly followed by a telegram from Cub, telling him to ignore the appeal for help in arranging his return. As Cub explained in a subsequent letter, although "I do not want you to think that my wish to assist you in your work has in any way diminished", he had just won a promotion (to GSO I) "which will enable me to hold my own with others of my age elsewhere". He was "almost scared" by the responsibilities, but his new role had convinced him that there was worthwhile work to do after all. He concluded with the hope that "you will not think me conceited if I say that I believe in a years' time I will be very much more valuable to you as a result of [the promotion] than I would be now".[8]

Cub did not know that his new job would give him the chance to return to Britain within three months of sending this letter, but when he was sent home for the War Office conference his excitement must have been increased by the prospect of seeing Rab again. Yet Butler was not the only correspondent he was anxious to meet. He had continued to write to Rachel Bingham, who was now a Petty Officer in the WRENs, serving on *HMS Caballa*, a shore station which, by March 1944, was at Warrington. To ensure that his news was fairly fresh when it reached Cub, Butler asked contacts who were flying to Africa to deliver his letters. Since Cub and Rachel had no such privilege, the time-lag between writing and receiving a reply continued to provoke confusion and (on Cub's part, at least) frustration. On 15 July 1943 a letter from Rachel was delivered to Cub, but it had been posted in April – since when Cub had sent yet another proposal of marriage. There was nothing for him to do but to dash off a letter which repeated the offer, although he knew that on its way to Britain it might pass a plane bearing a new refusal from Rachel. Her reply has not survived, but it contained a hint that his prospects were looking up; in Cub's next letter he wrote that "I'm sorry that you say that I have neglected you but I have written every week since the day I wrote saying that if you ever changed your mind and would marry me, you must send a wire". In fact Rachel's last letter had contained news of an engagement – that of her brother, Nigel. Cub slyly suggested that "your affection for Nigel was one of the reasons that you did not marry months ago" – or, for that matter, one of the reasons why she had rejected his own suit – but the idea that a serious obstacle to her own engagement had been removed plunged Cub into new despair at the thought that she might now accept the nearest eligible candidate. He reminded her to let him know if his hopes were gone for ever, and added as a postscript the confession that "I find it hard to strike my colours and let the ship sink while there is even the smallest vaguest chance".[9]

Cub's last surviving letter before returning for the conference was composed in November 1943, when he thought that Butler would be arranging for him to come home permanently. He told Rachel that seeing her again could do no harm, "Provided one insures oneself against the probable disappointment". In fact he had received further encouragement in a letter which Rachel posted on 15 August (and only reached Cub on 18 October). She had made it clear that whatever might happen she would always be his "supporter", but that "being fond of each other is not enough . . . One has got to love each other in all the senses of the word". This thinly veiled suggestion that Rachel's doubts concerned physical attraction can only have increased Cub's anxiety to shield himself "against the probable disappointment". He had already confessed that Rachel might detect alterations in his character; "I find myself developing rather like my papa", he wrote in September, "a little short of temper and sweeping in my criticisms, a little pompous (this is not a characteristic of Alport père) and not nearly as adaptable as I used to be". Since Rachel had yet to meet Cecil, this admission of ancestral vices was less damaging than it might have been. Cub's worries about his changing character had been triggered by a visit to a friend, whose young daughter had

> made me the butt of a series of practical jokes – every chair I sat on had a drawing-pin. She and a friend of hers put soapy water in my waterjug, which I duly drank, gravel in my bed, sewed up my pyjamas and spent a jolly morning either pushing me into the swimming-bath or ducking me when I was already there . . . I was quite horrifed how long it took me to enter into the spirit of the thing.[10]

When Cub arrived in London for the conference he found himself the youngest officer present – a pleasing discovery for someone acutely aware that some of his best years had been passing while he was in Africa. He tried to assert the importance of the East African forces, demanding 28 Saracen armoured cars for the reconnaisance regiment among other claims for reinforcements and war materials. The efforts which had been made by the Command to fulfil Churchill's orders by providing troops for the Far East had clearly made an impression in London, and Cub felt that the conference, chaired by the Director of Staff Duties, General Steele, was a great success.

When Cub was told to take ten days leave before returning to Africa his satisfaction was complete. He immediately sent a wire to Petty Officer Bingham, telling her that he was on his way to *HMS Caballa*. Later he was told that the arrival of his message had caused a great stir, and Rachel was given helpful advice on how to deal with this unusual visitor. Meanwhile Cub travelled by train to Manchester and established his headquarters at the Midland Hotel. On the following morning he boarded the vessel and presented himself at the guard room. As a Lieutenant-Colonel he was greeted by the sentry with a salute rather than the curse which might have been given to a lesser personage; even so, requests for advice on how to receive the intruder passed up the chain of command until Cub was manouevred into the Officer's Mess "where he was exhaustively interrogated over a series of pink gins".[11]

Eventually Cub left with his prize; Rachel was given leave to accompany him back to Manchester, where they danced to the hotel band and enjoyed the chance to relate their news without having to wait months for a reply. At the end of the evening Rachel had to return to Warrington, but before they parted Cub knew that the prospects for a fresh attack were bright. On the next day he returned to *HMS Caballa* and Rachel obtained leave for a week. They took an overcrowded bus back to Manchester; "having difficulty making myself heard above the din", Cub proposed once again and, this time, was accepted "without more ado". The couple travelled to Helmsley in North Yorkshire, where Nigel Bingham was stationed, then to Ryston in Norfolk to meet Rachel's aunt and uncle. Rab could not accommodate them in London, but for Cub the alternative was even better – a night at the Master's Lodge at Pembroke College, currently occupied by Rab and Jock's parents, Sir Montague and Lady Butler.[12]

The next stop was London, where Cub met his future mother- and father-in-law. He was warmly received; Ralph Bingham could have no objection to his daughter marrying a fellow Lieutenant-Colonel.

But Cub had always thought of his political prospects, rather than his military rank, as his greatest attraction for a potential partner. To emphasise the point he took Rachel to lunch with Butler, and also met the General Director of the Conservative Central Office, Sir Robert Topping. Butler and Rachel clearly got on well; after the successful lover had departed back to Africa, Rachel wrote a chatty note to Butler, inviting herself for lunches whenever she happened to be in London, and reminding him to write to the Treasurer of the Middle Temple stating that Cub was "a suitable person, in your opinion, to be called to the Bar". This was a clever precaution on the part of Cub, who knew that it would do no harm to call himself a barrister when applying for a constituency; and if all else failed he might even take up the law as a career. Although the overworked Butler remembered to do this favour, the effect must have been impaired by his (or his secretary's) misspelling of Cub's surname.[13]

Cub left for Africa on 7 March 1944, feeling that he could hardly have been more fortunate in his career to date. With hindsight, however, he might have made a slight mistake in not arranging to stay on in England. Not only had he attained a very suitable rank, but at the conference he had proved himself worthy of it. No one could be certain how long the war would last, but it was unlikely that there would be much more new work for him to do – and the greatest personal danger he was now likely to face would be the long flight back to Africa. In the meantime Butler would enjoy his triumph when the Education Act finally became law in May 1944 – after a parliamentary rebellion in March by members of the progressive Tory Reform Committee (including Quintin Hogg) leading to the passage of an amendment which would have ensured equal pay for women teachers. Only Churchill's personal intervention saved the situation for Rab, who had offered to resign. Butler's increasing prominence within the Conservative Party had earned him the predictable emnity of possible future leadership rivals, notably that of Anthony Eden; given his views he was unlikely to win favour from the Right of the party, and now he was ruffling feathers on the Left. Staying in England to "battle for the peace" with Butler would involve political risks, but Cub had already hitched his wagon to Rab's star and had he been with him through the passage of the Bill the bonds between them would have increased.[14]

On his return to Africa Cub broke the news of his engagement to his mother and father, who were now in Nairobi. While Cub had been starring in his own drama, Cecil had provoked his last and greatest furore. In Cairo he had been unhappy from the start with the conditions in the King Fouad I Hospital, where he directed the Medical Unit. Corruption was rife, with the poor (or "Fellaheen") often foregoing treatment rather than paying bribes to hospital staff. There was no central heating, the food was inadequate, and many patients contracted dysentery from "the myriads of flies in the wards". Years of protest brought no remedial action, and Cecil turned against the wealthy Pasha class, whom he regarded as the oppressors of the poor; to make matters worse, he was not supported by the Royal College of Physicians back in London, which could have withdrawn official recognition of the teaching hospital. At the end of March 1943 Cecil submitted his resignation, but just as his initial appointment had been delayed, the administrators of Cairo University now saw no reason to hasten a controversial departure. His letter of resignation was not accepted until early October.[15]

In the past, whenever Cecil had encountered obstruction from officials he made his grievances public. On this occasion he excelled himself, privately printing an "Open Letter to the Public", then scurrying around Cairo (with his cook) distributing copies to those who might help – and to those who would be most discomfited by his allegations. The Rector of the university, with whom Cecil had often clashed, published a reply in English and Arabic; the first was fairly temperate, but the Arabic version referred to Cecil's "psychotic condition", his "hatred for Islam and the Muslims", and accused him of believing that he was "a God-chosen man like Adolf Hitler". By no means all of this was accurate. In January 1944 a debate on Cecil's complaints was held in the Egyptian Senate, and, as if to prove his case that a whole class was ranged against him, the administration of the hospital was defended to general acclamation. By that time Cecil had retired to Nairobi, where he spent eight months writing a counterblast which was eventually published as the book *One Hour of Justice* (1946) – dedicated "to the twin gods of Decency and Justice", and giving him the chance to air his theory that Egyptians, having once enjoyed civilised life, were capable of having one again (and were thus worth fighting for), whereas the bantu tribesmen he had met in his

South African youth could not be made civilised for "three or four centuries". Whatever Cub might have thought about his father's previous antics (or his ideas on race), on this occasion he was rightly proud of the (almost unsupported) stand he had taken. He told Butler that the Open Letter "has been described as the most significant attempt at improving the administration of Egypt since Cromer". Cub did not name his source for this accolade; Lord Cromer was a great hero for Cecil, and one cannot resist the suspicion that his father's word was the only evidence Cub had received to suggest that "the resignation and the events subsequent to it can only be described as sensational".[16]

Presumably the writing of his book prevented Cecil from contacting his future daughter-in-law until May 1944. He then made up for the delay by composing a remarkable twelve-page letter ("In view of your interest in this youth of mine"). The letter contained a list of Cub's great merits, mixed with embarrassing anecdotes from his childhood; the reader was supposed to conclude that the positive points, at least, should be credited to the doting father. There was some justification for this, although at least one of the achievements was due entirely to the young prodigy's imagination. Cecil claimed that "He has given up alcohol of any sort to the great delight of his mother" – and, no doubt, to the astonishment of his fiancée. Hearing that this letter was on its way, the bogus teetotaller hastily advised Rachel to "Keep my papa in his place . . . he talks a lot and he doesn't mean all he says".[17]

In fact Rachel wrote a very diplomatic reply to what she called Cecil's "monumental letter", showing that she already knew a great deal about his son and had guessed many of the other accurate details which he had provided. On two counts, however, she already agreed with Cecil. He had written that Cub was "too inclined to hang onto the coat tails of the bigger people". Rachel took this as referring to Butler, and much as she liked her new friend she assured Cecil that she would try to stop Cub attaching himself "more than is necessary"; she had already warned her fiancé that he "mustn't just be content to rise on Rab's star". The other defect which Cecil had mentioned was that his son "is rather too diffident, and although he is a good mixer, he does not always trouble to do so. As a politician one must train oneself to be interested in even the most uninteresting people".

Rachel agreed, but thought that Cub would grow out of this. Indeed –
no doubt remembering his shyness after the Huntingdon races – she
thought that he had improved since first leaving for Africa. But her
optimism was misplaced here; Cub would always be "diffident", and
not just in the company of "uninteresting people".[18]

Back in Africa the diffident Cub was receiving advice about his
future state from the wives of some fellow-officers; one lent him
Marie Stopes' *Married Love* (1918), "which was then regarded as being
the latest textbook on sex". For the rest of the war his thoughts were
mainly occupied by the prospects of marriage and politics before him;
in June he told Butler that his "heart certainly [wasn't] in East Africa",
(although he was more taken with Salisbury in Southern Rhodesia
which he visited for the first time in October). News of the revolt by
the "Tory Reformers" on the Education Bill was received with a mixture of disappointment ("somehow one feels that they should not be
fighting a guerilla warfare against you in the House but that you and
they should be on the same side") and envy ("I dare say that many of
them were at our young mens' conferences at Ashridge. Well they
have got ahead but I have no doubt they can still be caught up").[19]
Cub's frustration at being far from the fray provoked an outburst
against a different foe: he told Butler of his hatred for "intellectuals"
and that he was glad to belong to "the stupid party", since "steadiness
and commonsense" were the qualities which were winning the war,
rather than utopian ideas. Whether or not the Conservatives were
right to blame the left-wing intelligentsia for their defeat in 1945, at
least Cub had named the scapegoats well in advance, and anticipated a
Labour triumph at a time when most experts thought that Churchill's
popularity would ensure a Tory victory at the next general election.[20]

By September Cub was feeling more doubtful of the "stupid
party's" virtues. "I don't think that the Conservative Party as it has
existed these last ten years has any future", he told Butler.

> I think that after the war – next year in fact – a Liberal–Labour
> coalition will come into power and I think that the opposition
> will comprise three elements – the Right wing (very small) an
> extreme left-wing (vociferous and turbulent) and the real
> "conservatives" or Tories – people like you and I. From that
> point we will have to start a new model party . . . We will then

breathe new life into it, re-clothe it with ideas, re-christen it with a name more consonant with its policy and purpose, and get to work to win the ground which has been lost to us. Don't laugh, but I'll organise the party for you … the idea of the combination – yourself in the House and I in the organisation – strikes me as an excellent one, like old times but on a higher plane.

Of course Cub was letting his enthusiasm run away with him; but it was not far-fetched to believe that after a Conservative defeat Churchill would retire, and pave the way for Butler rather than the "Crown Prince", Eden, who was supposed to lack the necessary expertise in domestic matters. It is unlikely that Butler would have been tempted to "laugh" at Cub's glittering prospectus, although it might have occurred to him that his protégé was rather too ambitious to be the "spaniel" he was looking for.[21]

In Cub's next surviving letter to Butler – undated, but probably written in March 1945 – his musings on the future took another turn. He confessed that "the lengthening shadows of the General Election are beginning to reach even these far off parts and stir up all sorts of hopes and ambitions". He had acted on his impulse, and written to Sir Robert Topping in the hope that a constituency was available. His letter to Butler was an attempt to enlist his help in the search for a seat. Aware that this might seem to contradict his earlier promise to run the Conservative Party for his friend, Cub added that he had not heard anything from Topping since their meeting in March 1944, and presumed "that there is not very much to be hoped for from that point of view". This argument could hardly have been more shrewd; if Butler really wanted him to spend some time as a "backroom boy", he would have to jog Topping's elbow and find him a suitable job, other-wise he would go all out for a seat. If his name was considered by a constituency he would have found a worthy reason for returning home. As he told Rachel, "The only reason why I ever think of stand-ing for the House is that it might bring me back to you". Although the insecurity caused by their separation had now given way to a romantic yearning, even in that love-letter his tactical self was visible; he went on to acknowledge that "After the next election would be the right time" to stand for Parliament.[22]

Before Cub's letter reached Butler the Americans and the British under Montgomery had crossed the Rhine, and the air-raid sirens sounded in London for the last time as Hitler's rocket assaults petered out. With victory now a certainty partisan conflict in Britain resumed in anticipation of an election which the Prime Minister would have preferred to delay until after the defeat of Japan, still apparently some way off. Butler's reply to Cub's letter arrived in late May, as the last German resistance was crumbling and the Labour Party was deciding to withdraw from the wartime coalition. Cub reported to Rachel that Rab had said "that the future of the Conservative Party was so insecure that it would be most ill-advised to try for the House at this late hour"; in other words, Butler had managed to combine a perceptive assessment of the political outlook with a response to Cub which fitted his own self-interest. While awaiting his letter, however, Cub had overheard a colleague in Africa telling his father back home that he was not prepared to put in for the Wirral constituency. Immediately he wired his own application, but he failed to make the short-list; the seat was won for the Conservatives by Selwyn Lloyd.[23]

With the war in Europe over Cub set about the task of undoing the previous expansion of the East African forces. As chairman of the Command Establishment Committee he had to review the ranks of the various units, "reducing Lieutenant-Colonels to Majors and Majors to Captains" at the stroke of a pen. This work would not have been to Cub's taste even if he had had nothing else on his mind. In fact he was so bored that he wrote a few chapters of a novel (in the style of John Buchan) entitled *The First Year Down*, which drew heavily on his Cambridge acquaintances, one of whom had turned out to be a German spy. With his own hopes of participating in the election dashed, Cub waited anxiously to hear the result. As news came through of a Tory rout, he heard a rumour that Butler had also been defeated in his Saffron Walden constituency, but this proved to be false although his majority was down almost 90 per cent, to just over 1,000. Having anticipated defeat for so long, Cub was jubilant at its scale. "One of the most interesting things", he told Butler in a letter to follow a telegram of congratulations on his own success,

is the list of the high level leaders who have been defeated. Almost without exception we are well rid of them all. So the field is clear and we can start building a leadership and a party for the next twenty years. What an opportunity, my dear Rab, particularly for you. For you have the opportunity of a well deserved rest – which I know you need urgently – and we can purge our organisation, refresh our minds and elevate our objectives ready for the next election in something like three years' time . . . I've no doubt the passage while in opposition will be bitter, but I'm glad we haven't had to put it off any longer in some ways.

Cub also speculated on the likely reasons for the result:

I suppose that if one views the election from a historical stand-point one should not have been surprised at the outcome [of course, both Butler and Cub had anticipated it well in advance]. Mr Churchill joins the Elder Pitt and Ll[oyd] G[eorge] as a great war minister who has been dispensed with as soon as the war situation permits and British politics reverts to colourless domesticity. I think the election is a vote for the people who are least likely to involve us in foreign adventures, or bring us up against Russia. . . . It is a vote for domestic security; it results from the swing of the pendulum and the desire for a change and it is a vote against the "brigands".[24]

Despite his pleasure at the result, Cub still had no certainty that he would be given an official role in the revival of the party which he longed for. He suggested to Butler that he might go into the City, and on 17 August he could only assure Rachel that "I daresay something will turn up". At least he was now pretty sure that he would be home in October, and the American bombs on Hiroshima and Nagasaki had made his return even more likely. This new development in war made Cub momentarily sombre; he told Rachel that "We'll have to bring up the little Alports in the atomic era". But on the day after his dispirited letter about the future Cub's Micawberite outlook was rewarded by a letter from Sir Robert Topping, asking if he would consider heading the Education Department at the Conservative Central Office.[25]

On hearing this news Cub seized his pen and wrote a four-part letter to Rachel. Without knowing the precise job that he might be offered, he had been planning for some time his strategy if he were to reach a position of influence. He told Rachel that he wanted "to divorce political education completely from the Central Office Organisation ... but retaining the good will of the agents and the professional politicians". He thought that he could run the organisation while sitting in the House, so he planned to seek out a suitable constituency as soon as his machine was up and running, although he was now very glad that he had not stood in the summer general election. The Wirral would have been far from ideal anyway; what he wanted was "a constituency reasonably near London where there is a Labour member with a majority of about 1000, but which returned a Conservative at the 1935 election". Once he had been selected he would work the constituency "for a couple of years, and I'm jolly certain we would get in without much difficulty". This remarkable wish-list coincided almost exactly with Colchester, the seat which Cub fought in 1950; it had returned a Tory in 1935, but in 1945 Labour had gained a majority of 2444.[26]

In the fourth part of his letter Cub returned to his plans for his party – and himself. "You see", he told Rachel,

the Conservative Party can only recover through a correct and farsighted use of political education. The Beaverbrook gutter-press type of propaganda has failed miserably and the last election has proved that a new sort of political approach is essential – that political approach is through education. I must have control of something similar to Ashridge. I must have sound finances, good writers and lecturers, educational agents in all constituencies called Educational Secretaries. New methods, new energy. My love, we're on the threshold of great things. The Conservative Party will honestly be very nearly in my hands if I can get what I want.[27]

In a later, but undated letter Cub let his imagination roam further: "Let us dream a little, [a] five-year Parliament, a Tory government, Under-Secretary of State for the Colonies, a ceremonial visit to East Africa". These prophetic visions had an uncanny element of accuracy mixed with their utopian quality; but before they could begin to be realised Cub had to get himself home. Ever aware of regulations, he had told Rachel that instead of revealing his precise travel plans in writing he would send her a message – "Will you marry me when I come home?" – when he was setting off.[28] In September General Anderson decided that Cub should accompany him to the conference of Commanders-in-Chief which was to be held at the Camberley Staff College. The telegram to Rachel, complete with the coded message, was despatched on 26 September 1945. The message was one which Cub had sent to Rachel many times before, only to be met with a negative response. At last he knew in advance that it would be welcomed this time. Now that Rachel had agreed to marry him, her expressions of love became, if anything, even more effusive than Cub's; in what was probably her last letter before their reunion, she told him "I love you so much that I can't imagine ever not loving you, or think why I didn't before, I suppose I did in a way but it was different and I didn't realise it". No doubt this explanation of the nine-year delay between meeting Rachel and marrying her was perfectly acceptable to the triumphant suitor.[29]

Cub had agreed to take the job at the Central Office, but his return from Africa did not mean that his war was over. The Camberley conference was attended by officers who had distinguished themselves in the various theatres of war; they included Lord Louis Mountbatten (whom Cub had already met on a visit to Burma), Field Marshall Montgomery, who had been a lecturer during Cub's first stay at Camberley, and Viscount Alexander, who had married one of Rachel's cousins. Cub records that despite the illustrious company he "was extremely bored by the whole proceeding, since the only thing I wanted to do was to claim my girl, get married and start on my postwar life". On 26 October 1945 the longed-for wedding took place at St Saviour's, Walton Street, London. The parents of both bride and groom were in attendance – Cecil having returned to London to act as "a consultant of some sort" to the Ministry of Pensions. What Lieutenant-Colonel and Mrs Bingham thought of their new relatives is not recorded, but Cecil must have reflected on the fortunate career of the son whom he had nearly christened in the garden bird-bath. Cub and Rachel were probably too happy to reflect very much, as they embarked on a honeymoon at Roman Camp near Callander in Scotland, before moving in on a temporary basis to share 3 Smith Square, London, with Butler and his wife Sydney.[30]

In August 1943 Cub had told Rachel that

I would like to be sitting in the top of an 88 bus going home from Parliament Square, up Whitehall, Lower Regent Street, with the prospect of warming a tin of Heintz [sic] Mushroom Soup on my gas stove when I eventually reach my flat. Yet when I used to do this, I always pictured myself watching the leaping flames of camp fires and loved to read about chaps like Sanders of the River who controlled with divine calm and faultless tack [tact?] a proportion of the black peoples of the empire.

Unlike his father, he had learned to respect native Africans during the war, although traces of prejudice remained. He was not yet finished with Africa: but although the landmarks he had passed on the 88 bus route soon became even more familiar to him, he would never again be forced to dine on a can of soup warmed over a gas stove.[31]

Chapter Four

Reviving Conservatism

Cub's anticipation of a Conservative defeat in the 1945 general election was a remarkable piece of forecasting, given his distance from the contest. Even more notable was his insouciant response to the outcome. Conservative strength in the Commons had been reduced to less than half the figure after the 1935 contest – 213 as opposed to 432 – and there was carnage in the senior ranks. Of those who served in Churchill's 1945 caretaker administration, 32 were now out of Parliament; 13 of these had held cabinet rank. Cub must have been one of very few Conservatives to choose the word "interesting" to describe this development. His analysis implied that the axe had fallen mostly on the party's old guard who were discredited in the eyes of the public, but naturally most of the survivors came from safe, traditional Conservative constituencies which tended to field safe, "traditional" Conservative candidates. Although after the election the average age of Conservative MPs was 41 years 4 months – more than four years below the Labour figure – the purge had claimed many young victims, notably the thirty-six year-old Peter Thorneycroft. Indeed the party had lost the services of over half the 41 MPs associated with the Tory Reform Committee, which during the war had emerged as the most progressive and promising Conservative grouping; Harold Macmillan, whose *Middle Way* was admired so much by Cub, had lost Stockton.[1]

When urged by his wife to look on the 1945 result as a blessing in disguise, Winston Churchill famously retorted that the disguise was pretty effective. It was not the case that Cub could see only blessings – he knew that the recovery would be difficult – but from his very different viewpoint he could regard the problems to come as a spur to effort rather than a cause for dejection. "The Conservative Party" might never hold office again; like Churchill himself, Cub was uneasy with the name. But whatever label might be chosen, Cub was convinced that a party representing his approach to political questions had a future worth working for. Socialism in his eyes remained a divisive creed, and however the majority had voted in the unusual circumstances of 1945 Cub believed that the real lesson of the war was that the British people had the will to work for the common cause as if class differences were unimportant – precisely the message he had tried to convey in *A National Faith*. Labour's triumph would prove to be nothing more than a temporary swing of the electoral pendulum, provided that the new opposition was properly organised and presented its ideas with clarity.

October 1945 was the most important month of Cub's life; he married the woman he had pursued for nine years, and he could not have chosen a more suitable job than his new position as Director of Political Education. In his first days he drew up a detailed plan of action which won the warm approval of the party vice-chairman, Marjorie Maxse. Before the end of the year his hopes for the future received three more boosts. In November Butler was asked by Churchill to take over the Conservative Research Department (CRD), which had run down so badly during the war that at the time of the 1945 election it consisted of just two staff members and two secretaries. As his biographer confirms, for the next eighteen years the CRD "was to provide the essential power base on which Rab's influence over the party rested"; its role as the Conservatives' own civil service was enhanced in 1948, when it was merged with the Parliamentary Secretariat to which Reginald Maudling, Enoch Powell and Iain Macleod had been recruited soon after the war. By the time of the 1950 election it had a staff of more than fifty, housed at 24 Old Queen Street near the House of Commons.[2]

Butler's central position in the party's policy-making machine was further augmented before the end of the year, when by a vote of the Central Council it was agreed that an Advisory Committee on Policy and Political Education (ACPPE) should be established under his leadership. In effect this would be the Post-War Problems Central Committee under a new name, and as before Butler could nominate its members. Officially the formation of party policy was the responsibility of the leader, but in the first years of opposition Churchill showed scant interest, arguing that the Conservatives would only open themselves to attack if they came forward with detailed proposals. Hence Butler had to tread cautiously, but the pressure from party members for some policy statements that would help to win back support before the next election ensured that his profile within the party would rise even further as a result of his new jobs. It was easy for both Butler and Cub to overlook an associated danger – namely that Rab, as a former lecturer, might have been labelled as more of an intellectual than a vigorous party leader-in-waiting by the time that he came under consideration for the top post.

Butler's chairmanship of the ACPPE meant that although Cub was based in the Conservative Central Office rather than the Research Department he would be directly responsible to his friend, and he was in close contact with David Clarke, the Director of the CRD. The work which Cub and Butler had begun before the war could now resume, and in December 1945 Cub received a third boost. The short-lived Conservative Political Circle was revived in the more ambitious form of the Conservative Political Centre (CPC), with Cub as its first Director. Due to the disruption of war the Central Office lacked suitable accommodation until a former hotel on Victoria Street, Abbey House, became available in August 1946; the CPC "began life in a semi-basement office at 11 Wilton Street" (loaned by an MP) before moving to another house on Victoria Street, number 58 (the site has since been redeveloped). According to Butler, the purpose of the Centre

"was not merely to develop political education methods and to influence public opinion indirectly by reasoned instruction within the party, but to create a kind of Conservative Fabian Society which would act as a mouthpiece for our best modern thought and attract that section of the postwar generation who required an intellectual basis for their political faith".

As Director of this new body, Cub was made a member of the ACPPE (as were his old tutor, Kenneth Pickthorn, and Charles Morgan, one of his favourite novelists). The minutes of the monthly meetings show that, apart from reporting on work approved by the committee Cub was always ready with suggestions of his own.[3]

Senior Conservatives had recognised the importance of political education before the war, and recent events had only served to enhance the prestige of the department Cub had left in 1939. However much they might dislike Labour's policy ideas (and attack the party because it peddled "ideology" rather than Conservative "common sense"), many Conservatives struggling for an explanation of the 1945 defeat could only conclude that their opponents had bamboozled the voters with clever policy presentation. In his angry and influential book *Our New Masters* (1947) Colm Brogan explained that anti-socialists had "largely ignored" left-wing propaganda, "in the belief that something so obviously mean and bilious was bound to defeat itself". In the short-term, the Conservatives would have to rectify this apparent mistake, but the need for political education would last far beyond a return to government. Butler's own 1944 Education Act meant that party strategists expected a more demanding and inquisitive electorate in future, and with Labour's allies in the Fabian Society constantly working on the minds of young enthusiasts Conservatives would have to remain equipped for what Cub called "the battle of ideas".[4]

Whether the 1945 election had been decided by "ideas" or not, the CPC was a welcome development in British politics which is still in existence more than fifty years after its formation. As before the war, Cub and Butler intended to produce something which rose above mere propaganda. True to its Fabian model, the centre published thoughtful pamphlets, starting with Butler's own *Fundamental Issues* (1946). David Clarke's brilliant tract *The Conservative Faith in a Modern Age* followed in April 1946. Clarke echoed Cub's prewar *A National Faith*; he rejected both "the anarchy of extreme individualism" and "doctrinaire collectivism", contrasting socialism, which relied on the "turgid brew" of Marx's theories, with Conservatism which was "rooted in the history of the British people".[5]

By the time of the 1948 Conservative Party Conference at Llandudno the CPC had been responsible for over 50 publications with a total circulation of more than 750,000. Four CPC bookshops had been set up; branches in Newcastle, Leeds and Cardiff had joined the one opened in November 1946 at Abbey House itself. This initiative was Cub's own idea, based on the success of another left-wing organisation, the Left Book Club, but it was not a financial success; as John Ramsden has pointed out, "it proved impossible to get party members to use [the CPC stores] rather than their nearest ordinary shop, and presumably political opponents refused to use them anyway". By the mid-1950s only the Abbey House shop remained, but the project illustrates the lengths that the party was prepared to go in its quest for renewed intellectual respectability.[6]

The highpoint of this campaign between the elections of 1945 and 1950 was undoubtedly the appearance of the *Industrial Charter* under the CPC's imprint in May 1947. The *Charter* was drawn up by the Industrial Policy Committee, which included Butler, Macmillan and the former Minister of Production, Oliver Lyttleton. While reaffirming the Conservative preference for free enterprise and promising that the industries which Labour had nationalised would be returned to private ownership if their performance had deteriorated, the document promised that a future Conservative government would try to foster co-operation in the work-place; trade unions were acknowledged to have a vital role in industry, and the party pledged to "ensure that the demand for goods and services is always maintained at a level which will offer jobs to all who are willing to work". In short, the *Charter* pointed "to a way of life designed to free private endeavour from the taunt of selfishness or self-interest and public control from the reproach of meddlesome interference".[7]

Thanks to the CPC, the party's leaders could claim to have a reasonable idea of the *Charter*'s reception from party members. Early in 1946 the party began "The Two-Way Movement of Ideas" (the name was suggested by Butler) as a means of establishing "a continuing partnership between the party leaders and its rank and file in the formation of party policy on political issues". According to one of

Cub's colleagues the intention was to establish "something more educational than a public opinion poll, but less academic than a correspondence course". Discussion groups in the constituencies were supplied with lists of policy areas and materials to inform debate on each subject. A series of pamphlets under the general heading *What do You Think?* was prepared by leading figures in the party, assisted by the CRD (and published by the CPC). Each of these included a bibliography and a number of questions to guide the constituency discussions. After collection by Area Education Departments the results were processed by the Research Department, then presented to the ACPPE. The participants in the process learned the overall results of their deliberations in a series of CPC reports entitled *What We Think.*[8]

On paper the "Two-Way Movement of Ideas" looks like a remarkable exercise in democratic practice. At Llandudno in 1948 Butler was to argue that "the days had gone by when policy was brought down from Mount Sinai on tablets of stone", but in a party which had traditionally deferred to its leaders it would take time for members to re-adjust. In 1961 Julian Critchley rather cynically described the "Two-Way Movement" as "a convenient means of discovering and then correcting any misconceptions or disagreements that the rank and file may have acquired". By contrast, a journalist who had worked in the CRD claimed in 1981 that the process had resulted in "a number of significant changes of policy or of emphasis within policy"; in his view neither Labour nor the Liberal Party "has ever created any system for the exchange and development of ideas remotely as sophisticated or as wide-ranging" as the "Two-Way Movement". Even assuming that the truth lies somewhere between these two judgements and that the great majority of party members maintained their traditionally passive role, at the very least they now had a far better opportunity to keep themselves informed about developments.[9]

The "Two-Way Movement" was the most significant achievement of Cub's years in Central Office. The Conservative Party was defeated, maligned and disorientated, yet Cub had to devise and run a process in which members were encouraged to participate in policy-making without letting this unexpected chance of influence go to their heads. The case of the *Industrial Charter* illustrates his difficulties. The extent of the newspaper coverage received by the *Charter* was gratifying to Cub and Butler, but they could not control its nature and at an ACPPE meeting two days after publication Butler was already expressing concern that the document had been presented in some quarters as an example of "milk and water socialism". Quintin Hogg's reply that this could only do the party good, because no one would be able to accuse it of being "reactionary", only emphasised the difficulty Butler had faced in producing a policy statement which would attract new supporters without alienating the old ones. The *Charter* owed far more to Baldwin than to Karl Marx or even Clement Attlee, but its appearance in the wake of Labour's crushing victory lent spurious colour to allegations that it represented a compromise with socialism.[10]

The *Industrial Charter* thus provided the first big test for the "Two-Way Movement of Ideas". If any issue could present the wider public with an impression of a disunited party riddled with "reactionaries" in the postwar period industrial policy was the most likely candidate, given the actions of the Attlee Government in that field. The prewar "old guard" of whom Cub had complained were not the doctrinaire right-wingers of Labour legend; at worst their views were founded on ignorance of the problems which most people faced in their daily lives. While the party was in government before the war this element had generally supported the progressive domestic policies of Baldwin and Chamberlain, but in opposition it was likely to demand a greater say in policy-making and the new consultation process provided its opportunity. In the political context of 1947 even an outside chance of trouble had to be guarded against if the party was to survive the years in opposition; Butler's concern that the document should be supported by a decisive vote when it was debated at the next party conference was heightened by the fact that he had identified himself so closely with it. As Butler's friend and ally, Cub's own future was now at stake.

Butler's *What do You Think?* pamphlet on the *Charter*, which appeared in the month before the conference, if anything protested too much in the face of his worries. Noting that the *Charter* had "received more attention than any recent political pamphlet", the brief foreword presented it "as the natural outcome of progressively-minded and up-to-date Conservative thinking". If this was not enough to guide the reader, the questions at the end were phrased to anticipate criticisms. The first one stressed that group leaders should take care to explain what Conservatives meant by the word "plan": "it is not a rigid totalitarian plan which the socialists favour but rather a series of broad decisions in which the government lays down the national interests while industry is left wide scope to put them into practice".[11]

In some quarters this soft-soaping acted as additional provocation; a rather tactless supporting speech by Harold Macmillan (still suspected for his prewar rebellions) cannot have helped either. One newspaper editor wrote before the 1947 conference that "all the branches are being hypnotised by central authority and accept anything that looks official". Looking back on the episode even so careful a historian as John Ramsden has taken his cue from this, reflecting that "it no doubt took considerable courage" to oppose the *Charter*; "recognising the inevitability of their defeat, many opponents cannot have bothered to vote" during the 1947 conference. "Courage" is surely the wrong word here: it implies that some fearful retribution could be visited on those who voted the "wrong" way, yet the Conservative Party of 1947 was hardly organised for an ideological witch-hunt. On the evidence of the "Two-Way Movement" it would be more accurate to say that many delegates must have voted with reservations, but that the mood in favour of the policy was genuine.[12]

In the conference debate, despite an appeal by the eccentric MP Sir Waldron Smithers for his audience to "save the Conservative Party and save England" by rejecting the *Charter*, it was approved with only three of the 3000 representatives voting against. Cub later claimed that one of the three had told him that he had put up his hand by mistake, "under the impression that he was voting for an adjournment for lunch". Thus, although Winston Churchill claimed not to agree with any of the proposals when Reginald Maudling showed him a summary, the leader in his closing speech referred to the *Charter* as "the official policy of the party". No doubt Churchill's show of reluctance arose from his negative attitude to policy statements in general; the *Charter*, after all, was wholly in sympathy with the social philosophy on which he had acted throughout his career. But in later years Maudling's report of Churchill's remarks could be used as further evidence to support the false claim that the party was bounced into accepting a policy which was alien to its traditions.[13]

Cub offered some suggestions about the content of the *Charter* to Butler – and much of it reads like an updated and more detailed version of *A National Faith* – but his main input concerned its presentation and production. In a letter enclosing the publishing timetable, for example, he offered his own ideas for the pamphlet's title: "A Fresh Start for Industry", "A New Lead for Industry", etc. In a later speech he jokingly disparaged the *Charter*'s dry content, claiming that "I personally have the greatest admiration for economists, but I only wish they were a bit more human and would speak English". When translating it for his audience he followed Butler's distinction between "totalitarian" planning, and planning which led to "abundance" and "fair shares for all" by enabling industry to "put its whole back into the task of production".[14]

In a letter to the *Conservative Agents' Journal* of May 1948 Cub defended the *Charter* against the party agent from Worthing, who had complained that money was being wasted on such exercises, which could only "pander to the intelligentsia". Cub retorted that the comfortable denizens of Worthing could not be expected to appreciate the value of a policy statement directed towards those engaged in industry. If the *Charter* was rather "highbrow", so much the better: "the Conservative Party have always underestimated the sort of people known as the intelligentsia, yet it is these people who in the past have been singled out by the Liberals, socialists and communists as being a most important element in the struggle to mould public opinion". The "intelligentsia" was not a body isolated from the rest of society; it included important elements of "the professional classes, school and university teachers, writers, scientists, economists". In many marginal constituencies the votes of these people on their own might be decisive, but as articulate "opinion formers" they were expected to exercise influence far beyond their own ranks. Apart from their political importance, the economic muscle of the professional classes was now recognised; Cub had been impressed by the arguments of James Burnham, whose book *The Managerial Society* (1941) predicted a world in which professional managers, rather than owners of firms, would dominate society. In both style and content *The Industrial Charter* gave the Conservatives a fighting chance to win the support of the crucial "managerial" classes, and through them the message would filter through to workers.[15]

The agent's letter had clearly touched a raw nerve. He had questioned the value of the *Charter*, to which Cub was passionately committed, but he had also attacked the CPC's publications in general for being "too costly". Public complaints like this could only play into the hands of people within the party who disliked both Butler and his growing empire; notable among these was the party chairman Lord Woolton, who recorded sourly that the CPC "was independent of Central Office until the bills came in". Woolton's strength, as demonstrated by his success in the wartime Ministry of Food, was propaganda, and this should have complemented Butler's more philosophical approach. Since the two men did not get on – as Rab characteristically put it, they were "never personally close" – what should have been a partnership turned into an attempt by Woolton to seize control of both propaganda and education.[16]

Apart from the threat posed to his CPC by the antagonism between Woolton and Butler, the situation must have been difficult for Cub because he had to deal with both men as his superiors. In a letter of late March 1947 he passed on to Butler the news that Woolton wanted to hold up the publication of *The Industrial Charter*. Attempting to be diplomatic, he reported that Woolton had said that "although he appeared to be antagonistic (he wasn't really), he was in fact quite the reverse". In the kind of double-edged phrase for which Rab himself would later become notorious, Woolton had added that the document would have to be carefully phrased because it "would win or lose us the election".[17]

If this skirmish between these powerful rivals resulted in something like a draw, Woolton had reason to cheer in November 1948 when ultimate responsibility for the Research Department passed to him (although in an unsatisfactory fudge Butler remained as chairman). In March 1949, "Against a background of some tension", as Rab put it, he wrote a stinging memorandum complaining that the Central Office had made an insufficient effort to publicise the *Industrial Charter*. This attack on Woolton's prized propaganda machine had no effect; indeed, when the report of the Maxwell Fyfe Committee on Party Organisation was approved in July 1949 Butler suffered another blow. The committee praised the work of the ACPPE, but added that it was "vital that the powers of the committee should be so defined [that] the party should have absolute confidence in it". The main recommendation was that political education should come under the supervision of a new committee responsible to the party chairman and his deputy. Butler was particularly hurt by his loss of control over the CPC, and with good reason. Having collaborated so closely with Cub in the formation of the Centre, he was bound to regard it with affection; and since Butler was so obviously the best person to supervise its activities, Woolton's *coup* seemed like a gratuitous and self-defeating way of clipping his wings.[18]

Years later the retired party chairman tried to land a further blow by claiming credit in his memoirs for the postwar revival of Conservatism in the universities, but to anyone with knowledge of the postwar party this could only be read as an inadvertent compliment to Butler, Cub and the CPC for whom the universities had always been a prime target. Although Cub's thoughts about the winding up of the ACPPE are not recorded, it was a serious set-back to someone who had dreamed of running the party for Butler. Fortunately by the summer of 1949 he had other distractions, but his last few months at the CPC must have been clouded by this first serious lesson about the influence of personal friction on the political battlefield.[19]

After first hearing about his job Cub had told Rachel that he wanted "sound finances, good writers and lecturers, educational agents in all constituencies . . .". As Woolton indicated in his memoirs, the CPC spent freely; whatever his personal faults the chairman was a legendary fund-raiser, and his control of the purse-strings gave him an invaluable weapon in his struggle with Butler. Cub could also draw on the services of numerous "good writers and lecturers"; the Llandudno conference was informed that in the first six months of 1948 "75 lecture series and 893 single lectures" had been given, in addition to the ambitious programme of publications which was soon augmented by Enoch Powell's *Conservative Policy for Wales and Monmouthshire* (published simultaneously in Welsh and English). In the same period, over 100 area and constituency conferences had been held. Cub spoke at many of these; this meant that he was often away from home, but (frustratingly for the historian) not long enough to make it necessary for him to record his daily life in letters to Rachel.[20]

To help organise this remarkable operation, Cub recruited full-time education officers for each of the 12 areas of England and Wales. His preference was clearly for strong (if not maverick) characters; the appointments included Ralph Harris, who was later chosen as the first Director of the Institute of Economic Affairs, and Humphry Berkeley, a nephew of Kenneth Pickthorn's who in the 1960s helped to design the party's process for electing its leaders.[21] Harris later recalled that Cub had taken his job very seriously indeed, running the CPC as if it were something like the military outfits he had dealt with during the war.[22] If Cub really had hoped for official "education agents in all constituencies" he was aiming a little high, but by the autumn of 1947 there were "557 local discussion groups usually meeting informally in a member's house, with about 6000 members taking part".[23] By the following spring, two-thirds of constituencies had a CPC group meeting regularly; in some constituencies more than one group was established.[24]

Cub also played an important part in setting up a Conservative college to succeed Ashridge, which became a non-political institution after the war. A replacement for Ashridge was always an important part of Cub's plans, and in 1948 Lord Swinton offered the use of part of his mansion near Masham in Yorkshire after promptings from Butler and Macmillan. Cub and Butler inspected the facilities and found Swinton quite as suitable as Ashridge had been; indeed, during the war it had housed Harrogate College. Cub appointed its first Principal, Reginald Northam who had been one of his tutors at Cambridge and was a friend of Butler's. The college was a great success, hosting the Ashridge combination of residential courses, weekend schools and discussion groups; over the year to July 1949 it was reported that 2000 students had attended 42 different courses. Cub continued to hope that there could be a southern counterpart to this "College of the North", but despite an intensive search he never found suitable premises.[25]

Apart from his strenuous and successful organisational efforts, Cub contributed some writing of his own to the CPC's list of publications. One of the *What do You Think?* pamphlets, a general survey of Conservative principles, appeared under his name. This followed the Baldwinian line, illustrated with historical examples, which he had laid down in *A National Faith* and which had been echoed so often since the war. At times, however, the tone of the pamphlet was too defensive. In his notes for group leaders, for example, Cub gave the important advice that "It is important to know the socialist point of view as well as our own. Try to get clear in the minds of your group where the conflict really lies. But . . ." he added as an unnecessary afterthought, "remember that Conservatism is something positive, having a definite philosophy of its own".[26]

This rather sheepish reference to Conservative philosophy was a symptom of a major problem for Cub. He had begun his work at the CPC with great enthusiasm, but he could not wish away the adverse circumstances at the time of his appointment. In *The Conservative Faith in a Modern Age* David Clarke had pointed out that "Conservatism does not spring from the works of any single philosopher. It is an attitude to life and an approach to private as well as public life". Cub agreed, and he denounced socialism because it owed too much to the thought of one man (Marx), and was too abstract to be applied to either private or public life. He thought that the Fabian socialists were a group of narrow extremists, who despite their boasted intelligence clung on to what they regarded as simple truths in defiance of practical evidence. Yet in late 1945, when Cub resumed his work for the Conservative Party, most observers agreed that the Fabians had made a significant contribution to Labour's victory. It was inevitable that Cub and Butler should coincide in their assumption that taking on and beating the Fabians at their own game would be an essential element of a Conservative comeback. Before long Butler's admirers within the parliamentary party and the Central Office had earned the collective name of "The Rabians".[27]

The difficulty for Cub was that if anti-socialists wanted to fight a "battle of ideas" in the postwar period they could draw on the work of a "single philosopher" for apparent "truths" which matched the misleading simplicity of socialism. In 1944 the émigré Austrian economist Friedrich von Hayek published *The Road to Serfdom* in an attempt to persuade well meaning people in all parties that their liberties were threatened by the economic interference of the state. The British people may have thought that they were fighting totalitarianism during the war, but according to Hayek they had already been taken a long way down that road by their leaders. Turning Labour's propaganda on its head, Hayek argued that the country "took the headlong plunge" towards a servile economy in "the inglorious years 1931 to 1939".[28]

Cub read Hayek's book, and believed that the principles of *The Road to Serfdom* would send the Conservative Party down the road to oblivion. Only someone with very limited knowledge of British political culture could have identified Stanley Baldwin as a totalitarian, which Hayek had done by picking 1931 as his pivotal year. But on one subject, at least, Cub and Hayek agreed. In 1947 Hayek told a disillusioned dairy farmer, Antony Fisher, that "the decisive influence in the battle of ideas and policy was wielded by intellectuals". He advised Fisher against standing for Parliament, recommending instead that he should set up a free-market version of the Fabian Society. It was not until 1955 that Fisher acted on this suggestion, helping to establish the Institute of Economic Affairs (IEA), and for some time this was dismissed by many commentators as a refuge for cranks. But as Britain's economic position deteriorated, Hayek's views, presented in a more accessible form by the IEA, filtered back to some Conservatives who had entered politics at the time when Cub's CPC was talking of a "battle of ideas" against socialism. With the distorted vision of hindsight they began to think that instead of fighting after the 1945 defeat Conservative leaders had simply surrendered.[29]

It was from this standpoint that Margaret Thatcher claimed in later years that "Documents like the *Industrial Charter* gingerly avoided the real battleground on which socialism ultimately had to be defeated". This was a conclusion which no one could have reached if Cub and Butler had been allowed a little more time to do their educational work before the war broke out, yet *A National Faith* had been forgotten to the extent that even Cub talked of postwar Conservative policy as if its broad outlines had been sketched *after* 1945. The message had not changed, but the fluent assurance of the earlier pamphlet had been erased by electoral defeat. Cub had come up against a paradox which has been integral to Conservatism since the time of Burke: the demand for statements of principle is always greatest at times of stress, but these are precisely the occasions when the Conservative "attitude to life" is hardest to express with conviction. For all his previous work as a moderate reformer, Burke sounded like an extreme reactionary when he wrote his *Reflections*.[30]

In his later years Cub found himself engaged in another "battle of ideas", against members of his party who had rewritten the postwar history of Britain on Hayekian lines. The work of the CPC certainly helped to postpone this right-wing reaction. But even before the conference which endorsed the *Charter* there was strong evidence that events, rather than ideas of any kind, would be the Conservatives' best weapon in the fightback against Labour. Severe weather affected Britain in January and February 1947, and despite the nationalisation of coal, fuel stocks had proved grossly inadequate. Rather than indulging in a "rigid totalitarian" planning exercise, as Butler had alleged, the Labour government had failed to plan even the output of the industry which they prized the most. Although Cub and Butler might have foreseen this – after all, they believed that unsound theory would lead to detrimental results – it would be a grave misuse of hindsight to criticise the decision to talk of a "battle of ideas" in the circumstances of 1945. The surprising thing is that their achievement lasted so long.

Cub's other CPC publication, *Imperial Policy*, was the last major Conservative statement to appear before the party's general programme was published in *The Right Road for Britain* (1949). By the time that Cub's pamphlet appeared (June 1949), Winston Churchill had begun to take more interest in his party's policy-making, but imperial matters had always been a priority for him and there was never any doubt that he would examine this document carefully prior to publication. Cub had originally written the pamphlet with the sub-title "A Statement of Conservative Policy for the British Commonwealth and Empire"; when Churchill got hold of the proofs, he changed the order to "British Empire and Commonwealth", and amended the phrase in red ink throughout the text. He found nothing else to object to, however, and the 1949 conference gave a "whole-hearted welcome" to the published pamphlet.[31]

A recent historian has judged *Imperial Policy* as the "least forward-looking of the series" published by the CPC before 1950, but this verdict was inspired by the standards of today rather than those of 1949. At the time only dogmatic opponents of empire could have called the pamphlet an exercise in nostalgia. *Imperial Policy* showed that the war had done nothing to dampen the idealistic views on Britain's future overseas which Cub had expressed in *Kingdoms in Partnership*. Having hailed "the British Empire and Commonwealth of Nations as the supreme achievement of the British people", he exhorted fellow Conservatives "to give our active support to all measures designed to promote [its] unity, strength and progress". By contrast, a Labour government heavily influenced by the Fabian Colonial Bureau could not be trusted in imperial affairs. Cub's specific proposals included more regular meetings of Prime Ministers; a new commonwealth tribunal with a supreme court to take over the under-used powers of the judicial committee of the Privy Council in cases involving disputes between commonwealth members; a British Empire and Commonwealth Defence Council with a commonwealth defence staff "which would recommend to the Prime Ministers . . . plans for action in the event of war"; and closer cultural and economic ties between the member nations.[32]

When Cub spoke of a close partnership, approaching to a federal union, between members of the old empire he clearly had in mind those nations like Canada and Australia which had long enjoyed dominion status. In a section which would later take on great importance for Cub, he discussed future constitutional developments in the more "backward" colonies which he had left out of *Kingdoms in Partnership*. The ultimate goal in each case was self-government, but

> Unlike the Fabians, we do not underestimate the difficulties which surround the application of democratic constitutions and ideas to peoples whose traditions are totally different from those of the western world . . . each colony will proceed at a different pace and whatever the pace, progress must inevitably be gradual.

He foresaw a danger of handing over control "to a small and clamorous political group who represent little but themselves"; of particular concern was the possibility that promising youngsters from the colonies might come to Britain to be educated, and after "falling an easy prey to communist doctrines, return to their country, embittered and disloyal, to spread sedition and unrest". Why they should fall "an easy prey" was not explained, but the best solution to this threat would be heavy British investment in education abroad, to ensure a literate and responsible electorate when self-government came. Cub was realistic enough to see that this was unlikely to happen on the necessary scale: "The plain, unvarnished truth is that universal education in the colonial empire must depend in the long run on the energies of the peoples themselves".[33]

These few pages of *Imperial Policy* contained the nub of the problem which was to haunt the remainder of Cub's career as a front-line politician. He saw enormous potential in the "empire and commonwealth", but while he was confident that mature partnerships could be established with the dominions – with Britain continuing its move from a position of control to the status of "first among equals" – he found it difficult to envisage the colonies in anything other than a subordinate position. Most of his contemporaries shared that belief – and it had no less a liberal authority than John Stuart Mill behind it. However, while the view that self-government should come at the appropriate time was fair enough in the abstract, the success of the operation would depend on the judgement being made by those who were impartial enough to decide on the evidence. In a world increasingly polarised between ideologues of Left and Right (and with Britain's own powers diminished by the ruinous conflict of 1939–45) there was a grave danger even in 1949 that the colonial constitutions would be shaped either by those who thought that the native peoples would never be ready to govern themselves – or by leaders who chose to rush all the remnants of Britain's empire towards independence, regardless of conditions.

By 1949 Churchill had already accused the Labour government of following the latter course – a policy of "scuttle", as he called it – over India, which became independent (along with the newly formed Pakistan, and Burma) in 1947. The Indian situation was a stark illustration of the problems of timing; early in 1947 the Viceroy, Wavell, was dismissed because he recommended a rapid withdrawal, yet his successor, Lord Mountbatten, announced in June that the British would pull out in August – seven months in advance of Wavell's timetable. The ensuing struggle between Hindus, Muslims and Sikhs resulted in the deaths of around half a million people. There was no chance of a "clean" break in Asia (or in Palestine, which Britain left in 1947 after a Zionist terror campaign) and in these cases ministers had good reason to act sooner rather than later. The typical Conservative response to these radical changes was to brood in silence rather than push their concerns to a vote, and in writing his pamphlet Cub refrained from partisan criticisms. Yet he must have been aware that many of his colleagues might lose interest even in the prospect of constructive partnership now that control over large areas had been ceded, and he deplored strong evidence of apathy among the wider public.[34]

To show how much the Conservatives had learned in the presentation of their programme, major statements like *Imperial Policy* were launched at press conferences which ensured immediate and prominent coverage in most of the national dailies.[35] Comment on Cub's pamphlet was divided on party lines. The Conservative-supporting press either praised it or simply summarised its contents at length; an editorial in the Conservative-leaning *Daily Graphic* enthused that the pamphlet "puts forward, not pious platitudes, but plans at once bold and practical. It is idealism stripped for action". On the other side, the correspondent from the *Daily Worker* exercised his imaginative powers to dredge out of it a worldwide attack on trade unions. Perhaps the most perceptive criticisms came from the Liberal *News Chronicle*, which pointed out that the author had not once mentioned the United States (although Cub had, like his party leader, applauded early signs of European co-operation). Even so, the correspondent welcomed the fact that "the roll of imperial drums [was] notably absent" from the document. Unfortunately for Cub, this meant that for all its idealism *Imperial Policy* lacked the kind of romantic appeal which might have stirred contemporaries like Enoch Powell to maintain their interest in the subject. In the circumstances, however, he had done everything possible to squeeze some hope out of a situation which bred dejection in others, without exposing his party to justifiable criticism from its opponents.[36]

The Right Road for Britain, which formed the basis to the 1950 Conservative manifesto *This is the Road*, appeared in July 1949, a month after *Imperial Policy*. In his foreword Churchill explained that with a "momentous" election looming the party had "not sought to embitter controversy but to present a broad and simple statement of the Conservative outlook and aims to those who are making up their minds". In reality, after a burst of hard drafting work beginning in April, a "rhetorical commitment to freedom" was injected at the last minute into a text which otherwise proved that the Conservatives had accepted most of Labour's policies as compatible with their own activities in government before and after 1939. Thus a policy statement supposedly innocent of any design to "embitter controversy" accused Labour of planning a society

in which all forms of power are to be centralised in the government, and the interference of government will pervade and dominate the private life of the citizen . . . If present policies are pursued to their logical conclusion, property with its rights and duties will be destroyed, management will be left without initiative, the trade unions will cease to be independent and local government will become a rubber stamp.

With an election looming, the Conservative propagandists had taken over.[37]

This kind of question-begging assertion was little better than Churchill's counter-productive "Gestapo" broadcast during the 1945 campaign. To claim that Conservatives stood for "freedom" while Labour stood for state control might have seemed like a cheap way of buying votes or of putting some extra spring in canvassers' steps; unfortunately it both overshadowed and contradicted the constructive suggestions which had arisen from the publications of the CPC. If voters subjected Churchill's slogans to the same logical test that they were invited to apply to Labour, they would conclude that the Conservatives believed in unrestrained *laissez-faire* – the very approach which the *Charters* had denounced, and which the fine-print even of *The Right Road for Britain* rejected. Ironically, despite efforts to show that the Conservatives had not simply fiddled during the 1930s while unemployment soared – efforts which included a persuasive pamphlet issued by the Central Office in September 1949 – the rhetoric of this pre-election publication implied that they now embraced the philosophy which voters associated with economic slump. Given the austere social conditions of 1945–50, the humiliating devaluation of sterling in September 1949, and the clear evidence that Labour had failed to bring about a New Jerusalem, the most interesting aspect of the 1950 general election was the fact that although the Conservatives recovered strongly they fell short of victory. When the other elements favouring the Conservatives – their vastly improved finances and organisation, as well as the constructive ideas published by the CPC in the years before 1950 – are taken into account, it is likely that the last-minute rhetorical assault on Labour lost more votes nationally than it gained, by convincing lukewarm supporters of the government that the beneficial legislation since 1945 would be at risk under Churchill.[38]

The section of *The Right Road for Britain* on imperial policy was a summary of Cub's pamphlet, but beyond this he played no part in the writing of the document. As the election approached he was also guilty of misusing the rhetoric of "freedom", if the notes he made for his speeches are an accurate guide. When he left the CPC in February 1950 he received warm congratulations from many of the party's "backroom boys"; had the Conservatives won the election, he probably would have been hailed as one of the chief architects of victory. As it was, his real achievement would not become apparent until the party returned to power in 1951, and since he was no longer in the backroom himself his contribution tended to be underrated. By stressing the value of constructive educational work until their voices were drowned in a hubbub of electioneering Butler and Cub had ensured that the next generation of Conservative leaders stayed within a party which was accepted as intellectually respectable by the important minority who paid close attention to policy ideas rather than slogans. They had brought this about in a party which tradition-ally had no time for the "intelligentsia", and which was led by a man who was far more interested in action than in thought. Cub's dream of a party led by Butler and run by himself had not been fulfilled, but in his five years at the CPC he had proved that this had been more than the fantasy of an overheated mind.[39]

⁓

The period before the general election of 1950 was particularly full for Cub. In 1946 he became a father, and within two years he was selected to fight his first parliamentary seat.

Cub and Rachel lived happily with Rab and his wife Sydney from the beginning of 1946. Butler was so busy that they saw far more of Sydney, with whom they had quickly established a strong friendship despite her natural reserve. Cub, who had known the former Sydney Courtauld since before the war, was particularly impressed by the affection between the Butlers; one day at Stanstead he had been astonished when on an impulse Sydney jumped on Rab's knee and kissed him. He remained convinced that her early and painful death when Butler was Chancellor of the Exchequer in December 1954 was a fatal blow to Rab's political career, although in 1959 the latter embarked on a second happy marriage with Mollie, the widow of Sydney's cousin.

The stay in Smith Square came to an end in September 1946, when Rachel gave birth to a girl, christened Cecilia Alexandra Rose (she was always known by the last name). The newly augmented family established itself in a spacious rented flat at 52 Cumberland Mansions, Seymour Place – close to Cub's old school and to a flat which he had occupied during the war. It was also very close to the South Paddington constituency, which in late 1947 began searching for a new Conservative candidate. Cub had embarked on his own quest, in the expectation of an election in 1948. Among the talented staff at the Parliamentary Secretariat, Iain Macleod and Reginald Maudling had already been adopted for seats in the London area, having been "blooded" in the 1945 contest; Enoch Powell, who fought an improbable and unwinnable by-election at Normanton in 1946, would soon find a berth in his native Midlands, and another promising Tory, Edward Heath, was chosen at Bexley in October 1947. The supply of seats was hardly drying up, but Cub had drawn up a list of specifications and knew that he had to act soon.

Cub could almost claim to be a "local boy" in front of the South Paddington membership; in addition to his own residence there (his flat had suffered bomb damage during the war), his father had worked at St Mary's Hospital for many years. However, the North and South Paddington seats had been re-drawn, and although South Paddington had returned a Conservative in 1945 Churchill's great friend Brendan Bracken had been heavily defeated in the Northern seat. Cub calculated that the Conservatives would be hard pressed to win after the recent revisions. Even so, he was pleased to discover in January 1948 that he had reached the final round of the selection process, with only one opponent; he told his parents that he considered the nomination to be "in the bag".[40]

Cub could afford to feel blasé about South Paddington because there was another constituency which he regarded as "in the bag". This second option was Colchester, where the selected candidate, Dr Pearl Hulbert, the wife of an MP, had been forced to step down "no doubt due partly to the Conservative Party's traditional male chauvinism and partly because they did not consider that she was a strong enough candidate to unseat the Labour member, Charles Smith".[41] Colchester constituency, which stretched from the River Stour on the Suffolk border to the sea coast at Mersea, contained 28 villages and had an electorate of about 52,000. For Cub it was love at first sight; as the oldest town in Britain, with strong Civil War associations, Colchester appealed to his sense of history, but it also combined "all the characteristics of English provincial life". Cub told his parents that "it would be a principality of its own", complete with a large military garrison. Equally important was its long-standing habit of returning Conservative MPs despite a strong healthy Liberal tradition in the area; the Tory candidate might have lost in 1945, but the Labour majority was small and vulnerable to even a slight opposition recovery. Strangely Butler, who was MP for the adjoining constituency of Saffron Walden, advised Cub against putting in for Colchester; on this occasion his views were politely ignored.[42]

Given a free hand Cub would have chosen Colchester, but his hand was forced in that direction anyway because the selection process moved faster there than in South Paddington where there were problems with the sitting Conservative MP. The first step at Colchester actually took place in a London hotel, where Cub was interviewed by the constituency executive with half a dozen other hopefuls. Looking back on this event Cub remembered none of the questions put to him, although he did recall that the panel contained several representatives of "the farming interest"; he would not see the *Agricultural Charter* through the press until June, so possibly he was stumped by their detailed inquiries. What Cub did remember was the "cherry coloured velvet suit" which he had recently bought for Rachel; his account merely states that "they asked me all the usual questions and it was clear that Rachel had made a very favourable impression". The field was whittled down to three after the meeting, and Cub was among those who proceeded to the next stage.[43]

The crucial meeting took place at Colchester's Red Lion Hotel in January. Cub gave his address accompanied by Rachel, who was asked to say a few words herself. Although the candidate later claimed that he was horrified by this request, his wife rose to the occasion. This, Cub felt, was the clinching moment; he also believed that their case had been strengthened by the fact that he and Rachel had a baby in their team, while one of the other candidates was a bachelor and the wife of his second rival was only just pregnant. His conviction that Rachel had been decisive in winning over the constituency party was later confirmed by the chairman, David Papillon, and by others.

Whether or not Colchester's "chauvinism" was peculiar at the time, it was an interesting first constituency for one of the local young Conservatives, Margaret Roberts, to encounter. In one respect, at least, the local party was fairly enlightened; although the "Maxwell-Fyfe" reforms that prevented candidates from subscribing more than £25 per year to constituency funds had yet to be officially endorsed, money was never mentioned during the selection process – much to the relief of Cub, who was prepared to sacrifice a large proportion of his income but could not go beyond a couple of hundred pounds. In the end he agreed to contribute just £10 a year – before the war Quintin Hogg discovered that one constituency demanded £3000 – and paid nothing at all towards his election expenses.[44]

When he put himself forward for Colchester Cub had been unaware that some members of the constituency party still favoured the claims of Dr Hulbert. On 4 February Cub's adoption meeting was held in front of an audience of 1500 at the Colchester Corn Exchange. Trouble was expected; the Central Office arranged for the area chairman Eric Edwards (later Lord Chelmer) to preside over the meeting. As Cub later recalled, "Captain Hulbert and his wife sat in the front row and after the adoption had been proposed and seconded he rose to make his protest which he did in forthright, even violent terms. On the whole", he added, "this probably did me good". A resolution demanding Dr Hulbert's re-adoption had been withdrawn, and Cub replaced her as the official candidate "with very few dissent-ers". Even so, it was inauspicious for someone who knew that he would have to attract a fair degree of cross-party support to know that he was beginning his campaign with divisions on his own side.[45]

Cub had promised that he would come to live in the constituency, but it was not until September 1949 that he rented a cottage in Copford, a few miles from Colchester. This temporary base was near Copford Hall, the residence of Brian Harrison who had considered putting in for the Colchester seat but instead became a key figure in Cub's campaign (in 1955 he won the nearby seat of Maldon). Before moving to Copford Cub commuted weekly to the constituency, and had proved himself a most active candidate long before the election date was announced. Less than a month after his adoption he told his parents that he had spent "four evenings and all Saturday" of one week in Colchester, making a total of eight speeches "most of which were reported". This was probably an unusual burst of activity – at the time Cub thought that the election would take place as early as July – but it was an early sign of a commitment to Colchester which Cub maintained for the rest of his life. Cub also showed the shrewd tactical sense which had first blossomed when he fought his election at the Cambridge Union. His Labour opponent was continually goaded in Cub's speeches and letters to the local press, but when Smith fell ill just before the poll Cub decided to call a halt to his campaigning – and made sure that the papers carried prominent stories about this act of charity. Cub also submitted to the familiar indignities of the hustings, on one occasion being paraded around the home of Colchester Football Club on match day "like a prize ox at an agricultural show".[46]

Attlee eventually called the general election for 23 February 1950, against an unpromising background for his party. Although the Conservatives had failed to capture a single parliamentary seat in by-elections – in February 1949 even the supposedly marginal seat of South Hammersmith held firm against an all-out attack – the party's share of the vote generally increased, and there were major gains in local elections. In the wake of devaluation the Conservatives held an opinion poll lead of almost ten per cent, but by January this advantage had disappeared as voters considered the likely consequences of a change, and the Conservatives were prepared in advance for a result which seemed to set them up for "one more heave" in the near future. Colchester was always going to be close, although the Conservatives could take heart from an increase in membership of 2665 between 1948 and 1949. Cub later claimed that he wanted to be an "inclusive" candidate and his election leaflet avoided excessive partisan comment, but as the battle approached he tried to encourage defections from the other parties by attacking them – particularly the Liberals, who (true to the generally negative Conservative campaign) were denounced throughout the country as potential splitters of the anti-socialist vote.[47]

In these days before elections were fought on television candidates worked hard for their seats in the full expectation that whatever the national outcome their personalities and ideas could make a real difference locally. In his 1949 report on Colchester the Conservative area agent described Cub as "a good candidate, very friendly and mixes well" (a judgement which would have surprised the candidate's father). The agent noted that Cub had "a reputation for being a little high-brow. He tries very hard to break this impression down". These efforts were not completely successful; Cub struck local canvassers as a very serious young man. Perhaps this impression was enhanced by the rapid thinning of his hair since the start of his military career. His local workers were exposed to the serious side of his personality, because he carried over from wartime experiences his exacting views on organisation. A typical day for Cub began with three hours of street canvassing, followed by meetings with representatives of local organisations or visits to factories and farms in the afternoon. The evening would be taken up by as many as five speeches at ward or village meetings; some of these orations were delivered on street-corners. These trips were tiring, but they also offered an opportunity for Cub to get to know all the parts of his constituency. Although the intensity of this campaign was something new to Cub, after the election the *Essex County Standard* praised him for his "confident, commanding treatment of a subject or an audience". His lessons with Captain Finn and his experience of the Union had laid solid founda-tions; all that was required, the *Standard* declared, was more experi-ence of these full-blooded campaigns to "make his armour entirely heckler-proof". Cub's exposure to professional campaigning also inspired his party's production of a daily campaign bulletin from the day on which official nominations were received.

At his eve-of-poll meeting Cub had another reminder of his Cambridge days; one of his supporting speakers was Charles Fletcher Cooke, who had converted to Conservatism after almost winning East Dorset for Labour in 1945. He introduced Cub to the audience of 2500 packed into the Corn Exchange as "a future Prime Minister". In a telling commentary after the election, the *Standard* differed from Fletcher Cooke, plumping for a "less fulsome" comparison – with Rab Butler. The paper's correspondent remarked that they both approached politics "from the viewpoint of the thinker, with the perspective of the historical example always in mind"; that each had been President of the Cambridge Union; that they exhibited "the same touch of formality, the outward indication of an inward shy-ness"; and that "Both are of the type most naturally referred to after the diffident public school tradition by initials or nicknames – 'Cub' and 'Rab'". Perhaps carried away by his acute analysis of the two men, the correspondent proceeded to notice "a facial resemblance" between them. Quite what Rab might have made of all this if he picked up the *Standard* that week can only be guessed; the direct comparison with the man he once invited to act as his spaniel was one thing, but the suggestion that Cub promised to be a second Rab *rather* than a future Prime Minister must have been difficult to take.[48]

While the "future Prime Minister" was being applauded at the Corn Exchange, a large group of Smith supporters had set up a chant of "We want Charlie" in the street outside. On the previous day the MP had been chaired around the streets to his own headquarters in Lion Walk. To those accustomed to stage-managed contests of recent times, accounts of the 1950 Colchester election seem hard to distinguish from the events at nineteenth-century contests – Charles Dickens' "Eatanswill" without the overt corruption. When Cub left his own meeting after an hour-long speech the Labour hordes gave him what the *Standard* described as "a stormy passage"; he was escorted from the hall by two policeman (assisted by the tall and athletic Brian Harrison) to the Cups Hotel next-door. He appeared on the balcony with Rachel "to the combined applause and boos of a very large crowd".[49] The Conservatives gratefully accepted the opportunity of milking the incident for sympathy votes; Cub's agent told the press that Smith's supporters had made "a concerted attempt to injure Mr Alport". In fact the only recorded injury in the Battle of the Corn Exchange was a kick in the back received by a policeman.[50]

In hindsight the last-minute demonstration by Smith's supporters seems like a final howl of anger against a candidate who had outclassed a much-loved Labour MP, although Labour's agent tried to blame the fracas on "the presence on the platform of an erstwhile socialist, Mr Fletcher Cooke".[51] On the day of the election all the main contenders expressed surprise at the large number of undecided voters; no one could be confident of the result. The count revealed that Cub had received 21,403 votes, beating Smith by less than 1000. Almost his entire majority could be accounted for by postal votes, which said a good deal for the organisation behind him.[52]

Nationally the Conservative Party had increased their support by 2,500,000 votes compared with 1945, but despite their patchy record in office Labour were also up by over a million; with 298 seats, the Conservatives had fallen short of Labour's tally by 17. In Colchester the Liberal candidate received over 4000 votes, but this was not enough to stop Cub winning. The 2,500,000 votes the Liberal Party received overall meant that only nine of its candidates were elected and over 300 deposits were lost. The Conservatives had tried to present the 1950 election as a straight fight between themselves and Labour, and this tactic was likely to pay further dividends in a renewal of the contest which could not be long delayed. On that February night these calculations must have given Cub more reason for cheer, as he contemplated the party revival which he had done so much to foster, and which had made him MP for Colchester.

Chapter Five

"One Nation"

On 2 March 1950 – less than a month before his thirty-eighth birthday – Cub was sworn in as a Member of Parliament. However, he had yet to reach the House of Commons: this was still being restored after war damage, so the MPs gathered in the "gothic splendour" of the House of Lords. At first Cub was uneasy in his seat; for some reason, at the start of every day's proceedings he "felt a slight quiver of apprehension – since it must, I thought, be a dream – that some burly Door-Keeper would tap me on the shoulder, seize me by the scruff of my neck and [drag] me through the great brass doors".[1]

Cub was one of 93 Conservative MPs who had never sat in Parliament before; perhaps he was not the only person to think that his presence was a mistake which would soon be ended by a door-keeper's hand on his collar. But he belonged to what even Nye Bevan admitted was "the finest Tory vintage in history" – Cub attributed its quality to the maturity which most had gained from war service – and soon the newcomers were playing a full part in what turned out to be a Parliament of only 20 months. On 14 March Iain Macleod delivered his maiden speech, on the National Health Service budget, and two days later Enoch Powell spoke on a Defence White Paper. Cub's opportunity came during a debate on the Army Estimates on 20 March.[2]

While the "Class of 1950" looked back with nostalgia on their early days (and held dinners to commemorate their entry to Parliament) they had embarked on their careers with uncertain prospects. Security of numbers helped the morale of the novices, as did the fact that the Labour government was clearly under pressure. But a long list of ambitious maiden speakers can foster an unusual degree of competition between members of the same party, and the sense that before long they might all be called to account by their constituencies must have added to the natural desire to make an early impression in 1950. The atmosphere was not improved by the first clash between Attlee and Churchill; with the scent of blood in his nostrils the old Conservative leader launched an ill-tempered attack on the Prime Minister, claiming that the two main parties were "separated by a wider and deeper gulf than I have ever seen before in this island". To say the least, this was an odd beginning to the exchanges of a decade which is usually seen as one of "consensus" between Labour and the Conservatives. In the circumstances it is greatly to Attlee's credit that within a few weeks he had singled Cub out as an old Haileyburyian, and invited him for a drink in the Smoking Room. The Prime Minister was rightly proud of his old school; for most of Cub's time in the Commons Haileybury was third (behind Eton and Westminster) in its tally of MPs.[3]

Cub delivered his first speech from a second-row seat below the gangway; from exactly the same spot 13 years later he made his maiden effort as a member of the House of Lords. Following the outspoken Labour MP Woodrow Wyatt, he drew on his wartime experience to suggest that African troops should be raised for service in the Indian Ocean area. This idea was not intended to save money, but to strengthen ties between Britain and the colonies; he noted that war had brought better facilities for health and education to many Africans, and this ought to be maintained in peacetime. He paid tribute to the performance of African soldiers in the war, and only rejected the idea that they might serve in Europe on the grounds that they would dislike the climate.[4] No good maiden speech would be complete without a warm reference to one's constituents; Cub managed this with the declaration that "We in Colchester like soldiers, and we think we understand them". His speech was well received; in addition to the usual compliments from the next speaker Cub was congratulated by another MP later in the debate. He also had the confidence to make an intervention, characteristically correcting a Labour member who referred to potential African recruits as "foreigners".[5]

Although Cub made several speeches (and numerous debating interventions) on colonial matters in his first Parliament, he had no need to advertise his expertise in this field to his party's leaders. Within two months of the election he was picked by Oliver Stanley, the former Secretary of State for the Colonies, as secretary of the Conservative back-bench Committee for Imperial Affairs. In the next Parliament he became vice-chairman of this committee; at the same time he took the chair of the Joint East and Central African Board, a non-party organisation which included many parliamentarians. The latter position (which he held from November 1953 to December 1955) gave him the opportunity of meeting many notable figures involved in African politics, including the nationalist leader from Nyasaland, Hastings Banda.

Work of this kind could lead to two very different careers in the House – the occupant might be seen as ministerial material, serving an apprenticeship in a responsible job until a vacancy arose, or as someone who would remain as a "good committee-man" on the back-benches, contributing his wisdom in relevant debates but generally keeping quiet on other subjects. The role of Oliver Stanley – himself strongly tipped as a future Conservative leader – in Cub's first appointment would suggest that he had been placed in the first category. Certainly that was his own view of the matter. Instead of sticking to his favourite topic of imperial affairs, he ranged widely in this Parliament as would be expected of an aspiring front-bencher. Before the general election of October 1951 he had made contributions on domestic subjects including underpaid workers, school meals, housing and the broadcasting of football matches. A notable effort in June 1950 was a speech introducing a short Adjournment Debate on the plight of former prisoners of the Japanese, who, he declared, felt "forgotten by the people of this country". He suggested that they should be given special compensation, perhaps through a special levy on Japanese imports, but although his speech was warmly received his argument was ignored by this government and by its successors.[6]

Cub's aim during this first Parliament was to make his mark as a frequent and knowledgeable speaker. By convention maiden speeches should be uncontroversial and listened to with respect by both sides of the House; the ideal would be to win similar attention for future efforts. But in the bitter atmosphere of 1950–51 this goal was far from easy, and the more often a tyro like Cub rose to his feet the more likely it was that he would run into trouble. Cub brought this on himself as soon as convention allowed – in his second debating speech of 8 May 1950. He decided that the motion on underpaid workers was a suitable platform for a lecture to the Labour members on the history of social reform in Britain. Taking aim once more at Labour's propaganda about the 1930s, he questioned whether socialists had ever heard of nineteenth-century Conservatives, such as Michael Sadler and Richard Oastler, who had fought for better working-class conditions. Evidently these well worn themes produced in Cub the illusion that he was back in the election campaign of 1950, addressing a hostile and ignorant crowd; instead of challenging Labour's boasted monopoly of good works he seemed to be setting up similar claims on behalf of his own party. Labour members were not in the mood to hear this, especially since Cub was slow to give way to those wishing to interrupt his speech. Some routine heckling provoked Cub into losing his temper and accusing his opponents of "wickedness". In the circumstances it was unlikely that he would make much headway with his argument that poorly paid workers would benefit more from low inflation than from large pay increases, nor with his accusation that Labour was working to prevent "the drawing together, [which] we on this side of the House hope for and work for, of the two nations that Disraeli noted".[7]

At least Cub had improved on Disraeli himself, who had caused outrage in the House with his maiden speech. But he knew that he had damaged his prospects. Some orators thrive on combat which gives them the chance to come to notice for their witty repartee. But this was never really Cub's style; besides, he meant what he said when he spoke of healing divisions in the House and in the nation itself. The speech had misfired and he had shown that he could become rattled under pressure; while not exactly a marked man, Cub was sure to be baited by Labour MPs in future when he strayed into controversial territory. In February 1951, for example, Charles Pannell protested that Cub "never gives way to other people and is usually unmannerly when others are on their feet"; when informed that, as a matter of fact, Cub had given way to another member on the previous day Pannell said he was making a general point about Cub's "bad manners". In an angry Parliament it was most important that clashes across the floor should not develop into feuds; before promoting even a promising newcomer party managers had to be certain that he would not be thrown out of his stride by enemy jeers every time he spoke from the front-bench. Although Cub's thin skin was hidden for the rest of this Parliament it was exposed on several occasions in the next one, and this could explain the delay before his first promotion.[8]

In the Parliament of 1950–51 it was unwise for Conservatives to generate hatred on the government benches, but causing exhaustion was another matter. Attlee and his senior colleagues were weary after ten years' ministerial service, and the government's slender majority meant that elderly or sick Labour MPs were required to attend and vote when they should have been resting at home. Two of the government's greatest figures, Sir Stafford Cripps and Ernest Bevin, were already ailing. The Conservative Robert Boothby threatened to make Labour members "sit day and night and grind away until they get absolutely hysterical and say 'We can't stand any more'". This attitude was unusually vindictive, but it must have occurred to most Conservatives that a few by-elections in winnable seats would do the party no harm.[9]

Of course, not everyone on the Conservative benches was fit for a sustained campaign of the sort suggested by Boothby – their own leader, after all, was seventy-seven in 1951 – but a war of attrition could be maintained by a handful of young enthusiasts calling debates late at night, backed up by the occasional full-scale ambush when the government was off-guard. The Conservatives could not defeat the most controversial legislation of the Parliament, on steel nationalisation, but they managed to beat the government in seven other votes. Almost certainly the ruthless tactics employed by the opposition in

1950–51 helped to persuade Attlee that the next election should be called early; it could not come soon enough for the Conservatives.[10]

Prominent in the attempt to wear out the government was a group of young Conservatives to which Cub belonged. The foundations of the group, which later took the name "One Nation", were laid by Cub before the election, when he had attended a meeting near Chelmsford. He was a member of a "Brains Trust" panel answering questions from local Conservatives, and another member of the team was Angus Maude, the Prospective Parliamentary Candidate for South Ealing. Cub discovered that Maude was deputy director of Political and Economic Planning – a non-party body with a high reputation for social and economic thinking. Cub recognised immediately that Maude's main interests were the perfect complement to his own.

Once both he and Maude had been elected, Cub saw no reason why he should not try to form a body along the lines of the CPC, but this time consisting entirely of MPs; after all, there were several good precedents, including the existing Tory Reform Committee (whose members belonged to the previous generation of MPs), and Labour's left-wing Tribune Group. As he put it,

> My aim was to assemble a group of like-minded members of the new 1950 entry who would work together to prevent the party from slipping back into the old ways of the past and ensure that its social policies continued along the lines developed by Rab Butler and those who were associated with him in the immediate postwar years.[11]

Once he had settled into the House it was only a matter of time before he began to put the group together. Ironically, the process began with a speech by Churchill's son-in-law Duncan Sandys, in a debate on housing on 22 May 1950.[12] Reading Sandys' speech many years later Cub considered that it had not been especially bad, but it was interrupted almost as often as his own unlucky effort of 8 May had been. At the time Cub thought that it exemplified all that had been wrong with the party in the years before the war, and he left the Chamber "seething with indignation". He spoke to Maude, and soon they had gained their first recruit: Gilbert Longden, the MP for South-West Hertfordshire, who had once been a pupil of Cub's at

Ashridge. According to one account, there were no free seats in the Members' Dining Room so the trio retired to the neighbouring Harcourt Room where they were joined by others.[13]

The order in which members were recruited for "One Nation" is sometimes treated as a matter of great importance – almost as if they had been the twelve disciples. Thirty years later Cub placed Iain Macleod next; Macleod suggested Powell who, after several near misses, now became a firm friend of Cub's.[14] Robert Carr was invited because of his practical experience of industry, Richard Fort because he was a scientist and had worked for ICI, and John Rodgers who had been an executive of an advertising firm and was presumed to know something about publicity. According to Cub it was Rodgers who suggested Edward Heath, whose attractions included a good war record and a Balliol College scholarship – some of the gloss was rubbed from the latter achievement in Cub's eyes when he learned that Heath had been an organ scholar.

Whatever the precise order in which the group was put together, as in most bodies of this kind an inner circle emerged fairly quickly; in this case Cub, Maude, Powell and Macleod seem to have been the most active members. Macleod had been commissioned to write a pamphlet for the CPC on the social services, and during the first meeting at PEP's offices at 16 Queen Anne's Gate he generously suggested that this should be put together by the whole group, with everyone contributing a chapter. Maude and Macleod would edit the resulting volume. They turned out to be particularly active editors; Cub later admitted that Maude had written the bulk of "his" chapter, on Education, and this was probably not the only example of editorial ghost-writing.[15] Cub told Nigel Fisher (Macleod's biographer) that Maude suggested the title to Macleod over the telephone; later he agreed with other accounts, which give Macleod the credit for thinking of "One Nation". It has been assumed that this apposite and eye-catching name was chosen some time during the summer of 1950, but a newspaper cutting from late August among Cub's papers announces the forthcoming publication under the title "The Strong and the Weak", which apparently came from a recent speech by Anthony Eden. This is one case in which the label was at least as important as the message; it is doubtful whether "The Strong and the Weak Group" would ever have achieved the prominence of "One Nation".[16]

When the pamphlet was launched appropriately at a CPC meeting before the 1950 Conservative Party conference it aroused interest, and the British public has been hearing the slogan "One Nation" ever since. In the 1980s it was adopted by Conservative opponents of Margaret Thatcher, and at the 1997 general election Labour's Tony Blair used it as part of his strategy of appealing to disgruntled Tory voters. To question the importance of "One Nation" would be to commit something like an historical blasphemy. Yet the philosophy behind the pamphlet was hardly new – in choosing their title from Disraeli's novel *Sybil* the editors claimed a distant ancestor for their ideas. Cub wanted the group to continue the work which he and Butler had done after the war, but this was unduly modest; he should really have referred to the work which he and Butler began *before* 1939. The acceptance of the Welfare State which Labour had built on the foundations laid by the Conservative-dominated Coalition was nothing new, either. The novelty of the pamphlet lay in the detailed thinking which the group undertook in showing how the Welfare State could be made more effective at a time when government spending had to be restrained as a result of Britain's wartime losses: before the pamphlet appeared the case for prudent management was strengthened by Labour's decision to boost defence spending to support American policy on Korea. As Cub put it in an article which contributed to the group's publicity campaign, the pamphlet showed that "we could make substantial economies while at the same time ensuring that the real purpose of the social services – to provide each person with a decent minimum standard of living – is faithfully maintained". In the optimistic atmosphere of the 1950 conference, with the party almost certainly on the threshold of a return to power, the kind of practical ideas embodied in *One Nation* showed that, whatever the Labour Party might say, the Conservatives once again looked like a natural party of government.[17]

Rather than being the major turning-point in the history of progressive postwar Conservatism, then, *One Nation* is only one of many milestones. From this more realistic perspective one can disentangle the personalities of the group from the debate about the meaning of "One Nation politics" which has raged in recent years. The fact that Powell and Maude were part of the original group has caused particular confusion here, since by the late 1960s both were regarded as being on the extreme right-wing of the party. As their collective name suggested, the members of the group were preoccupied with national unity; in 1950 differences between them were obscured by their agreement that the greatest existing threat to unity was the excessive taxation imposed on the wealthy by a radical Labour government. Shared optimism to the socialist idea of equality, and support for the concept of "minimum standards" for the poor, seems to have allowed the members to avoid debating the extent of inequality which each of them deemed to be tolerable in a united nation. Thus passages in the pamphlet can be read today as an argument for unlimited accumulation for the rich, so long as the poor received adequate provision – in other words, a manifesto for the "strong" against the "weak". Similarly it was common ground that private enterprise was necessary for a prosperous society; the fact that some members regarded this as a dogmatic principle while others based their views on practical considerations did not become apparent until later, when circumstances changed.

In short, it is possible to admire the style of politics upheld by the *One Nation* pamphlet without elevating the people responsible into oracles who somehow epitomised Disraelian "One Nation" principles for the rest of their lives, whatever they might have said or done. Many of the original group were unusually ambitious politicians, and as such were much more prone to opportunistic (or even sincere) changes of mind than even the average, irrational human being. If anything, it is still more mistaken to look for a persisting "One Nation" thread in productions of the group which appeared after most of the original members had departed; Cub, for example, was very unhappy with *Change is our Ally* (1954), which took a position somewhere between the first pamphlet and the "Two Nations" dogma later associated with Powell and Maude.

Perhaps the most interesting aspect of the "One Nation" story is the insight it gives into the divisions which can arise between politicians who at first feel a sense of unity. Cub once said that the group "was a sort of projection of those talks among friends at the university, sometimes until the dawn of a summer's morning lit the casements of our college room". It seems that memories of their former intimacy only served in later years to increase the bitterness of their numerous quarrels; in the reaction of Macleod and Cub to Powell's 1968 "Rivers of Blood" speech one can detect undertones of betrayal and sorrow born out of old comradeship. It was a feeling of collective responsibility, which caused Cub to reflect many years later that "we failed to provide . . . the sort of leadership which the Conservative Party and the country needed from the postwar generation of politicians".[18]

The foundations of friendship were laid as the members talked over their chapters during the unminuted sessions of summer and early autumn of 1950; it blossomed when they decided to keep meeting on Thursday (later changed to Wednesday) evenings when the House was sitting. This enabled them to discuss the forthcoming week's business, but also to relax and dine in congenial circumstances. The minutes of the first meeting, held on 23 January 1951 at the PEP offices in Old Queen Street, are typical of all the surviving records from this time in the impression they give of a dining-club which only occasionally lapsed into a serious mood. Macleod, Fort, Cub, Carr, Rodgers and Powell were in attendance; the last named was the group's secretary, and his minutes prove that despite his dour public image he was quite at home in this setting. He recorded that Alport and Macleod were given the task of approaching "A.B.B's" (Active Back Benchers, marshalled by John Boyd-Carpenter) who might associate themselves with "One Nation" in harassing the government, and it was agreed that at all meetings the group would study the coming week's programme to identify opportunities for holding the late-night debates which Labour's ministers found so irksome. Even at this first meeting of "One Nation" as a political dining-club rather than a drafting committee, differences were revealed between the members; it was "Agreed (with Alport dissenting) that any proposals for coalition be attacked and denounced". At the time, with party tempers high (and Cub himself a target of much Labour abuse) this was a strange hypothesis for discussion, but rumours had been circulating. Cub had made his mark at the Cambridge Union as a supporter of coalition and he was not prepared to relinquish what turned out to be a life-long preference.[19]

More serious divergences were revealed even when "One Nation" exploited the procedures of the House to "harry" the government. On 16 April 1951, for example, Maude proposed during evening "Prayers" an amendment to the School Meals (Charges) Bill.[20] This proposed legislation raised the price of a school meal to 7d.; it also gave ministers power to make further changes without consulting

Parliament. Maude's objection was not to the new cost of meals, but to the increase in ministerial powers. Cub, seconding Maude, attacked both the principle and the price. This short debate was something like the "Nation" against the government; other speakers included Longden, Powell and Macleod. On the following evening the group was at it again; during a twelve-minute speech from the Labour front-bench, they made a total of fifteen interventions. These incidents show how political friendships can be forged under fire, in spite of minor splits which in other circumstances could widen into gulfs between the members of the group. Cub remembered later that whenever he used the phrase "social justice" Powell attacked it as a meaningless cliché; at the time what could have been taken as a warning signal was regarded as a typical piece of pedantry from a classical scholar. The minutes suggest that the group swung to the right when Macleod, Alport and Heath were not in attendance; this was the case, for example, when a discussion was held in July 1953 which resulted in support (in the existing circumstances) for the principle of *laissez-faire*.[21]

In February 1951 the group moved its meetings into the dining rooms of the House of Commons. These were happy times: as Cub recalled, "We laughed a lot; the claret was cheap, but drinkable and there was always the satisfaction that, junior as we were in the party hierarchy, with *One Nation* we had made our mark".[22] This was no idle boast; they began to issue invitations to senior party figures in the confident expectation that these would be taken up. Now that they had some status to protect, the group decided at the beginning of March to restrict membership to twelve; in November it decreed that front-benchers would also be excluded. Another sign that "One Nation" had established an independent reputation was a visit in June from seven members of the Tory Reform Committee, who might have expected these striplings to join up with their own established group after the 1950 general election. Anthony Eden, still the Conservatives' "Crown Prince", visited in July.[23]

Cub must have been glad that the claret was cheap; dining once a week with his friends while the House was sitting put an additional strain on a budget which had been stretched by his election and his new family responsibilities, which increased in December 1951 with the birth of a second daughter. On 1 August the family moved into a new and larger home in the constituency. The Cross House in the quiet village of Layer de La Haye, a few miles south of Colchester itself, was originally a Tudor cottage, which had been expanded into a farmhouse probably during the seventeenth century. Additions were made in 1914; the young architect had been an early casualty of the First World War. By that time it was regarded as the manor house of Layer manor, since the original building, opposite the church, had been destroyed by fire. Even when the manor was no more, ownership of the Cross House could easily produce the illusion of lordship; by his middle-eighties Cub had become such a fixture in the village that, in a sense, he had grown into that role.

In 1950 this beautiful house was owned by the Round family, who rented it to Cub. He was unable to purchase the property until 1957. Cub had always wanted to put down strong roots; as he had remarked when explaining Anthony Eden's concept of a "property-owning democracy" before the 1950 election, a home could be said to constitute "the furniture of a man's life". In keeping with his Conservative principles Cub added very little to the "furniture" which he had acquired. He obtained a stone lion and a Tudor rose from the wreckage of the prewar House of Commons, and set them up in suitable places; in later years he had his coat of arms placed on a back wall. By that time he was High Steward of Colchester, and felt that such ornaments were fitting for the residence of someone who held that position. If property really should be considered "the furniture of a man's life", this element of Cub's furniture revealed a streak of pomposity which friends observed without feeling that he was any the worse for it. This might also be detected in the bust of Disraeli which he bought and placed in his substantial garden; but if anyone had a right to display Disraeli in this fashion Cub had certainly earned it.

While Cub was in the Commons during the week, Rachel remained at the Cross House. Cub was fortunate to be able to stay with his parents-in-law in Evelyn Gardens. Without the bonus of a free London base he might not have been able to sustain himself as an MP; as it was, he was in need of some supplement to his parliamentary salary of £1000 per year. The Conservative Party of 1950 was very different from its prewar manifestation in one respect, at least; the tendency even before the "Maxwell-Fyfe" reforms to select candidates on the basis of merit rather than wealth meant that many newly elected MPs were in need of assistance. Through Butler's contacts Cub found a very unlikely position as a director of a company which manufactured bags for cement. This brought him a much-needed annual supplement of £500, and the duties were something less than exhausting. He remembered that he visited the factory on one occasion, judged that the products were on the whole satisfactory, and dozed through a few meetings of the board. The only other evidence that he had ever held this position was a parliamentary question asked to the Minister of Works in May 1950, in which Cub demanded to know the reason for a continuing shortage of cement in North-East Essex – without declaring any interest in the matter. Even in the much later days of "cash for questions" scandals this omission would have rated as something less than sensational.[24]

These financial precautions were made in the expectation that, when the election came, Cub would retain his seat and would need both the Colchester base and his cement-bag sinecure. King George VI had told Attlee in the summer that he was concerned about the "unstable" political situation; the Prime Minister promised that there would be an autumn election to clear the air. Attlee finally called the election for 25 October 1951. At the start of the campaign the polling organisation Gallup identified a Conservative lead of seven per cent, but Labour had suffered bitter divisions during the Parliament, and hanging on in the hope that the position would turn around might have made matters worse for them.[25]

The Conservative campaign in 1951 was notable for the party's pledge to build 300,000 houses in a year – which had been adopted with some misgivings after a raucous debate at the 1950 conference – and the slogan "Set the People Free", which cleverly exploited public weariness with continued rationing. Historical judgements about elections are too often coloured by the overall outcome; any assumption that Britain turned against socialism in 1951 is refuted by the fact that Labour received more votes, but the Conservatives won more seats under the first-past-the-post system. Clearly the Conservatives lost a good deal of ground during the election; some potential supporters might have defected because of the *Daily Mirror*'s attempt to portray Churchill as a warmonger, but it is also likely that as in 1950 undecided voters were put off by the ambiguous Conservative rhetoric of "freedom".

For Cub the 1951 campaign was a mirror image of the previous election; he was now defending, rather than attacking, a marginal seat. There was no Liberal candidate this time – indeed two former Liberal mayors had declared their support for Cub – but he could not assume that a majority of uncommitted voters would float in his direction. As a result he played with a straight bat, welcoming the pledge on housing while stressing the difficulties of meeting such a target, and deploring the "warmonger" assaults on Churchill. A less predictable suggestion was that an all-party inquiry should look into possible reforms for the House of Lords, and his election leaflet included a declaration of war against "the shoddy materialism which is so alien to our way of life". He left nothing to chance with his local organisation; as soon as the election was called his headquarters in Museum Street boasted 30 workers, stuffing envelopes on trestle tables. He was also ready with some impressive statistics for a combative speech at his adoption meeting; he had spoken in 22 debates, asked 127 questions in the House and helped around 700 constituents at his weekend surgeries. His personal campaign slogan, "All for Alport", was slightly unimaginative, but he showed more flair in adopting the theme tune from the recent film *The Third Man* to herald his arrival in the Essex villages. The "Third Man" had the bonus of a second child for his publicity photographs; the new daughter was to be called Carole.[26]

As in 1950 every evening was filled with speeches and journeys from one village to another. Supporters from outside the constituency included Quintin Hogg and Barbara Cartland, whose MP brother had been killed in the war. One "photo-opportunity" went astray when all the candidates turned up at the same time for the football club's home fixture with Torquay; their chances of winning many votes were further reduced when the game ended as a drab 0–0 draw. A few days before the poll Cub enjoyed a typical stroke of luck, when a minor road accident happened in front of his car as he and Rachel were returning from a meeting in Dedham. He drove off to summon help as Rachel dressed wounds; undecided voters would have been interested to read about the heroism of Colchester's "Third Man" in the local paper of 23 October.[27]

The election brought Churchill back into power with an overall majority of 17. When the crucial result came through the BBC microphones caught Lord Woolton, yelling "We've won! We've won!

We've won! After six years we've beaten the socialists". These must have been expressions of relief, because the national victory only partially concealed troubling details. For example, in the south of England outside London the party was now even stronger than it had been in 1935, despite the fact that in that year it had benefited from its place in a National Government. In every other area it was much weaker – in the Midlands, for example, it won 35 seats, compared to 67 in 1935. Conservatives who simply wanted to win elections might be able to shrug off these trends, but for the "One Nation" group the figures showed that the party had a great deal of work to do.[28]

Cub won Colchester by an increased majority. He would still be vulnerable if the new government proved deeply unpopular, but he now had a cushion of 3846 votes. As he was carried around the town centre by supporters speculation grew that he would now secure his first government job, but if he expected a call himself he was to be disappointed. He had already proved his suitability for a junior post at Commonwealth Relations or the Colonial Office, and with Butler now Chancellor of the Exchequer something might have been found for him. But only one member of the "One Nation" group was skimmed off this time, and Edward Heath, who now embarked on his successful career in the Whips' Office, had found the cost of dining with his colleagues even more of a strain than Cub had done.[29] After Heath's departure the disruptions became more regular; his replacement Reginald Maudling had only been with the "Nation" for four months when Powell recorded that "at 9.45pm a waiter appeared and whispered to Mr Maudling (acting chairman) followed by a whips' messenger who announced – 'He wants to see you sharpish'".[30] Apparently the acting chairman thought at first that this was a practical joke, but Maudling abandoned his friends for the post of Parliamentary Secretary at the Ministry of Transport; a month later, after a blistering attack on Nye Bevan which impressed Churchill, Macleod was lured away to the Ministry of Health.[31]

Despite these changes, and the transition from guerrilla war against Labour to support for a Conservative government, Cub thought that the group was stronger at the beginning of the 1951–55 Parliament. They began to organise more carefully to win places on important committees, and even passed their own motions of censure against certain ministers during their private gatherings. Sometimes this would be no more than an idle prank – on 24 July 1952, for example, the list attached to a resolution "that the following members of the government be replaced" included almost everybody in the cabinet. But the group seemed fairly serious in its expressions of impatience at Churchill's refusal to step down from the leadership, and the discussion of 20 March 1952 concerning the "desirability of Woolton's dismissal" was certainly sincere – Woolton, after all, disliked Butler.[32]

Perhaps the group as a whole did grow stronger after the 1951 election, but Cub's commitment may have been wavering. In December 1951 he put his name to a pamphlet written mainly by a very different member of the 1950 "vintage" – the flamboyant right-winger, Gerald Nabarro. The pamphlet made a strong and prescient case for fuel economy, both in the home and at work. The reasons for Cub's co-operation on an issue far outside his main interests are now obscure, but he and Nabarro often raised the subject in the House. Almost twenty years later Nabarro branded Cub as "a prosaic and impressive parliamentarian" who "was never really at home in the Commons"; this shows how far time and ideological differences can distort the memory, because in December 1951 Nabarro was obviously pleased to have yoked his name to that of a promising colleague who was far closer to the mainstream of the party.[33]

Cub's flirtation with coal did not distract him from his infatuation with Britain's overseas role, particularly in Africa. By the time that the pamphlet appeared (December 1951) he was reported to be working on a book which was published in the following autumn as *Hope in Africa*.

Cub's previous full-length work on the subject, *Kingdoms in Partnership*, had in parts betrayed the fact that its author's knowledge of Africa was mostly derived from other people's books. Although the message of the later volume was very similar, the years that Cub had spent in that continent during the war ensured that *Hope in Africa* was more readable. He began by recording a depressing conversation with fellow officers on his outward journey in late 1941, which took place as the British Empire seemed on the edge of oblivion; later he mentioned another discussion, with the war correspondent who thought that whatever the outcome of the war only America and the Soviet Union now counted in world affairs – without confessing that he had lost his temper on that occasion. By the end of the book he had put pessimism to rout, declaring that "By our patience, statesmanship and success in Africa we can write a far greater chapter in the history of the contribution of the British people to world civilization than anything that has gone before".[34]

Cub's new vision took into account the scaling-down of the British Empire which had taken place under Labour. The goal now was to bring African states up to the standards of western civilization, in a partnership which would bring benefits to all the countries of the world. Cub deplored some of the Labour government's economic initiatives, such as the failed £25 million scheme to produce ground-nuts in Tanganyika, but he welcomed the 1950 Colombo Plan which brought international investment to Asia and called for a similar development in Africa. He urged that economic progress must pre-cede major political change; if the colonies were to become self-governing they must do so from a position of strength.

Cub's main interest was clearly focused on the idea for a federation in Central Africa, composed of Nyasaland and Northern and South-ern Rhodesia. Each of these territories enjoyed economic assets which were of limited use in isolation from each other; Nyasaland, the poorest country, had large reserves of labour, Northern Rhodesia had copper, and Southern Rhodesia could contribute its coal. Before the war the Bledisloe Committee had considered the future of these territories, and while rejecting amalgamation had encouraged the idea of close co-operation. The Attlee Government had followed this up with the Victoria Falls Conference (1949), and ministers favoured the idea of a federation, although they were concerned by the reported level of African opposition. The possibility that the white-governed Southern Rhodesia might dominate the Federation, applying its discriminatory laws to its neighbours which had massive black maj-orities, provoked genuine fears amongst the native populations whose leaders were now looking for independence. But the Labour govern-ment recognised the possibility that parts of Central Africa might be picked off by the racist South African regime led by Dr Malan; they believed that Southern Rhodesia might take a more liberal path if it was yoked to states which continued to be governed by the Colonial Office. A second conference at Victoria Falls in September 1951 was interrupted by Attlee's decision to call a general election, but Labour's Colonial Secretary James Griffiths reaffirmed his faith in federation and expressed the hope that hostility would disappear.

While others agonised over the problem of winning the active consent of the native population, Cub was all for instant action. "In an era such as this", he wrote, "a decision made firmly and in good faith is always better than weakness and vacillation". The benefits of federation would become obvious to all the inhabitants once the change had been carried out; if the will was lacking to go through with the experiment, the African population would remain in poverty and backwardness. Cub attacked those "internationalists" (the Fabian Colonial Bureau above all) who had made the concept of "self-determination" into their idol without thinking of the practical consequences; he claimed that although such people abhorred "imperialism", the ideals they upheld with words had been realised in action by the British over the centuries, whatever the misdeeds of isolated individuals.[35]

While Cub was working on his book the federation plan was dealt another blow. The new Conservative Colonial Secretary, Oliver Lyttleton, called a conference to produce a draft constitution in April 1952, but only two African delegates (both from Southern Rhodesia) turned up. It can be appreciated with hindsight that the boycott by representatives of Nyasaland and Northern Rhodesia placed the Federation in very serious jeopardy from the outset. While in office Labour had promoted the scheme as an enlightened solution to existing problems in Central Africa; now that the Conservatives were in charge they chose to denounce it as the source of any tension in the area. The opposition's new stance encouraged African leaders to step up their strategy of non-co-operation, and this in turn increased the volume of Labour's protests. For people like Cub this meant that the federal scheme had to demonstrate its benefits quickly; otherwise Labour would be able to wind it up as soon as the party came back to office. But the chances of success for the Federation were obviously reduced by the native opposition, which was left unmoved by promises that the governments of all three states would retain substantial powers to safeguard existing rights.

Cub believed that the potential prize of a well governed multi-racial state in Central Africa was so valuable that the government had to soldier on. He felt that he was engaged in a new "battle of ideas" with Labour, and was sensitive to anything which might give his opponents a cheap advantage. The delicate political balance in Southern Rhodesia forced supporters of the Federation to allay the fears of right-wing Europeans in advance of a referendum on the issue. As a result, the Southern Rhodesian Prime Minister, Sir Godfrey Huggins (later Lord Malvern), made a series of speeches which allowed Labour to claim that the Federation was designed for the sole benefit of white "settlers". Cub corresponded with the popular Northern Rhodesian leader Roy Welensky on the subject of Huggins' regrettable "witticisms"; he also contacted the Archbishop of Canterbury who had reacted strongly to reports of the speeches. Both Cub and Welensky recognised that unless the controversy died down the federal experiment would be denied a fair trial, but there was little they could do to quieten a debate with so many outspoken participants.[36]

In the House of Commons Cub spoke frequently during the prolonged and stormy debates of 1952 and 1953 – often losing his temper at what he regarded as unprincipled opposition from Labour members.[37] In their eyes the formal establishment of the Federation in September 1953 was far from being the end of the matter. Before then it had been decided that the position should be reviewed after ten years. This reflected the realistic assumption that Labour could not be out of power for much more than a decade and would scrap the Federation unless there was unequivocal evidence of progress. Even so, the decision ensured that as this deadline approached tensions would rise among both supporters and opponents of federation; it might be said that it provided a timetable for hostilities to break out. At the same conference, in January 1953, Lyttleton stated that the Federation could not be liquidated without consent from the UK, the federal government, and all three territorial governments. No one dissented from this verbal commitment, although it would have meant in practice that the federal government could only die if it agreed to its own euthanasia. Lord Swinton, the Secretary of State for Commonwealth Relations, commented that in theory no one could stop the UK Parliament passing an Act to dissolve the Federation, but this would only happen if a government had gone "off its head". Having planted these seeds of misunderstanding, the ministers left it at that; all that the supporters of federation would be able to do when it came to the crunch was to protest that Lyttleton's words "were taken as part of a contract by all who attended the conference".[38]

Within a decade these built-in flaws of the federal scheme would present Cub with his greatest political challenge. For the moment he felt very happy with the reception of his book. One reviewer exulted that in *Hope in Africa* "The belittlers of empire are shown up as ignoramuses"; the only weakness in the "brilliant book" was that in advocating an African version of the Colombo Plan Cub had implied that other countries beside Britain might have a role in developing the empire.[39] But the real weakness of the book was its timid treatment of racism. Cub criticised South African apartheid but made the astounding suggestion that if it had been given an English-sounding name people would not be so upset about it. Furthermore, for someone who wrote lyrically about partnership between the races he made too many concessions to Europeans (including those in Southern Rhodesia) who deplored mixed marriages, although this dubious interlude was tempered by some strong advocacy of improved treatment for African women. In the *Evening Standard* the historian Robert Blake applauded the book as "stimulating and free from the usual prejudices".[40]

Taking a leaf out of "One Nation's" book, Cub made sure that *Hope in Africa* was published in time for the Conservative Party conference, held in 1952 at Scarborough. Labour's earlier gathering had denounced the proposed Federation, and as if to mock Cub's idealism news had arrived that the vicious "Mau Mau" secret society in Kenya had attacked a retired British soldier and his wife. Atrocities had been going on for most of the year, but this outrage against Europeans produced special interest on both sides of the House. In Kenya Cub's wartime friend, the farmer Michael Blundell, was pressing for a genuine multi-racial society; in a country which contained 6,000,000 Africans and 50,000 whites this was always going to be a difficult task. Cub saw the problems at first hand when he visted Kenya as part of a six-man parliamentary delegation in January 1954; special security precautions were necessary amid rumours that the MPs would be the target of an ambush, and Cub slept with a loaded revolver on his bedside table. He was glad to renew his acquaintance with Blundell during the visit, and when Cub's son Edward was born in May 1954 Blundell joined Rab Butler as a godparent.[41]

The problems in Kenya gave an additional incentive for backbench Conservatives to regard colonial affairs as unwelcome in-

trusions in domestic politics. Having begun its existence with a publication on social questions the "One Nation" group was no exception
to a trend which dismayed Cub. The appearance of his book did nothing to change the priorities of his colleagues, and in late 1952 his
record of attendance at "One Nation" meetings slumped dram-
atically.[42] He returned at the end of January, but did not dine with the
group. The minutes for the meeting of 12 February 1953 record that,

> To the grief of his colleagues Cub Alport announced his inten-
> tion to withdraw from the Group forthwith for purely private
> personal reasons. He had no disagreement on policy or other-
> wise with the rest of the 'Nation' and it was agreed that he be
> invited to rejoin if the 'Nation' remembered the empire.[43]

As recorded by Powell, the minutes of that meeting look like a page
from *Tristram Shandy*: the secretary drew a black box around the news
of Cub's defection. At the next meeting the remaining members
speculated about the real reasons for Cub's departure, which as a voluntary decision provoked far more consternation than any of the earlier comings and goings. "Fears he'll lose his seat the election *after next*;
and now wants to 'save Africa'. Meanwhile he has to provide for a wife
and family". The minutes suggest that some doubt remained as to
whether these were the true reasons, but the cost of the dinners had
always been a problem for Cub and his loss of enthusiasm for the
"Nation" coincided with his new commitment to another time-
consuming task as chairman of the Joint East and Central Africa
Board. Although not by nature a "resigner" he lacked both the time
and the money to keep up his attendance, and preferred to give up
entirely rather than to maintain a half-hearted connection. The members felt that the balance of characters within the group had been
disrupted; Cub would probably have been heartened to know that his
former colleagues decided that a *bon viveur* should take his place to
ensure that the old mood was restored. Two weeks after Cub's departure only Powell and Fort turned up; this was the first time that
attendance had been so poor. As Powell recorded, they "dined pleasantly together and went home".[44]

The "Nation" continued to meet despite the absence of its founder,
but on 14 December 1954 it resolved "that Cuthbert Alport be invited

to rejoin the Group upon receipt of intimation that he was so disposed", and he reappeared at the next meeting.[45] Perhaps Mr Secretary Powell, or another member of the group, had already received such an "intimation"? The reasons for an approach by one side or the other at this particular time must remain obscure, but the minutes suggest that the "Nation" had not as yet "remembered the empire". Iain Macleod was doing well at Health, Ted Heath was proving himself to be a natural whip as Cub had predicted, and Maudling was Economic Secretary to the Treasury. Perhaps Powell and Maude, who had yet to receive the promotion which their talents deserved and were already known as awkward customers, were edging towards re-shaping the group into a base for malcontents. There is a clue that this was so in a remark which Powell made himself, and thought worthy of record, in the month before Cub was invited to rejoin: "the best change for us here would be a government defeat at the next election". Yet this, like so many of the entries in "One Nation's" early minute books, might have been intended as a joke. In later years Cub would only say that "The Group had become no less assiduous, but rather more light-hearted".[46]

To Cub and Rab Butler the postwar Churchill Government must have seemed both satisfying and infuriating. The Conservative Party had been all but cleansed of the "old guard", as they had wanted, and back in office it was following the broad principles they had laid down before and after the war. In 1953 Labour's Hugh Dalton noted the lack of respectable targets for the opposition to attack. Yet as the first postwar decade neared its end Butler was not leading the party, and Cub was a long way from running it as he had hoped. Indeed, despite its early promise the 1951–55 Parliament was an unhappy one for Butler, who had been defeated over his ill-advised scheme (nicknamed "ROBOT") to float sterling, had lost his mother, his father and his wife, and probably missed his best chance of becoming Prime Minister when both Eden and Churchill were seriously ill in the summer of 1953. At the same time an improbable rival, Harold Macmillan, was coming up on the rails having delivered on the promise of 300,000 houses per year.

When in April 1955 Churchill finally decided to call it a day, the long-suffering (and still ailing) "Crown Prince" Eden stepped into the inheritance rather than Butler. This was a further blow for Cub; Eden had visited both Colchester and the "Nation", but Cub was well known as a friend of Eden's rival, Butler, and he had a more personal reason for doubting whether the new Prime Minister would offer any favours. Back in the 1930s *Kingdoms in Partnership* had been given a fair review by the historian E. H. Carr, and when soon after the war Cub was asked to write about one of Carr's books on foreign policy "for some obscure periodical" he returned the compliment:

> A few days later and after I had been about half an hour in my office, the telephone rang and I was told that Mr Eden wished to speak to me. A voice said, hysterical with anger, 'That Alport? What the hell do you mean by writing that review [of] E. H. Carr's book?' I was so astonished that I stuttered some explanation. Then the voice said 'I regard it as bloody disloyal and offensive' and the telephone at the other end was slammed down. What I had not known was that E. H. Carr had written some fairly strong criticisms of Eden and his earlier policies and this had infuriated Eden.

Throughout his life Cub was liable to imagine that those he had offended were blessed with phenomenal memories; in this case, however, he knew that Eden had nursed a long-term grudge against Carr so he may have been right to think that the new Prime Minister would be at best a lukewarm friend.[47]

Having finally replaced Churchill Eden called an election for 26 May 1955. After what turned out to be a quiet campaign, Cub won in Colchester a comfortable majority of 4898 (again without Liberal opposition); overall the Conservatives led by 58 seats. When Parliament re-assembled "One Nation" seems to have become even more frivolous, as members of the great 1950 "vintage" realised that they might soon become overripe on the back-benches. On 13 July (in the absence of Powell and Cub) the only minutes recorded were as follows:

> [David] Orsmby-Gore: I haven't had hay fever this year. I think because I was hit on the head.
> [Angus] Maude: Perhaps I should hit my wife on the head with a poleaxe.

Towards the end of November things had become even more farcical, with Jack Simon launching an attack on a Bill which he had drafted himself.[48] On the following Thursday Cub introduced a more positive note, promising to draw up the outline for a collaborative book on the commonwealth. At last, the "Nation" was taking an active interest in "the empire". However, a cabinet reshuffle had been expected since Eden's appointment, and in the certain prospect of losing members the group had taken an oath to continue in some form whatever might happen in the coming weeks. Cub was sitting in the Smoking Room a few days later when a whips' messenger approached and asked him to see the Chief Whip as soon as possible. As Cub recalled,

I went along to Patrick Buchan-Hepburn's office wondering what I had done wrong. 'Oh, Alport' he said 'the Prime Minister has asked me to invite you to join his government as Asssistant Postmaster-General'. My face fell . . . the APMG was the lowest form of ministerial life even if, in the case of Mr Attlee, it had been the beginning of the road to Downing Street.[49] 'Don't be a bloody fool' said the Chief Whip, looking at me crossly, 'Get on the band wagon and next time you'll go upward'. I thanked him, mumbled that I was delighted to accept the Prime Minister's invitation and returned to the Smoking Room. I suddenly realised I was no longer just one of six hundred Members of Parliament, but a minister of the Crown and as such, no longer eligible to be a member of the 'One Nation' group.[50]

Chapter Six

Early Postings

Having decided not to be a "bloody fool" and to accept the Chief Whip's advice, Cub threw himself into the job of Assistant Postmaster-General as if it was the one he would have chosen for himself. He was given responsibility for telephones and the Royal Mail, and within hours of the appointment he was escorting the Mayor and Sheriffs of London around the Mount Pleasant sorting office. Cub's first inspection of his new empire came at its busiest time, because the Christmas mail was being processed. His initial misgivings were almost forgotten as he realised that he had been made "the *de facto* chairman of a major public service"; after his wartime experiences and his time at the CPC he knew a well organised machine when he saw one. "From that moment onwards", he wrote years later, "I was a devoted admirer of the British postal service".[1]

Cecil and Janet were spending the winter months in South Africa, as had become their habit. Cub told them his news in a telegram, and on Christmas Eve scribbled a letter which was a curious mixture of excitement and defensiveness. "Although it is a junior job", he told them, "the competition is fierce. The PM made only eight appointments from the back-benches . . . . Whatever happens in the future I shall at any rate have got myself out of the ruck". He went on to describe the "trappings of majesty" associated with the post: "I have a colossal office adorned by oils from the national collection. A private secretary and assistant, a car and a chauffeur and heaven knows what else".[2]

Cub believed that the main reason for his good fortune was "an extra push by a number of friends, particularly RAB". While others deserved his gratitude, he congratulated himself that "at the critical moment" he had made a Commons' speech "which was hailed as the best of the debate in which the PM, Foreign Sec, and eight senior Privy Councillors took part. [Eden] was particularly cordial . . .".[3] Yet this speech had been a plea for an even-handed approach in the Middle East as tensions grew between Egypt and Israel – an unlikely measure of someone's ability to debate the merits of the Hayes and Harlington telephone service on behalf of the government.[4] The most likely explanation is that Cub had always been regarded as a candidate for promotion, partly because of his connection with Butler (and later of "One Nation") but also because he had demonstrated expert knowledge in a key area of government policy. Unfortunately his performances in the House had raised doubts about his temperament, and although there was a vacancy in December at the obvious ministry, Commonwealth Relations, other candidates were considered to be more reliable. The solution was to try him out in a reasonably "safe" job, and if he proved himself equal to his parliamentary and administrative tasks he might be considered for a move later on.

Cub's immediate boss, the Postmaster-General, could not be counted among the "friends" who had canvassed on his behalf. Dr Charles Hill, who had been a popular broadcaster during the war, confessed in his memoirs that he was not consulted about Cub's appointment but would have opposed it if asked because "I suspected that we had little in common". His reservations lasted no longer than Cub's: "not only did he prove a first-rate minister", Hill wrote, "but we got on admirably together, despite any difference in outlook and personality. . . . I delegated a lot of work and responsibility to him, leaving him to get on with it as he thought best and to consult me when he thought fit. He had the obstinacy, as well as the ability, to get things done."[5] What might have been an unfortunate clash of characters turned into a mutual admiration society; in his own unpublished memoir Cub wrote that Hill was "an able and amusing person and we got on extremely well".[6]

Looking back, Hill regretted that the apparent achievements of a Postmaster-General are "for the most part determined by his predecessor, so long does it take to translate major policy into obvious action". This might have had something to do with the relatively brief tenure of most PMGs; Hill was the 28th occupant of the post in the twentieth century, and neither of his most famous predecessors, Attlee and Neville Chamberlain, stayed at the ministry for more than six months. To illustrate his point Hill recalled that he ordered an investigation into public attitudes towards the Post Office which was incomplete when he moved on; when asked about his aims in a television interview, Hill's successor Ernest Marples said "that he intended to investigate the public's attitude to the Post Office". As Hill remarked, "Ernest was always a speedy worker".[7]

Reflecting on his own record as Hill's assistant Cub felt none of these inhibitions. He remembered that less than a month after his appointment:

> I attended, in my constituency, a Burns' Night dinner. Inspired no doubt by the oratory and even more by the athol brose I came away thinking would it not be wonderful if Scotland had its own stamps . . . I therefore wrote a Minute suggesting that there should be regional stamps for Scotland, Wales and Ulster and supported it with such arguments as I could muster.[8]

The minute, written six days after the dinner, survives in the Post Office archives. Cub's arguments were:

1. The idea would be extremely popular in Scotland
2. It would provide variety for the United Kingdom issues
3. It would add to our postal revenue in a dignified manner.[9]

If this proposal seems a very modest one forty years later, at the time Cub knew that the odds were against him. Senior officials at the Post Office took pride in the smooth performance of their organisation, and any threat to their tranquility – particularly a threat with a strong political flavour – had to be resisted. Cub could also expect opposition from within his party. After a sensation in December 1950 when the Stone of Scone was repatriated by nationalists, sentiment north of the border seemed to have subsided. The beast might be asleep, but few Conservatives wanted to take the risk of waking it up.

Cub anticipated these objections in his cunningly worded memorandum: "So far from encouraging local nationalism", he wrote, "the policy of meeting such aspirations half way in matters of symbolism is always prudent". In fact he was not even suggesting that the nationalists should be met "half way"; the various stamps would still be dominated by the Queen's head. Yet when a paper drafted by Cub was discussed by the government's Home Affairs Committee in April the reservations of James Stuart, the Secretary of State for Scotland, were noted. Stuart had been reassured by the time the committee met again, and the Home Secretary (with responsibility for Wales), Gwilym Lloyd George, had been in favour from the beginning. But the Treasury claimed that the idea would lead to expensive demands for separate coins, and Butler (the chairman of the committee) reported that Eden himself "had expressed some misgivings".[10] In fact this was a typical Rab understatement, in what was a very skilful summing-up. The Prime Minister was allergic to nationalism in any form, and felt strongly enough to dispatch a stiff attack on the proposal to the Post Office.[11]

Butler had stepped down from the Treasury to become Lord Privy Seal in the December reshuffle – a move which his friend Henry Crookshank privately described as "sheer political suicide".[12] Despite this further setback to his ambitions, Rab's backing was powerful enough to sway the cabinet when it met to consider the national stamps. Cub had secured an unexpected victory; in his memoirs Hill generously gave him all the credit, although the Postmaster-General had helped to mobilise support and without Butler the proposal might never have got past the Home Affairs Committee. After all their work, however, Hill reflected that the stamps "had an unenthusiastic reception . . . nationalism, it seems, thrives on its grievances and is faintly resentful at their disappearance".[13]

Cub's second battle with Post Office inertia was also fought over stamps. He had noted that an elderly peer, Lord Elibank, made regular demands in the House of Lords for more British commemorative issues. Cub liked the idea; it would provide encouragement for designers, enhance the reputation of the Post Office and probably bring in extra revenue. His officials worked hard to produce counter-arguments; according to Cub, one of them claimed that office-boys would take twice as long to lick these larger stamps. Once again Cub's view prevailed, and a set in honour of a scouting jubilee appeared in the summer of 1956. If anything the reception was more hostile this time, at least in some quarters; one *Times'* reader felt that "The philatelic world must regard this as an outrage", and another denounced the "puerile folly" of a government which could fritter time away on such proposals.[14]

Cub would have liked to push beyond his commemorative issues and introduce pictorial stamps, but he had stirred up enough trouble for the time being and was advised to deny any such intention. It was left to a later Postmaster-General, Tony Benn, to take this radical step. The dynamic exemplar of Harold Wilson's drive for modernisation, Benn achieved so much at his department that it might seem as if Post Office reform only began in 1964. Cub rather resented this impression in later years; his own record showed that with "obstinacy and ability" even a junior minister could change things at the sleepy and self-satisfied Post Office.

If success in government is judged on a politician's ability to guide a proposal from the drawing-board to practical operation, Cub had disproved any doubts about his suitability for office. His efforts were not confined to the battlefields of Whitehall; in March 1956 his local paper reported that he had risen at 3am to accompany a postman on his rounds, and he visited numerous post offices from Wales to John O'Groats. In the meantime he was learning the parliamentary aspects of ministerial work, preparing himself for the occasional debates and regular questionings, and opening channels of communication with back-benchers on both sides of the House who supported his initiatives on stamps.

Although Cub enjoyed his work he might have begun to hanker for a role more suited to his real interests had he not been moved after just over a year. Ironically his chance came because of the government's Middle Eastern policy – the subject of the speech in December 1955, which the Prime Minister had appreciated so much. At that time Cub had advocated a neutral stance in the quarrel between Egypt and Israel, but during 1956 the Eden Government became increasingly hostile to the regime in Cairo, now led by Colonel Nasser. In June British troops were withdrawn as agreed from the Suez Canal area, but in the following month both America and Britain disowned their promise to supply funds for Nasser's Aswan Dam project. Nasser retaliated by nationalising the canal company on 26 July.

Cub had expressed strong views about the Suez Canal as early as February 1953, when the *Daily Telegraph* published a letter questioning Britain's strategic interests in the area.[15] He was making a virtue of what the Churchill Government regarded as at best a necessity; negotiations to pull out British troops were already in train despite the hardline views of MPs such as Julian Amery, who regarded the fortifications in the Suez area as "the keystone of the structure of imperial defence".[16] Cub had resigned from the "One Nation" Group just a fortnight before he wrote his letter; this was only a coincidence, but a fairly remarkable one since both Powell and Maude were fiercely opposed to Cub's views on Egypt. Their "all or nothing" approach, which made them worship the empire and deplore the commonwealth, led them to join with other Conservative back-benchers in the Suez Group. Cub cannot have been ignorant of their views; he also knew that his father saw a British take-over of Egypt as the only remedy for the corruption he had found in that country. Nevertheless, in May 1953 he repeated his message in a Commons' debate on foreign affairs; his speech was rightly described as "thoughtful and courageous" by Labour's Christopher Mayhew, who could not have known that Cub's courage was both political and personal.[17]

Like all politicians Cub had experienced convenient conversions in the past. When the Attlee Government introduced majority rule to the Gold Coast, for example, he warned against "so-called constitutional reform"; a year later he was speaking of the apparently successful changes "with a sense of pride".[18] Opposition members who remembered Cub's earlier opposition hooted at this brazen declaration, but hardly anyone else can have noticed. Suez was very different; it was the kind of issue which drove party whips to draw up lists of potential rebels, and even some constituents must have thumbed through *Hansard* to see how their representative had spoken in the past. Cub had always been an instinctive loyalist, but the Suez crisis must have been a sore trial for him; had he been in a relevant ministry, or even in a position to speak out from the back-benches, the tension between Eden's behaviour and his own views might have been too great even for him.

As the country lurched towards the disastrous invasion of November 1956 Cub was not much better informed than the average citizen. In September he and Rachel dined with Butler at Stanstead. As he later recalled,

> the conversation at dinner turned to the Egyptian problem. I said to RAB that I hoped we would not involve ourselves in some military action because I feared that the financial consequences to our somewhat shaky economic situation would cause us trouble . . . He had been Chancellor of the Exchequer only a few months previously and obviously knew the problem. He replied "Oh no, I can assure you that if any action is taken we will be able to stand the strain without difficulty".

The anecdote has a truthful ring – although Cub thought that Sydney Butler, who had been dead for nearly two years, was present.[19] Once the crisis ended Cub was horrified by the memory of the conversation, believing that if an ill-informed junior minister could anticipate economic problems the cabinet's complacency was inexcusable. In fact Rab's reply could be taken as a sign of detached disillusionment; he was excluded from any detailed planning, presumably because his senior colleagues sensed his own unhappiness with the Suez adventure.[20]

After the Americans used their financial power to force a ceasefire on 6 November Butler was left to clean up the mess; the ailing Eden fled to Jamaica. Cub had to join the salvage team in a Commons' debate on the BBC which illustrated the fearful rift within the Conservative Party; the impartial broadcasts by the corporation had infuriated Eden and his hawkish supporters, but Cub provided a robust defence of the corporation's public service role. With most Conservative voters supporting the military action he had a delicate task in his constituency. On the basis of what he knew (and what he believed) his only honourable course was to concentrate on a rebuttal of allegations that there had been collusion between the British, the French and the Israelis; even then his chief argument, that preparations had been so slow that there could have been no pre-arranged plan, was pretty desperate.[21] When he discovered that there had in fact been a plot between the three governments his only consolation was that he had always distrusted Eden's judgement.

When the stricken Prime Minister returned to the Commons after three weeks in Jamaica one obscure Tory MP leaped to his feet to welcome him, but soon sat down when he realised that no one else had followed his example. On 7 January Eden was advised that he was too ill to stay on at Number 10. As the man who had held the position in the Prime Minister's absence, Butler's hour seemed to have come at last; his main rival, Macmillan, had matched Eden for eccentricity over the last few months without the excuse of illness. Yet at least Macmillan was held to have acted decisively even if he had changed sides during the crisis. Butler had been caught between his loyalty and his doubts, and had left the impression of deviousness. He also failed to rally support in the smoking-room; when Cub urged him to raise his profile he shook his head sadly and replied that "one can never change one's character". In the battle for the succession Butler was comprehensively outmanoeuvred; once Macmillan had become Prime Minister he even managed to prevent his rival from becoming Foreign Secretary, sending him to the uncongenial Home Office instead.

Cub immediately sent his commiserations to his old chief; Butler, who was deluged by similar letters, sent what was a fairly standard reply explaining that "if the last three years have taught me anything, they've taught me to accept personal sorrows and disappointments".[22] Cub must have shared at least part of Butler's sorrow; he had admired Macmillan since the 1930s and thought on reflection that he was the right man to succeed, but after all that he and Rab had been through this must have been a difficult conclusion to reach. Macmillan was eight years older than Butler, and at the time it seemed unlikely that he would win another term as Prime Minister. Even so, it now looked as if the best outlook for Rab was to succeed Macmillan for a few years – as leader of the opposition.

January 1957 was certainly a month of mixed feelings for Cub. While he was still adjusting to the turn of fortune at the top of his party events at a junior level moved strongly in his favour. Anthony Nutting, the Minister of State at the Foreign Office, had honourably resigned from the government at the beginning of the Suez débâcle. His replacement, Alan Noble, had been Parliamentary Under-Secretary at the Commonwealth Relations Office. Cub was not offered his post at the time, but when the game of musical chairs provoked by Suez stopped there was a new vacancy at the CRO. There could be no denying his claims this time, and he was appointed on 18 January.

The Secretary of State at the CRO, Lord Home, was a member of the Upper House, so Cub would be the government's main spokesman on commonwealth matters in the Commons. Thus a policy which contradicted Cub's published views resulted in his promotion to a job which he coveted. As he embarked on his new responsibilities Cub must have blessed his amazing good fortune. He had inched his way further up the greasy pole, and *The Economist* named him among a handful of new appointments who guaranteed "a future supply of departmental heads".[23] He knew that the long-term repercussions of Suez would be grim, but at least he was in position to help rebuild a constructive role for Britain within the new realities of global power.

What he could not have anticipated was the extent to which Suez robbed him of the allies he would need in his task. The popularity of the Conservative Party recovered with remarkable speed, but the events of 1956–57 left a far more grievous wound to its self-image than the electoral reverse of 1945. The impulse among Cub's colleagues to abandon an ungrateful world to its fate, already strong once the impact of the Second World War had been digested, was now greatly increased. Not even Cub's idols – not even a Rhodes, or a Milner – could have stood their ground in the rush to cast away the lingering relics of empire after Suez. Despite the necessary compromises with his conscience, Cub's principles were unchanged by the episode; he might have felt that Suez would be helpful in dispelling some dangerous illusions. Yet the drastic loss of confidence on the "liberal" wing of the party meant that he was left in a middle ground which was almost deserted. To people like Iain Macleod, his continued insistence that Britain could keep up its paternal role in a partnership with its old colonies placed him close to the realm of right-wing fantasy occupied by the Suez Group. Cub knew better than to look for much assistance from those relics of the past, and for him the sorrows of Suez must have increased when his old friend Angus Maude tried to resolve his personal dilemma by throwing up his parliamentary seat and emigrating to Australia in April 1958. This breach never healed, and from that time Cub seems to have concluded that political disagreements would always bring on the severance of a friendship.

The Commonwealth Relations Office was established by the Attlee Government in 1947, to supersede the existing offices for India and the dominions. While the Colonial Office administered the remaining territories which had yet to be granted self-government, the CRO was responsible for relations between Britain and the independent members of the commonwealth. At the time of Cub's appointment the CRO dealt with seven countries in this category – Australia, Canada, Ceylon, India, New Zealand, Pakistan and South Africa. Before the end of 1957 these were joined by two more states, Ghana (formerly the Gold Coast) and the Federation of Malaya.

On paper, the CRO looked like a neat administrative response to the rapid changes affecting Britain's world role. In practice the Whitehall machinery was anything but tidy. Even the word "commonwealth" was a source of confusion. Although by 1957 most people assumed that it referred to the continued association between Britain and the self-governing dominions, when first used (by Lord Rosebery in 1884) it was merely a softer-sounding way of describing the empire as a whole. In the absence of a legal definition the word-jugglers at the CRO attempted a compromise, distinguishing between independent states which could qualify as "members of the commonwealth", and the rest which might be described as "commonwealth countries"[24]. However, the remit of the CRO extended beyond "members of the commonwealth"; the Office conducted relations with Eire, which had left the commonwealth in 1948, and ran Colonial Office-style administrations in the "High Commission territories" (Basutoland, Bechuanaland and Swaziland) which were seen as more likely to be absorbed by South Africa than to run their own affairs.

These were harmless anomalies when compared with the situation in the Central African Federation. Northern Rhodesia and Nyasaland were protectorates, administered by the Colonial Office; since 1923 Southern Rhodesia had been self-governing, so it dealt with the CRO.[25] When the Federation of the three territories was established in 1953 it was given autonomy in its foreign relations. Thus the CRO dealt with the federal government and with Southern Rhodesia, while the Colonial Office retained its responsibility for internal affairs in Northern Rhodesia and Nyasaland.

The situation called for smooth liaison between the two ministries, yet the relationship had never been easy. In part, the tension arose from their different functions. The main task of the Colonial Office was internal administration, while the CRO, dealing as it did with independent countries, was primarily concerned with diplomacy. Staff at the Colonial Office could be forgiven for thinking that they had to do all the hard practical work while CRO officials made small-talk at agreeable cocktail parties. To make matters worse, "success" for the Colonial Office in the postwar period meant preparing the territories under its supervision for independence; yet success in these terms would undermine the *raison d'etre* for a separate department dealing with the colonies, and increase the prestige and work-load of the CRO. From the perspective of the Colonial Office – which had won a high reputation for humane administration – the CRO must have appeared as an undeserving child waiting to enjoy a hard-earned inheritance. In Central Africa the situation was complicated further by perceptions among the population: since the CRO dealt with the white-dominated governments of the Federation and of Southern Rhodesia, there was a tendency to identify the Colonial Office as a defender of African rights, and the CRO as the champion of the European minorities. Even Lord Home remarked that although Colonial Office staff in Central Africa were loyal to the British government they could not conceal their dislike for the federal experiment.[26]

As a long-standing observer of African affairs Cub knew all about this inter-departmental friction, and had expressed his opinions in the House of Commons long before he joined the CRO. Having won the ballot to introduce a motion for Prayers back in April 1954, he used the opportunity to propose a reshuffle of responsibilities.[27] Pointing out that the Colonial Secretary (at that time Oliver Lyttleton) was fully occupied with constitutional developments, he urged that new machinery and extra resources were needed to ensure economic advance for the colonies and for the commonwealth. He deplored the fact that the existing CRO was "largely a liaison office and tend[ed] to be a post office in diplomatic communications"; it should be expanded into a Ministry of Commonwealth Relations and Resources, providing facilities for research and development across the commonwealth and empire. As under the more limited Colombo plan for South Asia, commonwealth countries could contribute their own expertise to what would be a carefully planned and coordinated programme of economic assistance[28].

None of this would have surprised MPs who were aware of Cub's previous speeches and writings on the subject. As in *Hope in Africa*, he was urging that the prospect of change should be seized as an opportunity; he focused his interest on a future which could be brighter than the past – provided that institutions were adapted in recognition of new developments. He had hit upon a difficulty which could not be solved under existing arrangements. Unlike the old dominions such as Canada and Australia, the territories now being considered for independence within the commonwealth required economic assistance if they were to survive. Yet on achieving independence they would be transferred from the ambit of the Colonial Office, which had experience in such matters, to that of the CRO which, as Nigel Nicholson complained later in the debate, was currently more concerned with "tact" than "initiative".[29] In making his own case, Cub showed that he could combine these characteristics; his sympathies clearly lay with the CRO, but he also made constructive suggestions for addressing the current low morale of Colonial Office staff. Unfortunately the debate soon lost its focus; Labour's Thomas Reid jumped in with the suggestion that the CRO and the Colonial Office should merge – a proposal which Cub had carefully avoided, knowing that it would ruin any chance of success. Other members thanked Cub for giving the opportunity for the discussion before galloping away from the main topic aboard their personal hobby-horses. This gave the Minister of State at the Colonial Office, Henry Hopkinson, the chance to sidestep the main issue with a bland promise that all of the points raised would be considered.[30] As so often during these years, Whitehall's petty priorities were more than a match for constructive ideas, whether they arose from the back-benches or from the cabinet.

After Cub's appointment to the CRO in January 1957 he retained his interest in economic development; in April 1958, for example, he asked his officials to brief him on the situation for a speech to the Annual Conference of the Conservative Commonwealth Council. Canada was perhaps the most advanced of the commonwealth countries in its aid programme, and Cub was persuaded by its example that the UK should establish a new ministry devoted to economic co-operation. Yet the political will elsewhere in Whitehall was still lacking, and when in July 1960 Labour's colonial affairs spokesman James Callaghan introduced a motion proposing the reforms which Cub had advocated back in 1954 the latter had no alternative but to trot out the official line of opposition to departmental disruption.[31] On the basis of a memorandum drawn up by Cub Duncan Sandys, the Commonwealth Secretary, won cabinet approval for a new approach to development funding which would bring in the new members of the commonwealth. But Cub had wanted a separate ministry with the power to distribute resources on the basis of need rather than political considerations, and it was not until 1961, when he had left the CRO, that the Department of Technical Co-operation (DTC) was set up.[32] When the Conservatives fell from office a new Ministry of Overseas Development (ODM) emerged from Harold Wilson's administrative reforms, and the old Colonial Development Corporation was reorganised as the Commonwealth Development Corporation. But the first Secretary of State at the ODM, Barbara Castle, found that despite the changes "Britain's aid programme had been fragmented among a cluster of departments", with the Colonial Office, the CRO, the Foreign Office and the Board of Trade all claiming a share of the (very limited) action. The "unplanned and uncoordinated aid programme" was left vulnerable to Treasury cuts.[33]

This was a far cry from the strategy proposed by Cub ten years earlier, and although in later years he felt a paternal interest in the ODM it could never be animated with the spirit shown on both sides of the House in the pre-Suez days of 1954. The muddle that greeted the dynamic Mrs Castle was a symptom of institutional decay in a policy area which Whitehall had virtually written off; in her year at the ministry even Mrs Castle and a high-powered team of advisers could not shake off this mood. Anthony Greenwood (with whom Cub had sailed to America in 1936) moved from the Colonial Office to replace her for a few months, but by the end of 1967 the ODM had lost its seat in the cabinet. In the previous year the Colonial Office and the CRO had been united in a new Commonwealth Office; this in turn was merged with the Foreign Office in 1968. This outcome had been rejected as unthinkable by all the participants in the 1954 debate, because it would send a signal to commonwealth countries that Britain had abandoned any idea of a special partnership. But in the year of Enoch Powell's "Rivers of Blood" speech few people cared about wounded feelings in the ever-growing and diverse commonwealth "family".

When Cub joined the CRO he felt that this doleful story could be avoided. His Secretary of State shared his views. Lord Home had been a surprising choice for the post; before his appointment in April 1955 his diplomatic record had been overshadowed by his part in Neville Chamberlain's policy of appeasement, and he had never visited a commonwealth country. But he blossomed in his new job, and Cub soon recognised in him a representative of the old governing class at its best. At the Colonial Office Alan Lennox-Boyd, who had succeeded Lyttleton in July 1954, was another congenial colleague. In the reshuffle which sent Cub to the CRO Lord Perth became Lennox-Boyd's Minister of State; he and Cub quickly established a close working relationship. The politicians in the two departments at that time made up a harmonious team, whatever the feelings of their civil servants.

As his PPS, Cub chose Keith Joseph, who had won the seat of Leeds North-East in February 1956. He later claimed that he had asked the whips to name the most intelligent available back-bencher, and chose Joseph when he learned of his All Souls fellowship. Although Cub may have been aware that his new aide was a member of "One Nation", it seems that he was not told about Joseph's opposition to the Eden Government over Suez, which he had carried to the length of joining ten Conservative MPs who signed a critical (but unpublicised) letter as the ill-starred attack began. A more outspoken rebel, Nigel Nicholson, was thrown out by his constituency party for his stand, and others were severely criticised; Joseph's punishment was to sit through a friendly lecture over lunch with the Earl of Selkirk.[34]

Joseph's biographer has remarked that in being offered this first government post "He could scarcely claim that he was being recognised as a high-flier, because the minister who took him on as PPS was a mere Parliamentary Under-Secretary of State".[35] The ambitious Joseph was sure to see things in that light, but at least Cub's duties were onerous for a junior minister and his profile both in and out of the House of Commons was high. In addition to his weekly surgeries in Colchester and the routine work of a ministry under pressure, he was often called to the dispatch-box in the Commons, attended cabinet meetings when Home was abroad, spoke at successive party conferences in 1957–58, and made several important journeys himself as the official representative of the British government.

The first of the trips was to the newly independent Ghana. As the British High Commissioner reported, "Mr Alport's task was not without its hazards"; as the first minister to visit since independence he had to ensure that the new relationship between the two countries began on a footing of friendship and respect. In his meetings with the Prime Minister, Nkrumah, and his senior colleagues he kept away from sensitive political issues and stuck to economics. His visit attracted a great deal of interest from the local press, and he gave a talk for Radio Ghana. The High Commissioner felt that Cub "steered his way skilfully through the shoals, and did everything possible in the short space of ten days to disarm suspicions and win confidence".[36] Diplomatic despatches are not the most reliable historical sources, but clearly Cub passed this first test without committing any blunders.

In September 1957 Cub was asked to undertake a more sensitive mission. Relations with India had been shaken by Suez – during demonstrations Anthony Eden was burnt in effigy – and Britain's sympathy for Pakistan in the dispute over Kashmir was a further source of tension. Cub believed that he was chosen to smooth things over because unlike Home he was "expendable". In fact, as Harold Macmillan predicted, Cub had "a jolly time" during his five-day visit, meeting Nehru and his daughter Indira Gandhi during a frantic round of meetings, receptions and banquets, before moving on to talks in Pakistan.[37] Cub loved India, and was glad of a further chance to visit as a CRO minister in the winter of 1959–60, when he had further talks with Nehru and attended the opening of an Anglo–India steel plant during a 17-day tour covering 20,000 miles.

These journeys were fairly typical of the CRO's work; Cub's task was to maintain or restore good relations, and, within the limited powers of his ministry, to foster economic ties. A more unusual visit took place in the summer of 1958, when he travelled to the High Commission territories to explore the possibilities of constitutional reforms. Given the proximity of the territories to South Africa, even the gradual introduction of democratic institutions would require careful management. The situation was particularly sensitive in Bechuanaland, whose Bamangwato tribe had suffered great disruption in a period which had seen the controversial banishment of both Seretse Khama and his uncle Tshekedi, who had led the tribe between 1926 and 1949. Before his departure Cub discussed with a delegation a proposal for a legislative council in Bechuanaland as a first step towards independence; after investigations on the spot he reported favourably on the scheme, and in April 1959 the British government announced its approval. In Basutoland he addressed 500 tribal leaders while standing on a rock; his polite reception convinced him that the territory was ready for change, and at a constitutional conference held in London after his return he threw his weight behind a proposal to give a Basutoland National Council more powers than some senior officials would have liked.[38]

The African visit featured a couple of hair-raising incidents which reminded Cub that he was "expendable". Flying over Brussels on the outward journey his plane was struck by lightning, and on one occasion he was forced to cross a crocodile-infested river in a dinghy because the ferry had broken down. His trip to Seretse Khama's home was memorable for a happier reason: Seretse's British wife Ruth gave birth to twins on the day of his arrival. The connection with the family was strengthened further in June 1959, when Cub visited Tshekedi in a London clinic. Tshekedi was dying of a kidney complaint, and had asked to see a British minister, possibly as an act of reconciliation after an uneasy relationship over many years. Cub "found him unable to talk, only able to register appreciation", noting that despite his illness he smiled as brightly as he had done at their previous meeting in Africa.[39] Later Seretse became Prime Minister of an independent Bechuanaland (renamed Botswana); before his death from the same kidney complaint in 1980 Cub presented him with an honorary degree on behalf of London's City University, and lunched with him at Buckingham Palace. Cub remained on friendly terms with the Khamas' son Ian.

Much as he enjoyed these trips, Cub looked back with most pleasure on a journey to the Maldive Islands, via Ceylon, which took place in February 1960. From Ceylon he travelled aboard a warship, *HMS Gambia*, and, as he had done on his last exciting sea voyage more than twenty years before, he hosted a party. Cub had visited this beautiful archipelago of around 2000 islands twice during the war; this time his business was to sign a treaty allowing Britain to lease an air staging post which it had built on Gan Island. As the first British minister to visit the Maldives he was greeted with almost royal honours; the Sultan's state barge was rowed out to greet the British warship, and women lined the streets as Cub drove through the capital, Male. The negotiations were complicated by the fact that Gan itself was controlled by rebels. Cub held talks with their leader, Afif Didi, who added to Cub's large collection of weapons by presenting him with a dagger. It was easy to form the illusion that he was a pioneer, pushing forward the outposts of empire. But the Maldives had been a protectorate since 1887, and although it was a useful staging-post between Britain and Australia the distant air-strip belonged to a strategic vision which had faded since Suez. By 1965, the Maldives had been granted independence and did not join the commonwealth until the 1980s.[40]

These successful overseas ventures provided confirmation to Cub that he had always been temperamentally suited to diplomacy. He also built on the reputation he had won at the Post Office for sound administration, and performed well in front of Conservative back-bench committees, dominated as they were by well informed MPs who were in broad sympathy with his outlook.[41]

Cub's greatest problems at the CRO arose from the debates on the floor of the House. Labour's colonial lobby had acknowledged his expertise and welcomed his appointment, but once the initial courtesies were over he could expect no mercy from them. Electoral considerations joined with genuine principle to sharpen their attacks. Despite the resignations in January 1958 of the Chancellor of the Exchequer, Peter Thorneycroft together with his junior ministers Enoch Powell and Nigel Birch, no economic crisis materialised to cheer the opposition; after an expansionary budget in April 1959 the general mood of optimism was summed up in a misquotation from an earlier speech by the Prime Minister: "You've never had it so good". The Suez card was available to Labour, but its leaders had no wish to appear unpatriotic. A preferable alternative was to leave aside that specific issue and move on to the general question of Britain's transition from imperial status. Here the practices which had either been taken for granted (or acclaimed for their humanity) less than a generation before had been exposed by events since 1939. The government was open to assaults in the name of high-sounding democratic principles; any attempt to counter this language could be condemned as the voice of reaction.

As the commonwealth spokesman in the Commons, Cub (along with Lennox-Boyd at the Colonial Office) was the owner of that "reactionary" voice. It was heard most often on the question of the Central African Federation. Superficially this had all the vote-winning features that Labour could ask for. The 1953 constitution provided for a federal legislature of 35 members; 26 of these would represent around 170,000 people of European origin, with only nine allotted to 6,000,000 Africans. The elaborate electoral system ensured an over-whelming majority of European voters. Since the Federation was not fully independent Labour could accuse the CRO of pandering to the interests of the Europeans, who were described as "settlers" no matter how long they had lived in Central Africa. Yet because the federal government enjoyed almost complete autonomy the only weapons available to ministers were persuasion or the dissolution of the Federation, which was likely to lead to the formation of a racialist state in Southern Rhodesia along the lines of South African apartheid. When the Federation was formed the attitude of the Europeans in Southern Rhodesia was already indefensible. As Robert Blake has written,

> Africans were only served in shops after every White had been served. Shops assistants were themselves always White. There were separate entrances and counters for Blacks and Whites in post offices. There was rigid separatism in state schools, hos-pitals, hotels, restaurants, transport, swimming baths and lavato-ries . . . an African was called "boy" whether he was six, sixteen or sixty.[42]

Undoubtedly certain right-wing Conservatives thought that life in Southern Rhodesia reflected the natural order of things, but others (in-cluding Cub) hoped that the federal arrangement would promote gradual reform and some of the worst abuses had been removed since 1953. The alternative was that Southern Rhodesia would simply an-nounce its own independence and move much closer to South Africa.

"A God-chosen man like Adolf Hitler": Cecil Alport in Egyptian Court dress at the time of his last battle with officialdom.

The dynamic president and his team: the Cambridge Union Society Committee, May 1935. Cub is seated in the centre, front row and to his right is the military historian, Basil Liddel Hart (visiting speaker). Also in the picture are Charles Fletcher Cooke (front row, extreme right), Jock Butler (middle row, centre) and John Royle (back row, extreme right) *(photograph courtesy of Mr John Royle).*

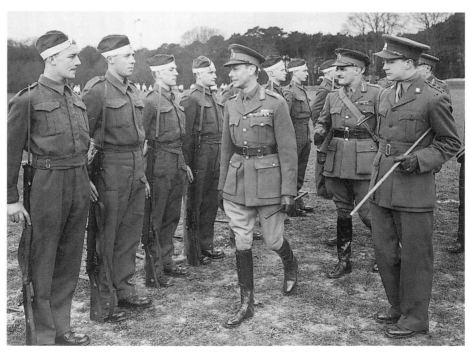

Captain Alport inspects King George VI, Aldershot, 1940.

"We will have to start a new model party . . .":
Cub launches the "Two-Way Movement of
Ideas", 1946.

The "One Nation" group, 1951. From left to right, Cub, John Rodgers, Gilbert Longden, Iain
Macleod, Richard Fort, Angus Maude, Robert Carr, and Enoch Powell. Of the original nine
members, Edward Heath is missing from the photograph.

General election, 26 May 1955: Cub notches a hat trick of victories in Colchester.

Cub, Under-Secretary of State at the CRO, arrives with the Minister of Aviation, Duncan Sandys, for a Baghdad Pact meeting at Karachi, January 1959.

Alec Home (seated), Secretary of State for Commonwealth Relations, with his junior ministers, Cub (Minister of State) and Richard Thompson (Under-Secretary) at the CRO, December 1959.

The new High Commissioner and his family display their new status. From left to right, Edward, Carole, Cub, Rachel, and Rose, on board the *Pretoria Castle* bound for Salisbury, April 1961.

The Northern Rhodesian police inspect the incoming High Commissioner, March 1961.

The man in the middle: Cub with Sir Roy Welensky (left) and his deputy prime minister, Sir Malcolm Barrow, at Salisbury airport.

A friendship under strain: Cub with Rab Butler, January 1963.

"Anything – anything at all – to declare?": Wilson waits to know what his policy should be on Rhodesia, *Sunday Telegraph*, 16 July 1967.

The bubble car Bevanite: Labour candidate, Pat Llewellyn-Davies, electioneering in Wandsworth Central, October 1959 *(photograph courtesy of Hattie Llewellyn-Davies).*

"The very best type of Englishman": Cub, in the Cross House garden, with his dog, Sadie, October 1997 *(photograph courtesy of Essex County Newspapers).*

If Cub had any illusions that this dilemma would be treated sympathetically by Labour they were dispelled during a debate held in November 1957. The federal government had proposed a constitutional change, which increased the number of legislators to 59 without altering the racial imbalance. Charles Fletcher-Cooke, now a Conservative MP, admitted that the reform was "not nearly so much of an advance as some members on both sides of the House would like". Cub privately agreed, knowing as he did that without some hard bargaining by Lord Home the reforms would have been even more limited; but as a front-bencher all he could do was offer a very lame defence without making his reservations explicit. The government won this vote, but not the debate. Its case had been seriously weakened by the opposition of the board established in 1953 to protect African interests, and Callaghan claimed that the original constitution had ruled out major reforms prior to the thorough review which was due to take place in 1960.[43]

The debate was typical of the many exchanges concerning the Federation in this Parliament, and sensing a weakness Labour members returned to the subject as often as they could. Ministerial question-time on commonwealth relations was normally dominated by inquiries about the situation of Africans in the Federation from such vocal critics as Fenner Brockway, and John Stonehouse (who provoked a particularly difficult debate for Cub when the federal government expelled him from Nyasaland in March 1959).[44] If the Federation had been exploited enough for the time being the opposition could always turn elsewhere. In the week of the debate on the constitution, for example, Brockway attacked the agreement for an airstrip on the Maldives on the grounds that 800 people on Gan would be "evicted from their homes and their fields" to make room for it.[45]

The Prime Minister regarded Labour's opportunity as a grave personal danger. Having spent the early part of his political career cultivating the image of an eccentric man of principle, Harold Macmillan was now relishing the game he had so unexpectedly mastered. It was presumed that the next election would be closely fought, and Macmillan had no intention of being edged out of office because of the stubborn "settlers" in Central Africa, whose cause had been embraced by his ally-turned-enemy, the Marquess of Salisbury. From some remarks he heard during a cabinet meeting Cub formed the impression that Macmillan sided with the "underdog" in Africa because of his own Highland origins; more likely, this trait merely reinforced an over developed sense of electoral calculation. Whatever the reason, Cub was not the only minister to feel exposed and uneasy at the dispatch-box. Lennox-Boyd decided to quit politics after the next election, and was badgering Macmillan to let him retire from the Colonial Office as early as March 1959; he was only disuaded by some extravagant Prime Ministerial flattery.[46]

Lennox-Boyd offered to resign again in July 1959, and with good reason. For their perseverence, if for nothing else, perhaps Labour deserved a stroke of luck in the Federation, and it had arrived in March with the declaration of a state of emergency in Nyasaland by the governor, Sir Robert Armitage. Many leaders of the Nyasa Congress Party, including Hastings Banda, had been detained; in clashes with local troops nearly 50 Africans were killed. It was also alleged that the houses of Nyasa Congress Party supporters had been burned, in a heavy-handed response to information received by the federal government indicating that nationalists were plotting an uprising and a massacre of Europeans and Asians. A Commission of Enquiry was established under Lord Devlin; on 17 March an attempt was made to defuse the problem in the short-term by setting up a more general inquiry into the federal constitution, supposedly in preparation for the 1960 review. Devlin found no evidence of a nationalist plot; instead he concluded that "Nyasaland is – no doubt temporarily – a police state where it is not safe for anyone to express approval of the policies of the Congress Party".[47] The anxious government had intervened before publication in the hope of stripping the report of value-laden comment; the notorious passage slipped past the scrutiny of Lord Perth. The affair was deeply embarrassing to Macmillan, who had provisionally booked the date of the next election; perhaps he also considered the effect on the reputation of the responsible minister, Lennox-Boyd. The latter was already under attack over the murder of 11 members of the terrorist Mau Mau organisation at Hola detention camp. On 27 July Enoch Powell joined the government's critics over Hola, and on the following day Lennox-Boyd was obliged to defend the police actions in Nyasaland. As even Powell pointed out Lennox-Boyd had done nothing wrong himself, but constitutional convention in those days could still force a minister from office.[48] Fortunately for Macmillan, the unlucky minister had been persuaded not to resign at a meeting on 20 July, when the whole cabinet urged him to stay on.

Cub was not present at that tense cabinet meeting, but he deputised for Home on 8 September when Macmillan decided to call a general election for 8 October. By now Cub was fairly safe in Colchester, and newspaper coverage presented him as a seasoned statesman. His majority rose to 7500. The government's overall lead of 100 seats made a nonsense of Macmillan's fears; this comfortable position was achieved despite what most observers acknowledged to be an excellent challenge by Labour under its combative leader, Hugh Gaitskell.

With the retirement of Lennox-Boyd a new Colonial Secretary was needed after the election; Macmillan chose Iain Macleod, who had enhanced his reputation with a stint at the Ministry of Labour and National Service. In a typically theatrical phrase Macmillan told Macleod that he had been lumbered with "the worst job of all". Cub had an inkling of what was to come because he had noticed his old friend listening to several recent debates on colonial affairs. But the appointment caused general surprise; although Macleod's brother had a farm in Kenya the new minister was inexperienced in African affairs, which left him exposed to criticism from members of his party who claimed expertise through their own acquaintance with this key area. In spite of their assumptions none of these old hands really "knew Africa", but Macleod had never visited that diverse continent and the Colonial Office was under pressure for rapid decisions. Macleod was also a brilliant bridge-player, which convinced his critics that every action he took was a gamble based on abstract calculation rather than research. After just three months at his post Macleod chaired the Lancaster House conference on Kenya, which he opened with a commitment to majority rule. Given the extent of the Mau Mau problem this decision was unavoidable, but the character and background of the Colonial Secretary increased the rancour of those who opposed his move. After Lancaster House this personal edge surfaced in every controversy affecting Macleod, which made life more difficult for policy-makers in associated departments.

In addition to the political troubles of 1959, Cub had suffered a personal loss. Cecil and Janet spent the winter of 1958–59 in South Africa as usual, but Cecil was troubled by a chest complaint which would not respond to treatment. He was later found to be suffering from cancer. When Cub met his father at Heathrow after the homeward flight in March he took him straight to his old work-place, St Mary's Hospital, although he realised that there was no hope. He stayed at Cecil's bedside for most of the last week of his life. In recent years their relationship had been strained by Cecil's outspoken criticism of British policy after Suez, but as always Cub had tried to avoid argument and in November 1957 the family enjoyed a private dinner party at the House of Commons to celebrate Cecil and Janet's golden wedding anniversary. An author to the end, Cecil had written a violent critique of Suez, but (fortunately for his son) this last effusion did not find a publisher.[49]

Two snatches of conversation from these last days stuck in Cub's memory. At one time he told his father that "you have had great success in your life"; the dying man retorted, "Well, that doesn't help me much now". Then, as Cub recalled, "two or three days before he died he suddenly turned to me and said, 'Cub, don't let them make you a life peer'". Cub later recorded that he was astonished, because "nothing was further from my thoughts or expectations" despite the passage of the Life Peerage Act in the previous year. He considered that the remark might have arisen from "the extraordinary prescience which sometimes seems to be associated with death" – or Cecil's hope that his son might achieve an hereditary peerage, making him the founder of a great dynasty.[50] A more prosaic explanation would be that it was a sarcastic parting shot against a once-great country whose proudest institutions were fast dissolving. Ironically, Cecil did not know that he had won an immortality of his own through his work during the 1920s on the disease Nephritis. In 1961 an article appeared in *The Lancet*, naming the hereditary variation of the disease as "Alport's Syndrome".[51] By that time Cub had acted against Cecil's advice, and accepted a life peerage. No doubt the author of *The Lighter Side of the War* would have appreciated the joke – eventually.

Cecil died on 17 April 1959. He was buried in the family grave which Cub had purchased in the churchyard at Layer de La Haye, with an epitaph he had chosen himself: "This man endeavoured to be just". His son was determined to continue that struggle; but the ministerial office they had both dreamed of was proving as much of a handicap as his father's hot temper.

Chapter 7

"Political Suicide"

The government reshuffle after the 1959 general election provided an opportunity for the original members of the "One Nation" group to take stock of their careers. They had been in the House for almost a decade, and with younger Conservatives now filling up the back-benches this Parliament would decide whether or not their early promise would be translated into solid achievement.

From the founding nine, Richard Fort was already dead, the victim of a car accident before the 1959 election. Gilbert Longden and John Rodgers, who had entered the Commons comparatively late, were still on the back-benches. Both Powell and Maude had interrupted their careers with acts of rebellion; Powell would return as a cabinet minister under Macmillan, but Maude only got back into Parliament in 1963. They were already well known for being too brilliant to ignore – or to trust. Having served as Eden's PPS in 1955, Robert Carr was working his way through junior offices; the youngest of the original group, he still had a good chance of higher honours. Cub had every reason to be

143

satisfied with his own progress; after the election he was promoted to Minister of State, the first time anyone at the CRO had held that rank. But Ted Heath and Iain Macleod had prospered the most. Having done so much to hold the party together as Chief Whip, Heath succeeded Macleod at the Ministry of Labour after the election. Both men were already being spoken of as possible future leaders of the party.

Already the original "Nation" enjoyed near-legendary status, standing as an example for each new intake of Conservatives. Yet they no longer enjoyed much of each others' company. Maude and Powell remained good friends, having collaborated on a book together; but in 1959 Maude was still in Australia. Heath had never been personally close to anyone in the group, and was destined to remain a political loner. The good-natured Carr worked with Macleod at Labour, but even he could not make the members of the original group maintain their close relations against the powerful solvents of departmental responsibilities and conflicting ambitions. Cub had seen little of Macleod since the latter's appointment to Health in 1952. At that time any friendship between them had been restricted because their interests were so different; from 1959 to 1961, although they retained their mutual respect, they were pushed further apart because their interests were the same.

Cub thought that Macleod's Highland blood made him a kindred spirit to Macmillan; having heard the Prime Minister compare African tribes to Scottish clans, he thought (without much evidence) that Macleod drew the same analogy.[1] Certainly the new Colonial Secretary was very different from Lennox-Boyd; Macmillan thought that "imagination, even genius" would be required to sort out the problems in Africa, and whatever his other qualities Lennox-Boyd fell short of that standard.[2] Although colonial affairs had scarcely featured in the general election campaign, in September General de Gaulle had announced that the principle of self-determination would be applied to Algeria, after five years of bitter conflict. Macleod agreed with the Prime Minister that at all costs Britain must not be saddled with an Algeria of its own. Kenya remained the leading candidate for the role but the Colonial Secretary was also troubled by the prospect of serious disorder in the Central African Federation.[3]

Before the election Macmillan had struggled to recruit a Labour representative for the Commission on the Federal Constitution.

Gaitskell replied that he would only co-operate if the terms of reference were expanded to include the possibility of territories seceding from the Federation. The Labour leader was right to suspect a trap; Macmillan was keen to neutralise Central Africa as an election issue. Yet the Prime Minister's game was deeper than that; he hoped to dupe both the opposition and members of his own party who were worried about the future of the Federation. When discussing the terms of reference in the Commons in July, Macmillan's words were deliberately vague. After appointing his friend Walter Monckton to lead the commission in November, he declared that he regarded it

> as free, in practice, to hear all points of view from whatever quarter and on whatever subject. It will, of course, be for the Commission to decide what use to make of the material which reaches them. . . . In these cases, I do not think that it is ever wise to be too specific or rigid in interpretation.

These obvious nods and winks in the direction of Labour carried the risk of provoking a back-bench rebellion on the Conservative side; so Macmillan ensured that the opposition would offer no official co-operation by telling the astonished Gaitskell that there would be no change in the terms of reference after all. The Prime Minister had realised that the ideal person for his Commission would be someone who would give it a more balanced appearance, without being under the influence of Gaitskell. On the following day Labour's former Attorney-General Lord Shawcross agreed to serve, and promptly announced on television that he considered himself free to recommend the dissolution of the Federation if he "felt that that was the right conclusion".[4]

From Macmillan's point of view there was nothing reprehensible about his behaviour. Central Africa was a difficult problem which required careful handling; after all, the Algerian crisis had caused the downfall of the French Fourth Republic. Yet his integrity was compromised, because he already had a strong indication of the conclusions Monckton would reach. In October 1959 the civil servant Burke Trend produced a damning report after a visit to the Federation. He identified the Federation as the root cause of unrest in Central Africa; it had been "imposed against the wishes of the Africans as they expressed them at the time and still express them". Commenting that this was "a most interesting paper", Macmillan asked for copies to be sent to Home and Macleod.[5] In fact, although Trend provided new details of the Federation's failure to advance the position of Africans, most of his report would have been very familiar to ministers – they had heard it all from Labour's spokesmen ever since the federal scheme was approved by a Commons majority in 1953. At that time it was recognised by Conservatives that progress towards equal civil rights would take time – and that until standards of education had improved it was difficult to make any assumptions about African opinion. Trend was an astute public servant, who would not have written his report in such forceful language unless he felt sure that his political masters had changed their minds about the Federation only six years after embarking on the experiment.

Macmillan was a skilful actor, but he was now playing to too many audiences and began to fluff his lines. Having set out on a tour of Africa in January 1960 he told reporters in Ghana that the people of Northern Rhodesia and Nyasaland would be given "an opportunity to decide on whether the Federation is beneficial to them".[6] This contradicted assurances which he had given to federal ministers, but he knew that he would be meeting them within a week to smooth their feelings with declarations of commitment to the Federation. Despite the absence of bankable guarantees these words acted like a charm, especially when delivered with the emotion which Macmillan could summon at will. Some trickery was clearly in the air, but a meeting with Macmillan could beguile federal ministers into thinking that other people would be the victims. If Macmillan was not entirely trusted in Salisbury, Alec Home was much respected, and the Monckton Commission had been his idea; he had used his charm to persuade the federal government that it should co-operate with the Commissioners, on the assumption that the question of secession would not be considered.

After a rowdy visit to Nyasaland (where he snubbed the governor, who was a convenient scapegoat for the Devlin Report) Macmillan passed on to Capetown. On 3 February he spoke of a "wind of change" – a phrase which he had previously employed in Ghana. Lord Kilmuir later claimed that "neither Macmillan nor his colleagues had any conception of the mine he had unwittingly exploded"; the responsible minister, Lord Home, was certainly caught unawares because he was not consulted about the final text. What has been hailed as a courageous attack on apartheid was, according to Kilmuir, "essentially a speech designed for home consumption, and in this it admirably succeeded in its purpose". In 1961 South Africa voted to become a republic, and declined to make the necessary reapplication for commonwealth membership; a major source of political embarrassment had gone.[7]

Cub has left no record of his feelings at this time, but he had indicated his concern with the new pace of events in a memorandum to Home written in December 1959. The immediate problem was whether or not Hastings Banda should now be released from the federal prison which had housed him since the Nyasaland riots. Cub felt that this should not happen

> until such time as we are quite certain of the policy we intend to carry out in Nyasaland for the period ahead . . . we must not get into a position in which we find that in six months' time or less we are negotiating with Banda because the Colonial Office has come to the conclusion that there is nobody else to talk to.[8]

Macleod was already sure of the Nyasaland policy "for the period ahead"; he had put his trust in Banda on the grounds "that there is nobody else to talk to". A fortnight earlier he had told the Prime Minister that "I am convinced, although this might sound paradoxical, that Banda is the most likely African Nyasa leader to keep Nyasaland within the Federation".[9]

Macleod's judgement was "paradoxical" because Banda loathed the Federation, but the priority for the Colonial Office was the maintenance of order in Nyasaland. In the belief that Banda was more of a threat to peace while he was in prison, Macleod assured him of a speedy release. This brought a plea for delay from Home who regarded Banda as the main source of trouble in Nyasaland, and on 23 February Macleod threatened to resign. A compromise was reached before matters got out of hand, and Home managed to win the agreement of the federal government to a release date of 1 April for Banda. Almost certainly Home saved the government at this time; as Cub had warned in December, back-bench Conservatives were "beginning to talk about Africa as being likely to occupy in this Parliament the same role as India did in the 1930s".[10] If Macleod had moved too fast the Prime Minister had done nothing to discourage him; he might serve as a useful sacrificial offering to the right-wing of the party at some point, but not yet. A voluntary resignation at this time would have made life very difficult for Macmillan, and a sacking would have been worse. The symptoms of the disagreement were cured, but not the root cause; Home renewed the battle at a press conference on 26 February, declaring that the government was opposed to any proposal for the secession of a territory from the Federation. The majority on the Monckton Commission, now beginning their work, were un-shaken in their confidence that they could say whatever they liked in their report.[11]

Macleod's threat of resignation was kept out of the papers – it even was omitted from the cabinet minutes – and possibly Cub never heard of it. If he had been unhappy before the election things had already become a good deal worse for him. He had never liked the idea of the Monckton Commission, but now he was having to defend it against both the opposition and back-benchers from his own party. Replying to a debate on commonwealth affairs in March he made the remarkable claim that Macmillan's words on the Commission's terms of reference had been "extremely clear".[12] A week later he answered on behalf of the Prime Minister a Private Notice question from Hugh Gaitskell about rioting at Sharpeville in South Africa; he enraged the House by sticking closely to an agreed text, but Macmillan sent a note of praise for his "sure touch in choosing which questions to answer and which to ignore".[13]

Winning plaudits from the Prime Minister was gratifying, but dead-pan statements of this kind could not endear Cub to the House. Presumably this occasion was one of those which Gerald Nabarro had in mind when he wrote that Cub "would have made a better Foreign Office official than party politician"; a Private Notice question from the opposition leader would ensure a better attendance than the normal debates which Cub addressed, so he was exposing his "pompous" streak to his biggest parliamentary audience.[14] In May Cub was given a tangible reward for acting as a shield for the Prime Minister, along with his other services at the CRO; Macmillan offered him the rank of Privy Councillor, an unusual accolade for a junior minister.[15]

Cub could be forgiven for prizing this symbolic honour; after all, his job had brought him few other consolations, and the tension in Africa was rising. On 30 June the Belgian-run Congo was declared independent, and immediately collapsed in disorder; the province of Katanga, which bordered on the Federation, declared its secession from the Congo and its President, Moise Tshombe, appealed for assistance from British and federal troops. Macmillan and his Foreign Secretary, Selwyn Lloyd, decided not to intervene and made the same decision on behalf of the federal government, which regarded Tshombe as the main hope of restoring order in Katanga. Later in the month there was more dismay in the Federation when Lord Home left the CRO, to replace Lloyd who had been a lame duck at the Foreign Office since Suez. Churchill's son-in-law Duncan Sandys took over at the CRO.

By this time Cub had shifted his position. The Monckton Commission was still deliberating, but early indications suggested that it would recommend that the right to secede from the Federation should be granted. In these circumstances Hastings Banda would become the key figure in the Federation. A constitutional conference for Nyasaland was held in July; Cub suggested to Home that some way should be found of "getting Banda and his associates into posts of executive power without all the rigmarole of complicated eighteenth-century franchises and checks and balances". Having known (and argued with) Banda for many years, Cub shared none of Macleod's enthusiasm, but superficially he was now in step with his old friend who was soon pressing on the federal government his view "that office would make Banda a responsible person". An important remaining difference was that Macleod and Macmillan saw tactical advantages in hopelessly complicated "eighteenth-century franchises" for a legislative assembly which Cub regarded as a red herring; while Macleod assured Banda that the new arrangements would give his Congress Party a majority, the Prime Minister was able to juggle with the figures and reach a different conclusion in private letters to Sir Roy Welensky (who had succeeded Huggins as federal Prime Minister in 1956).[16]

In his memoirs Alec Home claimed that he was perfectly happy with the work of the Monckton Commission. But a well informed source confirms that he was furious when he learned that the report would favour the right to secede from the Federation, and he protested to Macmillan.[17] It was time for Home to move on; he left the

CRO before the Monckton Report was published in October 1960. The report praised the economic performance of the Federation and agreed that there had been some progress towards multi-racial partnership, but as expected it argued for the right to secede. Sensing trouble ahead Home had suggested that a British minister might go out to the Federation when the report appeared, and the expendable Cub was chosen for this job. But at the last minute the visit was cancelled by Duncan Sandys, when the Federal Chief Justice Sir Robert Tredgold resigned over the introduction of emergency powers legislation by the Southern Rhodesian Prime Minister, Sir Edgar Whitehead.[18]

The cancellation of his trip infuriated Cub. It would have been much more than a courtesy visit; in addition to discussing the Monckton Report he was due to talk over possible changes in the Southern Rhodesian constitution in advance of the long-awaited Federal Review to be held in December. After months in which rapid and grave decisions had been taken by those around him he had glimpsed a chance of affecting the course of events himself, but it had been taken away for what he considered to be a petty reason. He liked the decision-maker no more than the decision; Sandys had no track record on African affairs and Cub still remembered his poor speech on housing which had inspired "One Nation". The atmosphere between them had not warmed during a trip they took together in January 1959 to Karachi for a meeting of the Baghdad Pact. Since that time Sandys had been moved to Aviation for a few months, and when he landed at the CRO it looked like a case of another job being found to keep his father-in-law happy. He was a ponderous administrator, and after a few meetings with him Cub made it his policy to leave the room if no decision had been taken within two hours. No doubt the antipathy he felt was increased because he had worked so easily with Home, and he must have felt some pique because Sandys' appointment deprived Cub of his status as the CRO's spokesman in the Commons. But he was not alone in his frustration: Macleod, whose relations with Home had been strained, disliked Sandys even more.

Cub was in a sombre mood for the Review Conference, which turned out to be a fiasco. As Cub related, "Its main effect was to make all those who took part in it determined never to hold a similar function again. Seventy delegates attended the opening session and nearly all insisted on making a series of unrelated speeches, some of which were highly provocative and others merely boring". When exposed to "the patent hates and conflicts" in Lancaster House Cub became even more depressed about the future of the Federation. His mood was not improved when Sir Roy Welensky called out to him "Come and sit down, Cub – you at any rate are one of us". Cub was well known to Welensky as a long-standing supporter of Federation, but this did not mean that he necessarily agreed with the conduct of affairs by Welensky's government. He was also troubled by the implicit assumption that there could be no compromise between Welensky's views and those of the African nationalists – in short, that people were either for or against him. With an attitude typical of the Cambridge graduate dealing with a self-educated man, Cub assumed that Welensky relied too much on his feelings rather than rational considerations. He should have realised that Welensky himself had been struggling for years to sustain a middle position between white supremacists and those who demanded immediate majority rule.[19] Cub went on to attend a Southern Rhodesia constitutional conference which made some progress despite a walk-out by one of the African delegates, Joshua Nkomo.

In late January 1961 Cub called on Sandys in his enormous room ("at least twice the size of a modern three-bedroomed house") in the CRO.[20] The British High Commissioner to the Federation, Rupert Metcalf, was about to come home due to his wife's illness and his own fatigue after some difficult years. No obvious replacement came to mind, and it occurred to Cub that he might suggest his own name. Sandys agreed to discuss the proposition with the Prime Minister.

In describing this incident for his memoir published in 1965 Cub implied that the suggestion had come from Sandys.[21] He thought that it would look like arrogance on his part if he revealed that he had helped to appoint himself to a well paid and prestigious post. Unfortunately Cub's published account gave rise to rumours that he had been appointed because Sandys was anxious to dispose of an uncongenial colleague. This was an unlikely speculation, since as High Commissioner Cub would continue to be in very regular contact with the Secretary of State. But Cub was surprised that his unorthodox suggestion was accepted within 48 hours. Now that the government records for the period are available this can be explained. On 20

January 1961 Sandys had discussed Metcalf's replacement with the Prime Minister. They decided that the next High Commissioner in Salisbury should be an experienced politician rather than a career diplomat, and drew up a short-list of four possible candidates. Since "it was agreed that Welensky would not like to have a minister who had been in the Colonial Office", the Earls of Perth and of Munster were ruled out. This left Lord John Hope as the only alternative to Cub: but Hope had served at the CRO for just two months and was now out of touch with developments, at the Ministry of Works. Thus in offering himself as Metcalf's successor Cub had pre-empted a request from his colleagues.[22]

Macmillan expressed his gratitude to Cub, and offered him a choice between a knighthood and a life peerage; his own preference would be for the former, since a peerage "makes people think you are so old".[23] Cub chose the latter in defiance of his father's advice and of his own reply to a question at a recent public meeting near his constituency.[24] During their conversation Macmillan referred with typical grandiloquence to the great public servants from Britain's imperial past such as Lords Cromer and Milner. Cub "did not take the bit about Cromer and Milner seriously"; perhaps he should have remembered that these great "Pro-consuls" made their reputations in spite of what they regarded as unsupportive and ungrateful governments at home.[25]

In his book Cub rehearsed all the arguments for and against his sudden idea. Rachel was "passionately opposed", and his daughter Rose burst into tears when she heard about the move; he told neither that he was the guilty man who had suggested this violent upheaval in their lives. He reasoned that the "man on the spot" would have far more power than a Minister of State stuck in Whitehall; but then, "particularly if he had aspired to influence rather than reflect HMG's policy, [he] was bound to be caught up in the consequences of failure". Cub knew that "the chances of saving the Federation were very small"; within a week of his decision to take the job he was told by the Federal Justice Minister Julian Greenfield that the mood among Europeans was one of "utter dejection". But Cub remained hopeful that something could be salvaged – probably some form of economic association between the territories – and that with his political background he might contribute more to this task than the officials who had preceded him. For all his admiration of the British Empire he knew that it was coming to an end; but if the Federation failed the final chapter would be inglorious for Britain and tragic for Central Africa, which he had loved since his first visit. The Federation had many faults, but Cub still considered that in the short-term any alternatives would make life worse for all the people of the area – particularly for the Africans in Southern Rhodesia.[26]

As for being "kicked upstairs" to the House of Lords, Cub knew that someone else would take over his Commons seat while he was away and becoming Lord Alport of Colchester would be the best way of maintaining a link with his beloved constituency. He might never hold office again, but relations with senior ministers were good, and if the worst came to the worst (as Alec Home pointed out) he would always have a political platform in the Lords.[27] Ironically, if Cub had hung on until Home himself became Prime Minister something good might have fallen into his lap; after all, he had the warm approval of the party's "big three" – Macmillan, Home and Butler – at the time of the handover. But that would beg the question of how he could have marked time at the CRO for nearly three more years, and as he confessed many years later he found it hard to keep up his life as a commuting minister and a family man. He always felt that he made the correct decision, and on balance that comforting view was justified.[28] The more interesting question is why Macmillan agreed to an appointment which brought on a potentially awkward by-election and another (albeit small-scale) ministerial reshuffle.[29] Undoubtedly the Prime Minister had a high opinion of Cub; many of the judgements in his memoirs are suspect, but Macmillan had no ulterior motive for the tributes he paid to Cub in his sixth volume. As Macmillan said at the time, Cub was "eminently the right man for this important task"; the affairs of the Federation were causing him so much vexation that "the right man" would have to go, even if this brought some inconvenience to the government.[30]

The appointment was announced on 2 February, and an exchange of letters appeared in the newspapers. Macmillan praised Cub for "putting the good of the public service first", but hinted that he had been motivated at least in part by a regard for his own future prospects: "You are acting in the knowledge that this will add to your value subsequently in public life here when you return again". Press reaction was mixed. The *Daily Mail* thought that Cub's appointment proved that "the Federation will not be allowed to dissolve as easily as some people think", and the *Daily Express* welcomed the presence of "a key man" on the spot. James Callaghan described the appointment as "not very reassuring", claiming that Cub had been sent to appease European sentiment in Central Africa. Actually the federal government's distrust of Macmillan was now so deep that any decision he made was scrutinised to see if it would fit into a conspiracy theory; one of Welensky's colleagues claimed that the change had only taken place because the previous High Commissioner, Metcalf, had been recalled for showing too much sympathy to the Europeans.[31]

The most interesting reaction came from the local papers in Essex. The *County Standard* described Cub's new job as "formidable, dangerous, complex and probably thankless"; it reported that people in Colchester were asking "What is that Mr Macmillan doing to our Mr Alport?". The *Colchester Gazette*, congratulating itself for having predicted a place in the Lords for Cub back in May 1960, also pointed out that it had accompanied its forecast with the comment that taking a peerage would mean "political suicide" for "one of the hardest workers in the Conservative Party". The writer of the piece was only prepared to revise this judgement slightly in view of Macmillan's stated desire that Cub should resume his career on his return. As a parting salute both newspapers expressed regret that Cub would no longer sit for Colchester; he was praised for his accessibility to the press and his attention to the problems of constituents. His popularity was attested by a turn-out of around 1000 people at his farewell party; many more subscribed to presents.[32]

It had been agreed that Cub's tour of duty should begin in April. In the meantime he remained at the CRO, and stood in for Sandys while the latter attended the resumed Southern Rhodesian Constitutional Conference which had now moved to Salisbury. At the same time a similar meeting had begun in London under Macleod's chairmanship, to discuss constitutional change in Northern Rhodesia. Two conferences of crucial importance to the Federation were thus taking place 5000 miles apart, under the auspices of separate (and antagonistic) British ministries; at the same time the conference which was supposed to be examining the future of the Federation stood adjourned (it was never reconvened). Although Cub acted as a kind of liaison officer between Sandys and Macleod, the results of the two meetings underlined the absurdity of existing departmental arrangements. After tough negotiations Sandys produced proposals for Southern Rhodesia which would increase African representation without alarming the European population – a gradualist approach which was necessary because the new constitution had to be approved by a referendum on the existing franchise. But the leader of the African National Congress in Northern Rhodesia, Kenneth Kaunda, had demanded immediate majority rule in his country – otherwise there would be an uprising which, he declared, "would make Mau Mau a child's picnic".[33] Macleod was responsible for Northern Rhodesia and left to himself would have pressed for an African majority. However this would have a serious effect on European opinion in Southern Rhodesia, almost certainly leading to a negative vote in the referendum followed by an illegal declaration of independence by a European-dominated government in Southern Rhodesia. Macleod was well aware of this factor, but given the division of responsibility he had to put the interests of Northern Rhodesia first.

In January Macmillan had told Cub that Central Africa "had caused him more anxiety than almost anything else".[34] The events of February threatened to tear his policy apart, with catastrophic results for the people of the Federation – and for his own government. The nightmare prospect for the Colonial Office was an outbreak of African violence which would spread to Kenya; naturally the CRO feared an alternative disaster, in which the Europeans of Southern Rhodesia would seize all the economic assets of the Federation and leave the less prosperous areas to their fate. Sandys was seconded in this quarrel by Lord Home, who naturally retained his CRO sympathies despite his move to the Foreign Office. But Macleod had the stronger hand; the "winds of change" speech had tied Macmillan to a policy of rapid African advance, however much he might now regret it, and anything else would be difficult to reconcile with South Africa's imminent departure from the commonwealth. When Macleod threatened to resign once again on 17 February – on the justified grounds that "he was not being allowed sufficient freedom in his own sphere of responsibility" – Macmillan was forced to allow the publication of a White Paper which envisaged majority rule in Northern Rhodesia[35].

Despite the release of most of the cabinet documents the crisis of

February 1961 has received inadequate attention from historians, presumably because subsequent events have made it too easy to assume that it was a straight-forward battle between the forces of the future (led by Macleod) and a bunch of rather desperate reactionaries (whose main spokesman outside the cabinet, suitably enough, was the Marquess of Salisbury). When these dubious judgements are set aside, the records reveal a period when the heavy and conflicting pressures on British ministers caused a suspension of the usual standards of political morality. Poor decisions and administrative muddle had created a situation which precluded an honourable settlement; the inevitable results were personal clashes, a search for scapegoats – and more mistakes.

Welensky's response to Macleod's White Paper was to mobilise some army reservists. On 23 February, the Governor of Northern Rhodesia Sir Evelyn Hone warned Macleod that the federal government might be planning a *coup d'état*. Later that day Macleod met Macmillan to discuss the crisis, while a meeting of CRO ministers and officials took place in Sandys' room. Cub argued that Welensky would stop short of unconstitutional action, especially since he was due in London in a few days for a conference of commonwealth leaders. Sandys was less confident and, prompted by Macleod, the Prime Minister shared his worries. Welensky was soon receiving reports of unusual British troop movements at Nairobi airport. As the minutes of the CRO meeting confirm, these forces were on stand-by to supress any move from federal troops. A Conservative government had brought itself to the verge of war against its own creation, and if conflict had broken out the party would have been fatally split. After the cabinet meeting of 24 February which endorsed the decisions of the previous day, Macmillan wrote in his diary "We are preparing for the worst event in Rhodesia . . . I am very tired".[36]

If Welensky had been set on a violent course his intelligence reports could have been leaked to rouse the European population for war. Instead he took the news calmly, judging that the British forces might even be helpful if a nationalist rising broke out in Northern Rhodesia. He attended the Prime Ministers' conference as planned, and referred to the incident at dinner with Macmillan on 5 March. With tears in his eyes (or, according to Welensky, rolling down his cheeks) Macmillan protested that the troops had been assembled "in case you needed help" and that he could not have given orders for soldiers to fire on "Britishers, their brothers". He had no moral qualms about the bugging of Welensky's hotel suite, to check on the extent of his contacts with influential "Britishers".[37] As a fitting climax to this phase of the drama, Lord Salisbury launched a savage attack on Macleod in the House of Lords on 7 March, branding the Colonial Secretary as "too clever by half". To personalise the issue in this way was a serious error, to which government spokesmen could reply with offended dignity. Salisbury's serious point – that loyalty to the British government among the European population had been transformed into a feeling "of suspicion, of contempt, almost of hatred" could be ignored; the feelings stirred up by Macleod's strong personality prevented his critics from seeing that he had done little more than prefer the interests of his own ministry to those of the CRO. It was the departmental system which needed to be changed, not the personnel.[38]

Cub had planned to visit the Federation on a reconnaissance mission before taking up residence there. A party was held in his honour by Duncan Sandys; among the guests was Enoch Powell, who told Cub that "this is the most romantic thing that has happened to any of us". In fact Powell had always felt that the Federation was an "absurdity", only deciding not to attack it because that would damage his standing within the Conservative Party: later he regretted his reticence.[39]

Cub arrived in Salisbury just before Welensky flew off for the commonwealth conference. They had time for a brief meeting at Welensky's modest home in Greendale, a suburb of the capital. Cub was encouraged to find that whatever the underlying difficulties his own part in recent events had not been held against him; Welensky made light of the Nairobi incident, and showed that he could match the British government's imaginative powers by claiming that his own army reservists had been called up to cover a possible reaction from Europeans in Northern Rhodesia. Cub trotted out the official explanation that the British preparations had been provoked by possible trouble from Africans – an account which he apparently came to believe, such is the convenience of memory.[40] The new relationship between the two men had thus begun with diplomatic falsehoods on both sides; but they were now working in a complex hall of mirrors, and when Welensky began his journey to London Cub was hopeful that they would be able to do business together.[41]

The convoluted problems of the Central African Federation had been made far worse for Harold Macmillan by the personality of Sir Roy Welensky. The thirteenth product of a marriage between a Polish Jew and an Afrikaner, Welensky had been an engine-driver, a successful heavy-weight boxer and a trade unionist before entering politics in his native Northern Rhodesia. While no one could have accused him of being "too clever by half", Welensky was shrewd enough to know when he was being duped. His great difficulty was that unless he deployed his doomsday weapon of an illegal declaration of independence – which would hurt his own people at least as much as the British – his only defence was angry rhetoric. Like most honest men he struggled with this tactic – one accidental aside from Rab Butler could be more damaging to the government than hours of bluster from Welensky. But his conduct infuriated Macmillan, who would have preferred to deal with a brute or a hypocrite in a situation where his government could be accused of behaving like both. A recent historian of Macmillan's Government has solved the dilemma by presenting Welensky to his readers as a bigotted white supremacist, going so far as to identify him as a member of the Dominion Party, which he despised.[42] In reality Welensky's popular appeal meant that no one else could have brought about true partnership within the Federation. Over time his stated belief in Cecil Rhodes' dictum of "equal rights for civilised men" might have been exposed as an empty slogan which excluded the possibility of democratic politics, but the letters he wrote to Cub in his retirement – when neither man had any reason to disguise his true feelings – show Welensky to have been at least as enlightened on this point as many of his left-wing critics. Historical misjudgements on Welensky's character have only arisen because Macmillan's policy ensured that time would be denied to him; after his fall from power very few cared to defend him.[43]

In Welensky's absence Cub called on the Prime Minister of Southern Rhodesia, Sir Edgar Whitehead. In 1958 Whitehead had seized power from the liberal Garfield Todd; Whitehead had built on Todd's reforms without appearing to move too fast in the eyes of most Europeans. A skilled financier, Whitehead had much more diplomatic sensitivity than Welensky, although in a typical misjudgement

Macmillan convinced himself that Whitehead was the more dangerous man. Cub appreciated the contrasting qualities of both, and
wished that it were possible to merge them in a single person. He
moved on for talks with the two Northern governors, Hone in
Northern Rhodesia and Armitage in Nyasaland. The latter was on the
point of retirement; his understandable gloom after recent events was
an object lesson in the pitfalls of government service. At least Cub
won the agreement of Hone to his proposal of regular conferences
between himself and the governors. He calculated that if the men on
the spot understood one another some of the friction between the
CRO and the Colonial Office might be by-passed. Predictably the
idea was frowned upon by officials in the warring departments, but
common sense prevailed on this occasion; only when Cub was about
to leave the Federation did Welensky claim that these meetings had
disrupted his own contacts with the governors, but by that time he
was ready to find fault with all of Cub's initiatives.[44]

Cub's account of this trip in *The Sudden Assignment* is dominated by
two lurid images. He travelled to the Matopos Hills to lay a wreath on
the tomb of Cecil Rhodes, and found this "a disturbing experience" in
the midday heat:

> I had paid my respects at Jinnah's tomb in Karachi, at Gandhi's
> shrine in Calcutta and at Bandaranaike's grave on the Kandy
> road in Ceylon. Nowhere except beside the sepulchre of this
> Englishman in the heart of Africa have I had this sense of being
> in a haunted, sinister, pagan place – despite the solemnity of its
> associations and the grandeur of countryside around.

Still more troubling was a visit with his private secretary Brian Unwin
to an old European farmstead in Nyasaland:

> our host [was] a gallant, lame old gentleman still suffering from
> a wound received in German East Africa 45 years before. He had
> buried his wife a few weeks previously. His dairy farm, built in
> the hope and optimism of a generation earlier, where they had
> raised their family and lived the happy years of their lives, was
> falling into disrepair. There was nothing to look forward to in
> what remained to him of his life. We sat watching the sun setting

in a sulky, blood-shot sky and the creeping shadows gathering beyond the lamplight on the *stoep*. I felt, as I have felt in other places as far apart as Basutoland and Peshawar, an overpowering sense of loneliness amounting almost to despair. As we left it began to drizzle, and by the time we reached Government House it had developed into an oppressive tropical storm. . . . It took more than one glass of the Governor's excellent whisky to restore, to both of us, a better sense of perspective.[45]

These flashes of memory across a barren landscape show the depths of feeling which Cub – with his Haileybury training – managed to conceal throughout his political life. They stand as authentic testimony to the misgivings he felt as he embarked on his self-selected mission.

In April Cub and his family sailed to Africa on the *Pretoria Castle*. They travelled first-class, suitable for their new status. Cub had rightly asked for a salary in keeping with the equivalent rank in the diplomatic service and he was now on an annual rate of £5000 (as a Minister of State he had earned £4500). His new residence, Mirimba House in the Salisbury suburbs, lacked the associations of the Cross House but there were plenty of compensations. It was a long two-storied house with spacious reception-rooms, a swimming pool, two tennis courts, a detached indoor playroom and ten acres of parkland running down to a river. In the swamps of Serbia Cecil Alport had constructed a golf course; his son did the same in this more auspicious setting. The only difficulty was that the rough became somewhat overgrown, and when Sandys visited in February 1962 he soon gave up his game because he kept falling over in the long grass. The play-area was turned into a classroom, where the family's nanny Edith Hammond presided over a school for the children of local residents and the staff of the house. By the time that the family left there were over 50 pupils; the fact that African children in the area lacked any other educational opportunities was a reminder to Cub of how much progress needed to be made in Southern Rhodesia. Rachel helped with the school and made herself as popular in Salisbury as she had been in Colchester; staff at Mirimba, so used to talking about "Her Ladyship", thought it natural that Cub should be addressed as "His Lordship". For security there was only a Rhodesian Ridgeback puppy which Cub bought; when he returned to the area in the 1970s he found that the British High Commissioner had moved to another residence protected by a high fence with strong security gates, alarms and lights. There were times during his own stay when he would have appreciated similar defences.

Cub arrived in Salisbury with definite ideas about his role. Before his reconnaissance trip he had asked Sandys for a statement of his terms of reference. After some prevarication Sandys had replied that there was a need for "someone in Rhodesia who would help the government to evolve a coherent policy" – a tacit admission that the existing approach fell short of a rational strategy. Cub told reporters on his arrival that he was "a diplomat, not a politician", but for him there was no sharp distinction between the two roles. He felt that he should take the initiative with suggestions of his own from time to time, always making it clear when he was speaking for himself and when his instructions came from the government. The trouble with this approach – apart from the fact that anything he said was likely to be opposed by either the CRO or the Colonial Office – was that at times of greatest stress communication was liable to break down, especially with an impatient man like Welensky. As Cub told Butler after a few months in the job, he believed that good diplomacy depended on personal relationships.[46] Complete trust was essential, but it was hard to maintain in the prevailing atmosphere. Misunderstanding was built into the changed relationship between the two: Welensky had adopted an "us and them" approach to Central Africa and still regarded Cub as "one of us", but Cub was determined to at least appear impartial, telling his deputy, David Scott, that "the best we are entitled to hope for in this job is parity of disesteem. Once either side gets the idea that we are the cat's whiskers, we've had it".[47] Once trust had gone, private ideas which Cub advanced as his own would be interpreted by Welensky as tentative approaches by ministers in London; if he liked the suggestion, but no subsequent action was taken, he would take this as a sign that Cub had been insincere – or that he had no weight in Whitehall. On the more frequent occasions when Cub delivered messages which Welensky disliked, the wrath of the federal Prime Minister would be sharpened by his knowledge of Cub's real feelings.

For two months after Cub's arrival the situation was relatively calm within the Federation. He was involved in negotiations over Southern

Rhodesia, and although the nationalist leaders Nkomo and Sithole walked out of another conference in mid-May Cub was fairly confident that the referendum, scheduled for July, would bring a satisfactory result. Sandys, who visited in May, also discussed Northern Rhodesia, apparently with the blessing of Macleod. He and Cub favoured a compromise to break the deadlock between Welensky and the Colonial Secretary – the so-called "60:40" solution in which the upper (European dominated) roll of voters would elect 60 per cent of the legislative members in Northern Rhodesia while the lower roll (mainly African) were left with the remaining 40 per cent. While the "50:50" arrangement preferred by Macleod seemed fairer, it did not address the problem that the European population was already deeply divided along party lines. Even if British ministers had seriously hoped to engineer a pro-federal majority in the Assembly while giving a better deal to Africans, the hideous complexity of the situation on the ground would have defeated their efforts. But one reason for the improved atmosphere was that Welensky believed that the moderation (as he saw it) of Cub and Sandys would prevail over Macleod's radicalism, despite the rows of February. On 14 June Cub pressed his arguments on Butler, stressing that "if we can get through this particular phase it is not impossible that the Federation, in a revised form, can be kept in being and a lot of trouble avoided in this part of Africa".[48]

On 18 June Cub suffered a rude shock. He received an unexpected summons to see Welensky and his senior advisers, who informed him that they had reliable information to the effect that the 50:50 formula would be introduced after all. According to his account Cub replied that he had no such information himself, and repeated arguments he had already used in favour of 60:40. Apparently he had not been told that Macmillan, Sandys and Macleod had opted for 50:50 on the previous day – a decision which Sandys had relayed to Welensky through the Federation's High Commissioner in London.[49] Welensky saw this as a death-blow for the Federation before it had been given the chance to prove itself; he declared that he would go in person to argue his case in London. If he did not get his way he would dissolve the federal Assembly and call a general election.

This new proposal horrified Cub. In his memoir he claims to have felt most concern for the future of the Federation, and records that

Welensky himself admitted that impulsive action might damage its prospects. But the graver threat, in the short-term at least, loomed over the British government. Welensky was likely to whip up support among back-benchers by making one of his numerous barn-storming appearances before the Conservative Commonwealth Committee; there the mood was generally antagonistic towards Macleod, and harsh words behind closed doors could be quickly translated into a rebellion in the House. Even so Macmillan might have preferred this to having to meet Welensky himself; they saw quite enough of each other at their regular meetings, and Macmillan was unlikely to relish the prospect of an unscheduled harangue.[50]

For the next few days Cub maintained close contact with Welensky and his office, arguing against this provocative gesture. By 23 June he had been assured that Welensky's journey would not take place, and took a relaxing bath in preparation for a military dinner. While soaping himself he decided that he ought to check on Welensky, and rang him as soon as he finished his bath. Welensky answered the telephone himself, and said that he had changed his mind again; his luggage was at the airport and he would follow in 15 minutes.

Cub put through an urgent call to Sandys in London while scrambling into his dress-suit, weighed down with medals. According to Rachel, Cub was "seething with anger" at the lack of information from London; he "told [Sandys] where he got off, threatened resignation and the Secretary of State was very contrite". Sandys revealed that he might have a proposal which would make Welensky's journey unnecessary. Rachel contacted the airport to warn the Prime Minister that a messenger was coming, while Cub was driven rapidly through crowded streets. When he darted into the VIP lounge he found Welensky saying his goodbyes to friends, relatives and the press. Cub delivered his message ten minutes before the departure time; simultaneously Welensky's private secretary announced that Sandys was on the telephone and wanted to speak to him. Welensky returned to say that his journey was cancelled, thanking Cub warmly for his help. Lady Welensky was not so happy about the sudden change; as she left she whispered, "What have you done, High Commissioner? I've not a thing in the house for the old man's dinner". Cub went on to his own meal in high spirits; as Rachel recorded in her diary, when they spoke later he told her "that he expected to be sober for at least another hour". He was not the only one in a celebratory mood; two days later Macmillan rang Buckingham Palace to say that "he had solved Rhodesia".[51]

Macmillan's optimism was based on the calculation that, after further negotiations, a settlement had been reached which met both Kaunda and Welensky half-way. The reaction in the House of Commons was favourable, although as Brian Harrison confessed to Cub, "I don't think any of us really understand the constitution". The labyrinthine system of percentages was irrelevant, after all; what mattered was the government's perceived attitude to the Federation, and clever presentation had convinced MPs that all was well. But the obscurity of the new proposals, announced by Macleod on 26 June, produced wildly contrasting headlines in the press; as Harrison reported, the *Daily Express* had proclaimed that "Sir Roy Welensky wins", while the *Daily Mail* had hailed a "victory" for Macleod.[52]

Cub told Harrison that "we have got through that particular period much more satisfactorily than I ever thought possible . . . [the constitution] provides as good a compromise as possible".[53] But the language of the press should have alerted him to the fact that the grounds for any sort of "compromise" had disappeared. The changes made after the scene at the airport were minimal, and both sides had been assured in private that their own views had prevailed. Before the final negotiations Kaunda had warned that any concessions to Welensky would be opposed by a campaign of passive resistance in Northern Rhodesia; after the revised White Paper appeared he confirmed that this threat would be carried out, and denounced Welensky as a "political idiot". The nationalist leaders within the Federation admired Gandhi, but in Africa it proved impossible to match his peaceful methods. The campaign, which opened in mid-July, soon led to violence, although (to the relief of British ministers) Whitehead was still able to secure a majority in the Southern Rhodesian referendum, held on 27 July. Macleod's response to the disorder was to propose more concessions to Kaunda.[54]

By this time, in the words of Macleod's biographer, "Macmillan had had enough of Macleod on Northern Rhodesia".[55] The new crisis cast an ironic light on the Prime Minister's merry message to the Palace back in June, and he wanted to concentrate on the government's application for membership of the European Economic

Community (EEC), which itself had serious implications for the commonwealth. At the CRO Sandys was also losing patience. The only solution was an even more dramatic compromise; Macleod would get his way over Northern Rhodesia, but he would lose his job. A statement was delivered in the House on 14 September, noting the disorder and promising that once calm had been restored a new look would be taken at the constitutional proposals. Macmillan told the Queen that "Sir Roy Welensky will, of course, be upset by it, but then everything upsets him".[56] Sir Roy was not upset in early October when he heard that Macleod would move from the Colonial Office.

The strain on Macmillan at this time was considerable, but at least he was not meeting Welensky on a daily basis. The role of unwelcome messenger was thrust upon Cub, who delivered an early warning of the government's change of mind on 9 September. He had warned London against any decision on Northern Rhodesia which might look like a capitulation to violence, predicting that what seemed to be an expedient decision would lead to a total collapse of the British position; but these arguments were overruled. To make matters worse, the news from London arrived during the second of his periodic conferences with the Northern governors, ensuring that this meeting ended with a row. Cub's conversation with Welensky was even more unpleasant. Welensky must have been aware of Cub's difficulty – after all, he knew that the High Commissioner had originally pressed for the 60:40 franchise, which was far removed even from the abortive deal of late June. Presumably this added to Welensky's irritation, which produced a diatribe against the British. Cub (ever the loyal servant) deeply resented this. He relayed news of Welensky's complete rejection of new talks on 11 September, then set off for a brief golfing holiday to refresh himself after recent strains. His rest-cure was ended after just one day; news reached him of serious fighting in Katanga province, and he hurried back to Salisbury to face a more spectacular disaster.[57]

In the context of the continuing troubles of Northern Rhodesia the Katangan crisis of September 1961 has a surreal quality. The United Nations had been struggling to maintain some order within the independent Congo, but in June 1961 the Katangan leader Tshombe repudiated an earlier agreement (which he had made while under arrest) to submit to the unstable central government. The situation caused great concern in Whitehall, where the break-up of the Congo was feared as a possible pretext for intervention by the Soviet Union. The CRO (and the Europeans in Southern Rhodesia) regarded Katanga as a grim warning of what might happen if the British gave premature independence to any of the territories of the Federation. While sharing these fears the federal government saw that the crisis might work out well for Central Africa; Katanga shared a border with Northern Rhodesia, and if it secured independence from the Congo this copper-rich province would be a useful ally (if not a new component) of the Federation.

In August the UN increased the pressure on Tshombe, but was met with strong resistance. Welensky was itching to help Tshombe, and Cub had to warn him against any provocative actions while Britain attempted to use its influence with the UN. On 12 September the UN presented an ultimatum to Tshombe, who went into hiding. In response Welensky moved some forces to the border, despite Cub's "not very energetic attempts to dissuade him from doing so". At least this action could be passed off as a precaution in case Europeans in Katanga had to be evacuated, but the potential for a catastrophic clash between Welensky and the UN was obvious.[58]

Meanwhile Welensky continued to pour out his anger over Northern Rhodesia; after delivering a message from Macmillan on 13 September Cub reported that "the atmosphere was worse than it had been on any previous occasion". He sent another message to the CRO on the 14th, advising that Welensky's anger should be allowed to burn itself out: the anxious Macmillan scrawled "This is a very sensible telegram" on his copy. Cub proposed that he should return to his golf for 24 hours, but rightly guessed that the Katanga situation would ruin his plans.[59] The Marquess of Lansdowne, Under-Secretary at the Foreign Office, was holding talks with the UN Secretary-General, Dag Hammarskjold; on 17 September Cub, who had located Tshombe on the border between Katanga and Northern Rhodesia, was asked if he could arrange a meeting between Hammarskjold and Tshombe to discuss arrangements for a cease-fire. The talks were to be held in the Northern Rhodesian town of Ndola, where there was a small airport.

To Cub it was astonishing that such a meeting was planned at all. Even if Hammarskjold could persuade his supporters on the ground to stop fighting, it was unlikely that a deal struck by the UN

Secretary-General would be honoured by the Congo government, which regarded Tshombe as a stooge for European imperialism. By this time Hammarskjold was worried enough by divisions between his own officials, some of whom were anxious to destroy Tshombe. To hold the meeting in Northern Rhodesia, of all places, made it even more unlikely that a lasting solution could be devised. Despite his doubts, Cub made the necessary arrangements, and travelled to Ndola in a plane provided by the federal government.

Tshombe arrived at about 5pm, and had dinner with Cub who found him an impressive figure.[60] Lord Lansdowne was due between 10pm and 11pm for a quick check that suitable arrangements had been made, before leaving to avoid the impression that the British were interfering in the talks. The British minister flew in a DC-4 originally assigned to the Secretary-General; Hammarskjold was to follow in a faster plane. After Lansdowne arrived there was a slight embarrassment, because Cub had assured Tshombe that he would meet the British minister, whereas Lansdowne would have preferred to avoid any suspicion that he and the British government approved of Tshombe's actions; however, a brief conversation did take place before Lansdowne's departure at midnight.[61]

Left to himself Cub began to hope that this strange rendez-vous would work out well, although there was still no sign of Hammarskjold and there had been no recent radio contact with his plane, whose flight path was unclear. By 3.30 am he felt sure that the Secretary-General had changed his plans, perhaps diverting to the Katangan capital of Elisabethville for discussions with UN command-ers; he respected Hammarskjold, whom he had met on a previous occasion, and thought that this was the only sensible thing for him to do. He dozed for a few hours in his aeroplane, and on waking heard reports that a flash had been seen in the sky. Further inquiries were being made, but Cub was not unduly concerned because he felt certain that Hammarskjold had called off his unlikely mission. Tshombe was now anxious to leave, and Cub decided to fly back to Salisbury.

On his arrival he was met by Lansdowne and the Deputy High Commissioner David Scott, who told him that the wreckage of Hammarskjold's plane had been found and the Secretary-General was dead; the plane had failed to clear some trees a few miles from Ndola.

There was little time to reflect; Cub reported the news to a shaken Welensky before flying back to Ndola to patch together some new arrangements for talks between the UN and Tshombe. He also helped to organise a suitably dignified ceremony for Hammarskjold, and umpired a bizarre contest between two local UN officials for possession of the Secretary-General's briefcase.[62]

The shocking death of Hammarskjold gave rise to some wild accusations; the Indian and Ghanaian press carried articles naming Welensky, Macmillan and/or Cub as murderers, while Kenneth Kaunda thought that the incident was "a serious indictment of the British Government". Conor Cruise O'Brien, the UN representative in Katanga, entertained a more subtle theory – that Hammarskjold's plane had been shot down by extreme supporters of Tshombe. This allegation even cropped up during the proceedings of South Africa's "Truth and Reconciliation" Commission in 1998. But Cub treated all of these notions with contempt. Despite the political pressures an official UN inquiry found no evidence to support allegations of foul play; an investigation by the federal government concluded that pilot error was to blame, although naturally this cut no ice with people who thought that the government had been responsible for the tragedy. The strange death of Dag Hammarskjold will continue to interest those who think that no accident can ever befall a famous person, but in this case the least sensational explanation must be the right one. Cub's sole regret was that he did not order a search as soon as the first suspicions arose; but his authority in Northern Rhodesia was uncertain, the evidence of a mishap was slight, and the only survivor of the immediate impact was so seriously injured that a rescue team would probably have failed to save him.[63]

Even before Hammarskjold's death Cub's predecessor Metcalf had written sympathetically of the "fiendish time" that Cub was having, but at least October and November were "relatively peaceful months" in Central Africa.[64] The main political development was Whitehead's pledge to repeal the Land Apportionment Act which cemented the European domination of Southern Rhodesia, but this important initiative would be overtaken by events. Briefly Cub's attention was caught by developments at home. In August he had received hints that Rab Butler was about to cut down his numerous responsibilities; he felt that it would be "extremely wise" for his friend to enjoy "a quiet period where other people make the running and the mistakes". Rab thanked Cub for his advice, confirming that he would shortly relinquish the chairmanship of the party, which he had held in awkward combination with the office of Home Secretary and the Leadership of the House of Commons. He did well to keep up the pretence that his decision had been voluntary; the letter was written only two days after Butler had discussed the problem with Macmillan, who had made the wounding suggestion that his old rival might like to retire with a peerage.[65]

After the October reshuffle it was clear that Butler would no longer have to "make the running". In addition to losing the party chairmanship he was no longer Leader of the House. Both of these offices fell to Macleod, Butler's protégé, who in the greatest speech of his life affirmed his belief in "the brotherhood of man" at the party conference as a defiant parting shot at his critics. The press response to the reshuffle was a barrage of articles hailing Macleod as a certain future leader of the party, and friends noticed that he was now much happier. Butler was deeply upset: Brian Harrison reported to Cub that he refused to give up his room behind the Speaker's Chair to his successor as Leader of the House. Macleod's dual role revealed his power over Macmillan; he had insisted on taking the Leadership of the House after the Prime Minister offered only the party chairmanship. Yet as Robert Shepherd comments his new jobs left him "effectively marginalised" from key policy decisions. Cub's correspondents from both wings of the party were bemused at the press reaction to what they regarded as an effective demotion for Macleod, whose decisions over Northern Rhodesia were now described even by moderate Conservatives as "deliberate double crossing". Cub felt it necessary to warn Welensky against any "crowing" over Macleod's departure.[66]

Cub was now in the curious position of reading about his friends clambering over each other on the political ladder while he laboured on his own middle rung 5000 miles away. Even Edward Heath, from his post in the Foreign Office, had been drawn into the Katanga situation. Now another old "One Nation" colleague, Reginald Maudling, was summoned to replace Macleod at the Colonial Office, and toured the Federation in early December. Cub welcomed the appointment as a chance for a new start; he explained to Lord Home that "for psychological reasons" federal ministers would "like to see Maudling succeed where Macleod has previously found himself up against a brick wall".[67] These hopes were misplaced; although Welensky and his colleagues never felt towards Maudling the hatred they had shown to his predecessor, this was only because they attributed his decisions to ignorance rather than malice. Once again, Welensky and his colleagues had confused the intentions of individual ministers with the settled policy of the British Colonial Office, and Macleod's allies on the left-wing of the Conservative Party now rivalled Labour in their dislike of the Federation.

By the time of Maudling's visit Cub was distracted by new clashes between Tshombe, Welensky and the UN. He was told (against his own judgement) to advise Welensky that UN observers should be allowed to guard the frontier between Northern Rhodesia and Katanga against possible infiltration by mercenaries. As Cub had predicted, the interview only increased Welensky's antipathy towards London; in his phrase, the federal Prime Minister was "shrill with indignation and self-righteousness" when he conveyed the government's message. In October Cub had boasted to Butler that Welensky had always been "completely frank" in their dealings, but after this incident relations deteriorated sharply. The Katangan stalemate dragged on, and when in January Welensky was told to rest by his doctors Cub felt at least partly responsible for his exhaustion.[68]

Hardly anything had gone right in the year since Cub suggested his move to Central Africa. At least there were signs that his work was appreciated by British ministers; in early January 1962 Lord Home sent a message of condolence over the Katangan situation, telling Cub that he was "doing magnificently". An old adversary, the Minister for Air Julian Amery, wrote that he was "tremendously impressed" by the quality of Cub's telegrams, confided that the Prime Minister felt the same way, and acknowledged that it must have been "damnably frustrating to have to give advice to Roy which so often seems to be neither in his best interests nor ours". "Isn't the time coming", he continued, "when we should pay Welensky for any further concessions to the Africans by the promise of very early independence? It seems rather absurd to hand independence out all over the place with very dubious safeguards for the minorities and yet to hold it up indefinitely in Central Africa".[69]

Amery's letter was an unwelcome reminder of the deep splits

within the government, and if Cub felt any temptation to talk treason he resisted it. If the Federation were to be given immediate independence, he pointed out, it would fragment. His aim now was to try "to provide a transitional period between its present form and something which is politically and economically viable".[70] This meant coming to terms with the changed situation and at least trying to introduce an element of stability. He began negotiations with Hastings Banda over a scheme to produce electricity at Nkula Falls in Nyasaland, hoping that the clear economic advantages would make the nationalist leader look more favourably on co-operation with neighbouring states. Banda, whose Congress Party had won elections held in August, replied that "the people of Nyasaland would rather starve on their own than have full stomachs under the Federation". On a more hopeful note he declared that it was "a real joy" to have constructive relations with Cub after years of disagreement, but despite the thaw between them it proved impossible to set up a meeting between Banda and Welensky in February.[71]

However irrational the decision-making process might have been over the past year, it seemed that a remorseless logic was driving the Federation towards break-up. Despite his cool reply to Amery, at the third meeting with the Northern governors on 10 January Cub declared that "definite action was needed soon if anything was to be salvaged from the federal concept". A settlement in Northern Rhodesia was still urgently needed. Maudling had produced some ideas after his visit which went even further than Macleod had done; in a rather bitter telegram of 19 January Cub argued that the original deal of June 1961 would have worked if given the chance, but now thought that Maudling should be supported since his ideas at least had the virtue of (relative) simplicity.[72]

His message arrived at an unfortunate time for the government. Dismayed that Maudling had proved to be more radical than Macleod, Macmillan wanted to face down the new Colonial Secretary. Yet this would lead to the resignation of Maudling and his junior ministers; it was thought that Macleod would follow them out of the government. The long-suffering Butler was sent to sound out Macleod; afterwards he noted characteristically that "I did not find him especially keen to give up all his new honours", but for Macleod there would be no honourable alternative to resignation if Maudling was sacked for carrying further the policies he had fought for. Butler was also shown Cub's telegram, which Macmillan had read "with considerable interest and some sense of disappointment"; Rab told Macmillan's private secretary that "however constructive Alport's views may be we *must* remember the situation and the reactions here". This cruel reminder to the Prime Minister that his Central African policy had trapped him between two wings of his party implies that Butler was rather enjoying his new task; but as usual Macmillan was a step ahead of him. Without noticing what had happened Butler had been tricked into taking an active interest in a subject for which Macmillan no longer had much taste.[73]

As the cabinet limbered up for another showdown over the Federation, Cub prepared an initiative of his own. He knew that Welensky would reject Maudling's proposals in isolation, but he had thought of a way in which the deal might be sweetened. He had always deplored the fact that the map of Africa reflected the legacy of nineteenth-century power-politics rather than any geographical logic. It occurred to him that Northern Rhodesia could be partitioned and a constitution similar to that of Southern Rhodesia granted to the central area, where the European population was concentrated; as part of the deal a chunk of territory could be allotted to Nyasaland, which would please Banda. He put this plan to the federal ministers, who were impressed. This was no surprise, since the central area contained most of Northern Rhodesia's copper reserves. If the rest of the Federation territories seceded, Southern Rhodesia would be able to survive in a close alliance – if not a union – with this new creation. The partition scheme was also approved by Whitehead, although he favoured the immediate absorption of the central area into Southern Rhodesia.[74]

Cub's presentation of this idea in *The Sudden Assignment* is understandably sheepish. Hindsight makes it look like an attempt to produce exactly the result which was demanded by the hard-line Europeans in the Southern Rhodesian Dominion Party – a prosperous state carved out of the Federation under permanent white rule. Actually Cub was being "too clever by half"; he was calculating for the medium-term while the British government was muddling through from day to day. The problem was no longer one of saving the Federation; unless something was done the concept of racial partnership in Central Africa was finished. After secession Nyasaland and the whole of Northern Rhodesia would become "African" states, and Southern Rhodesia would retreat towards South African conditions. Whatever happened in the other territories, the only chance that Southern Rhodesia might steer a course towards a multi-racial state would be some assurance of future security to the European population. The partition plan, Cub thought, would help Whitehead to fend off the growing popularity of the Dominion Party.

Duncan Sandys visited the Federation in February, fresh from a row with Maudling which not even Butler could smooth over. His tumble on Cub's golf course was a suitable beginning to a disastrous stay. It has been claimed that when he met Hastings Banda Sandys confirmed that Nyasaland would be allowed to secede from the Federation, although Cub was never sure about this. What he did witness was a conversation over lunch on 15 February with Welensky and the hard-line minister Julian Greenfield, during which Sandys was told that Nyasaland could be kept within the Federation by "firmness". "No, Roy", the minister replied, "You see, we British have lost the will to govern". Cub later recalled Greenfield's "somewhat theatrical interjection, 'But we haven't'".[75]

In his memoirs Welensky admits that Sandys' remark annoyed him so much that he suffered an attack of migraine; someone told him that Cub had gone home to vomit. In his own account Cub denied that his reaction had been quite so spectacular, but he was "extremely angry" at the time. The first draft of *The Sudden Assignment* recalled that he "took advantage of [Sandys'] good nature later that night to tell him in somewhat brutal terms" the reason for his vexation. When the book was scrutinised prior to publication by Sandys and the CRO Cub was advised to cut this passage. Regrettably he agreed, and also strengthened the excuse advanced on Sandys' behalf – that the remark was taken out of context by the federal ministers. The impression left by the published text is that Cub was furious with Sandys only because he had offered Welensky a stick with which the British government could be beaten; but if the words had no truth in them there would have been nothing to worry about.[76]

Sandys took back with him Cub's plan for partition, but it was shelved pending a new constitution for the whole of Northern Rhodesia – a decision which effectively killed the proposal. After some more horse-trading a deal over Northern Rhodesia was thrashed out

by the British cabinet on 27 February; it guaranteed an African majority, although once again enough concessions were made to the federal
viewpoint to ensure that Kaunda would be dissatisfied. A telegram
containing Maudling's statement was sent to Cub at Mirimba House.
When he took it to Welensky's home at Greendale he found the Prime
Minister with his bags packed for another journey to London. Cub
read the telegram to Welensky, and urged him not to leave; he would
be "throwing away a card which he might wish to play in more propi-
tious circumstances at a later stage". This time Welensky would not be
turned back from the airport, although he had been hoping for a concession which would allow him to unpack. He showed his displeasure
to Cub; perhaps he failed to notice that, for a moment at least, the
High Commissioner had thrown off the guise of servant to the British
government and become an impassioned friend to the federal Prime
Minister.[77]

Welensky's trip was unsuccessful; although he later claimed that
"my resolution had thoroughly shaken the British cabinet", he did not
realise that he had done that so many times that even his well wishers
were anxious for some peace. Even so, Duncan Sandys managed to
see him off at the airport with an assurance that "I am still a good
friend of the Federation and I still believe in it". Welensky stormed
home to dissolve the federal Assembly, and on 9 September
Macmillan asked Rab Butler to head a new Central African Department.[78]

Chapter Eight

"More Trouble with the Government, Daddy?"

I n October 1961, six months into his "sudden assignment", Cub had told Butler that "in this part of the world, there is still considerable *panache* in being the British representative".[1] He was enjoying the ceremonial aspects of his job, the gossip at cocktail parties and, above all, the sense that he was an important source of information for the government back home. Writing and receiving telegrams was a pleasure to him; letters were not such fun, because they were often out-of-date before they arrived. As High Commissioner he had faced acute political problems in his first few months but the excitement of living at the centre of a storm had compensated him for the regular frustrations. Having come through the double trouble of Katanga and Northern Rhodesia in September Cub must have felt equal to anything else that might be thrown at him.

Even so, "*panache*" was a curious word for Cub to choose. From the beginning he had sensed hostility from the European population of the Federation. In May 1961 a correspondent complained that he had felt "ill with revulsion" on hearing Cub deliver a speech which consisted of "Bloody sales-talk – and of a low order".[2] During Sandys' visit of the same month a federal politician attacked British ministers, "attributing to them every form of baseness of motive and method"; he rounded off his sally by telling Cub "with a deep and bitter emotion, 'You know, I *hate* your government'".[3]

With radical changes under way it was unlikely that European attitudes would improve, but Cub took up the challenge. For the rest of his time in office he tried in his public speeches and broadcasts to justify the ways of Britain to hostile audiences. His efforts might have made some difference if the European population had shared his desire to cherish Britain's remaining virtues while being a little blind to its faults. But even Cub recognised that Southern Rhodesia, in particular, had changed since his first wartime visit. Long-established families deplored British policies which they had no power to change; convinced as they were that Britain had collapsed into decadence, their former respect for "the old country" sharpened their new sense of grievance. Their outlook could not be shifted by a few speeches from the High Commissioner, and Cub had even less hope of mollifying the young, or recent immigrants from South Africa who had been attracted to the Federation by its postwar prosperity. Many of these were Afrikaners who had no traditional loyalty to complicate their feelings; they were happy to add their voices to the swelling anti-British chorus.

The constitutional changes which brought about the new antipathy to Britain also led to heightened tensions between the races in the Federation and threatened to destroy any chance of partnership. The Southern Rhodesian Prime Minister Edgar Whitehead was trying to bring Africans into his party, but Welensky and his colleagues had few contacts with nationalist politicians, believing that dialogue would be fruitless with people whom they regarded as intellectuals who did not speak for the mass of their people. Cub disagreed, and in November 1961 he held discussions with the Southern Rhodesian leaders Joshua Nkomo and Robert Mugabe in addition to his attempts to establish a better relationship with Banda. He was willing to talk, but his status made him an excellent target for demonstrators; in the following month he was trapped in the High Commission offices by a hundred African women – including Mugabe's wife – protesting about the

Southern Rhodesian constitution. This was not an occasion to display the *panache* which Cub had boasted of so recently; he made his escape in his chauffeur-driven Austen Princess while the bare-breasted protesters washed their babies' nappies in the High Commissioner's ornamental fountain. They were still there when he returned and he was forced to listen to their complaints for twenty minutes, later telling reporters that "odds of 100-1 against is more than a mere male – even though a diplomat – should be expected to take on".[4]

Cub clearly needed all the friends he could muster, and he was delighted by Butler's appointment. "Looking back over the last thirty years", he wrote to Bill Deedes, "it really is astonishing how time and time again Rab's path and mine have crossed. The coincidence is so remarkable that it must mean something though I have no idea what".[5] The coincidence became even more improbable when Charles Fletcher Cooke, now a junior minister in the Home Office (where Butler continued as Secretary of State) began to assist Rab on Central African affairs. But although Cub knew that Butler had shared his deep misgivings about the Monckton Commission he was right to wonder what this strange reunion might mean, and to hold back any suggestion that he and Butler could reproduce their success in reviving the Conservative Party after the war. Butler himself recognised how far the situation had moved since the Monckton Report, and was far from enthusiastic about his new challenge; at first he suggested the unlikely names of Peter Thorneycroft and Julian Amery as preferable candidates. Eventually he took on the job because of his remarkable sense of duty. Macmillan had tried to convince him that he could make his name in Central Africa – as if Butler was still a political novice consumed by personal ambition. Butler was more inclined to listen to Alec Home, who pressed him to accept in the hope that he could save something of the federal idea.[6]

Cub's new optimism was increased by the fact that the Central African Department was designed along lines he had recommended for many years. It promised to bring to an end the friction between the CRO and the Colonial Office by taking over from both of them in dealing with the Federation. Cub claimed in *The Sudden Assignment* that on 17 March he had "dictated a long letter to the Permanent Under-Secretary at the CRO", reminding him of the arguments for a new department, only to hear that same evening of Butler's appointment. In fact he had known of the change on 10 March, when he sent a telegram congratulating his old friend: either he mixed up the dates when he wrote his memoir, or the "long letter" to the CRO was an invention to add some drama to this section of the book. Perhaps Cub feared that the CRO had not preserved his earlier communications on the subject, and resorted to a white lie to "prove" his wisdom to posterity. If so he need not have worried. A letter written to Sandys on 16 August 1961 was found by the present writer at the front of the file on the formation of the Central African Department held by the Public Record Office; although in this letter Cub argued not for a wholly new department but for a transfer of Colonial Office responsibilities to the CRO, the effect on policy-making for the Federation would have been the same. As the file records, his suggestion ran into the usual Whitehall obstructions. These could have been anticipated, but having advocated such a change for so long Cub would have been dismayed to see a scribbled civil service note which pointed out that "The time to have made such a transfer was at the start of the Federation and if this had been done the Federation might be in a much stronger position than it is today". The note was written in October 1961; when the transfer took place six months later the Federation had weakened still further, mainly because of the divisions between the CRO and the Colonial Office. Even so, in his official telegram announcing Butler's appointment Macmillan allowed himself to claim that the switch had been agreed because constitutional advance in the Rhodesias and Nyasaland had reached a suitable stage. According to Butler, the Cabinet Secretary Norman Brook had provided the true explanation: "the Prime Minister could not stand the ceaseless competition and rivalry between the Colonial Office and the Commonwealth Office and the Foreign Office" over the Federation.[7]

Reaction in the Federation was mixed. Roy Welensky knew and liked Butler, and had also recommended a change in departmental responsibilities. Cub reported that after his initial surprise he seemed pleased. But Welensky also protested that he would not have called a federal election had he known that the reshuffle was imminent; Cub chose not to retort that the change had only happened *because* he had called the election. Still, the advent of Butler gave Welensky some positive news to present to the federal electorate. Cub found Sir Edgar

Whitehead "even more astonished than Welensky"; he also was an old friend of Butler's. In Nyasaland Hastings Banda was at first "puzzled and suspicious". This confused response was exactly what the British government wanted, since it bought a little time to plan its next move. Acute observers outside the Federation had no doubts about the meaning of the appointment; a British journalist told Welensky that Butler had been brought in as an "undertaker", while Fenner Brockway gave him the dubious accolade of "Britain's de Gaulle".[8]

In late March, at Cub's suggestion, he and the Northern governors flew to London for talks with Butler. During an eight-day visit the party spent a weekend at Stanstead Hall, which must have evoked many memories for Cub; it also gave him the chance to visit Colchester and Layer de la Haye, where the Cross House was now occupied by tenants. The national press, hungry for any news connected with the Federation, dispatched reporters to the area; the best the *Daily Express* could do was to inform its readers that "Lord Alport . . . yesterday bought a bag of sweets at the village shop in Layer de la Haye". Cub's home base had never been far from his thoughts while he was in Africa, and the news of a decision to found a University of Essex in the area was one of the few cheering things he had heard; he had been calling for a university in the Colchester area since 1948. In a telegram to the local newspaper he proclaimed that it was "the most important thing to happen since the Emperor Claudius built his temple".[9]

The weekend at Stanstead included a visit to the nearby church of Greenstead Green for matins. For both Cub and Butler this was a place with poignant associations; Jock, Sydney and Butler's parents lay buried close together in the churchyard. During the service the dignitaries sat in the front pew, but soon wished they had chosen less prominent seats. After the third hymn the vicar began his sermon: as Cub later recalled,

> I suddenly woke up to the fact that the subject of his discourse was the problems and record of another colonial governor, named Pontius Pilate . . . I am sure that no members of his congregation ever listened more intently to any of the good vicar's sermons than we three did on that occasion – all struck by a guilty sense of fellow-feeling with the wretched Pilate in his dilemma.[10]

During the talks in London Pilate's sympathisers were relieved to hear that Butler "did not want to desert the Federation straight away, which would be a betrayal"; more exactly, as he admitted in the second meeting, there would be too many political problems if an early decision was taken. Throughout the meeting Cub advocated what he called a "composite solution"; Nyasaland should be given the right to secede, but this should be announced in tandem with similar permission for the two Rhodesias. While the territories decided on their next action there would be a transitional period in which the British government took "direct responsibility for certain federal functions, including defence"; a future form of association could be negotiated in this breathing-space. At one point in the second meeting Butler offered to announce this initiative before Hastings Banda arrived on a scheduled visit to London in May, but the suggestion was dropped.[11]

Cub at least felt that he had established the general principle that the British government should announce the secession of Nyasaland as part of a wider settlement, rather than dealing with that problem in isolation. Even so, from his point of view the main outcome of his brief trip was the "somewhat unattractive task" of telling Welensky of Butler's intention to announce that he "acknowledged" Banda's wish to secede from the Federation. By now it was clear to everyone that the existing form of association could not continue; the outstanding issues were those of timing and tactics. The British government knew that Welensky was seeking a new relationship between Northern and Southern Rhodesia, and thought that he only wanted to avoid being saddled with the responsibility for giving up Nyasaland. Butler's statement would be a holding move; it included yet another British commitment to the idea of some kind of association in Central Africa, and although the remarks about Nyasaland were intended to please Banda they stopped short of granting the right to secede. Instead, an advisory committee would examine the problem and report to Butler.[12]

Seeing things from this perspective Cub thought he had given Welensky exactly what he wanted at a meeting with federal ministers held on 13 April. According to Welensky's own account, Cub became "visibly indignant" when faced with criticism of Butler's proposal to appoint the advisory committee. Cub might have been "visibly indignant" to those in the room, but he was invisible to Welensky who was not present at this meeting; the Prime Minister fabricated his own side of the imaginary conversation from a letter which he wrote to Cub later that day. But the gist of their exchange is accurately reported in Welensky's book. Cub told the ministers that "My government has a responsibility which they cannot evade; and since you are taking this unconstructive line, they will have to make their own decisions".[13]

Unfortunately for Cub Welensky's priorities had changed while he was consulting with Butler in London. The federal election was turning into a fiasco, boycotted by almost everyone including the right-wing Rhodesian Front, an alliance put together in March under the leadership of Winston Field. Originally Welensky had sought a mandate to lead the Federation into a new series of negotiations, but with so many of his United Federal Party candidates unopposed he bitterly regretted his gamble. Instead of a contest between different political approaches the election would be a referendum on himself, and his best hope was to present voters with the image of a brave leader battling against the unscrupulous British. Conciliatory gestures from Butler had no place in this desperate strategy, which threw a new impediment between Cub and Welensky. Cub thought that Welensky was now playing the role of Samson, determined to cause the maximum destruction with little regard to his personal fate.[14]

The federal election took place on 27 April. The result was a humiliation for Welensky; the United Federal Party won 54 out of the 59 seats, but only 13,397 voters from a minuscule European-dominated electorate of 120,000 bothered to cast a vote. A Northern Rhodesian nationalist leader exulted at the news: "Hallelujah – Sir Roy has killed the Federation himself". A few pillars were certainly beginning to topple around Samson. Although Welensky coasted home in his constituency of Broken Hill, only 721 people voted for him. If, as he suspected, the British government wanted to allow Northern Rhodesia to secede along with Nyasaland – leaving him as a federal Prime Minister without a Federation to govern – the election had helped to clear their path. Butler could proceed with his statement, which was delivered to the British House of Commons on 8 May; three days later the Secretary of State flew in to Salisbury with his wife Mollie.[15]

Rab Butler's visit to the Federation in May 1962 was one of the oddest episodes in his long career. He was met by an African demonstration, and a cool reception from Europeans who now thought of him as the "liquidator" of Central Africa. When he left a fortnight later he had earned the honourable name of "Large Elephant" from African leaders, and retained the respect and affection of Welensky, who lamented years later that such an able minister had been handed "a stinking kettle of fish" by Macmillan. Remarkably, this public relations triumph was achieved without Rab giving anything of value to the people he met; Banda was told that he would have to wait for secession, and Welensky was so relieved that the Federation had survived the visit that he overlooked the lack of any firm promises for the future. Cub was heartened by his friend's success; he told Bill Deedes that the public responded to Rab because it made them feel that "he was not doctrinaire or defeatist and that he wished to help".[16]

During his visit Butler stayed with Cub at Mirimba House, and the relationship seemed to be fully restored on their shared understanding that partnership in Central Africa was desirable. There was a danger signal, though, in the good relationship struck up between Rab and Banda, who did not go so far as to praise the Secretary of State as a "Large Elephant" but rated him higher than Iain Macleod. Butler was certainly not "doctrinaire", but the trip made him more "defeatist" in his attitude to the Federation. Perhaps he was impressed by Banda's use of a surprising card; he threatened to resign from the leadership of his party unless he was given some concrete assurances of secession. Whitehall was now convinced that Banda was at heart a reliable figure in an unstable territory; his threat rekindled visions of a British Algeria. Cub had tried to arrange meetings with nationalist leaders in other territories, but Joshua Nkomo of the Zimbabwe African People's Union (ZAPU) refused; he had recently attacked the Southern Rhodesia constitution before a sub-committee of the UN, and thought that he could safely snub a mere British minister. UN hostility made it harder for Britain to contemplate letting Southern Rhodesia go it alone without radical change, while Banda's clever tactics pointed to early independence for Nyasaland; thus while Butler enjoyed his successful tour Cub's "composite approach" was seriously undermined.[17]

After returning to London Butler appointed a four-strong advisory team on Nyasaland; the group, led by Sir Roger Stevens of the

Foreign Office, included Cub's deputy David Scott. Macmillan had refused Butler's request that Burke Trend should be included; since Trend had written the 1959 report which started the unravelling process, Butler's attempt was a significant indication of the way his mind was now working. The advisers were intended to act as a revived Monckton Commission, and to put a more "objective" stamp on conclusions which would best suit the British government. Cub was clearly uneasy about the body from the start; on 12 June he sent a mild complaint to Butler, ostensibly because he lacked information about the advisers to pass on to Welensky and Whitehead, but really because he sensed that decisions were being made without his participation. On this occasion Butler was able to offer reassurance, but the renewed partnership between the two men was already under strain. In July Cub floated a detailed timetable for future developments, based on the assumption that Butler was still following the "composite approach"; significantly Butler could only reply that "I will bear in mind what you say", noting that plans had to remain fluid in advance of a report from the advisers, who had begun their work.[18]

July was another bad month for Butler; on the 13th (Friday) the Home Office was added to the lengthening list of positions taken from him. He would now be known as "First Secretary of State", and the unofficial title of "Deputy Prime Minister" was thrown in to guard against the possibility that this fresh humiliation would at last provoke his resignation. Butler satisfied his feelings by drafting a letter to Macmillan in which he protested that the new arrangements left him "out on an African limb". His biographer claims that this letter "exposed the streak of self-pity" in Butler's character, but having missed many chances to upset the government's apple-cart from a position of strength, for him to have done so on this occasion would have looked petty. There was already considerable panic in Downing Street – hence Macmillan's dramatic cabinet reshuffle ("The Night of the Long Knives") which also removed Cub's old friend Charles Hill from the government while bringing in Bill Deedes as Minister Without Portfolio to help with policy presentation. Butler had been undone by a desire to serve his country rather than himself; having chosen this honourable course he was right to stick to it, and his draft letter was the strongest protest he could make – it was a pointed reminder to Macmillan that they were actuated by different standards of conduct.[19]

Cub had been alerted to the smell of decay surrounding the British government by a prescient letter from his friend Brian Harrison which arrived earlier in the month. "We have lost our sense of purpose and idealism", Harrison wrote, "All around us our policies are beginning to come home to roost. This, of course, is the danger of being in power for so long". Surprisingly Cub made no reference to the reshuffle in his private letter of 18 July. Butler might have regarded his task as nothing more than "an African limb", but more than ever Cub was convinced that the problem of the Federation would be the major challenge of his own political life. After the first month of promise his old friend was proving to be no more helpful than Sandys had been. The prospect of a lasting breach between them loomed larger in August, when Cub despatched a 27-page letter repeating his arguments about the timetable for change in the Federation. He now gathered that Rab planned to announce the secession of Nyasaland at the start of a constitutional conference to be held in November, and rightly pointed out that this would kill off any chance of a "composite approach". Whether consciously or not, for the first time since he had first written to Butler as a student in 1932 he signed this letter with his full name. Butler picked up the hint, and followed suit in a reply which contained no concession to Cub's arguments. It closed with a request for advice in dealing with Welensky in a way which would preserve Butler's integrity: this, he wrote, "is vital". Years later readers of Butler's autobiography must have been puzzled by his decision to reprint this letter almost at full length, taking up two pages of a short book; by that time the master of double-meanings obviously hoped that the publication of the letter would "preserve his integrity" against allegations that Cub was not consulted properly at the time.[20]

This exchange of letters blew away Cub's happy illusion that he could exercise much influence over future developments. On 5 September he wrote that he understood and fully accepted Butler's views, but reserved the right to keep expressing his own. Two days later he brought up for the first time the question of leaving his post. Originally he had undertaken to serve until March 1963 with the idea that he might stay until early June at the latest, but he had realised for some time "that the natural break comes in July and that therefore if you wish me to do so, I would be very happy to stay on until the

beginning of August". Choosing his words carefully he reminded
Butler that by moving to Africa he had given up his "old line of
business"; he had been aware of the risk he was taking, but it was a
risk all the same. If Butler wanted to make an earlier change Cub
would understand, but if not he would appreciate a public announcement of the extension before Christmas.[21]

On the surface it might seem from this letter that in the absence of
any other weapons Cub had resorted to emotional blackmail in an
attempt to prise some kind of positive commitment from Butler.
Perhaps there was an element of this, but it took a curious form; he
was telling Butler that he possessed a more powerful weapon –
resignation – and that he was handing over this blunt instrument
unused. Always sensitive to subliminal messages, Butler was happy to
interpret Cub's letter as a formal act of disarmament. Assuring Cub in
a handwritten reply that "I have long understood your own personal
position", he acknowledged July or August 1963 as a provisional date
for his return, adding that "This letter is not intended to be an official
one to that effect" given the uncertainties about the Federation's
short-term future. He went on to say "how much we have valued
your sterling work and services", although after the exchanges of
August Cub must have known that in future he could expect to be
treated as little more than a titled messenger boy.[22]

Butler's political star might be fading, but there was still no chance
of equality in his relationship with Cub. This must have been particularly irksome to the latter, who recognised Butler's knowledge and
diplomatic skills but thought that when it came to the situation on the
ground in Africa he had the greater expertise. Even if they had been
strangers when Butler took over Central African policy Cub felt that
his advice should have been respected; instead it seemed that Butler
was taking advantage of their long friendship, and turning down
suggestions which he might have accepted from a different source.
The truth was more complicated; for obvious reasons Butler's priority
was a settlement which would be most acceptable to British and world
opinion, while Cub still felt a sense of personal mission which
prevented him from forming what Butler regarded as a realistic perspective on the future. Both men were aware of the reasons for their
disagreement, but after so many years of friendship any dispute
between them was sure to have a personal edge.

In October Butler's advisers reported, finding little hope of anything more than an economic association between any of the territories in Central Africa; unlike Cub, they recommended an early decision on Nyasaland's departure from the Federation. Cub did not at that stage have a copy of the report, which was submitted to ministers in London, but he knew through Scott the gist of its conclusions. He suggested to Butler that he might pay a brief visit home to discuss the next steps. At the end of the month he flew to London and made a final stand on behalf of the composite approach. Butler, however, was concerned that any more delay before secession might spark off serious trouble in Nyasaland. After several days of argument Cub returned to Salisbury, defeated once again. After seeing Welensky in private he was summoned to the federal cabinet meeting of 5 November, and read out a statement which he had drafted himself. Welensky later wrote that Cub read out the message with "great solemnity"; no doubt the word he used at the time was "pomposity", which best described Cub's manner when taking a line that he did not believe in. The most provocative phrase was a claim that Butler's decision did not "result from weakness in the face of pressure from Dr Banda or anyone else". The federal ministers knew of Butler's decision in advance, and were no doubt prepared for an artificial burst of anger against the unlucky messenger. But Cub was clearly protesting too much in his passage about Banda; the "hysterical and high-pitched denunciation of the British Government" which followed from one (normally placid) minister may even have been genuine. Cub "retired in a somewhat ruffled frame of mind".[23]

Cub had known from the outset that the "man on the spot" could end up being abused, but it was difficult to sit through a verbal assault brought on by a decision which he had strenuously opposed. When he visited Welensky on 7 November he knew that he could expect another round of kick-the-commissioner. According to Welensky, Cub claimed that the British government had not changed its goals: it still wanted "the closest possible links between the two Rhodesias and some sort of economic association with Nyasaland". To Welensky it no longer mattered what the British wanted; he could only see that their ultimate objectives were at variance with their policies. His response to Cub's well meaning remarks was to hurl against him every accusation which came to mind, dredging up Duncan Sandys' gaffe about Britain having lost the will to govern. Cub replied that Welensky "simply did not understand the British mentality and that Mr Sandys' statement was typical of the British tendency towards exaggerated self-depreciation". In the tension of the moment he forgot the usual explanation, that Sandys' words had been taken out of context.[24]

Reflecting on the incident two days later, Cub compared Welensky to "a wounded buffalo". Previously he had been attracted by a different animal image provided by one of Welensky's advisers:

the Prime Minister is a youngish bull-dog surrounded by old, toothless bull-dogs, who run about barking and growling and encouraging him to rush out into the street and bite the first person he sees. It's just an unfortunate coincidence that usually the first person he sees is you, High Commissioner.

Cub was right to notice a change in Welensky in early November, and probably attributed it to a fresh blow for the Federation. While he was in London an election in Northern Rhodesia produced a very narrow lead for Welensky's UFP over Kaunda's UNIP. Some seats remained unfilled and were to be decided in December; these were unlikely to fall to the UFP, which looked sure to require a coalition partner if it was to have any say in the new government. The party holding the balance of power was another nationalist grouping, the Northern Rhodesian African National Congress.[25]

Welensky's mood cannot have been helped by an election result which threatened to leave both Nyasaland and Northern Rhodesia with anti-federalist assemblies. But the new hostility detected by Cub had a more potent and personal source. Unknown to him, while Cub was travelling back from London Butler had written to Welensky, explaining that he had "called the High Commissioner home in order that he could take back to you our latest government thinking on the many issues involved"; in a fateful moment he added that "Alport has been able to influence our deliberations. I will not go into detail here but leave him to explain".[26]

Why did Butler claim that Cub had influenced government decisions, when he knew that his advice had been rejected? Perhaps he was trying to give a boost to Cub's credibility with the federal ministers – or, more likely, to present a plausible explanation for Cub's sudden journey to London, which had aroused Welensky's suspicions. Whatever his motives, Butler's remarks ensured that Welensky and his cabinet would hold Cub responsible for a decision on Nyasaland which he had spent the last few months trying to resist. At his meeting with Cub on 7 November Welensky referred to Butler's letter and accused him of going beyond his remit as High Commissioner. Instead of spelling out his real part in events Cub gave a flustered response which Welensky had no means of de-coding. The minutes of the meeting record that Cub "was satisfied that what he advised [i.e. the opposite of what Butler had decided] had been in the best interests both of the Federation and of Britain. His conscience was clear. If the need arose he would defend himself from public criticism in whatever way the circumstances might require".[27]

For Cub the situation was already farcical but worse was to follow. Having infuriated Welensky with his decision on Nyasaland Butler was now having second thoughts. Disorder in Southern Rhodesia during August and September had led Sir Edgar Whitehead to ban Nkomo's ZAPU. For over a year Whitehead's "Build a Nation" campaign had been making some progress towards a genuine multiracial society, and Africans were encouraged to register for a vote under the new constitution. Whitehead decided to call an early election for December in the hope that his party could attract sufficient support from moderate Africans to take the sting out of continuing attacks from the UN and local nationalists. Before the election he flew to New York to address the UN Assembly, and believed that this intervention had improved the image of his country. He held talks in London on his way home, and pressed for a delay in the announcement of Nyasaland's right to secede from the Federation. Whitehead was worried about the effect of such an announcement on the Southern Rhodesian election; although he now regarded the political connection with the Northern territories as an obstacle to his liberal programme, he recognised that Southern Rhodesian extremists on both sides would gain support if Dr Banda were to be given all he wanted at that crucial time. Whitehead faced a considerable challenge from Winston Field's Rhodesian Front; on the other side he was threatened by an African boycott of the election, encouraged by Nkomo and backed by a campaign of intimidation.

The situation in Southern Rhodesia was the main reason for Cub's opposition to an early announcement on Nyasaland. But having lost his battle and faced up to Welensky's anger he should have left the matter alone. In *The Sudden Assignment* he claimed that he merely sent a telegram after his meeting with the federal cabinet, urging Butler to carry through his new policy. It is possible that such a telegram was sent, but it does not appear in the relevant government file. This contains a copy of another telegram which Cub mentioned in his book without saying exactly when he sent it. In this message he asked "for discretion to act as might seem most appropriate" after the "explosion" which he expected to follow the announcement. On reading the telegram, David Scott had gasped "My God, this will give them kittens". It did: a meeting of senior ministers was convened in London to discuss the telegram in the context of Whitehead's plea for delay.[28]

On the evening of 9 November Cub was told to stand by for two emergency telegrams. As he wrote later:

> At 9.35pm the messages were delivered. I recollect that the one addressed to me began by saying that the decision which it conveyed would cause me 'some surprise'. It then said that it had been decided to postpone the announcement on Nyasaland until just before Parliament rose for the Christmas recess at the end of December. I was invited to inform Welensky of this decision without delay.

In his memoir Cub wrote that his alarmist telegram might have been a mistake. As it affected his position as High Commissioner, it would be better described as a monumental blunder. His fears about Southern Rhodesia were quite genuine, but from his own point of view the time for extreme language had passed once he received the instruction to inform Welensky of Butler's decision. Now Cub had helped to get the decision he wanted over Nyasaland – too late to salvage his relationship with Welensky, who could only think that Cub's arguments for an early announcement had been overruled at the last moment by his masters in Whitehall. On the next day Cub dragged himself off to tell Welensky about the new twist. The federal Prime Minister was delighted with what he took to be a victory for his own arguments; in the heat of the previous days he had threatened to withhold his support from Whitehead, but this would have been counter-productive even by Samson's standards. Now he could go and speak on Whitehead's behalf in Bulawayo (as he had always intended) without any loss of face. He arrived at the meeting later than advertised: "For this he invited the audience, a little sourly, to blame the British High Commissioner".[29]

Cub was left to reflect on "a problem which was both political and personal. . . . How long can a political representative tender advice on issues of considerable importance and, seeing his advice regularly rejected, continue to serve in his post?". His duties were increasingly stressful, and this was beginning to affect his home life. One morning when his son would not eat his breakfast he had delivered a particularly sharp and undeserved reprimand. Young Edward innocently asked "Are you having more trouble with the government, daddy?". Cub might have replied with a question of his own: "Which government do you mean, son?"[30]

There was a good deal to be said for resignation, but, as Cub told the British Ambassador to South Africa, the Nyasaland affair was so complicated that his departure would be "quite inexplicable from the public point of view". Besides, Cub's sense of duty was at stake; he was expressing a life-long view when he told David Scott that "I don't believe in resigning; if they want to get rid of you let them sack you". Ironically, although Cub and Butler were now causing each other deep irritation they were both ensnared by their shared principles of public service. Just as Butler had consoled himself in July by drafting a letter of protest to Macmillan, Cub tried to alleviate his own frustrations in a letter to his old friend. Having rehearsed recent events with brutal clarity, he wrote:

> while in other circumstances I think that I would have been justified and, indeed, compelled to offer you my resignation, at the same time there are considerations of loyalty to the Prime Minister and his government, of which I have been a member, and to you personally after nearly 30 years of friendship. I think, however, that I should let you know that if you feel that it would be of advantage to the government and in the public interest that someone else should replace me as British representative here in

Salisbury, I would not regard this as a breach of any agreement there might be between HMG and myself as to the length of the tenure of my present office.[31]

Butler's reply was prompt; he had read Cub's letter "with great care since I attach so much importance to our working together in what we both described as a great adventure – probably the greatest adventure of our lives – during your short visit home" (evidently Butler had not shared with Cub his belief that the job was nothing more than "an African limb"). Of course there should be no question of a change, and he would not even discuss the matter with the Prime Minister. Cub later wrote that this "generous and reassuring letter . . . found me in a somewhat unreceptive frame of mind so that I did not perhaps draw from it the consolation which I now realise it was sincerely intended to convey". In fact Bulter's words of "consolation" were restricted to the familiar remarks about Cub's excellent service; buried amongst all the praise was a reminder that although the Nyasaland statement had been postponed after all, the future of the territory would still be addressed in isolation from the problems of the Federation as a whole. In short, Cub's "composite approach" would not be revived.[32]

The strange logic which had governed events in the Federation since the Monckton Report was now driving it faster towards dissolution. Butler felt that the Nyasaland conference, which closed on 23 November, was a success – by which he meant that the British government had escaped without serious embarrassment. On the day the conference ended Cub tried for over an hour to dissuade Welensky from despatching a telegram to Butler which included a threat to "use every means available" in his fight to save the Federation. Welensky assured Cub that this was not a hint that force would be used; indeed he had already told Butler that he would never contemplate an armed clash with Britain. But the British government was jumpy, and afflicted by a guilty conscience as it moved to wind up the experiment it had started so recently.[33]

Having chosen to stay on his uncomfortable perch, Cub, as so often, decided that he should make the best of it. In mid-November he had held talks with Kenneth Kaunda and Harry Nkumbula of the ANC. His conclusion, that after the second round of voting in

Northern Rhodesia there would be a coalition between these two nationalist parties, was borne out by the new elections on 12 December. Cub managed to dredge some hope out of the result, feeling that Kaunda had matured as a leader and that at least the new government "would not have the dangerously monolithic character which had been achieved so rapidly in Africa elsewhere". He was also encouraged by clear signs that having secured his political aims Banda was now ready for constructive talks about economic links between the territories.[34]

Understandably, the desire to find some cause for optimism had begun to colour Cub's judgements. Power was slipping away from Welensky and his colleagues; if Cub wanted to provide constructive service for the future of the area he needed to get on terms with the emerging power-brokers and to translate whatever they might say into a message of hope. He assumed that at least one of the familiar faces would remain; although the ZAPU-inspired boycott of the Southern Rhodesian elections had succeeded and only 20 per cent of qualified Africans registered to vote, Cub still predicted a victory for Whitehead.[35] But whereas he had for some time expected a transfer of power to nationalists in the Northern territories, the political prospects in Southern Rhodesia were far more uncertain – and Whitehead's survival was crucial to the cause of multi-racial politics in Central Africa.

Cub had tried to shore up Whitehead's position earlier in the year by helping to negotiate a substantial British loan for Southern Rhodesia, but his anxiety as the election approached led him to make the most dubious suggestion of his whole political career. Back in October he had asked Butler if the British government would provide "£20,000–£25,000" for Whitehead's election fund, to compensate for the fact that the Rhodesian Front had raised a much more substantial war-chest. Butler replied that "I am personally most reluctant to embark upon this operation. Even assuming it were kept fully "watertight" I sh[ou]ld not feel happy about it". Apart from the question of personal integrity which always carried so much weight with Butler, the consequences if the news leaked out would have been disastrous both for Whitehead and for the British. Cub's telegram may have helped to undermine Butler's trust in his judgement, just as the First Secretary was deciding on the best strategy for dealing with the Federation.[36]

Whitehead's election was held two days after the Northern Rhodesian poll, on 14 December. Cub told Butler that "provided all goes well at today's election I think we can all relax over Christmas", but it was not to be. The result was an overall majority of five seats for the Rhodesian Front. As Cub remarked, a different outcome might have been achieved with only a slight shift of votes, "but this fact was quite immaterial". The Front "was a party ruled largely by emotion, prejudice and narrow self-interest"; its new popularity among Europeans marked the end of liberal politics in the area, even if Whitehead had clung on to power. As usual Cub adapted himself to new realities, finding it easy to work with Field and even convincing himself that his deputy, Ian Smith, was "a quiet-mannered, pleasant person". But Smith symbolised the failure of moderate Europeans to hold their precarious advantage of 1953; before his lurch into right-wing politics Smith had been a prominent member of the Southern Rhodesian branch of the UFP, the party of Welensky and Whitehead. The British had set up the Federation as the best way of dealing with Southern Rhodesia. Many factors were involved in Whitehead's defeat, but undoubtedly the most important of these was British policy towards constitutional change in the federal area. With the arrival in power of the Rhodesian Front, Africans in Southern Rhodesia would soon be worse off than they had been before the Federation.[37]

For some time the main purpose of the federal cabinet had been to make life as hot as possible for the British government; the fear that they would soon lose everything made them protest against the slightest erosion of the doomed federal structure. Events – the remorseless enemy of political friendship – had driven Whitehead and Welensky far apart, but the latter regarded the Southern Rhodesian election as grim confirmation of his long-held belief that the British cared nothing for the inhabitants of Central Africa. As the Federation moved towards dissolution the opposing forces concentrated on the debates which surrounded its birth. Officials in the Federation pored over the minutes of meetings in search of evidence to support their argument that the Federation could not be dismantled without the consent of all the governments concerned; ministers and civil servants in Britain laboured to prove that this was a false interpretation.

Butler had still to make his announcement on Nyasaland. On the day before Whitehead's defeat Welensky wheeled out his biggest guns in preparation for an all-out attack if the result went the wrong way. Lords Salisbury, Chandos and Boyd visited Butler and pledged to use a debate in the Upper House to support the federal government's case. Even the ageing Lord Malvern, the first Prime Minister of the Federation, was imported to join the battle; his intended visit was supposed to be a secret, but his cover was blown when Cub met him by chance in the VIP lounge of Salisbury airport. When Whitehead's fate was known Welensky released his government's research into the history of the Federation as a White Paper, which contrasted the various stages of the British "betrayal" with the promises of 1953 and 1957.[38]

Welensky's offensive reached its climax on 19 December, the day on which Butler made his long-delayed statement to the Commons. Cub attended the federal Assembly to hear the Prime Minister's pre-emptive strike. As he later recalled, Welensky's speech

> was full of familiar invective. I did my best to remain motion-less, expressionless, so as to give no hint of my personal reactions to curious onlookers or to a vigilant press. What does a diplomatic representative do when he hears his country accused of treachery and deceit? To walk out seemed a trifle melodra-matic, to remain unmoved would smack almost of disloyalty.

His solution was a compromise; he "stalked out of the Stranger's Gallery" as Welensky finished his speech. With Butler's permission he called a press conference that evening and replied to Welensky's allegations; this, rather than the Prime Minister's speech or the on-slaught of his elderly shock troops in the British House of Lords, domi-nated the coverage by federal newspapers. When the debate resumed on the following day Welensky plunged into deeper controversy by revealing that British troops had assembled at Nairobi airport to enforce Macleod's policy back in February 1961; again Cub won the major headlines with a robust reply, which included the scarcely relevant allegation that Welensky had always preferred the idea of an amalgamation of the two Rhodesias to the existing federal structure.[39]

Reflecting on this period in his memoir, Cub wrote that

> The stronger and more widespread became the criticisms of the country I represented, the more powerful became my sense of

loyalty and patriotism. In England one has no difficulty in seeing the mistakes and weaknesses of British policy, but a couple of years abroad, subjected to all manners of taunts and sneers, turns even the most phlegmatic Englishman into a passionate patriot.

This reads like an expression of regret for actions taken in the heat of the moment, when his judgement was affected by the constant stream of recriminations; Cub later recalled that on one off-duty occasion during these few days in November 1962 he became seriously drunk for the only time in his life. In hindsight he could admit that some of Welensky's attacks were borne out by his own knowledge; the Nairobi incident, for example, was not a figment of Welensky's overheated imagination. Cub also questioned the wisdom of the White Paper which the British published in February 1963 as a reply to Welensky's story of betrayal; this undignified document "seemed to be intended to demonstrate that either no pledges [on secession] had been given; or, if they had HMG had not broken them; or if it had, it had a right to do so anyway". Back in London his misgivings were echoed by Burke Trend, who concluded that the record was "not entirely satisfactory from the government's point of view". But as the confrontation reached its climax there was no room for scepticism; Cub was a servant of the British government, and therefore, as Welensky might have put it, no longer "one of us".[40]

Welensky had regarded Cub with new animosity ever since Butler's misguided letter of early November; during another row at the end of that month he interpreted a remark of Cub's as further proof that the policy of the British government was covered with his finger-prints. After the clashes of 19 and 20 December rumours circulated that Cub was about to be declared *persona non grata*. In a letter to Lord Colyton, who as Henry Hopkinson had been a Colonial Office minister until 1955, Welensky revealed the extent to which Butler's letter had affected his thinking as he sought an appropriate target for his anger. He told Colyton that Cub, "to a very large extent, is responsible for what has occurred here . . . My cabinet almost to a man, hate the sight of him and, of course, the general public think him extremely pompous". In his sympathetic reply Colyton deplored Cub's recent behaviour, adding that Welensky would have been justified in asking for his immediate recall. Colyton was particularly bitter at the time, having joined the abortive House of Lords attack on Butler. When David Scott was researching for his memoirs in the early 1980s he came across Colyton's letter, and drew attention to what he rightly considered to be "a fairly remarkable piece of advice" in the published volume without naming the author. Even Colyton must have been abashed in the following March, when during a visit to the Federation he was taken ill and visited by the sympathetic Cub, who knew nothing of his treachery.[41]

Having offered Butler the chance to sack him Cub could hardly object if he was sent packing by the other side. His position with the federal government was clearly untenable, and life was being made even more unpleasant in other respects. He took his telephone off the hook every night to avoid being woken up by spiteful callers, and was advised to take down the British flag from his residence in case it attracted gunfire. Personal abuse only made Cub more determined to defy his critics, but now the physical safety of his family was a matter of serious concern. It was something of an anti-climax when Welensky issued public denials that Cub was to be declared *persona non grata*. To Colyton Welensky claimed that Cub was so unpopular that his continued presence in Salisbury was an asset to federal ministers in their campaign against the British.[42]

With exquisite timing the figure of Moise Tshombe now re-emerged on the stage. On Christmas Eve Cub heard of new fighting in Katanga; Tshombe's supporters had shot down a UN helicopter, and retaliatory action forced the rebel leader to flee into Northern Rhodesia. After consultations with Alec Home Cub arranged for Tshombe to be given a guarantee of safety if he returned to Elisabethville. By early February the UN was in control of Katanga, and Tshombe exiled himself to Paris. The new Katangan outbreak helped to bring a partial thaw in the relationship between Cub and Welensky, who were able to agree on the handling of this issue. Yet Cub had to apologise to Butler; he, rather than Home, should have been consulted about Tshombe's flight to Northern Rhodesia, but he was on holiday when the trouble began. Home sent a warm note of thanks for Cub's help in defusing the situation, noting that he had "never dealt with a more complicated situation or with more hopelessly incompetent people"; he closed with the parrot-formula that he hoped "something federal" could be saved from the Central African experiment.[43]

On 18 January 1963 Butler left London for a planned visit to the Federation. Given the recent furore his decision to go ahead with the trip required great courage, but the mood he left behind in London was equally grim after General de Gaulle vetoed British membership of the EEC on 14 January. Butler went through the ritual of talking to Welensky before departing for Nyasaland, which gave him a warm reception, and Northern Rhodesia where Kaunda's supporters pressed him for an early decision on the secession of their territory. While Butler was in the North Welensky wrote to Lord Salisbury, blaming Cub for the "somewhat strained atmosphere" that greeted the First Secretary in the federal capital and claiming that Cub had only been appointed because Sandys wanted rid of him. "Alport", Welensky wrote, "is behaving in a very strange manner . . . he senses the dislike of him by all sections of the community here". Despite his bitterness Welensky had asked Butler when Cub's duties would end, instead of demanding his instant recall; greatly to his credit, Butler replied in the terms of his informal promise – that Cub would leave in "July or August". Welensky replied "that that was far too long . . . outside of the fact that he no longer enjoys any personal relationship with me – if enjoyment is the word in those circumstances – I don't think he's doing your government any good". After further reflection Butler informed Welensky that he was thinking of "removing Alport much sooner". On 4 March the federal cabinet discussed Cub's position, and decided that further representations should be made to London. Eventually it was agreed that he should return at the beginning of June. Welensky probably interpreted this as a victory for himself, but this was the date which Cub and Butler had envisaged before their correspondence of the previous September and represented a three-month extension of the period agreed with Duncan Sandys.[44]

Cub's "sudden assignment" was coming to a sorry end, but the Federation was dying and there was little more for him to do. The looming nightmare was now the prospect that Southern Rhodesia would make an illegal declaration of independence; Britain was not prepared to relinquish its remaining powers without extensive reforms, and with a right-wing government in Salisbury Whitehead's "Build a Nation" strategy was finished. Europeans in Southern Rhodesia noticed that South Africa had prospered since cutting its links with Britain in 1961; its successful defiance (and its treatment of an African majority) looked increasingly attractive, particularly to recent immigrants.

Both Cub and Butler were on friendly terms with Winston Field, but like Welensky this genial farmer was far more moderate than the majority of his supporters. A delegation from Southern Rhodesia visited London in March – part of a succession of awkward guests who made these days "some of the most laborious and painful" of Butler's career. The result was a stalemate; Butler laid down conditions for independence which the Southern Rhodesians would not accept. Kaunda and the Northern Rhodesians arrived on 24 March; Butler saw that they were far too interested in an independent Zambia to consider economic association with their southern neighbour, and a political connection was out of the question. Welensky and his federal colleagues were the third group to enter Butler's office; on the 29th they were told that "any territory must be allowed to secede if it wished", and Butler issued a public statement to that effect. As Butler's advisers had suggested, there would be a conference, preferably in Africa, to discuss what happened next; while they had hoped that at least some kind of deal could be struck between the two Rhodesias this now seemed a forlorn hope. Even that would leave no room for a federal government. After providing a record of these discussions with Butler in March, Welensky's published account of the Federation jumps to the official dissolution in December 1963.[45]

Cub continued to look on the bright side as far as Central Africa was concerned, but his own future was becoming a concern. In early March he heard from Bill Deedes, who reported that "No one I have spoken with has anything but sympathy with and praise for your own handling of all this. If you have not got the amount of kudos I think you should have got, it is because Central Africa is thoroughly off the boil in Parliament now". The implications of de Gaulle's veto were still being digested; a fortnight earlier Butler had told Cub that "the breakdown in Brussels has produced a wave of depression" in the Conservative Party. Both Butler and Deedes promised to do all they could to help Cub in his search for employment. Butler explored the possibility of another job in the commonwealth, but (unsurprisingly, perhaps) drew a blank, and there was even an abortive suggestion that Cub might return to work for the party's Central Office. It was difficult to see what use there might be for an unemployed ex-High

Commissioner. As usual, Cub was forced to sustain himself with the philosophy of Mr Micawber.[46]

In his last months at Mirimba House Cub was mainly concerned with preparing for the conference which would wind up the Federation and persuading the various governments to attend it. The most difficult problem was to coax Winston Field into turning up; without a Southern Rhodesian delegation the conference would be futile, and Field had given strong indications that he would use this advantage to prise from the British a promise of immediate independence. Matters which would have been quite trivial in happier circumstances, such as finding a replacement for the Federation's Governor-General Earl Dalhousie, occupied much of Cub's time as Welensky was now keen to read deep meanings into every decision of the British government. As tempers stretched in the dying days of the "great adventure" this question provoked new friction between Cub and Butler. Welensky complained that he had not been consulted on Dalhousie's replacement, and Butler sent a handwritten note to Cub suggesting that he had not followed his instructions. In his reply Cub was forced to point out that while he had kept to Butler's script Dalhousie had leaked the government's decision to Welensky in advance. With grim satisfaction he treated his old mentor to a lecture: "I hope by now that the situation is clear but in case it is not, I will go over the main points again". Butler hastened to assure Cub that "nothing in my previous letters or telegrams was intended as anyway a criticism of your handling of the matter". There were no more collisions; the old friends now agreed on the best way to handle their government's damage-limitation exercise, and the official files show that Butler invariably took Cub's advice throughout these final months. In his memoirs he paid tribute to Cub's "assiduity and dogged sense . . . of sticking to the last".[47]

In Cub's account of his last period in the Federation only one incident is recounted with any zest. On 3 February, after leaving Butler at the airport, he and Rachel set off on a 30-mile journey for lunch at a cattle ranch. Rachel said that she "felt like having an adventure", and they waded across a river near their destination rather than risking the car. On the way home they tried to repeat their successful crossing, but the current was more powerful and Rachel fell in. With the help of their guide they all reached the other bank of the river, but

Rachel was soaking and decided "as there was no one about, to take off most of her clothes" which she hung from the car window. They set off again in the car, only to encounter another swollen river, in the middle of which the vehicle stalled. Cub got out and attempted a push-start; instead he slipped and fell into the water. They had to be rescued by an African fisherman who helped to pull the car out of the water. Assisted by local villagers they restarted the engine, "and with Rachel's lingerie still floating provocatively in the evening breeze we proceeded on our way".[48]

Obviously Cub wanted to enliven his final chapter with an amusing incident, but the undignified end to Rachel's "adventure" suggests a symbolic, if unconscious significance in his treatment of the episode. The last few days of Cub's residence in Salisbury were taken up with farewell dinners and the cocktail parties (or "sundowners") which had occupied so many evenings. He had no desire to stay on, but leaving filled him with more than a sense of personal failure. He realised

> that with the end of the Federation would end, to all intents and purposes, the long adventure of the British in Africa . . . the era of constructive statesmanship, of nation-building, of planting in Africa the ideas and inspiration which the British people had evolved for themselves over so many generations and which had already transformed so much of the continent from the helpless chaos of the past – that was finished and perhaps for ever.

In fact, the "adventure" had ended with Suez, at the latest. After 1956 Britain had residual responsibilities, but no real power; this meant that even if policy-makers had any ideals left their decisions could only be driven by expediency.[49]

The Alport family left Salisbury on 7 June 1963, amid the tears of the school-children of Mirimba and songs from the women of Harare township with whom Rachel had worked. The whole of the High Commission staff were at the station to see them off, though it was conspicuous that none of the political or official figures with whom Cub had negotiated for two difficult years took the trouble to attend. Just three days before Cub finished his assignment John Profumo, Macmillan's Secretary of State for Defence, had been summoned back from a holiday in Italy to resign from his post, having lied to the House of Commons. The inquests occupied Parliament for some time, and London was far too preoccupied with rumour to notice Cub's arrival, even though the Bill to dissolve the Federation had its second reading on 17 June.[50]

Cub returned to Britain in relative obscurity, but in the context of Central African politics his departure could not have happened at a more intriguing moment. In *The Sudden Assignment* Cub wrote that by the beginning of June he was "satisfied" that the winding-down conference could go ahead. Macmillan had privately conceded that if Winston Field refused to attend the conference and made a unilateral bid for independence there was nothing that the British could do about it, but this would prove to the world that his government's policy had failed. On the other hand it was most unlikely that the Rhodesian Front would offer anything more than cosmetic improvements to the constitution, which meant that if Britain gave independence to Southern Rhodesia the commonwealth would break up. The only way forward was to engage in clever diplomacy while hoping that something would turn up. The sense of panic in Whitehall now that the full implications of the federal break-up were at last becoming clear was reflected in a draft letter from Butler to Field which referred to a "common objective . . . to secure independence for Southern Rhodesia as soon as possible after the final dissolution of the Federation".[51] On Cub's advice a more sensible (and vague) form of words was included in the final draft; he also pointed out that Britain could have a bargaining chip in the fact that Field was over-confident about the continuation of economic links between the two countries even if he made an illegal declaration of independence, and suggested that Butler could invite Field to London to make this point. Butler acted on his old friend's advice, and during the London talks refused to give Field any guarantees for the future.[52]

On the day before Cub slipped away from Southern Rhodesia Field returned from London. He astonished the federal cabinet and his own Southern Rhodesian colleagues by announcing that he would attend the conference after all, despite the tough stance of the British. To the hard-liners in Salisbury it seemed that Field had thrown away his final card by agreeing to attend on this basis. When Albert Robinson, the federal High Commissioner in London, met Butler to discuss the situation the First Secretary of State "literally danced round the table" in his joy at the *coup*. The partnership between Cub and Butler had lasted more than a quarter of a century, and when Winston Field appeared at the Victoria Falls conference in June 1963 it bore its final fruit.[53] But Cub had only helped to shore up the situation; he had no chance before the end of his tour of duty to contribute to a long-term solution. Victoria Falls was just the end of one chapter in the Rhodesian story, and he would have a part to play in the next one.[54]

Chapter Nine

A Freelance Diplomat

Cub's fears about his employment prospects were confirmed when he completed his journey home. He lunched with Butler and saw Macmillan in Downing Street, but, as he delicately put it, "my political friends were, on the whole, more concerned with their own survival than with helping me". The idea that he might return as a cabinet minister had been floated by the *Manchester Guardian* in November 1962, but only to prove to its anti-Conservative readers that Macmillan was desperately short of options – there were too many titled people in his government already. In one of Cub's obituaries it was claimed that he expected to be made Lord Chancellor on his return; evidently the source for this story was unacquainted with Cub's sense of humour. In 1963 no pension arrangements existed for ex-MPs, and Cub's unorthodox career allowed the CRO to refuse him the financial help due to diplomats after service overseas. A visit to the under-secretary responsible for public appointments was fruitless; his contacts in banking and business could do nothing either. He received one offer, from a subsidiary of the mining company Lonrho, which was buying influence and cheap assets in Central Africa while other investors fled from the area. Having disliked what he heard of the company's activities Cub rejected the idea; Duncan Sandys, Hastings Banda and even Roy Welensky proved to be less resistant to the blandishments of Tiny Rowland.[1]

It seemed to Cub that, having been an active politician all of his life, he was suddenly cut adrift without skills of any market value. This was unduly self-critical; as more recent ex-ministers have found, political experience is very useful in the boardroom, and finding a niche there is largely a matter of timing. Cub was identified with a governing party which looked to be heading for the rocks – and with a political experiment in Africa which was clearly bound for the same destination. He had three children to educate and a substantial house to maintain. His only resource was the small expense allowance which he earned through attendance at the House of Lords. If his financial position did not improve he knew that he would have to sell his beloved Cross House.

In his predicament Cub drew once again on the support of his family and his own resilient character. Throughout his political life unemployment had been the social problem which most concerned him, and he also felt that it would be beneficial to bring home to himself the reality of his plight. He went to a Labour Exchange "somewhere in Holborn" and applied for an interview. He discussed his position with the manager, who was astonished that a peer of the realm should ask for employment advice; all he could suggest was that Cub should use "the old boy network", but that had already failed his visitor. Cub later recalled that "sitting in that unemployment bureau gave me some idea of the frustration and helplessness felt by those out of work".[2]

Fortunately there was one way for Cub to keep himself occupied while he waited for something to turn up. During his stay in the Federation he had kept in sporadic contact with his old PPS, Keith Joseph. In October 1961 Joseph became a Minister of State at the Board of Trade, and Cub wrote to congratulate him. In his reply Joseph noted the troubles which Cub had encountered in his dealings with Welensky and Tshombe, and consoled him with the thought that "you certainly must be collecting plenty of material for your autobiography!". The idea of writing an account of his time in the Federation might have crossed Cub's mind when he took up the post; after all, he had written about so many of his previous experiences. The interview with Welensky in November 1962, when he spoke of defending his actions regardless of the circumstances, indicates that the suggestion became a settled plan once things had gone irretrievably wrong. Cub's father Cecil would have resigned at that point and gone public as soon as he could; Cub tried to do his job for as long as he was needed, reinforced by the knowledge that he would tell his tale when it was prudent to do so.[3]

Cub was an experienced author and he had a strong motive to unburden himself. Even so, *The Sudden Assignment* – originally drafted as *The Dream that Faded* – took at least a year to complete, and was not published until May 1965. He felt that "a memoir should be written close as possible to the events which it describes and yet not so near that the emotions and prejudices which they aroused in the mind of the writer distort his perspective". This advice is helpful for those who want to produce a readable text, but inappropriate if the main purpose is money-making. Cub was beaten to the punch by Welensky, whose *4000 Days* caused some embarrassment to the British with its creative quotations from official documents. But Welensky proved Cub's point about "emotion and prejudices"; his book fell between the stools of sorrow and anger. The ex-Prime Minister had fired his most dangerous shots in his White Paper of December 1962; now he seemed like yesterday's man. Events had moved quickly after Cub's departure; the Victoria Falls conference of June 1963 had gone very well for the British, and after the break-up of the Federation both Nyasaland and Northern Rhodesia received their independence as planned. Having allowed their policy to be driven by the Northern territories since the Devlin Report, the British were now obsessed by Southern Rhodesia. Butler clearly regarded Winston Field and his "cowboy cabinet" as soft touches; according to Ian Smith, he promised immediate independence at a meeting which took place before the main conference, but put nothing in writing. Once the trick had been exposed Field was left vulnerable to right-wing accusations that he was a push-over for the British; in April 1964 he was toppled, and Smith replaced him.[4]

Like Welensky, Cub seemed to be a relic from the last Rhodesian crisis. By July 1965 his story had also lost topicality from the point of view of British politics. He had guessed that the next general election would be held in the autumn of 1963, but for once his gift for political prophecy let him down. His conversation with Macmillan in July was interrupted by a telephone call bringing news that a nuclear test-ban treaty had been signed in Moscow, but the year of the Profumo scandal brought no other cheering news for the Conservative Party. Macmillan's attempt to steer through to better times was halted by illness on the eve of his party conference in October; he resigned, and after the very public battle to succeed him Alec Home was pushed forward as the candidate least likely to upset the already leaking boat. Cub's old colleagues Iain Macleod and Enoch Powell encouraged Butler to make one last stand, but Rab had no stomach for the fight and accepted the post of Foreign Secretary from Home. Macmillan had kept him away from this job, which he had always coveted; it proved to be the last of his cabinet appointments.

Cub, who had once offered to run the party for Butler, watched the unfolding drama without making contact with any of the participants; although some kind of consultation was held with Conservative peers, there is no indication that his opinion was asked. Had he remained in the Commons – as a minister or back-bencher – his views would have commanded respect, because he had a strong connection with all of the possible candidates except Quintin Hogg (the once and future Lord Hailsham, whose chances were scuppered because of his alleged "showmanship" at the 1963 party conference). Presumably Cub would have spoken up for Butler, despite his worries that his old friend was not a suitable captain for troubled times. Much as Cub liked Iain Macleod he had a privileged insight into the enmity he had aroused, and Cub had never felt close to the other candidates from his political generation, Reginald Maudling and Edward Heath. He regarded Home as a man of integrity, but thought it a mistake to replace a Highlander with a Scottish Laird; Home was unknown to the electorate, and despite his virtues he was an unlikely man to lead Britain in a period of rapid modernisation. When Home finally called the election in October 1964 the voters ended thirteen years of Conservative rule, but the result was close and Cub was not alone in thinking that Butler's cross-party popularity might have led to a narrow victory despite all the difficulties faced by the Tories.

Soon after the election Duncan Sandys received a draft copy of *The Sudden Assignment*. Sandys told Cub that the book was "most absorbing. Your crisp, clear style makes it easy and interesting to read". His placid response was fairly surprising, since Cub had used his opening chapter to make his feelings plain by mentioning Sandys' speech on housing which had provoked the formation of "One Nation" back in 1950. Sandys observed that he had "no recollection of this speech but, whatever I may have said, I hope you will not feel it necessary to focus criticism upon it after all this long time". In the published version of Cub's book the offending front-bench spokesman is left unnamed. Cub also removed a sentence describing his argument with Sandys after the latter admitted to Welensky that Britain had lost the will to govern, and toned down his account of Sandys' verbal slip.[5]

Another interested reader prior to publication was Rab Butler. More than a quarter of a century after he had read the proofs of *A National Faith* during the Geneva conference, he looked through *The Sudden Assignment* to see how it might affect his reputation. His main objection was raised against the inclusion of Cub's "resignation" letter from November 1962. After a meeting between the two Cub agreed that the letter should not be reprinted verbatim, but insisted on presenting a summary of its contents. Rab agreed that Cub had "every justification in preserving your integrity which we all so deeply respect", but regretted that "the book should appear to create a division between us"; in truth, he regretted that the book should appear at all. "With so much trouble in the world", he wrote, "one does not wish to quarrel with one's friends".[6]

In fact Butler was referring to a "quarrel" which had already taken place; their relationship could not recover from the strains of Central Africa, and Butler was only concerned that there should be no public comment. He told Sir Saville Garner of the CRO that Cub was "obviously seeking to justify his own actions. It is a pity from my point of view that this difference of opinion should be brought out in public, but I do not see any means of stopping this". Butler had to wait until 1971, when his own memoir was published, for a chance to defend himself against the subtle criticisms contained in *The Sudden Assignment*.[7]

The subject-matter of Cub's book meant that it had to be checked for possible breaches of the Official Secrets Act. After being dispatched by Macmillan during "The Night of the Long Knives" both Lord Kilmuir (formerly David Maxwell-Fyfe) and Cub's old friend Charles Hill had recently published their memoirs; Kilmuir's book had ruffled feathers, and the literary critics at the CRO were on the alert. Naturally their private reflections on the book were covered by the same Whitehall rules of secrecy, and Cub only found out what they really thought when the documents were released in the mid 1990s. After reading Cub's synopsis one official remarked with truth that "it is difficult to see how far Lord Alport is likely to break the rules. If he doesn't [the book] will lose a lot of its bite". Cub would have been amused and flattered by the comments of his friend Garner who thought that "It is certainly an extremely lively account with many quite brilliant descriptive passages. His method is very direct but he is careful to make [it] clear that he is merely giving his personal impressions". Even so Garner felt that there was too much criticism of British policy in the book: "the last few chapters about the final phase are the most controversial and unwise". But he noted that Welensky had already come out with a much more damaging account; if *The Sudden Assignment* had "bite", Garner thought that most of the tooth-marks were left on Welensky. In the end Cub was only asked to make a few changes.[8]

Garner was right about Cub's style. Although he had written nothing of substance for a decade, Cub was sure of the kind of book he wanted to produce and his prose was fluent and authoritative. *The Sudden Assignment* is not always accurate in its details, but the broad picture is borne out by records which were unavailable to Cub at the time of writing; on his return from Africa he deposited with the CRO most of the documents connected to his work. The book was widely reviewed and generally welcomed, although it was attacked in the left-wing journal *Tribune* whose critic claimed that "most of us have already forgotten" that Cub was ever High Commissioner. Conor Cruise O'Brien, whose part in the Katanga crisis was recorded in Cub's most rancorous passages, strove for revenge in the *Observer* with a sneer at the expense of "a man emotionally bound to a dream of the past, to Kipling and Rider Haggard and the high imperial adventure of ruling justly and dangerously over dark peoples". Yet even O'Brien was forced to concede that "Lord Alport has written rather a good book".[9]

Few reviewers agreed with Garner's assessment that *The Sudden Assignment* was intended as a counter-blast to Welensky; indeed one suspects that Garner had used this argument to protect the book from the censors. If Cub had wanted to floor his old sparring partner he would not have rushed through his time at the CRO in a single chapter; Welensky, by contrast, had devoted more than two hundred pages to those years (1957–61), in the belief that they clinched his case against the British. Elspeth Huxley, who had served on the Monckton Commission, thought that Cub's inquest on the Federation had produced a verdict of death by natural causes; she wrote that "the problems were (and are) too big for the people", but that no one individual or government was to blame. From a different viewpoint John Connell noted that Cub and Welensky were now "reconciled" (in fact, Welensky was acknowledged for his help with the book); Connell used this as his springboard to reach the opposite conclusion from Garner. He defended Cub's own part in "this squalid episode", and claimed that "in the Central African Federation we, the British, suffered our nastiest defeat since the fall of Singapore in 1942 . . . we let down good people – our own people – and what we did still stinks in our nostrils". This was a caricature of Cub's message, but reading between the lines there was enough in *The Sudden Assignment* to make members of the previous British government feel uncomfortable. Garner had located the potential for damage when he noted that although ministers had hoped for "some continued association be-tween the two Rhodesias" up to March 1963, "Lord Alport is perfectly entitled to his view that the Nyasaland decision in December 1962 in fact spelt the end of Federation". In short, while Welensky had at-tacked the government on the score of integrity, presenting the federal break-up as the product of a deliberate design, Cub's account implied that his old colleagues had been far too incompetent to achieve the settlement they wanted. This point was missed by reviewers, pre-sumably because Cub had avoided direct criticism wherever pos-sible.[10]

Had *The Sudden Assignment* appeared at the time of UDI its real message might have been appreciated more widely. Even so sales were respectable, but Cub's financial outlook had brightened before he submitted the final draft. A chance meeting with a former constituent who had become a stockbroker brought the suggestion that Cub might become chairman of a new unit trust with East Anglian inter-ests. This enterprise was administered by the Dawnay Day Group.

Having no experience in finance or company organisation, Cub listened to the idea with a mixture of gratitude and apprehension. In his position he could scarcely refuse the offer, but to make sure of his ground he arranged for a tutorial from a senior accountant whom he had met in the army.

Cub's worries were soon dissipated. He proved to be a great asset to the unit trust and was offered a position as non-executive director with Dawnay Day itself. This turned out to be more than just a welcome source of income; Cub enjoyed the work and the "sense of comradeship" so much that he found himself looking forward to the end of his holiday breaks. Dawnay Day had a strong reputation for sponsoring young companies, providing them with financial support and corporate advice; it was coveted by several larger groups, and eventually was taken over by RIT, chaired by Victor Rothschild's son Jacob. In later years Cub felt that he had been particularly fortunate in playing a part in a group which had a high reputation for integrity even in the days of exacting standards in the City. With typical self-deprecation Cub described himself as "a sort of ennobled office boy though I do not think I ever stuck on the stamps or made the tea". In reality he was an effective non-executive director, chairing several of the companies associated with the Group and winning respect for his views across the range of Dawnay Day's activities. Occasionally he invited senior politicians (including Enoch Powell) to lunch with the board when prominent industrialists were in attendance: these were remembered as particularly useful and lively occasions.[11]

When he returned from Rhodesia the prospect of idleness was as frightening to Cub as his financial position. Now he had the security he craved, and, as so often happens, he faced the opposite hazard of having too much to do. In April 1964 Alec Home asked him to serve as a British delegate to the Council of Europe and the Western European Union Assembly. Cub had always supported closer European ties – unusually for someone whose heart was in Africa – and had kept himself informed about Ted Heath's ill-fated negotiations for EEC membership. Participation in the Council of Europe at least gave Britain the chance to show that it had a constructive outlook, but it had always been an arena for talk rather than action – and, to Cub's chagrin, much of the talk was conducted in the European languages which he had never mastered. His attendance at the Council lasted for only a year.

Far more important to Cub was his association with a famous City livery company, the Worshipful Company of Skinners. Having discovered that a member of the family had been a Warden of the company in the seventeenth century, Cecil Alport had tried to arrange an apprenticeship for his son, then at Cambridge. At first his attempt was unsuccessful, but about a month later one of Cub's friends was asked to find someone to make up a party of four for a game of bridge at Field Place near Horsham – Shelley's childhood home. Cub was recruited, and discovered that one of his partners in the bridge game was Alfred Bowker, who had just rejected Cub as an apprentice. Bowker quickly saw that he had been too hasty, and Cub began a long association with the Skinners' Company.[12]

When Cub returned from Rhodesia he was invited to join the Skinners' Court as a "Renter Warden" – a junior office which led in successive years to Third, Second, and First Warden, then the Mastership which, unusually, Cub was asked to take up for a second time when a prospective Master died. The position of Master involved a good deal of committee-work, attendance on the Lord Mayor of London, dinners with other Companies, and various charitable activities. When Cub became Master he found himself chairman of the governors of Tonbridge School – the scene of his bloody boxing match nearly half a century before – and Pro-Chancellor of the City University, a position that he held for seven years. He considered this an appropriate berth; Butler became Master of Trinity College, Cambridge in 1965, and Cub thought that the universities were now providing the retirement homes which public figures once found in the medieval monasteries. In fact Cub was a very active pro-chancellor, attempting to revive the Elizabethan institution Gresham College as part of the City University. He won support for his idea from the Mercer's Company and the Corporation of London, but his ambitions were defeated by a lack of funds.

The Skinners' Company meant a good deal to Cub, but it could hardly displace his affection for Colchester. Over the years he managed to contribute to almost every aspect of civic life. At one time or another he was president of the Minories Art Gallery, the British Legion, the Royal Naval Association, the Essex Association of Local Councils and the Business Enterprise Agency. In addition, he chaired the Archaeological Society and the Bishop's Commission which re-organised the 28 parishes of Colchester. He was also a founder-member of the Essex University Council, and served as a Deputy Lieutenant for the county of Essex (along with his "political twin" Tony Greenwood, who rounded off his imitation of Cub's career by serving as a university pro-chancellor). He helped to establish a hospice, and as chairman of Colchester Theatre Trust played a leading role in drumming up the finance for a new playhouse – the impressive "Mercury", which was built between the Roman Wall and his favourite Colchester landmark, the massive water-tower nicknamed "Jumbo". Much of this work took place after his services to the town had received full recognition with his unanimous election to the post of High Steward of Colchester in July 1967.

Cub was only fifty-one when he left Africa; he had been in Parliament for only thirteen years, and felt that he had a great deal more to offer in national politics, despite the time he lavished on the affairs of Colchester. When his old "One Nation" colleague Edward Heath became leader of the Conservative opposition in July 1965 Cub offered his congratulations. Despite the apparent difference in their fortunes Cub was sympathetic rather than jealous. The new Conservative leader faced an uphill struggle projecting his message against the populist Prime Minister Harold Wilson, while Cub enjoyed a dignified soap-box in the House of Lords. After his maiden speech in November 1963 he began to contribute to debates as frequently as he had done in his early days in the Commons, and in April 1965 he was offered the position of opposition spokesman on agriculture in the House of Lords. This was not a subject close to Cub's heart and he had enough to do already; he turned down the approach from Lord Carrington.[13]

Cub had never been a "man of one idea", and agriculture was almost the only topic outside his repertoire at this time. But from an early stage he participated in debates on Central Africa. Many of his old adversaries – including the Marquess of Salisbury on one side and Fenner Brockway on the other – were in the House of Lords, and Cub was determined that the case for a "Middle Way" should not be lost by default. In December 1963 he spoke in a debate on the Order in Council which wound up the federal experiment, arguing that Britain should lend special financial support to the three territories and repeating his familiar pleas for partnership in Africa. He was heard with respect – as he rose the Earl of Listowel intervened to request that the Lord Chancellor be summoned back into the chamber to hear him – but he was unlikely to win over die-hards like Lord Colyton, the former colonial minister Henry Hopkinson, who preceded him with a typically intemperate performance.[14]

For years the Labour Party had opposed the Federation without giving much thought to what might succeed it, and after the 1964 general election its leaders discovered why the Conservatives had agonised over the problem for so long. The situation deteriorated further when Smith won a decisive victory in the Rhodesian election of May 1965, and, desperate to stave off UDI, Wilson flew to Salisbury in October. He tried to convince Smith that the inevitable sanctions would destroy the Rhodesian economy, but threw away his main negotiating card when he denied that Britain would use force against an illegal declaration of independence. Smith and his supporters were confident that their regime would survive sanctions, and the declaration was made in the following month.

With a commonwealth conference scheduled for mid-January 1966 Wilson was faced with the prospect of uncomfortable conversations with African leaders who were outraged by the rejection of force. His own party was divided over armed intervention, and given Wilson's constant concerns about an internal revolt it was scant consolation to him that the split within the Conservative Party was even more damaging. If the Rhodesian problem could not be solved overnight it was necessary to take the heat out of the situation somehow; with a diplomatic venture by a senior Labour figure unthinkable at this stage the idea of choosing a moderate Conservative to put out feelers appealed to Wilson. Cub was the perfect candidate, and when the Lord Chancellor asked him to take on the job in early January he readily agreed.

Subsequently Cub met Wilson in company with Burke Trend, the Commonwealth Secretary Michael Stewart, and the Chancellor Lord Gardiner. This was his first encounter with Wilson, who he later described as "a good Prime Minister on the whole" – Cub's way of saying "not very good at all". At the time he was impressed that Wilson could overlook party differences in pursuit of a fair settlement in Rhodesia. Wilson explained that he needed to discover the thinking of the Rhodesian government and public; this task demanded someone of standing and objective outlook. Cub realised the sensitivity of his proposed mission, and suggested that his widowed mother, who was about to return to South Africa, could provide "cover" for his departure.[15]

According to plan Cub flew to Johannesburg via Luanda on 11 January. He was greeted with the news that his journey was in doubt because the Governor of Rhodesia, Sir Humphrey Gibbs, had raised objections. He hung around in Pretoria for a day before Wilson advised him to call off the mission. This was a serious disappointment to Cub, who had relished the prospect of a new adventure; to make matters worse, he suspected that his journey had been sabotaged by Gibbs and the Rhodesian Chief Justice Sir Hugh Beadle, who wanted to replace the Smith regime with a government of national unity. Normally this idea would have appealed to Cub, but Beadle's notion of "national unity" excluded the African majority and he wanted to set up Gibbs as the temporary ruler of Rhodesia. As Duncan Sandys observed, "this would be a concealed form of direct rule from Whitehall and the Rhodesians would fight to the end rather than accept it"; with little prospect of African support Beadle's government of national unity would have triggered off a brutal civil war.[16]

With the blessing of Ian Smith Beadle himself flew to London soon after Cub's return, and over lunch told Wilson that "Lord Alport had made a very poor impression as High Commissioner and there was no confidence in him in Rhodesia". On 21 January Duncan Sandys inadvertently discredited this view by telling Michael Stewart that "he did not think [Beadle] was a very clever or clear-sighted man". Sandys had been sacked from the Conservative front-bench by Edward Heath, and promptly redesigned himself as a fearless champion of the Europeans in Central Africa; if even he disowned Beadle there was little hope for the "national government" idea. Cub entered the Commonwealth Secretary's room as Sandys left it; he accepted Stewart's apologies for his wasted journey, and protested that "he knew that he was rather unpopular with certain sections in Rhodesia, but there were a number of people who had wanted to see him and he might have been of some assistance in the present situation". He suggested to Stewart that the British should include in any statement of its aims the notion that "the deal would get worse from the Rhodesian point of view as time went on. In other words, now was their chance for a settlement".[17]

At the end of his meeting with Stewart Cub received permission to discuss recent events with the Conservative leadership. At a subsequent meeting with Heath he advised his old colleague to avoid personal involvement in the Rhodesian quagmire and hand over the subject "to someone like Selwyn Lloyd" (who was nearing the end of his career). Heath's thoughts were already moving that way, and he authorised a futile visit to Salisbury by Lloyd in February 1966. The Conservatives had nothing to gain from Rhodesia; after all, Wilson was only sipping at the poisoned chalice which Macmillan had prepared. But in his discussions with both leaders Cub seems to have underestimated the extent of their anxieties about extremists within their parties. Given the kind of freedom enjoyed by Cub Heath would have paid no attention to his right-wing on Rhodesia, but this luxury was denied to him. The interview was amicable, but there was fertile ground for future misunderstanding between the pair.[18]

Cub's cool advice to negotiate was certainly wasted on a government which was hoping for a "quick kill". At the commonwealth conference in Lusaka Wilson had foolishly announced that the Rhodesian crisis would be ended by sanctions in "weeks rather than months", and despite the warnings from Cub and Sandys he embraced the Beadle plan in a speech to the House of Commons on 25 January. Like Macmillan in 1959, Wilson was desperate to neutralise Central Africa as a domestic issue; he wanted a spring election to cash in on his "honeymoon period" with the voters, and for short-term gain he threw out statements which would come back to haunt him in his second term. Also like Macmillan, Wilson discovered that his fears were unfounded; at the election on 31 March Labour won an overall Commons majority of 99. Heath fought bravely in a hopeless cause, but the result left him more vulnerable than before.

With less reason to fear his left-wing Wilson was now ready for a settlement, and before the end of the year he believed that Smith would strike a deal. In December 1966 the leaders met aboard the British warship *Tiger*, stationed off Gibraltar. Wilson suggested a more liberal version of Edgar Whitehead's 1961 constitution (which Smith had opposed at the time), but the deal fell short of the established British principle that Rhodesia could not secure independence without majority rule. Despite this vital concession – which would have been very difficult to sell to the commonwealth – Smith insisted on consultations with his cabinet before signing. The result was a rejection of terms which Whitehead himself denounced as a victory for the white supremacists. The Rhodesians had taken Wilson's stance as a sign of weakness, and knowing that he would never launch a military offensive they had decided to hold out for more. Meanwhile their country was sliding towards an apartheid system, reinforced by strict censorship and arbitrary arrests of political opponents. Wilson's response to the failed agreement was an ill-conceived attack on the Conservatives for wanting the end of his own government more than the deposition of Smith. By this time British voters were as sick of Rhodesia as they were ignorant of the problem's complexities; the idealism of the early Federation days had been replaced by a general feeling of resentment against the intrusion of Rhodesia on the nightly news bulletins.[19]

In the House of Lords there was no escape from Rhodesia. The Marquess of Salisbury continued to press his line that sanctions had done no good and should be removed. Cub was now a hate-figure to the die-hards associated with the Joint East and Central African Board which he had once chaired; he had begun a series of radio broadcasts aimed at the European population, urging them towards a moderate settlement. In the month before the *Tiger* talks he enraged them further, declaring that "there can be no agreement which the present government, or any government in this country, could reach with the Smith regime and still maintain its self-respect, its sense of confidence and its integrity". He warned that Rhodesia might soon become a new Katanga – before long the United Nations might intervene and impose its own one-sided settlement. The only chance seemed to be the replacement of Smith by moderates, but liberal Europeans were being starved of information by government censorship and unless something was done Smith's siege mentality would spread throughout the European population. Desperate measures were needed; as Cub put it, it was time to become "a dove in hawk's plumage". He recommended that unarmed aircraft should drop leaflets over Salisbury and Bulawayo, spelling out the real implications of the present crisis and offering alternatives to apartheid and war. The desperate British government took the hint, and made secret preparations to bombard Rhodesian cities with copies of a conciliatory speech by Wilson.[20]

After the failure of *Tiger* the Rhodesian stalemate resumed. By April 1967 new feelers were being put out towards Cub by the British government; he responded once again, reflecting that "although Rhodesia has been a dead loss as far as my career has gone", it was only human "to want to get back on the act". On 18 April he met Herbert Bowden, the new Commonwealth Secretary, for a private discussion. Bowden listened carefully while Cub outlined his ideas for a settlement; refreshed by the thought that his lonely stand had produced a positive response, Cub went off to broadcast to Rhodesia reflecting how curious it was "that the socialists should give me credit when my own party gave me none".[21]

Cub at this time was attracting numerous visitors to his home; the majority were members of "the liberal upper-class in Rhodesia; well meaning but ineffective". Cub deplored their lack of influence in a country which had been taken over by the "lower middle-class and crypto-fascists determined to hang on to power at any cost", but he understood their predicament; their capital was tied up in Rhodesia, and he acknowledged that "I would not risk anything if I had livelihood and hope to lose". On the day after his meeting with Bowden a Rhodesian liberal visited him at the Cross House. Recording his feelings after his friend's departure Cub was reminded of his own good fortune;

> the garden with a wonderful display of spring flowers and blossoms looks just what an English garden should look like. I have tried to build a family in a traditional atmosphere of an English country house and despite many worries and the pressures of life I think that for at any rate yesterday I succeeded. It's part of my act. I hope I can keep it up.[22]

There was one thing that Cub had never been able to "keep up" – a diary. The meeting with Bowden had inspired him to set down his thoughts, and he sustained the effort for twelve days – by his standards, a remarkable display of stamina. By 28 April the strain was showing – his writing on that day was barely legible. But these were interesting times for Cub, and if he wanted to leave an impression of his character at fifty-four a whole year's endeavour could not have provided more clues than these few scraps of paper. He saw himself as the upholder of values, notably that of public service, which were shrinking away in a country which now caused him more dismay than delight. Yet his melancholy was mixed with the pleasure which often accompanies a sense of principled defiance. On 25 April he went to a memorial service for his old friend from Swinton College, Reginald Northam; Robert Carr and Enoch Powell sat in front of him, and Lord Swinton himself was propped in the front pew "looking very aged". The sight of these old friends brought a moment of regret that "after all the common efforts of the 1945–51 period we should all have drifted apart". The days of "One Nation" were over, but he felt that he had not changed; he was still making a useful contribution to public life. Walking back to Westminster with another old friend, John Tilney, his self-esteem was given a further boost. Cub asked Tilney what he was concerning himself with at present: "'Oh', he said, 'I'm pressing the government to grow rambling roses up the wall round Buckingham Palace. I think that they have agreed'". "This", Cub lamented, "was an ex-Commonwealth Office minister!" Rhodesia might have been "a dead loss" for his own career, but at least his eyes were still fixed well above the rambling roses of Buckingham Palace.[23]

On 27 April Cub was asked to see the Lord Chancellor. It seemed to him that Gardiner had been advised to call this meeting as a result of the previous conversation with Bowden; by maintaining his independent line on Rhodesia Cub had pushed his way back into the inner councils of government. It was understandable that he should contrast his achievement with the plight of ungrateful and impotent Conservatives, but his triumphant mood quickly ran out of control. On 28 April he went to Colchester's Moot Hall with his daughter Carole, to hear a speech by Lord Hailsham. "On two occasions", he wrote

[Hailsham] has been unforgivably arrogant to me; once in cabinet. If I were a less prickly character I would have forgotten all about it, but I have not. It was sad to see the poor, old, moth-eaten bear made to go through his tricks . . . I was thankful that I no longer had to perform in that way though I enjoyed the fact that when I entered a few minutes late and was directed to a front seat followed by an attractive little daughter there was a pleasant sound of clapping from the audience. At the end I was going out when [Hailsham] called out to me in a friendly manner so I shook him cordially by the hand, but I disliked his speech as much as I dislike him.

Two days later Cub attended a party given in Hailsham's honour: "He asked me how I was getting on and I said that I was living like a Lord. He said that I was lucky to be a Lord and to live like one. He was himself tired and over-worked". True to form, Cub now felt "rather ashamed of the fact that I had been so off-hand with him". But he soon recovered his feeling of virtuous hostility: after all Hailsham was "one of Macmillan's protégés whom I regard as being the cause of the decline of Britain and partly the architects of this period of decadence and rootlessness". He regretted that Hailsham was seen as almost the best that "the aristocracy of Britain – the governing class – could produce. Led by that wicked old man Macmillan". Cub was unaware that after the Rhodesian UDI Hailsham had pressed on Heath almost an identical moderate line to the one which had produced the transformation in Cub's own political fortunes. The knowledge might not have made much difference; torn at this time between the bitterness of rejection and the gladness of recognition Cub found his judgements on people and affairs sent reeling from pole to pole by nothing more than a glance or a gesture.[24]

In early June 1967 Wilson received strong hints (from Sandys and others) that Smith was ready for a new initiative on Rhodesia, and it was agreed that Cub should finally make the visit which had been planned back in November 1965. On 13 June the cabinet discussed the proposal. The discussion was led by Bowden, who stated the official line that Cub had been invited for talks with Gibbs; however, he would be ready to discuss the current situation with "all sections of Rhodesian opinion" – including members of the Smith regime if they wished to see him. Barbara Castle noted in her diary that Wilson chipped in with strong support for the idea. She wrote that "My heart sank as I heard all the familiar noises from Harold: there was no question of instituting 'talks', but we were under pressure from the opposition and from [Gibbs] and this would head them off". Castle challenged Wilson to reiterate his support for the guiding principle that there should be no independence before majority rule – known in political circles by the acronym "NIBMAR". Wilson's reply was ambiguous, but Castle guessed that, as in the *Tiger* talks, he was prepared to see how far the principle could be stretched. Ever the tactician, Wilson even suggested that it would help the British case against Smith if Cub were refused entry to Rhodesia.[25]

To some extent Cub saw the point in Wilson's cynical thinking, but he intended to get into Rhodesia and do anything he could to promote a settlement. On the day of the cabinet meeting he visited Hastings Banda, who was staying at the Dorchester Hotel on his way home from the United States. Banda, who had asked Cub to see him, seemed unchanged in appearance, but now that he was President of an independent Malawi there was no need for him to trot out the liberal clichés which had served him so well in the past. Once he had refused to co-operate with Welensky's government; now he confided that he enjoyed close relations with Smith, whose views on race made Welensky sound like Fenner Brockway. Banda thought that there would be no settlement unless Wilson dropped his commitment to NIBMAR; Cub assured him that the British government was flexible on this point, and asked if Banda would support his own mission. The President agreed, and promised that he would send one of his European supporters to Smith with a personal message.[26]

Meanwhile Wilson announced Cub's proposed visit in response to a parliamentary question from Sandys. The news was badly received by the Conservatives, as Cub had anticipated. There was some bitter laughter from the opposition front-bench when Cub was mentioned; Sir Gerald Nabarro shouted "Aubrey Jones" – the name of the former Conservative MP who had been recruited by Wilson to deal with another thorny problem, prices and incomes policy. Cub's old "One Nation" colleague Sir John Rodgers asked whether Wilson had consulted Heath about the appointment; the Prime Minister confirmed that he had not, but asserted that Cub had been chosen because he had "unrivalled knowledge of the situation in Salisbury and of the personalities . . . I would have thought that Lord Alport's appointment would commend itself to the House". It did not commend itself to Lord Salisbury, who tactfully described Cub as "hardly an ideal envoy". On balance the adverse reaction was pleasing to Wilson, since it made the opposition look obstructive on this sensitive issue, and Cub sent him a note to reassure him that although he had heard the reception of Wilson's initiative in both Houses this had done nothing to put him off.[27]

Smith's response to the appointment was equally negative. He described Cub as "almost a listed enemy of Rhodesia", who had been "cold-shouldered out of the country by the federal government". He had written a "scurrilous book" (which Smith himself had never found time to read: it included an amusing vignette of Smith as a finance minister, "looking somewhat blankly at the columns of figures produced by his Treasury officials and giving the impression that they would have made just as much sense to him if he had held the pages upside down"). All this fitted with the plans of the British Prime Minister, but Smith strayed dangerously near to the truth when he added that "I cannot help wondering that when Mr Wilson chose this man he was hoping and planning for the mission to fail". If that was Wilson's game Smith was not prepared to play along, at least for the time being; he stopped short of a refusal to allow Cub into the country. Back in England Cub refused to trade insults, telling reporters that "I'm really going as a sort of litmus paper. If I turn red you'll know something's gone wrong. If I turn blue then everything's all right. Perhaps those aren't very appropriate colours . . .". In other interviews he dropped the litmus paper and compared himself to a thermometer.[28]

Cub arrived in Salisbury on 22 June. As expected, the Rhodesian government failed to send anyone to meet him – although when Selwyn Lloyd had visited on behalf of the Conservative Party in the previous year he had been greeted by the Minister of Information. The weather was as chilly as his reception; it was the Rhodesian winter, and the fact that Cub arrived in a light-weight suit was noted as a sign that he was desperately out of touch. The "thermometer" had failed to gauge the temperature on this occasion.[29]

Cub drove from the airport to discuss the situation with Gibbs, who was marooned at Government House. This time Gibbs had acknowledged the case for a visit from Cub, and, as the head of Britain's residual mission in Salisbury reported, he proclaimed that "he was happier than he had been for months". In his "euphoria" he even wondered if Rachel could accompany Cub and charm the Rhodesian women. Despite the misunderstanding of January 1966 Cub admired Gibbs for his stubborn sense of duty; an Englishman who had gone to farm in Rhodesia at an early age, Gibbs refused to budge from his lonely post in the hope that events would force the Rhodesian government back to legality. In his report for Wilson Cub compared himself at this stage to "Sir Colin Campbell approaching the relief of the Residence at Lucknow, without the advantage of pipers or troops behind me". He established his own base at the Ambassador Hotel, where an armed Rhodesian security man sat in the foyer in case of trouble. As Cub expected his researches started slowly; he was able to fit in a round of golf. Smith pointedly left town for the first days of his visit, and the only people who were willing to visit the hotel were known supporters of Britain. Letters were a safer means of communication; he received a friendly note from an old Haileyburian, and one African liberal even sent him a ticket for the Rhodesian lottery (as usual, Cub won nothing). Some of the messages were less welcoming; one man declared that "you have the hide of a rhino and the personal dignity of an engorged tick and your uninvited presence on our soil is a contamination". At least Cub was discovering something about the range of Rhodesian opinion, as he had been asked to do.[30]

On 27 June Cub decided to break the deadlock. Smith had returned to Salisbury, and a courtesy call on the Prime Minister was permitted. An important part of Cub's brief was to discover what was happening within Smith's Rhodesian Front and to assess the mood of the Prime Minister himself. This was the kind of personal diplomacy which Cub enjoyed, but Smith was a very different animal from Welensky. He was a cold, hard man and Cub found it impossible to like him; the antipathy was mutual. The first meeting lasted for just over half an hour; the *Rhodesia Herald* commented that while Cub "appeared in good spirits" on his arrival he seemed "considerably less jovial when he left, appearing grim-faced and tense". When he read that report Cub resolved to come out smiling from the next encounter, even if it went badly. Actually he was pleasantly surprised by the meeting; in a telegram to the Commonwealth Office he described the mood as "cordial, if reserved, on both sides". There were two more business-like discussions with Smith, on 5 and 12 July.[31]

It was thought in London that Smith had rejected the *Tiger* proposals because of pressure from the wilder spirits in the Rhodesian Front. The party was always capable of splitting; Smith himself had only reached his position because of a *coup* against Winston Field. There was some reason to hope that if a reasonable deal was offered Smith would be strong enough to turn the tables on his right-wing, and appeal over their heads to the Rhodesian people; he had told Selwyn

Lloyd in February 1966 that once independence was settled he would expel the die-hard racists from his party. Cub thought that "despite an outward display of confidence, Mr Smith was an anxious, even frightened, man", and sensed that suspicion was growing among the members of the cabinet. Support for the Front was still high, but it seemed to have passed its peak as the reality of long-term sanctions hit home. Cub also thought that there was a clear majority in the country in favour of a settlement, but confirmed his previous view that there would have to be some movement from the rigid NIBMAR position. Most Europeans in Rhodesia accepted that African rule was coming, but very few wanted an immediate hand-over.[32]

These were little acorns of hope, but they were better than nothing and Cub was struck by Smith's remark during the second meeting that if the British government could produce a revised version of the *Tiger* proposals he would fight a general election on that basis. Cub believed that some exploratory talks could proceed; indeed it was necessary to take the initiative if Britain wanted to prevent a further deterioration in the position. Without some fresh move moderate opinion would be squeezed further, and Cub saw evidence that the sanctions policy was falling hardest on Africans and those who continued to be well disposed towards Britain. He felt confident that he had seen a representative sample of Rhodesian opinion, with the exception of African leaders, including Nkomo and Robert Mugabe, who had been detained by the illegal government. By the end of his first week the antagonism towards him declined markedly; one journalist noted that he was "spreading geniality and goodwill on all sides", and the *Rhodesia Herald* conceded that "viewed as a reconnaissance exercise, Lord Alport's visit is a success". Reporting back to the CRO, the head of the British residual mission praised Cub's diplomatic skills. By the end of his visit he had seen around 1000 people, from old friends like Welensky, Winston Field and Garfield Todd to African trade unionists and, individually, the members of Smith's cabinet. His stay was extended to 13 July to accommodate all of these visitors; many more who wrote asking for interviews were denied access through lack of time.[33]

Cub's flight home was preceded by newspaper headlines in Britain which predicted correctly that he would recommend further negotiations. He presented his report to Wilson on 17 July; two further meetings were held to discuss a statement for the Commons and Cub's own ideas for progress. He believed that Wilson was impressed by his suggestion that Smith should hold an election on a "Tiger Mark II" platform, after which he could dispense with his right-wing and put together a relatively broad coalition government. Once these changes had been carried out negotiations could begin on a return to legality; in the meantime Wilson should maintain sanctions to mollify the commonwealth. Despite Cub's optimism this was far too visionary for the Prime Minister, who chose in his memoirs to describe the report as "totally negative". When the cabinet met to discuss Cub's report it decided that Gibbs should ask Smith about his proposed amendments to the original *Tiger* programme, and that steps should be taken to intensify the sanctions in order to appease international opinion. Barbara Castle opposed any further contact with Smith, claiming that everyone in the cabinet agreed that such gestures would be "merely presentational". In his statement to the House Wilson paid tribute to Cub's work, but stressed that the initiatives arising from the visit would be "extremely limited". When he read the statement Smith must have felt that the mission had been a waste of everyone's time; soon after Wilson's performance Cub heard that Smith had "turned right about over the ideas he suggested to you about the way forward", and had told Gibbs that he would like to prevent majority rule for 1000 years.[34]

This was a disappointing outcome to all Cub's efforts, and there were other unwelcome repercussions. He had promised Wilson that he would see Heath and Lord Carrington, but would not reveal the contents of his report. Instead, he would say that he was opposed to the publication of his findings, and read them a message from Ian Smith stating that the antics of the Conservative Party were "a source of embarrassment to him". Heath invited Cub for lunch at his flat; Cub remembered a delicious meal, with salmon and strawberries and cream. Unfortunately the conversation fell below the quality of the food. Once they had finished eating Heath said "Well now Cub, spill the beans". In obedience to his promise Cub refused, telling the leader of his party that "if he wanted to know the details the right procedure would be for him to ask a question of the Prime Minister in the House of Commons". He did not record whether he followed this upper-cut with the right-hook of Smith's curt message.[35]

Cub's relations with Heath had never been very warm; now they entered the deep freeze. Cub's refusal to spill any beans followed some miserable weeks for the Tory leader; on the day before Cub's return from Rhodesia an article in the *Sunday Express* anticipating a positive outcome to his talks appeared on the front page next to a piece which predicted that Heath would shortly be replaced as leader of his party by Sir Alec Douglas-Home. The uncomfortable meal was not Cub's first offence; in April he had sent Heath some well meaning advice, pointing out that the Conservatives would suffer if they continued to attack everything Labour did and singling out a speech by Enoch Powell as particularly "lamentable". Cub guessed that his strictures would be supported by "a number of highly experienced professionals in the party establishment". This was a fairly cheeky lecture for a member of the House of Lords to deliver to someone faced with conflicting pressures from a divided and disillusioned party; Heath would have been even more annoyed had he known that in April Cub was on the verge of intimate discussions with cabinet ministers.[36]

In later years Cub felt that Heath's behaviour over the trip to Rhodesia was another instance of Conservative ingratitude. But at the time he recognised that he had treated both Heath and Carrington "a trifle cavalierly". As with so many of his personal quarrels, this one had arisen because he was at cross-purposes with an old acquaintance; from their different perspectives both Cub and Heath had good reason to feel injured. Cub thought that he had travelled to Rhodesia as a trusted Privy Councillor, and on these terms he should honour his oath of secrecy; Heath agreed with a Rhodesian newspaper which observed that Wilson "has certainly covered himself very well by picking a Tory in case attempts at negotiation fail; he can then pacify his own party by blaming the Tories". Since there was more than a grain of truth in this Heath was quite justified in overlooking the fact that Cub himself had gone out with the national interest at heart.[37]

Not until October 1968 did Wilson make another serious attempt to resolve the Rhodesia crisis. Again the meeting took place on a warship – *HMS Fearless* – but, possibly because Smith had to resort to seasickness tablets on *Tiger*, this time the craft lay at anchor. The result was no different, although Wilson pushed his concessions much further than on the previous occasion; according to a well informed

British source a deal on these terms would have left Britain with only one other commonwealth partner – Banda's Malawi. The next step for Smith was to sever his remaining connections with Britain by declaring Rhodesia a republic; this had been the situation in practice since March 1968, when the rebel government proceeded with the execution of three Africans despite an intervention by the Queen.[38]

Cub's speech back in November 1966, denying the possibility of an honourable peace with Smith, seemed to have been verified by events. Even so, he continued to nag away, and in January 1968 he made public the plan he had outlined to Wilson. He was rewarded with an approving editorial in *The Times* and a quantity of hate mail from right-wing Britons, including a Christian Scientist who had deduced that Cub was "a heathen, pagan, or communist – the anti-Christ!". Copies of his speech were circulated among members of the Rhodesian government, but a lengthy report in the *Rhodesia Herald* was excised by the censors. Feeling emboldened rather than deterred by the reception of his ideas Cub continued to make regular BBC broadcasts to Rhodesia, including a memorable dialogue with Roy Welensky which demonstrated how far events had pushed the pair together again. Welensky no longer counted in Rhodesian politics, and now that his former right-wing colleagues – the "old bulldogs" – had left him alone he was free to express the typical views of the liberal Europeans.[39]

In the autumn of 1970 Cub made another trip to Africa, taking in Kenya, Zambia, Tanzania, Malawi, South Africa and (inevitably) Rhodesia. This time he travelled in a private capacity (although he kept the British government informed of his plans) and was told by the Rhodesians that "you may find it difficult to see anyone in government or official circles". Smith decided that this would be a good time to leave the country. As a result Cub only saw at first hand what he already knew – that the moderates were increasingly desperate and that sanctions were damaging the wrong people. The polarisation of opinion was revealed in press reaction to the visit; a liberal newspaper praised Cub's courage after he had delivered an uncompromising speech, while the ferocious publication *Property and Finance* made the unlikely claim that Cub was "a dedicated intellectual militant . . . hatchet-man for Mr Macmillan and Mr Ian (sic) Macleod in the subtle destruction of the Federation. . . . He should be sent packing". Back in Britain the

Daily Telegraph retailed the story that Cub had been nicknamed "Lord Pomposity" by right-wing Rhodesians. At least Cub once again met up with Welensky and saw Mirimba House, where a jacaranda planted by Butler was now twelve feet high. Everything else in Rhodesia looked sterile; by contrast, Malawi seemed to Cub to be thriving, even if Banda had proved to be no more liberal than Smith.[40]

It was a remarkable achievement for Cub – who depended entirely on his own energies and capacity for research – to keep up his constructive interventions on Rhodesia, which occupied so much time in well staffed Whitehall departments to so little effect. Reading about the situation was no substitute for seeing it at first hand, but finance was a problem for a private individual; for his 1970 visit Cub put together a package of business meetings and newspaper articles to cover his expenses. But at least Cub knew the recent history of Rhodesia as well as anyone else in the Lords; his views would always be listened to, if not universally shared.

During the 1960s Cub built a reputation in another field from scratch, and once again chose a subject which would increase his unpopularity in some quarters. Since his return to Britain he had been musing over the state of the constitution. In November 1964 he roughed out a proposal for a book on Parliament (*The Way to Westminster*) which, like so many of his ideas, went no further than a sketch. But it was easier to persist in the House of Lords. Reform of the Lords had featured in his 1950 election leaflet, but as an MP he had given little thought to the matter. Membership of the House brought new enlightenment. The introduction of life peers had ensured that the quality of debate rivalled that in the House of Commons. Even so, the chamber continued to be dominated by Conservatives and the hereditary element left it vulnerable to criticism. Over the century the House had been stripped of its meaningful powers, but Cub saw the election of a Labour government committed to "modernisation" as a threat to its continued existence even in this emasculated state.

Clearly the best way forward for the Lords was to reform themselves before their enemies moved in. In April 1965 Cub argued for a thorough review of the Lords' procedures. Astutely swerving around the question of hereditary peers, he claimed that the existing House could contribute more to the legislative process if its routine work was handed over to standing committees; the whole House

227

would only be involved if issues of constitutional gravity were being discussed. The leader of the Labour peers, Lord Longford, was clearly sympathetic, but despite a full and well informed discussion the proposal got nowhere.[41]

In the following year Cub tried again, and, since Labour now enjoyed a thumping Commons majority he produced more detailed and radical proposals, including the novel idea that the House of Lords should be televised. Although he claimed to be "very bad" at lobbying, Cub enjoyed dispatching circular letters urging attendance on those peers who shared his passion for reform; as a matter of courtesy he sent a copy of his motion to Lord Longford. Longford already appreciated Cub's point about the advantages of the Upper House reforming itself, and a correspondent passed on to him a report that senior Conservatives were coming round to the same view. Wilson's Cabinet Secretary Burke Trend was brought in; he advised that the government should prepare its own case for far-reaching reform in advance of Cub's motion, since Labour had promised action on the Lords in its last two manifestos.[42]

Cub's original intention had been to save the House of Lords, not to embarrass the government. But the official documents show that his motion of 4 July 1966 started a chain of events which led to a humiliation for the Prime Minister. The case for reform of the Lords seemed obvious; after Trend's intervention Longford submitted a memorandum to Wilson which knocked over all of the objections he could think of. But the major British parties had mixed feelings on the subject. Labour had predictable objections to this bastion of privilege, but many MPs were tempted to leave it in its current state; it was not powerful enough to do lasting damage, and if a serious conflict did arise with the elected government Wilson could make capital out of the claim that he was the champion of "the people" against the forces of the past. For the Conservatives the peers were a potential source of embarrassment, but after the 1966 election they had few cards to play and a principled stand in the Upper House on a suitable issue was an option to hold in reserve if morale continued to slide. The position was neatly summarised by a Labour peer before the 1964 election, when asked by Cub what his party would do with the Lords if it returned to power. He replied: "Same as you have been doing since 1951: use it as a means of helping out when things get sticky". Cub thought that these devious party priorities were reinforced by a generalised feeling of envy on the part of MPs towards the peers, who had no worries about re-election; he had felt the same way during his time in the Commons.[43]

Sensing that this time his efforts might lead to government action Cub decided for tactical reasons to drop his radical motion and fell back on the more modest proposal that a select committee should look into the question. But his real intentions were now known and few Conservatives were willing to contemplate such an upheaval. Lord Carrington expressed the hope that "we shall not rush into change because change is in the air", and averred that the House had more urgent matters to discuss. The Marquess of Salisbury, who had offered some private encouragement on reform in 1965, reverted to his old opinion that Cub was a dangerous meddler in many matters. He pointed out that his noble friend was relatively new to the House; although new brooms could be useful there was a danger that they might sweep too roughly. Cub's reforming zeal was defeated again; he withdrew his motion without a vote.[44]

Yet House of Lords reform was now progressing from the political drawing-board. *The Times* and *The Economist* published leading articles in support of Cub's stand, and, prompted by Longford, Wilson's cabinet debated the matter for the first time in the run up to Cub's motion. For the time being a majority opposed any moves, but in August Richard Crossman became Leader of the House of Commons. Crossman was a well known writer on constitutional subjects, and he soon became a rival to Cub in his enthusiasm for reform. He persuaded Wilson that this was an appropriate time for action, and before the end of 1967 an inter-party committee, composed of senior figures from both Houses, was sitting to consider possible changes.[45]

This development delighted Cub; instead of being a political football as so often in the past, it looked as if the Lords might be bringing the parties closer together. Cub was worried about mounting pressure on Heath to use the Lords for a strike against the government, and in May 1968 wrote to the party leader urging that nothing should jeopardise this excellent chance of a moderate reform. But senior Tories could no longer restrain their dogs of war. In June Salisbury led a successful rebellion in the Lords against the renewal of sanctions against Rhodesia; Cub was one of five Conservatives who voted with the government. In fact the Order was only defeated by nine votes despite a sudden invasion of the House by Tory "back-woodsmen", and Crossman took this as a sign that the old Conservative dominance was being worn away by life peers. Wilson was more impressed by the need to look tough in the eyes of his MPs; he responded by calling off the inter-party talks.[46]

The break-up of the committee in the face of irresponsible behaviour from Conservative peers raised the possibility that Wilson would appease his own wild men, and propose outright abolition of the Lords. But the White Paper which eventually appeared (after fifteen drafts) on 29 October 1968 dismissed this idea. Instead, there would now be a two-tier Upper House, where voting rights would be restricted to selected peers. These working members of the House would be paid life peers; they might include some hereditary peers, but only if the government of the day decided that their knowledge and regular attendance was of proven value to the House. The others would have the right to turn up and speak, but not to vote. The House would be able to delay legislation passed by the Commons for no more than six months; the government of the day would have more supporters in the House than the other parties, but it would not be able to command an automatic majority. To win votes the government would need to persuade cross-benchers, of no party allegiance.[47]

Critics complained that the White Paper had been concocted by constitutional boffins who had transformed a simple idea into a lengthy and complex menu of reforms. Others were concerned that the proposals gave too much patronage to the Prime Minister, and even Crossman suddenly realised on a visit to the Lords that MPs would be annoyed that the peers in "the best club in the world" would still have a much more comfortable life than their own. But Cub was quite satisfied with the White Paper, and was particularly pleased when the Lords gave its approval with a majority of almost 200. The procedures of the Lords would be examined by a committee, as he had suggested, and the new power allotted to cross-benchers was exactly what he hoped for. But, ironically, the Bill fell a victim to the procedures of the House of Commons, and a cross-party alliance of a destructive kind. Enoch Powell deplored this root-and-branch assault on a venerable institution; from Labour's left-wing Michael Foot objected to anything which fell short of outright abolition. They set out to destroy the Bill through delaying tactics; the government was unable to stop them, because a vote to curtail debate would have been opposed by the united Conservative Party and its own back-bench rebels. After twelve sessions of the Bill only the preamble and five clauses had been covered. On 16 April 1969 this serious disruption to the government's legislative programme forced the cabinet into surrender; Crossman agreed that the Bill should be dropped.[48]

Cub was not prepared to give up the battle. He introduced the Bill in the Lords, hoping that if it passed its early stages unscathed it might be sponsored by the front-benchers who had backed the White Paper. But now that the danger of abolition had passed their lordships could show what they really thought of the reformers; in the first Lords' vote since 1939 on the First Reading of a Bill, Cub was defeated by 54 to 43. Cub had told Rachel that in his next *Who's Who* entry he would list "reform of the Lords" among his recreations. Rachel replied that no one would ever take him seriously again. His championship of what seemed to most people a hopelessly lost cause after the government surrender suggests that on this matter his judgement had failed him. But his small band of supporters made up in quality what they lacked in numbers; eight Labour front-benchers voted for his reintroduced government Bill on First Reading. In any case, he understood that success or failure was less important than the task of keeping the issue alive; as he told the political scientist Max Beloff, he considered "that the only contribution somebody like myself can make is to voice ideas which those whose political careers lie ahead of them are unable to do". His interest in Lords reform outlived these temporary setbacks.[49]

The hostility shown towards Cub by fellow Conservatives in the Lords increased his disillusionment with the party he had served for so long. But this feeling did not prevent him from rebuking Labour; within months of his friendly talks with Wilson over Rhodesia he was attacking the government's economic policies, which led in November 1967 to a devaluation of sterling. The crisis caused him to reflect

> that most of the things which I came into politics to pursue and forward, most of the problems with which I was familiar when I came into politics thirty years ago as a professional politician in

the Conservative Party . . . no longer matter or make sense in the contemporary political scene.[50]

Cub's rhetoric clouded his message on this occasion. The domestic problems of the days before the war – unemployment, prices, social disunity – had not gone away. Rather, the end of empire had exposed underlying flaws – notably, in Cub's view, those which afflicted Britain's party system and parliamentary institutions. He proposed the remedy which he had yearned for since the beginning of his political career – a government animated by a truly "national faith". For many years he had believed that the Conservative Party could fulfil that need; now he was certain that neither of the major parties was an appropriate vehicle. They were both preoccupied with petty competition, unaware that their antics merely drove Britain further into decline. Cub noted that after he had made an earlier plea for a government of national unity "one noble Lord, of great political experience, warned me that I should choose the timing of my speeches with great discretion. Such a theme, he said, might be appropriate two or three crises from then". But immediate action was needed – unless the British people enjoyed being mocked and misgoverned.[51]

In his speech Cub made an historical, and personal, digression. "Between 1956 and the Election of 1964", he said, "the Conservative Party was forced to take actions which ran directly counter to the basic tenets of its faith: in the commonwealth, in overseas policy, and, to some extent, in Britain". As a result, "the party suffered what can only be described as a breakdown". This remark, which might have been interpreted by Cub's audience as an attempt to seem even-handed in a speech which dwelt mainly on Labour's failures, explains the nature of the change he had undergone since his days of unflinching loyalty to the Conservative Party. As High Commissioner he had received regular bulletins from a wide variety of party colleagues; after his first year the "nervous breakdown" of the Conservatives, and the dismal prospects of the country, had emerged as common themes in their letters. Cub's correspondents were "off-duty" when they wrote; in their daily work as parliamentarians they had a professional interest in pretending that the customary ways of transacting political business could survive the transformation of Britain's place in the world. While his parliamentary friends were sheltered by the familiar rules of the game, Cub had been buffeted by every wind when presenting British policy to Welensky. If he had remained within the diplomatic service Cub might have continued to adapt, living from hand-to-mouth as his masters changed his orders on a daily (or even hourly) basis. But his re-engagement in British politics meant that after 1963 he was an insider with an outsider's perspective. From that viewpoint, he had concluded that Britain would never emerge from its present toils without radical reforms in the way it made law and in its system of industrial relations.[52]

In short, Cub had contracted what (in honour of a later sufferer) might be called "the Jenkins Syndrome". The victim of this condition is sent on a lengthy overseas mission. He or she may or may not harbour doubts about the political scene, but while serving abroad will become convinced that only drastic changes can save the situation and that it would be wrong to stay silent. In November 1979, three years into his term as President of the European Commission, Roy Jenkins delivered the BBC's Dimbleby Lecture and began his quest to "break the mould of British politics". Jenkins found that distance crystallised his previous thinking on constitutional and party-political matters: significantly, the title of his lecture was "Home Thoughts from Abroad". Naturally there were important differences between these two cases: by 1979 Jenkins' argument had been strengthened by the fact that Britain had passed through rather more than the "two or three crises" which Cub sought to avoid, and having held three of the most senior posts in British government Jenkins was sure to win wide publicity for his views. Cub tailored his own ambitions to his circumstances; he could only chip away at the mould in the hope that more powerful hands might arrive to smash it. But the differences between the methods and prospects of the two men cannot disguise the common features of their experiences on their travels.[53]

Cub's activities after his return from Rhodesia provide an interesting contrast with the activities of his old friend Enoch Powell. Despite his analytical mind Powell rejected constitutional change and in April 1968 became the most celebrated (and reviled) figure in British politics with a speech on immigration – a problem which, at most, was a symptom of the problems facing Britain. Powell had rarely travelled abroad since his remarkable wartime exploits. Perhaps all of

Britain's legislators should be sent in mid-career on a contemporary version of the "Grand Tour" enjoyed by eighteenth-century aristocrats.

Powell's "Rivers of Blood" speech dismayed Cub as much as his later wrecking tactics against reform of the Lords. He confided his worries about a perceived drift to the right in the Conservative Party in a letter to Rab Butler, who had encouraged his House of Lords campaign without troubling himself to vote for it. Cub had backed his words about a national government with a strong letter to *The Times* and some discrete preparations for action; Reginald Maudling was sounded out, but counselled delay. Maudling shared Cub's concerns about the Tory party; at the time of his letter to Cub he reportedly felt that a third of Conservative MPs would choose Enoch Powell as their leader rather than Ted Heath (Powell had received only fifteen votes when he stood against Heath in 1965). But if the Tories threatened confrontation, Labour offered only capitulation; in June 1969 Harold Wilson withdrew the government's proposed legislation to curb trade union power. The concerns which Cub had felt since his return from Rhodesia were now more widely shared; the journalist Cecil King thought that MPs of all parties "don't see how things can go on like this – nor how they can alter!". Suddenly all kinds of wild ideas – including a military dictatorship – were being canvassed by people on the fringes of Westminster. Cub, who wanted a temporary coalition which would safeguard democracy, was distressed by such fantasies which were used to discredit the case for any form of national government.[54]

When Wilson called a general election for 18 June 1970 the situation had stabilised – thanks largely to Roy Jenkins' management of the economy – and most people expected another Labour victory. But the Prime Minister was handicapped by a long list of failures – a second veto against British membership of the EEC was added to the climb-downs over the House of Lords and trade union reform, while in Rhodesia Ian Smith continued to defy the man who had predicted the downfall of his regime within weeks of the imposition of sanctions. While the press (and some in his party) wrote him off, Heath stumped the country pointing out Labour's failures to the voters, and gradually his message filtered through. The Conservatives achieved an overall majority of thirty.

Two decades after the "One Nation" group began those meetings which reminded Cub of his best university days, one of their number had climbed to the top of the greasy pole. Cub knew that Heath was a decent man, but wondered if he had the necessary powers of leadership to pull Britain through the troubled days to come. If he found the task too much Cub expected that the party would look to the right for his replacement, and in private conversation Rab Butler had identified the most likely successor: the man who had taken the "One Nation" minutes, Enoch Powell. Cub had other ideas; at the first "One Nation" meeting all those years ago he had been the only member to support coalition government, and if Heath failed he was quite prepared to repeat his lonely stand.[55]

Chapter Ten

Gains and Losses

After his unexpected victory Heath appointed a cabinet which featured many of Cub's old friends. Apart from the Prime Minister himself, Iain Macleod (Chancellor of the Exchequer) and Robert Carr (Employment) represented the original "One Nation"; Reginald Maudling at the Home Office had been an early recruit to the group. Margaret Thatcher, the former Colchester Young Conservative, was made Secretary of State for Education, and Cub's one-time PPS, Keith Joseph, went to Health and Social Security. Cub's old boss at the CRO Sir Alec Douglas-Home was the obvious candidate for the Foreign Office. As soon as the ministerial line-up was complete Cub sent his best wishes to Heath, Thatcher and Carr; clearly in a good letter-writing mood, he also dispatched congratulations to Butler on the first election of his son Adam, and even consoled Enoch Powell on the "rotten time" he had gone through in recent months. There was genuine sympathy in the latter message; Powell's friendship had once been important to him, and he regretted that poor judgement had deprived the nation of his talents. Ominously Powell replied that "I fear I may yet have to make further calls on your friendship and charity as the stock of torpedoes is not exhausted".[1]

Powell's "stock of torpedoes" was far more lethal than anything Cub had to offer; besides, unlike his old friend Cub wanted to give the new government the benefit of the doubt before he engaged in any form of combat. Even so, when Lord Hailsham (now Lord Chancellor, rather than a "moth-eaten bear") offered him the chance to join the list of Deputy Speakers in the House of Lords Cub interpreted this as a sign that he was regarded as "a bit of a bore" and that the suggestion was an attempt to muffle him. He therefore made it clear when he accepted the position (which meant that he had occasionally to preside over the Lords from the Woolsack in Hailsham's absence) that he would continue his troublesome activities. To prove his point, within days of his appointment he convened a cross-party meeting of peers on Lords reform. His group included Lords Longford, Shinwell and Boothby, but without any prospect of assistance from the new government legislation seemed as far away as ever. In February 1972 he confessed to Lord Perth that "I have ceased to be emotionally involved in the problem . . . I have made myself so unpopular that some of my colleagues tend to react against any views I may have whatever the issue may be".[2]

Predictably one of those issues was Rhodesia. Soon after the 1970 election Home told Cub how much he regretted that independence had not been granted to Rhodesia on the basis of Whitehead's 1961 constitution; this view must have worried Cub, since Home had apparently forgotten that the only election held under Whitehead's arrangements had produced the fateful victory for the right-wing Rhodesian Front. Cub's own thinking had changed with the realities of the situation. In August 1972 Lord Brockway, who previously thought that Cub was "ill-tempered, snobbish, patronising and unhelpful", acknowledged that he had "now reached a stage where he is more pro-African than I am". But Cub had no influence over Home and renewed negotiations produced exactly the outcome which he expected – proposals which were acceptable to the Europeans and anathema to a clear majority of Africans. As Cub pointed out, the Land Tenure Act which secured European domination – and which Whitehead had promised to repeal nearly a decade earlier – remained untouched by the proposed agreement. From this perspective the deal with Smith could not be seen as an attempt to settle the Rhodesian problem; rather, Cub claimed, the British government had decided to sever its last link with Central Africa so that it could stand aloof from the inevitable civil war. Fortunately the opinion-sounding Pearce Commission established by Home could not disguise the extent of African opposition. The agreement was scrapped, and Home left office in 1974 judging Rhodesia to be his greatest disappointment.[3]

Both Labour and the Conservatives had wrestled with Rhodesia for so long that the issue no longer aroused the old passions between the parties at Westminster. Domestic policy was the main political battleground throughout the Heath Government. Cub supported Robert Carr's Industrial Relations Act, but was pessimistic about the chances of union reform. The government's main problem, as he saw it, was that of communication with the public. Much later he recognised that the death of Iain Macleod within a few weeks of taking office had been a crucial blow. Heath's election victory against the odds made him feel that the electorate was instinctively sympathetic to his views; disliking what he saw as political gimmickry he tended to appeal for public support when crises arose rather than cultivating goodwill in advance. Cub felt that Macleod would have avoided this mistake; his inspirational oratory would have rallied the party, and his image of competence and compassion might have acted as a focus for a sense of national unity at a time of economic peril.

Without Macleod the government's good intentions were wasted; a Prime Minister who sought to promote the national interest was successfully portrayed by Labour as an ally of the bosses against the workers. Once the unions had refused to co-operate with his industrial relations policy Heath had to resort to legislative control over prices and incomes as Wilson had done. Yet as Cub pointed out in the Lords, this kind of measure could only succeed "if the nation can be persuaded that we are facing a major national crisis – and such a crisis, whether in peace or war, has always produced in the past a political situation in which party government has been superseded by a national government". While Heath remained Prime Minister Cub believed that a coalition was out of the question. Since his days in the Whips' Office Heath had been the favourite of the Conservative establishment, and now his public image was that of a stern, unbending Tory. As Cub knew, this label was unfair; Heath had never changed his views, and had been a conciliatory Minister of Labour. But it was a sad reflection on a determined follower of "One Nation" policies that many people believed him to be uncaring. Cub thought that the Conservative Party could only renew itself under a different leader who was capable of inspiring non-Conservatives as Britain faced its most difficult days since the war. Years later he confessed in private conversation that he had lost his faith in Heath over commonwealth affairs; he was appalled by the Singapore conference of January 1971, at which Britain refused to abandon its policy of selling arms to South Africa.[4]

On 25 September 1973 Cub told his friend Julian Ridsdale that he expected a major crisis around Christmas, although he was still on good enough terms with Heath to invite him to attend Colchester's annual Oyster Feast in the following month. Before Heath could sample the oysters his government suffered a fatal blow, when fighting broke out in the Middle East and the Arab oil producers announced drastic price increases just as Britain's coal miners were preparing a massive pay demand. As in 1968 Cub sought to establish a nucleus of support for a coalition, this time concentrating his efforts on East Anglian dignitaries as if preparing to hold the area for the monarch in an impending civil war (indeed, he often drew parallels between the existing tensions and politics in Britain under Charles I). While these eccentric endeavours came to little, an intriguing note amongst his papers indicates that powerful people were ready to listen to him. In November 1973 he called on Lord Rothschild who as head of Heath's "think-tank" had warned the government of a looming energy crisis. Cub thanked Rothschild for an "interesting conversation" in Whitehall; unfortunately he left no record of their talks, but they must have ranged beyond Cub's tentative suggestion that Rothschild might take some position with the City University. There were plans to take these conversations further, but Rothschild suffered a heart-attack in mid-December; when he finally resigned from the think-tank in the following October he made an impassioned plea for a national government.[5]

Feeling as he did that the nation was crying out for political unity, Cub thought that Heath had made a fatal mistake by calling a general election in February 1974 and allowing it to be dominated by the theme "Who Governs?". His previous disagreements with Heath played no part in shaping his thoughts; indeed he wrote that it was "tragic that someone with so many qualities for valuable public service should have been cast in a role for which he is temperamentally unsuited". Cub was confident that the public would rally behind Britain's democratic institutions if it felt that these were under attack from unelected forces – they would even prefer their politicians to the miners, with whose case for special treatment Cub had a great deal of sympathy. But a desire for democratic leadership was not the same thing as wanting to be ruled by the Conservative Party. In the election the Conservatives attracted more votes than Labour, but won only 297 seats compared to Labour's 301. Since no party could govern alone Heath rightly tried to put together a coalition, but his policy on Northern Ireland had alienated the Unionist MPs who had been traditional supporters of the Conservative Party. Talks with the Liberals broke up without agreement, and Heath resigned as Prime Minister.[6]

Commentators claimed that the election had been indecisive. Cub disagreed, and sent a letter to *The Times* to explain his point of view. "The election", he wrote, "shows that British people do not want Mr Heath or Mr Wilson as Prime Minister. They do not want 'firm government' on Mr Heath's terms nor do they want the doctrinaire socialist policies of Mr Benn's Labour Party". The people had voted "with absolute clarity and authority" for a "grand coalition" embracing all of Britain's parties, including Labour and the various nationalists whose support had risen at the election. Both Wilson and Heath would have to stand aside, since they symbolised the conflicts of the immediate past and could not possibly work together. If they refused this sacrifice they would suffer the consequences: "Public opinion will not easily forgive persons or parties who, at this juncture, allow self interest to frustrate a development which is so clearly in the interests of the nation as a whole".[7]

Cub followed this public challenge with a private letter to Heath. He recounted his own experience in Rhodesia, where he had tried to produce a political outcome "by force of character". In the short-term his efforts seemed to have failed, but ultimately (he asserted) he had been proved right. Heath was invited to take consolation from this. "My advice to you now", Cub wrote is to resign from the Leadership of the Conservative Party and to offer, as you would do, to serve the nation and the party in any other capacity which seemed to be right. If you stay on as Leader, the movement against you would increase and, if you get thrown out, you may never be able to return . . . the Conservative Party must get itself into a position of being seen to be a spearhead of national unity and being able to attract back to it the support that it has lost to Liberals and Labour . . . you will find yourself in difficulties during this period and will be regarded as an obstacle to this development within the party and in the country at large. If, on the other hand, you withdraw from the stage for a period it will do you personally a great deal of good and will put you in a position of reserve against the time when we will need your services again.[8]

In his enthusiasm for coalition Cub had overlooked his earlier remark that Conservatives tended to react against his views on every subject. On this point he could hardly hope to make a willing convert of Heath, and his letter to *The Times* was a very public breach of the Conservative Party's surviving code of loyalty. Even Edward du Cann, whom Heath had sacked as party chairman, sent Cub's suggestion of a change of leader straight back up the pitch: "While Ted is the leader of the party", he wrote, "I shall support him as strongly as I can". Almost the only Conservative to agree publicly with Cub, ironically, was the right-winger Lord Coleraine with whom he had clashed over Rhodesia many times in the Lords. Coleraine felt that they "must make the most of the common ground" between them; since he wanted a government which would drive out inflation regardless of the cost in unemployment, his only "common ground" with Cub was their shared belief that Heath must go.[9]

Heath himself sent Cub a cool reply, acknowledging the constructive intention behind the letter but pointing out that he was receiving advice from a wide range of people and would make up his own mind about the leadership. He stayed at his post, believing that there would soon be another election and that Labour's left-wing programme would alienate the people. But Wilson had made a reasonable impersonation of Stanley Baldwin during the February campaign, and although the voters preferred Heath's policies they felt safer with his rival. By the summer of 1974 Heath had been persuaded by colleagues in the shadow cabinet to adopt a platform of national unity in an attempt to win back voters who had defected to the Liberals in February. This was the only card remaining for Heath, but it made no impression on Cub who believed that the leader, rather than the programme, had to be changed; there was still no sign that Heath's concept of national unity included Labour, or indeed that he had any enthusiasm for power-sharing. When Heath visited back-bench Conservative peers in July Cub repeated to his face the unwelcome advice in his letter; news of the incident leaked to the press, and although Cub was rebuked for his disloyalty in some of the letters he received the majority of his correspondents praised his courage.[10]

In April 1974 Cub met Sir Keith Joseph in the street. It was a symbolic encounter; in political terms both men were travelling on the same road at the time – but in opposite directions. Joseph, who had been a high-spending minister at Social Services, was deeply affected by the late government's failure and by his own sense of having sinned. After their chance meeting Cub summed up the remedy now proposed by Joseph: "you told me that you were engaged in trying to persuade people, on behalf of the Conservative Party, that profit is an essential factor in our life". Cub's response was discouraging; "from a political point of view", he wrote, "this sort of effort is a waste of time". Undeterred, Joseph asked if they could meet. Cub put him off until June; when they finally met he made clear his own preference for a change of leader, but lamented to a friend that "quite obviously [Joseph] is a committed Heath man". Possibly the conversation helped to weaken Joseph's loyalty; this would be ironic, because Cub never considered his old PPS as a potential leader. Over the coming months Joseph sent him advance copies of speeches in which he agonised over the failure of postwar governments and sketched out his free-market ideas. These speeches, particularly the one delivered at Preston in September, joined with Heath's own pronouncements in undermining the attempt to present the Conservatives as the party which would bind the nation's wounds. Cub had once told Joseph that he had "no judgement"; Joseph's persistent attempts to interest him in right-wing policies must have reinforced his suspicions. These received public confirmation later in the year when Joseph made another speech, implying that the poor of Britain were breeding too much. This was the political equivalent of the letter written during the war by Cub's father-in-law, protesting at the quality of working-class army recruits; it destroyed Joseph's ambitions to succeed Heath.[11]

While Joseph was brooding over his Preston speech Cub was preparing a very different document. The *Spectator* published his "Draft manifesto for a National Government" on 14 September 1974, accompanying the article with a statement that while the journal "has no commitment to his opinions . . . we think it right that at this time he should have the opportunity of ventilating them through our columns". The manifesto contained broad themes for action, rather than specific policy ideas. There were some differences between Cub's approach and that of the last Conservative government; he embraced Labour's idea of a "social contract" (while arguing that this should cover employers as well as workers), attacked the tendency for ministers to think that "big is beautiful" (exemplified by Peter Walker's reorganisation of local government), and – predictably – called for reforms of both Houses of Parliament. Cub would also have gone further than Heath in ensuring the devolution of power to the regions. Yet there was no retreat from Heath's tendency to search for governmental solutions to economic problems: indeed Cub's coalition would have exercised more detailed control even than Attlee's postwar Labour government. Like Heath he hoped to tame the unions by offering them full consultation on economic matters, even suggesting that some union leaders might be brought into the cabinet without having to stand for election. His appeal was addressed to those of his countrymen who had retained their sense of public spirit, despite his acknowledgement that in an acquisitive society "a sense of vocation and pride of service have tended to be submerged in a struggle to acquire higher material rewards". He thought he sensed a reaction among the young against what he had denounced back in 1951 as "shoddy materialism", but he was wrong. His view that life was about more than money was shared by a dwindling minority; the trade unions certainly preferred their material interests to the well being of the nation, which might explain why so many of them later voted for Margaret Thatcher. The "irrational prejudice and purely partisan ideas" which had fostered Britain's decline could not be reversed by the words of a peer who had been out of full-time government service for more than a decade, and no prominent public figure supported his line.[12]

With hindsight Cub's manifesto looks like a quixotic gesture, but if the general election of October 1974 had produced another hung Parliament a coalition was a strong possibility, and it must have acted along the broad lines he had sketched. As it was, Wilson squeezed home with a tiny overall majority. Heath campaigned hard and the result was better than the Conservatives expected; Labour's continued vulnerability encouraged him to stick to his task as opposition leader. But this time he had to submit himself to re-election by his party; his chances of winning were apparently strengthened when Joseph knocked himself out of contention with his ill-advised venture into eugenics. But Cub had been cultivating a leadership candidate of his own.

Cub hit on the idea that Richard Wood should succeed Edward Heath as leader of the Conservative Party early in November 1974. Wood, the son of Neville Chamberlain's Foreign Secretary Lord Halifax, had been seriously wounded during the war, but he had defied the loss of both legs and when Cub got to know him in the 1950s he was a back-bencher respected on all sides of the Commons. He had never held a cabinet post – in Heath's government he was Minister for Overseas Development – but in Cub's eyes this was an advantage rather than a drawback. As Cub told him in December, Wood was one of the few people who could "give the traditional leadership for which the country looks to the Tory party . . . You are a North Country member; you have served in both home and overseas departments". Then came what Cub regarded as the clinching point: "You don't want the job". This was necessary because Wood's role would be a "sacrificial" one, "to make a clean break with the immediate past" and to prepare the way for a new generation.[13]

Clearly the example of Alec Home was in Cub's mind, because Wood was another old-fashioned Conservative from the shrinking school of public service. On 16 December the *Sun* reported the emergence of Wood as a dark horse; he had told reporters that he was thinking the matter over after "one or two people at Westminster" had urged him to stand. Cub approached Home to find out whether he would add his name to the "one or two people", but the ex-Prime Minister replied that although he had the highest regard for Wood "it is not fair to cast him in this role and to press him to consider it . . . I have been close to him for years now and I think that this would kill him in no time".[14]

Home's gloomy assessment of Wood's survival chances was rather ironic given his own performance back in 1963, when he tried to hint at his intention of standing for the leadership without seeming vulgar by telling people that he was planning to consult his doctor. At fifty-four Wood was six years younger than Home had been when he made his artful bid for the leadership, and if his health really was as bad as Home implied he could surely be trusted to make his own judgement. But Home had a valid point when he added that the next election might not take place for some time. In fact, Cub was trying to slam the stable door on a horse which had bolted when Heath succeeded Home in 1965. At that time there had been a case for keeping Home as a transitional leader in a short Parliament when there was no prospect of success at the next election. But after the election of October 1974 there was a chance that the Labour government could last for five years, giving plenty of time for a younger Conservative to make an impression on the voters as leader of the opposition. In these circumstances a transitional leader might delay any Conservative revival.

Cub seems not to have spelled out either to Wood or to Home the real reason for his unlikely choice of candidate. After four years of firing his "torpedoes" at Heath Enoch Powell had ruled himself out by stepping down from his Wolverhampton constituency in February and winning a seat as an Ulster Unionist in October. But Cub still feared that someone might win the leadership on the basis of policies associated with Powell – hard-line economic liberalism and the repatriation of immigrants. Even when Heath was in office he had worried about this, and had told the Prime Minister that it was the duty of the remaining "One Nation" members to fight off "the Powellite – Monday Club – right-wing of the Conservative Party". Despite his gaffe Joseph was still in the running in early November, when Wood was first approached. Cub was still on friendly terms with Joseph but the idea that he could emerge as the elected leader of a great party still appalled him; Joseph obviously hoped to pose as Powell's heir, but Cub saw him as a mediocre copy of a flawed original. Most moderates in the party pinned their hopes on William

Whitelaw, but Cub had no faith in him. Cub wanted a break with the immediate past, and a decisive reversal of the rightward trend he had noticed since the late 1960s. Wood was a man of the centre, who would lead the party into a coalition if the need arose. Cub hoped that under Wood's leadership the Conservatives would become once again a national party, and that when the time came for him to step down there would be no chance of a divisive successor.[15]

These hopes quickly evaporated. Although Joseph pulled out, on 25 November Margaret Thatcher told Heath that she intended to stand against him after making a brilliant attack on Denis Healey in the Commons. Although Heath was still leader Edward du Cann discovered that his loyalty had limits after all, but his own bandwagon soon stalled and by the end of January 1975 Mrs Thatcher was the only declared challenger. Cub had seen little of Mrs Thatcher for many years; he bore her no personal ill-will ("pretty and bossy" was his crisp summary of the impression she had made as a Young Conservative), but he was dismayed by an interview she gave to the *Evening Standard*, trumpeting the virtues of the middle-classes. In his frustration Cub sent to *The Times* a letter of which Ralph Bingham (or his own father) would have been proud: "If Mr Heath, a formidable and dedicated personality, is a political liability", he thundered, "Mrs Thatcher, as his principal opponent, is living evidence of the poverty of leadership material in the present establishment of the parliamentary party". It was a last-ditch attempt to summon a unifying candidate from the back-benches, and it failed. Margaret Thatcher became leader of the Conservative Party after a second ballot on 12 February; although the precise nature of her support is still unclear, undoubtedly many opponents of her policies helped her to knock Heath out on the first ballot in the mistaken view that this would facilitate a victory for Whitelaw.[16]

Cub's behaviour during the twelve months after the general election of February 1974 had been manic; even he thought that he had become something of a "loose cannon" in British politics. Actually his efforts to bring about a coalition and a change in the Conservative leadership showed that he was thinking more clearly than most moderate Tories, however unrealistic his actions. In February 1975 the "One Nation" tradition within the party suffered a conclusive defeat. What made this possible was the fact that the moderate majority failed to organise for battle; after the leadership election more and more ground was conceded to Mrs Thatcher while traditional Tories convinced themselves that she would be forced one day to retreat from her preoccupation with middle-class interests. In superficial hindsight Cub's fierce attempts to prevent this outcome make him look out of his depth. But if he wanted to draw attention to his views he had to be outspoken; and, having done so much to help Rab Butler to rebuild the party after the war, silence was not an option for him. Ironically, he appeared in the guise of a determined (if ineffectual) rebel only because of his excessive loyalty to the party he had served for so long.

During the leadership crisis Cub had received some proof that, even if he had doubts about his own judgement, others regarded him as a reliable figure. At the end of November 1974 the Labour cabinet responded to the increasing level of IRA attacks on the British mainland by preparing emergency legislation. The Prevention of Terrorism (Temporary Provisions) Bill was rushed through both Houses; it gave to the British government powers which the Home Secretary Roy Jenkins called "Draconian". Among other devices it enabled the government to deport residents of the United Kingdom and to prevent other suspected persons from leaving Northern Ireland.[17]

In the words of Labour's Attorney-General, the powers of deportation "introduced a principle of banishment from Great Britain which had not existed since the Middle Ages". The government was sensitive to criticisms from the civil rights lobby, and the system had to be run with something better than medieval standards of fairness. On 3 December Jenkins telephoned Cub and asked him to be one of two assessors of deportation orders. Cub had never taken an active interest in the Irish troubles – perhaps, on balance, that made him more suitable – but clearly he was regarded within Whitehall as a shrewd judge of people. As he told Richard Wood, he regarded the proposition with "particular distaste", but as a Privy Councillor he felt unable to refuse this new assignment. At least his new job allowed him to tell Wood that in his small way he, too, was prepared to make sacrifices in the national interest.[18]

Within 48 hours of his appointment Cub was asked to review his first two cases and received secret documents setting out the reasons for deportation. Since there were no precedents for this kind of work he had the right to make suggestions about procedure; drawing on his old ideas about personal diplomacy, he insisted on seeing the two men concerned before reaching his decision. This was agreed, and he travelled to Brixton prison where the men were being held. He decided that he should avoid any questions which might give the suspects an impression that he was trying to tease out additional information; in his first interview, with a well known IRA commander who had been living in Bristol, he asked about the local football team which had recently been in the news. With the second man sporting topics were out of the question; Cub was dragged into "a long talk about the philosophic and political background to Sinn Fein and the IRA". During this useful tutorial Cub reflected on a strange coincidence: the mild-mannered Irishman had the same name as a person who had been hanged by Rachel's Tudor ancestor, the Governor of Connaught Sir Richard Bingham. Cub's decision this time was less drastic; he confirmed the Exclusion Orders on both men. The incident generated a lasting interest in Sir Richard Bingham, and he researched a biography which allowed him to indulge his interest in Elizabethan times and his pride in his family connections. He was encouraged in his task by the historian A. L. Rowse, but (as usual) abandoned the book after a publisher rejected the manuscript of the first chapter.[19]

There were interesting aspects to his work as an assessor, but it involved serious risks. On one occasion Cub returned with Rachel from a wedding to find several policemen patrolling his gardens. There had been a secret warning that a "judge" was to be assassinated when he came home from a wedding on that day; after eliminating everyone else who fitted the vague description Special Branch concluded that Cub must be the target. The information proved to be false, but as in Rhodesia Cub felt that it was unfair to place his family at risk. The "Temporary" Act soon took on a permanent appearance, and Cub believed that nobody should be asked to stay in such a hazardous position for very long; the security precautions even came to affect his colleagues at Dawnay Day. But Jenkins wanted him to stay on, describing his reports as "a model of wisdom and thoroughness". Once or twice the government decided to act against his recommendations, but more often the Home Secretary was swayed by Cub's arguments into changing his original decision. In April 1976 it was agreed that Cub would continue for two more years. He was not allowed to escape so easily; despite occasional hints that he would like to retire he did not leave the job until forced to do so by family circumstances in 1982.[20]

Despite this new burden and recent setbacks Cub plunged back into his various political campaigns after the Conservative leadership had been settled. He decided to change his approach to the question of a national government, becoming in April 1975 the first Conservative to introduce a parliamentary motion in support of proportional representation. This reform, he felt, would spark off a long-delayed realignment of British politics. The major parties had always been coalitions in themselves, but they no longer enjoyed any principle of association more elevated than organisational inertia. The campaign which had been started to secure a "yes" vote in the forthcoming referendum on membership of the EEC had already revealed that moderates in all parties had more in common with each other than with their extreme colleagues; at the same time, the referendum was a constitutional innovation which could be followed up by more radical changes. Cub backed his speech in the Lords with a letter to *The Times*, which produced the kind of supportive editorial which had greeted so many of his unseasonal suggestions. He also received congratulations from the Liberal leader Jeremy Thorpe, who looked forward to "a fresh start in politics – which I believe could throw up a social democratic party and could throw out a quasi-marxist one".[21]

Cub, as usual, had been thinking about the situation within his own party rather than Labour, which in power had proved a good deal less than "quasi-marxist". He tried to interest Margaret Thatcher in proportional representation, but despite a friendly exchange of letters and a commitment to call a Speaker's Conference on the subject he expected no help from her. Having seized the leadership of one of Britain's great parties she was unlikely to drive through any reforms which might endanger the existing system. At the 1975 party conference in October Angus Maude – now restored to the Commons and the shadow cabinet – made clear his own opposition to proportional representation. Reflecting on this with Anthony Wigram, who had recently founded Conservative Action for Electoral Reform, Cub doubted whether the Tories could win the next election and added that "I have no confidence in the ability of Thatcher, Maude and Co. to govern the country if they did". Soon he was writing to Peter

Thorneycroft – brought out of retirement to fill the role of party chairman – to complain about Mrs Thatcher's style of leadership; Thorneycroft replied that his fears were quite unfounded.[22]

Amid all the party controversy Cub had not forgotten Rhodesia. On the tenth anniversary of UDI he confessed in a radio interview that he was "baffled" at the survival of the Smith regime; an anonymous Rhodesian showed that his views could still provoke passion by informing him that he was "a blithering stupid illiterate old fool". But events were turning against Ian Smith. Communist uprisings in Mozambique and Angola endangered Rhodesia's illegal supply-routes and worried the Americans; in 1976 Henry Kissinger joined the British in pressing Smith to agree that there would be majority rule within two years. Despite initial progress these talks broke down. By the end of the year Cub was planning a new tour of central and southern Africa, again with official approval. The visit occupied the first three months of 1977. This time Cub met some members of Smith's government as well as his old (and increasingly doleful) friend Roy Welensky; by contrast, Hastings Banda was clearly enjoying his status of Life President in Malawi, and was thriving although Cub had recorded his obituary for the BBC more than a decade earlier.[23]

Cub returned from Rhodesia with new worries. The country was now engaged in a brutal guerrilla war which eventually claimed 20,000 lives. Although most Africans apparently preferred the moderate Bishop Abel Muzorewa to the Patriotic Front leaders Nkomo and Mugabe, it was felt that the Bishop would be tainted if Smith tried to reach an agreement with him. Cub also picked up warnings about a possible civil war between the Shona and Matabele tribes once majority rule had been secured. On his return he floated the idea that the country could be partitioned between the tribes. This time he was lambasted by African leaders, one of whom described the plan as betraying "colonial mentality at its height". Cub might have responded that the existing national frontiers in Africa, which took no account of tribal loyalties, were the real legacy of the "colonial mentality".[24]

During his visit Cub made a short speech at the Three Feathers Club in Salisbury. He had been given a hostile reception at the club during his 1967 visit, but this time Rachel noted that "only a few refrained from clapping". In the past Cub had tried to defend the

British government against attacks from Europeans; he no longer felt this responsibility, because as he made clear in his speech "the time [is] past when we had any power". As Cub had feared since the break-up of the Federation, Rhodesia looked set to become a venue for a proxy war between the Americans and the Soviet Union. Against the super-powers not even Ian Smith's defiance could last long, and although Cub continued to offer suggestions to Labour's Foreign Secretary David Owen he had limited knowledge of the new players in the game. Elections were eventually held on the basis of universal adult franchise; the outcome was a victory for Muzorewa, but the Popular Front had resorted to its traditional tactic of a boycott. When Cub visited Central Africa for the last time in 1981 the Popular Front leader Robert Mugabe was Prime Minister of an independent Zimbabwe.[25]

There had also been changes in Britain, where the Conservatives replaced the unpopular Labour government after the general election of May 1979. Mrs Thatcher agreed with Cub that Muzorewa would have been preferable to Mugabe, but that was the limit of their harmony. In 1980 Cub tried to introduce a Bill which would ensure that a future Labour government would not be able to abolish the Lords without holding a referendum, but the Prime Minister gave a very cool response and the Bill was destroyed by her supporters in the Upper House. But the differences between them went much deeper; Cub always had a dim view of economists, and deplored the fact that the new Conservative government was following the abstract teach-ings of a narrow "monetarist" clique. In their name the government increased interest rates at a time when sterling was already rising due to Britain's possession of North Sea oil; although this forced the efficiency gains in manufacturing industry which the government expected, it also bankrupted many firms which would have survived had it been possible for them to export their products or to borrow money on reasonable terms. These hard-nosed policies became a badge of honour for Mrs Thatcher's supporters, who knew that her political fate depended on the success of the monetarist experiment. Her opponents were derided as "wets", as if to dare them to topple her. Cub had already fought to the best of his ability, and had no reason to regard the label as a personal insult; he drafted an article ("The Anatomy of a Wet") to show that the triumphant right-wingers were the real traitors to the Conservative tradition.

At the time of the 1979 election Cub was sixty-seven years old and after his long record of public service might have settled down to enjoy a retirement which, thanks to his investments and the generosity of Dawnay Day, was safe from the policies of the new government. Those who thought like him had lost the battle for the soul of the Conservative Party, and having made so many enemies during his various struggles he was entitled to think that others should rally around the tattered standard of "One Nation". But Cub's temperament ruled out the prospect of quiet acquiescence; he continued to attend the House of Lords, and he could never vote for policies which, he believed, contradicted everything he had stood for since he supported Stanley Baldwin in the debates of the Cambridge Union. He recognised that those who thought like him within the cabinet were vulnerable, but, as he told one of them in February 1980, he was in a position to "sound a warning", and, "by standing up and being counted among the 'wets'", he could "encourage the others to do likewise". His carefully prepared speeches on the effects of the recession were the most eloquent of his career. During a debate on the economic situation in February 1982, for example, he declared that

> All of us, I think, navigate our public careers by certain stars and, as one gets older, I suppose that some stars become more firmly fixed, and in other cases they disappear, perhaps forever, below the horizon. For me, the commonwealth is a fading star; but the social consequences, the sheer waste of national resources, the human misery caused by mass and long-term unemployment, is a star which burns as brightly in my political firmament as it did 50 years ago.

In his speech he pleaded that the government should now change its priorities, from the control of inflation to the conquest of unemployment. But ministers were following their own star – the implementation of a counter-revolution in economic thinking – and in their eyes there could be no other light in the sky. No amount of eloquence from the "wets" could distract them from their course; this dogmatic style, as much as the content of Conservative policy, dismayed Cub. Even so, he was not tempted when in January 1981 Roy Jenkins and his allies set up the SDP in an attempt to bring about a realignment of British politics. He declared that he would "live and die" as a Conservative, and continued to encourage ministers he admired (notably James Prior). In July 1981 he even sent a letter of congratulation to Edward Heath, who had encountered the customary sniping from his critics in the press after attacking the government in the wake of inner-city rioting. Heath wrote a very warm reply, but there was no lasting rapprochement. Mrs Thatcher's reply to the arguments of the wets was to remove from her cabinet two of their number, Ian Gilmour and Christopher Soames; Jim Prior had warned Cub that he might "have to go into the wilderness" after the reshuffle, but the Prime Minister prefered to send him to Northern Ireland as a preliminary push in that direction. At the 1981 party conference she declared that there would be no change in policy.[26]

Cub well knew what unemployment meant to its victims, but as some regions of Britain returned to the despair of the early 1930s he was struck down by the worst kind of personal blow. In the spring of 1982 Rachel was taken ill, and cancer was diagnosed. After the family returned from Rhodesia she had continued her work for the Girl Guide movement and her civic duties; in Colchester she remained at least as popular as her husband, frequently appearing in the local press. The partnership was as close as it had been at the beginning and although Rachel's health was sometimes delicate she was Cub's junior by four years. Cub, who remained a valiant smoker despite the health warnings which had appeared in recent years, had assumed that he would leave Rachel a widow. But after a holiday in the Western Isles Rachel's doctors warned Cub that her illness was incurable. He gave up his Deputy Speakership of the Lords, and his responsibilities under the Prevention of Terrorism Act, to be with his wife through the final crisis: but Rachel's condition brought side-effects for which Cub was unprepared. Rachel had been brought up as a Christian Scientist, and although none of the diaries of her adult life show any trace of excessive devotion to this sect she expressed a desire to be nursed by fellow-believers, far away from the Cross House. To the grief Cub felt while nursing Rachel through these days was added the agony of apparent rejection; the cloud only passed in the final stages of her illness. Rachel died on 14 July 1983, with her family around her; she was buried in the family grave at Layer de la Haye.

Rachel was only sixty-six years old when she died; the couple had been together nearly forty years, but could have expected more years of contentment at the Cross House. Cub's mother had died in 1976, followed by Sir Ralph Bingham in the next year; both were full of years. He was also beginning to lose the political colleagues of his early days. On 4 January 1982 he went to see Rab Butler at his home in Great Yeldham – not far from Stanstead Hall, where Rab had once asked Cub to be his "spaniel". Butler was very frail – indeed he was dying, although this had been concealed from him by his doctors. As Cub recalled after Rab's death in March, "I sat almost literally at his feet, as I had done so often in those far-off days before the war, while he advised me how I should conduct my political activities and made some characteristically perceptive comments on the personalities in the present government". He noted that events in Africa had left "a certain feeling of estrangement", but "by the alchemy of time, the old affectionate relationship of nearly half a century seemed to be completely restored". Unfortunately time had not quite finished its alchemy. A year after Rab's death a massive, well researched and highly partisan account of the Federation was published, based on the papers of Roy Welensky. Cub was alive to the bias in the author's judgements – despite his renewed friendship with Welensky he was criticised as harshly as anyone – but the book convinced him that he had been betrayed. He told a friend that "Rab, after ignoring my advice and rejecting my ideas offered to recall me in disgrace in order to appease Welensky". He had done so although he had told Welensky about the strong personal bond between them: "no wonder Rab avoided me during the last 20 years". In fact it was Welensky who had demanded Cub's head, and Butler only agreed that he should be recalled one month earlier than planned; but Cub had known nothing of these discussions and the revelation was a bitter surprise. The wound lingered but he did his best to cover it up, and from the memoir he began to draft in 1984 no one would be able to guess that there had ever been a falling-out with Rab.[27]

Butler had been left a widower at an earlier age than Cub, and had found great happiness with his second wife Mollie. As Rachel succumbed to disease Cub thought that his own life was ending too. He accepted – perhaps too readily – that his children would be preoc-cupied with their own families (the youngest daughter Carole had continued the political theme between the two 1974 elections by marrying Ian Taylor, later a Conservative minister). But Rab's good fortune would soon be his own.

Patricia Parry had studied at Cambridge (reading English on a scholarship) while Cub was at Pembroke College. But Patricia (always known as Pat) preferred the Cambridge Apostles to the budding statesmen in the Union. After both had made false starts with partnerships which ended in divorce she married one of the Apostles, Richard Llewelyn-Davies, who later won fame (or notoriety) as the chief planner of Milton Keynes. Another close friend was Pat's Cambridge room-mate Tess Mayer, who subsequently married Lord Rothschild. Pat was a fiery socialist who had often clashed with her Conservative father; she remembered shouting "Down the drain with Chamberlain!" during a demonstration before the war. She was also a noted cricketer. In the unusual circumstances of war interesting characters like Pat were welcomed into the civil service. She reached a senior position in the Ministry of Transport; when her minister, Philip Noel-Baker, moved via the Ministry of Air to the Commonwealth Relations Office Pat went with him. She fought three elections for Labour in the 1950s, including one contest against Enoch Powell at Wolverhampton West. In those days even the most able women found it hard to find winnable seats, and Pat's friendship with the rebellious Nye Bevan further narrowed her chances of selection. Instead of forging a career in Parliament she poured her energies into Great Ormond Street Hospital and the African Education Trust. In the latter capacity Pat visited Central Africa while Cub was at the High Commission, but she deliberately avoided contact with this representative of a reactionary imperialist power.

In 1967 Pat became a life peer in her own right. Richard was already in the House of Lords but his political interests were limited; on the first anti-nuclear Aldermaston march he took a prolonged and unauthorised rest in a pub. As her friend Richard Crossman predicted, Pat soon proved that the chauvinism of the selection committees had robbed the Commons of an excellent MP; within two years she had become a whip, in 1972 she was made Deputy Chief Whip, and a year later took the top job. These positions lumbered her with some arcane titles; at first she was a "Baroness in Waiting", and when Labour returned to power in 1974 she was addressed as "Captain of Her Majesty's Bodyguard of the Honourable

Corps of Gentlemen-at-Arms". The bodyguard consisted of retired soldiers, most of whom, Cub suspected, were dedicated Conservatives: the arrival of a left-wing female at their head "initially caused great consternation in their ranks". But resistance to Pat was always short-lived; David Scott, who worked with her at the CRO and later became Cub's Deputy High Commissioner, remembered her as "attractive and dynamic" and the years did nothing to diminish her charisma.[28]

If Pat had forced her way into the Commons during the 1950s she would have formed a chorus of criticism against Cub with the likes of Fenner Brockway. She joined the Lords at a time when Rhodesia was frequently debated, but by 1967 Cub was far more popular with the Labour left than with his own party's right-wing. There was enough common ground to allow friendly discussions, although Pat was an early admirer of Robert Mugabe and felt that the future lay with people regarded by Cub as extreme nationalists. In a 1972 debate on sanctions which Cub had instigated Pat strayed beyond the usual courtesies of the House; the words she used in connection with Cub's own speech included "fascinating", "astonishing", "absolutely right", and "extraordinarily interesting", although she managed to quibble on one or two points. In November 1973 Cub sent Pat a note to congratulate her on a speech on Rhodesia and on becoming Chief Whip. The final settlement in Rhodesia was broadly welcomed by both, and they were unlikely to fall out over the early domestic policies of the 1979 government.[29]

In October 1981 Richard Llewelyn-Davies died after a long illness. Despite her many admirers and friends, of whom one of the dearest was the ennobled Tony Greenwood – Cub's "twin" to the last – Pat responded to her loss by retreating into what she called an emotional cocoon. In 1982 she gave up her post of Chief Whip, although she continued to participate fully in the work of the Lords as Principal Deputy Chairman of Committees; she also chaired the Lords' Committee on European Affairs, which had a high reputation for well informed debate. Cub kept in touch with her, but Rachel was now ill and he only appeared in the House of Lords when urgent business took him to London. There were similarities between the illnesses of Rachel and of Richard; towards the end of Rachel's life Cub sought advice from Pat concerning the sad estrangement which the disease had caused. Pat's reassurance was helpful to him in the most difficult weeks of his life; her special knowledge of Cub's position complemented the loving support of his family.

After Rachel's death the bereaved couple lunched together on a more regular basis. By the autumn they were seeing each other whenever they could, although Pat's work on House of Lords committees often sent her abroad. The friendship, cemented by so many mutual interests despite the apparent disparity between an outgoing socialist and the shy, old-fashioned Cub, had torn off Pat's protective cocoon; thanks to her help at the crucial time Cub had never needed to develop one of his own. His gratitude might have made him fall in love with Pat without any other assistance; in combination with her strong intelligence and her beauty it left him dazed. He had agreed with Rachel's view that if something happened to one of them the survivor should feel free to marry again if the circumstances were right. The idea of seeking out a replacement for Rachel was odious to Cub, but the only other person he could love had crossed his path before he realised that he was lost.

Cub sensed a special "affinity" between himself and Pat, and a holiday in Kenya proved that they were compatible. He was desperate to marry her. But there were two major obstacles. Pat had her own homes (at Tring in Hertfordshire and a flat in London close to her friend, the actress Peggy Ashcroft); as a professional woman she was used to her independence. The Cross House meant as much to Cub as Tring did to Pat. Negotiating the logistics of a marriage would be as difficult as any problem Cub had faced as High Commissioner; and, Pat reasoned, if their life-styles were going to stay as they were why bother changing their status?

The more serious difficulty concerned the cross-party nature of their alliance. They agreed that Cub's reputation would suffer if he married a socialist; his opponents would use it as evidence that he had never been a true Conservative. In fact the couple's disagreements on most issues were camouflaged by their mutual dislike of the Thatcher Government, which was re-elected in June 1983 despite its initial unpopularity – but that counter-argument would not have impressed the critics very much. A marriage would have affected Pat, too; Cub suspected that she had won the hearts of many (if not all) of the male Labour peers, and their misery at seeing her married at all would be multiplied by the thought that she had been carried off by one of the enemy.

This second argument was a great threat to their happiness, because it ruled out any public displays of affection whether they were married or not. The only solution was to embark on a clandestine affair which turned out to be a source both of frustration and of extra piquancy. This, Cub felt, was the love affair which he should have experienced at Cambridge instead of making clever speeches about the institution of marriage and the future of the House of Lords. They could meet in her room at the House, or exchange glances across the Chamber, but there were a limited number of excuses for a Tory peer caught hanging about the office of a senior member of the Labour Party, and too much staring would give them away. After Cub's gaze had wandered during a debate when he deputised for the Lord Chancellor Pat sent a note with a postscript: "I'm sure it's improper even to *think* of knees while presiding over the Woolsack!". Even travelling abroad – what Cub called their "elopements" – brought unexpected hazards. In Kenya they found themselves in a hotel next door to the former Lord Privy Seal, Humphrey Atkins, and his wife. Cub recalled that "we had dinner with them one night giving the impression that our presence together in Kenya was entirely fortuitous". Feeling that they had managed a narrow escape, the guilty couple were dismayed to find themselves booked on a flight home with the Atkins'.[30]

Cub had to conceal his feelings from colleagues but found an outlet in an amazing stream of love-letters. He produced almost a hundred of these in the first year of their relationship; thankfully for the postal service they spent more time together after this. As he confessed, he was "bombarding" her, and he made numerous proposals of marriage. Pat kept Cub at her mercy by refusing either to agree or to say that she would never marry him under any circumstances; occasionally the amorous peer rebelled under this treatment, but gradually came to think that so long as his intentions were honourable it was permissible for him to be Pat's lover. He made other concessions, trying (unavailingly) to stop smoking and remembering to wipe his feet before going in to the house at Tring; to show that life went on at the Cross House he had it painted pink (a gesture which, he joked to Pat, might prove to his neighbours that his politics had always been dubious). The adjustment he made to accommodate Pat's character was remarkable; whenever she made a decision which irked him he responded with nothing more than a teasing reference to the phrase which she used when she was feeling stubborn – "I will if I want to". He rejoined the panel of Deputy Speakers to show Pat that he still wanted a place in political life, and he considered fresh political causes to channel his renewed energy.

A suitable outlet far from the usual topics of party controversy soon suggested itself. In the summer of 1983 there had been a public outcry against the effect produced on air quality by the tendency of some farmers to burn off straw and stubble in their fields. Cub had never taken much interest in environmental questions, but he decided that this topical problem would provide a suitable legislative challenge. In November 1983 he introduced a Bill in the Lords to control the practice. His move brought many letters of support from environmentalists, and it was also adopted in the Commons by the Conservative MP Roger Gale. But it earned him a fresh group of enemies – the farming lobby, whose members felt that the adverse publicity had arisen because a very small minority had ignored the safety and comfort of the public. They were already subject to local restrictions and had no wish to be burdened with new regulations. At least the farmers' spokesmen in the Lords were better-humoured than Cub's opponents on the Rhodesian issue: Lord Stanley of Alderley, for example, engaged in a constructive correspondence and delivered a jovial rebuke to Cub's "straw lust".[31]

Cub tried hard to master the technicalities of his new hobby, taking advice from experts on alternative means of disposing of the straw and stubble. So often in the past he had introduced motions in the House of Lords just to draw attention to a problem; now he had landed himself with the challenge of guiding a Bill through its various stages. His persistence was all the more creditable because public interest in the problem soon flagged; when the Bill received its second reading only 48 peers voted, despite the fact that 250 of them had taken part in a division on education only a couple of hours before. The vote was close even though Cub had accepted a series of amendments; he won by 27 to 21. Among his supporters was one member of the Lords not noted for her interest in such matters – Baroness Llewelyn-Davies of Hastoe. Perhaps her vote was a present – this crucial division took place on Valentine's Day 1984.

The Bill passed all its stages in the House of Lords, and was promptly killed off by the government in the Commons. Cub made another attempt at the end of 1984 and in the following year but ministers were still opposed and the Bill made no further progress, although the regulations governing the straw-burning process had been tightened. By now he felt that he had taken his campaign as far as he could; besides, having tried to play a part in so many great issues of state he felt that it would be rather ironic if he were to be remembered as the man who put a stop to the burning of straw and stubble. But the story had an interesting sequel. In the summer of 1989 there was a new public outcry, and Cub dusted down his Bill, complete with the concessions he had been forced to make by the agricultural lobby. Under his proposals farmers would be allowed to burn stubble under licence. However, the government had realised that many of its supporters were anxious about the environment, and that even if it upset the agricultural lobby farmers were unlikely to transfer their support to other parties because of stubble and straw. In November 1989 the Environment Secretary John Gummer told the Commons that straw and stubble burning would be outlawed within three years. After all the opposition that he had encountered Cub was amused to read in *Hansard* that hardly anyone protested against Gummer's statement – even though the measure finally adopted was far stricter than his own proposals.[32]

Advised by Pat, Cub had decided in 1984 to help his Bill by avoiding speeches and votes which would provoke the government. But this self-denying ordinance was no easier to sustain than his renunciation of tobacco. Unemployment was still rising, and the government's moves to curtail the powers of local authorities offended against his belief in decentralisation. In the event his reluctant silence made no difference to the fate of his Bill; the government's unfriendly attitude allowed him to join six other Conservative peers who voted against the abolition of the Greater London Council. By November Cub was in a truculent mood, and had an ideal opportunity to express his feelings in the debate on the government's legislative programme for the coming year.

Before Cub made his contribution to the debate the frail Harold Macmillan, now Earl of Stockton, delivered his maiden speech. The proceedings of the Lords were now televised, which added to the drama of the occasion. But on the printed page Stockton's speech was dramatic enough. Cub's old tutor Captain Finn would have approved of Stockton's opening joke; the old interventionist also included a humourous explanation of the controversy between monetarists and Keynesians, although Cub remembered with a shudder a cabinet meeting at which Macmillan, pressed by the Treasury for spending cuts, had merely shrugged and said "Well, during the whole of my life I have always spent more than my income". But this time Macmillan's message was very serious, and damaging to the government. The mineworkers led by Arthur Scargill had been on strike for several months; Stockton referred to them as "the best men in the world", who had beaten the Kaiser and Hitler. "The strike is pointless and endless", he claimed. "We cannot afford action of this kind".[33]

Cub, sitting on his familiar bench just behind Stockton, praised his old leader and kept his own speech shorter than usual. Unlike Stockton he toned down his rhetoric, but the facts he produced were damning. The government talked about its record of good housekeeping but the taxpayer had to pay for three and a half million unemployed; the cost to the nation of this unnecessary and demoralised army was estimated to be more than £7 billion. Stockton had referred to the experience of the 1930s which Cub remembered equally well; he called for something like Roosevelt's "New Deal", which he had praised as a student, to solve the problem of unemployment. Cub had made more eloquent speeches, but Stockton was moved by his warm tributes and by the strange fate which had brought them to fight once more in a battle which they seemed to have won thirty years before. The old Earl turned around and grasped Cub's hand when his speech was over. Ironically the next speaker was Lord Harris of High Cross whom Cub had recruited to the CPC in 1947; for many years Harris had been a champion of the monetarist creed which both Cub and Stockton blamed for Britain's troubles.[34]

The government was increasingly worried about the Lords, which was asserting the stubborn independence which made it a defensible anachronism. Stockton's speech was widely publicised, and repeated rebellions by their lordships convinced party managers that they should impose some order. While this was a fairly straight-forward matter in the House of Commons there was very little that could be done with the peers. "The machine", as Cub called the party's officers, could hardly carpet the Earl of Stockton: but Cub was not so eminent, and in his case the charge-sheet was much longer. Back in November 1981, as a gesture of support to the wets, he had announced that he felt free to vote as he wished in the Lords. Subsequently he was a frequent visitor to the opposition lobby, and, as the Chief Whip Lord Denham complained, on 12 December 1984 he spoke and voted for the opposition on "what amounted to a vote of censure covering [the government's] whole economic policy". In that debate on unemployment Cub argued that "policies which serve the interests of the middle classes are just as dangerous and divisive as the policies which are designed to give domination to the working class"; if Mrs Thatcher continued on her present course she would "end up destroying the party she leads. Behind her she will leave anger, disillusionment and a nation divided against itself".[35]

Cub was seated on the Woolsack at 8.30pm on the same day when the Deputy Chief Whip, the Earl of Swinton, informed him in what he considered to be "peremptory and discourteous terms" that he should attend the Chief Whip after the debate. Cub indicated that he would prefer to go home after a long session, and that he could not be in London on the following day because he had to make preparations for a visit from Carole and Ian Taylor – complete with two children, a nanny and an unruly parrot. Lord Denham himself now appeared, and to the astonishment of the other peers a heated discussion was conducted on the Woolsack. Denham was happy for the Lords to defeat the government now and again, feeling that this provided justification for a "revising" second chamber: but the truculent Cub was a different matter.[36] Denham felt that he had made a reasonable request in asking for an early interview, and said that unless Cub turned up within 48 hours he would see him next week "as a Crossbencher". On the following day Denham wrote to Cub, informing him of the decision to deprive him of the party whip which was confirmed after a conference with Whitelaw. The "loose cannon" had been tipped overboard.[37]

It was thought that the government's action was unprecedented in the history of the Lords – no one could remember anyone losing the whip for political reasons, although one or two might have been black-balled by their parties for personal indiscretions. As Denham probably expected his action produced a wave of goodwill towards

Cub, although one self-professed (and confused) socialist wrote to tell him that "You asked for what you got . . . You will never destroy Thatcher. Long may she live!". He received a warm letter of support from the hardened dissident Sir Ian Gilmour, but even some junior MPs with more to lose felt that they should record their dismay at the government's actions: these included the pro-European Hugh Dykes but also Tim Yeo, later a minister. Cyril Townsend MP enclosed a copy of a protest he had sent to Lord Denham. The press coverage was also sympathetic, and some papers published the exchange of letters between Cub and Denham. In the *Guardian* Hugo Young hinted that the move was really inspired by Lords Whitelaw and Boyd-Carpenter who wanted to turn the Upper House into a muffled echo-chamber for the thoughts of their mistress.[38] In fact the Chief Whip had acted on his own initiative, but the incident could be woven into a plausible story about a government incapable of tolerating dissent from any quarter. There had already been moves to tighten discipline in the Lords; the old back-bench Association of Independent Unionist Peers, to which Cub was proud to belong, had been remodelled under a new name from which the word "independent" was pointedly removed.[39]

On balance Cub enjoyed the fuss. It made no difference whatsoever to his conduct in the Lords, where he was now regarded with great affection. The former Conservative minister Lord Renton sat beside him on the bench from which Cub had made his first Commons speech in 1950, and described him to the author as "always a fine speaker: lucid, audible, sincere but always determined to speak his own mind". After losing the whip Cub told Denham that the decision allowed him to speak and vote as he wished, but he had been doing that since 1963 and he merely continued to call himself an Independent Unionist. There was an awkward moment when an Essex Conservative denounced Cub for his "public display of disloyalty", but Cub was far too popular in the Colchester area for this to damage him and when he repeated his views in articles and letters to the press his own mail-bag showed overwhelming support. Had he been alone at the time he might have been depressed once the adrenaline of the first few days had worked through his system. But despite her refusal to become his wife Cub now felt secure in the love of his "enchanting, wilful, rebellious, independent, brave, clever, and adorable" Pat. This gave him the necessary platform to resume his attacks on the government, which culminated in a debate on education reform in June 1988. Cub, who had been prompted by the Skinners' Company and the memory of Butler's 1944 Education Act, was prominent among the peers who moved over 450 amendments. The session of 28 June began at 3pm and ended at 9am the following morning. The seventy-six year old Cub continued to propose amendments after 2am. Not even the youthful "One Nation" group had "harried" its opponents with such determination.[40]

Even since his friendship with Angus Maude had foundered over Suez Cub had struggled against a feeling that political differences must mean an end to cordial personal relations. After a quarrel which almost led to a fight Cub could tell Denham that he regarded him "as one of the nicest men I know"; Denham replied that "it would make our relations closer and more friendly than ever". The knowledge that Welensky had wanted Cub sent home in disgrace from the Federation had no effect on their renewed friendship; in August 1985, after a few months without a letter from Cub, Welensky (now living in Dorset) expressed his relief that Cub was not ill. By contrast Cub felt certain that Mrs Thatcher would hate him for his persistent criticisms. When he dined at Number 10 in November 1980 he was glad to be seated well away from the Prime Minister. After being deprived of the party whip he met her in a narrow corridor at Westminster. He felt that he had no alternative but to try to sneak past and hope that she would not recognise him. The strategy failed; she asked him how he was, and he muttered that he was very well before brushing past. Afterwards he felt ashamed of himself and wished that he had stopped for a few words.[41]

In his position Cub was less affected by a major problem for "wets" in the House of Commons: if Mrs Thatcher was so wrong, what was the alternative? Like Sir Ian Gilmour he believed that trade union reform was fully justified, but this ran into the "Thatcherite" argument that mass unemployment was the necessary price for securing a shift in power-relations in the workplace. The wets could reply that in 1979 the country was so sick of industrial disputes that Heath's compromise of restricting union power while using government intervention to keep unemployment down would have been accepted if Mrs Thatcher had cared to try it. Cub also stayed loyal to the idea of a "property-owning democracy", but was deeply troubled by the policy of privatisation. Like other wets he had to acknowledge that each state sell-off seemed to be popular, and this took the edge off his complaint that the government was introducing a form of "casino capitalism" only suited to American conditions. Whether the wets were right or not in their criticisms is a matter of personal judgement, but Cub's contribution to their case was both sincere and consistent with what he had always thought. If he had a weakness, it was his refusal to accept the possibility that society had changed since the 1930s – that by 1979 Britain had already become more like the United States, and that the average citizen was no longer moved by appeals to the national interest. This much he might have gathered when his call for a coalition passed unheeded in 1974–5; but the recognition would have extinguished the last remaining "guiding star" of his political life, and he continued to think well of his fellow countrymen.

After the fall of Mrs Thatcher Cub continued to attend the House and was a regular speaker until 1994, when he returned to his old theme of overseas development and attacked the misuse of aid in connection with the Pergau Dam affair. The aid budget had been intended to help economic development, he argued, not to promote dubious arms deals. It seemed that all the measures to which he had contributed were now being undermined; in a rare intervention in 1996 he bemoaned the fact that the selective commemorative stamps he had championed as Assistant Postmaster-General had been super-seded by a "flood" of "vulgar and ugly" issues. "On the whole" (to use one of his favourite phrases) he welcomed the election of "New" Labour in May 1997, not least because the Major Government seemed to have clung on to power for far too long; his hope that the Conserva-tive Party would be revived by a period of opposition received a jolt when his favourite candidate, Kenneth Clarke (like himself a former President of CUCA and the Cambridge Union) was defeated by William Hague. During the Lords' Debate on the Address in 1997 he concentrated on the new government's plans for constitutional reform, supporting proposals for devolution, an elected Mayor of London (but not for other towns), and – inevitably – changes to the House of Lords. As usual he had something else to add; casting his eye back to the "long, dreary and bilious" final year of the Major Government, he recom-mended that parliaments should last a maximum of four years.[42]

In his eighties Cub stepped up his contributions to *The Times* letter-page; it was as if this was a substitute for the House of Lords on those days when he was unable to attend. Euthanasia was notable among the new causes which he urged on his readers, and he introduced a Bill on the subject in the Lords that led to the establishment of a select committee.[43] Pat, a firm supporter of this cause, served with distinction on the committee; she had once made a semi-serious pact with Tess Rothschild that when they had both reached the age of eighty they would push each other off Beachy Head. Cub also began to scour the obituaries, as more of his friends departed. Roy Welensky died in 1991, after years of ill health; with the death of Enoch Powell in February 1998 the original "One Nation" line-up had been whittled down to three. Even Hastings Banda proved to be mortal in November 1997 having lost the Presidency and suffered a short period of house-arrest as a token penalty for his years of tyranny in Malawi. By the mid-1990s Cub was appalled to find that he met most of his old acquaintances at memorial services, and only there; he resolved to give up these macabre excuses for token reunions. After meeting Pat he was certain that he was "A Man Born Lucky", and chose that title for the memoirs which he abandoned, as usual, after the first chapter (later he put together a very informal record, not intended for publication). Yet the health of those closest to him jarred against this feeling of good fortune. Carole was taken seriously ill in the mid-1980s, but in typical Alport fashion struggled gamely against her difficulties. Worse was to follow: Rose died very suddenly in 1993, after many happy years with her husband Geoffrey, an independent-minded clergyman.

Pat herself had suffered a stroke before the remarkable love-affair began; her work at the Lords was also hampered by ME. But until 1995 she and Cub enjoyed an active life together; their "elopements" included regular visits to the West Indies and Greece, which would have been unlikely destinations for Cub without Pat's firm guidance. Cub had been accepted by Pat's inner circle of friends – on further acquaintance with Lord Rothschild he judged him to be the most gifted man he had ever met – and inevitably their secret began to seep out. In the last two years of Pat's life there was no reason to continue the subterfuge; further strokes gradually eroded her ability to speak, although since she could still understand what others were saying her situation caused her great frustration. Cub was determined to nurse her at the Cross House, with the assistance of professional carers. He now prided himself on his ability to look after himself, although his catering skills were questionable; on one occasion he was alleged to have started to cook a kipper while it was still in its wrapper.[44]

Cub already had a road named in his honour in his adopted town (he would have preferred to see a public house called "The Lord Alport", and kept a temporary inn-sign of that name which was used for a while in the Southern Rhodesian town of Gwelo). In March 1992 he received further recognition of his contribution to life in Colchester when he was made an Honorary Freeman of the Borough. Tributes were delivered by old friends and representatives of all the parties, but Cub was most impressed with the newspaper article describing the ceremony: this bestowed upon him the wholly undeserved rank of QC and saluted his youthful career as "a distinguished Cambridge academic". He had won so many honours and served in so many positions that the local reporter could be forgiven for adding to or subtracting from the list here and there; if he had been asked to invent a couple of distinctions he might have chosen these. Typically he exploited the renewed attention to himself by launching a crusade to bring more employment to Colchester.[45]

The article celebrating Cub's new honour noted that he was looking fit. He had certainly been lucky in that sense; he once had appendicitis, and in 1985 he was shaken in a road accident, but otherwise he had avoided serious afflictions. In 1996 he underwent major surgery after a life-threatening illness, but recovered fairly soon and bounced into the Lords to tell his old friend Lord Harris (a defender of the right to smoke) that if anything happened to him it should be advertised that this had nothing to do with his life-long habit.[46]

Pat, however, was not so lucky. She sank gradually and died at the Cross House in November 1997 after further strokes. Cub's second chance of happiness had been snatched away. But he kept himself busy, arranging a memorial meeting which was held at the House of Lords in February 1998. Cub had always enjoyed organising people, whether or not they wanted to be organised, and the event was a great success. But few people in Cub's position could have coped with the emotion of this ceremony, at which he was finally acknowledged as Pat's devoted lover after years of secrecy. His public school training carried him through a difficult day, and he was amused when Pat's great friend Lady (Nora) David revealed that most people had known about the relationship anyway.[47]

Pat had filled up the hole which yawned in front of Cub when Rachel died. As it turned out, she had only delayed his encounter with this void; and the sweetness of their love-affair deepened his sense of loneliness once she had gone. He went through with his routine of opening fêtes and attending functions which went on far past the time when he wanted to sleep; he continued to sit on his familiar bench in the Lords, enjoying above all the chance to see Carole for lunch at Westminster and to gossip with his son-in-law Ian. He had the company of his golden retriever, Sadie, and looked forward to visits from his housekeeper and confidante Mary; he was delighted when Pat's daughter Hattie called her son "Cub", and he recognised the likeness to Pat in Cub's sister Sarah. Faithful friends such as Brian Harrison and his neighbour Mary Fairhead, who had once defaced the posters of his political opponent in Colchester, saw him as often as they could. But he had always hated the thought of returning to an empty house, although he was far too proud to admit it. In April 1998 Cub expressed the view that the present spring might be his last; his biographer was relieved to find in the course of his researches that he had been saying the same thing since 1967 – at the latest. By that spring of 1998 some memories of his past life had begun to fade, but he was proof against any argument that at some points during his career he might have profited from a different decision: and on this matter (if nowhere else) the subject of a biography should be allowed to put forward a point of view.

He was still the same "diffident" Cub of whom his father had gently complained, and was always surprised to be told how much he was loved and respected. In addition he was self-willed, impulsive, careless of his own interests and – just possibly – a little pompous on occasion. But he would always be, as his friend Charles Fletcher Cooke once told readers of *The Granta*, "the very best type of Englishman".

Notes

Chapter 1: Father and Son

1 A. Cecil Alport, *The House of Curious* (1938), p. 220.
2 *Ibid.*, pp. 235–41.
3 *Ibid.*, p. 303.
4 *Ibid.*, pp. 303–7.
5 *Ibid.*, p. 30.
6 *Ibid.*, p. 29.
7 Family papers suggest 1888, but in *The House of Curious* Cecil places his father's death just before he left for Edinburgh University, which indicates that the penultimate digit should be a nine.
8 *The House of Curious*, p. 108.
9 *Ibid.*, pp. 186–88.
10 Obituary of Cecil Alport, *The Lancet,* 2 May 1959.
11 *The House of Curious,* pp. 147, 313.
12 Manuscript memoir, p. 6, Alport MSS.
13 *Ibid.,* p. 63.
14 A. Cecil Alport, *The Lighter Side of the War* (1935), pp. 107–8.
15 *Ibid.*, pp. 17, 102.
16 *Ibid.*, p. 108.
17 *Ibid.*, pp. 160–62.
18 Undated letter from Cecil to Janet; Report from Lieutenant-Colonel Kidd, 20 June 1917, Alport MSS.

19 The Serb officers based their affection for Cecil on a party which he had arranged for them for which the wrong drinks were provided; as a result the Serbs got drunk for the first time in their lives. To express his gratitude to Cecil for bringing about this unique experience, one of the Serbs presented him with a magnificent revolver, which was bequeathed to Lord Alport.

20 Undated letter from Cecil to Janet, Alport MSS.

21 A. Cecil Alport, *One Hour of Justice* [1947], p. 8.

22 Obituary of Cecil Alport, *The Lancet*.

23 Autobiographical fragment, "The Furniture of One Man's Life", pp. 5–6, Alport MSS.

24 *The House of Curious*, p. 181; Trevor Burridge, *Attlee* (1985), pp. 14–15.

25 "The Furniture of One Man's Life", pp. 7–8; Burridge, *Attlee*, p. 15.

26 *The House of Curious*, pp. 197–98; Lord Alport, manuscript memoir, p. 5; Cecil Alport to Rachel Bingham, 24 May 1944.

27 Report of boxing match, *The Tonbridgian*, March 1929; Cecil Alport to Rachel Bingham, 24 May 1944; Geoffrey de Freitas, unpublished memoir, de Freitas Papers, Bodleian Library.

28 School reports, Alport MSS.

29 Manuscript memoir, p. 5; "The Furniture of One Man's Life", pp. 8–9, Alport MSS.

30 School report, Easter 1931, Alport MSS.

31 Cub to parents, 4 October 1931.

32 *The Granta*, 12 January 1934.

33 Geoffrey de Freitas, "The Thirties", in Percy Craddock (ed.), *Recollections of the Cambridge Union 1815–1939* (1953), p. 144; *The Granta*, 29 November 1933, p. 168.

34 *The Granta*, 28 February 1934, p. 307.

35 In December 1933 Julian Bell wrote in the *New Statesman* that at Cambridge "a very large majority of the more intelligent undergraduates are communists, or almost communists". As a Marxist himself Bell was a poor witness; presumably he denied that anyone who disagreed with his ideology could be "intelligent". See Robert Skidelsky, *John Maynard Keynes: Volume Two, The Economist as Saviour, 1920–1937* (1992).

36 Cecil to Rachel Bingham, 24 May 1944.

37 "The Furniture of One Man's Life", p. 13; *The Granta*, 22 May 1935, p. 423.

38 *The Granta*, 6 March 1935, p. 329; 24 October 1934, p. 54; 22 May 1935, p. 423.

39 "The Furniture of One Man's Life", pp. 11–12.

40 Manuscript of unpublished novel, "The First Year Down", p. 1, Alport MSS.

41 "The Furniture of One Man's Life", p. 15; Cub to General Sir Reginald Hoskins, 25 August 1935.

Chapter 2: A National Faith

1 *The House of Curious*, p. 25.

2 Diary of trip to the United States, Alport MSS.

3 Kay-Shuttleworth held his peerage for less than a year – he was killed on active service during the war. I am most grateful to Mr John Royle for his help on this and other matters.

4 Cub was never very musical, but years later he claimed that he slept through most of the performance, tired out from his journey.

5   M. J. A. [sic] Alport, "New Ideals from the New Deal: A Young Conservative Looks at America", *The London Imp*, March 1936. Speeches delivered by Cub and Royle at Morgantown, West Virginia, are reprinted in E. Phelps and J. Johnsen (eds), *University Debaters' Annual 1935–1936* (1936), pp 11–58.

6   Diary of trip to the United States, Alport MSS; M. J. A. [sic] Alport, "New Ideals from the New Deal", *The London Imp*, March 1936.

7   John Royle has pointed out that they occasionally rose before eight to catch trains.

8   Diary of trip to the United States, Alport MSS; John Royle's diary, 1 November 1936.

9   "New Ideals from the New Deal".

10 Manuscript memoir, p. 2, Alport MSS.

11 *Ibid.*, p. 1.

12 H. W. J. Edwards, *Young England* (no date: 1938?), p. 33; notes in Rachel Bingham's exercise book, in the possession of the Alport family; conversation with author, February 1998.

13 Edwards, *Young England*, p. 33; Cub to Rachel Bingham, no date (autumn 1945?); Manuscript memoir, p. 29, Alport MSS.

14 Cub to Butler, no date (June 1937?).

15 Geoffrey Ellis to R. A. Butler, 27 October 1937, Butler MSS. H87; Cub to R. A. Butler, 15 December 1937, Butler MSS. H87/11; Lady Falmouth to Butler, 17 December 1937, Butler MSS H87/9.

16 [C. J. M. Alport], *A National Faith* (1938), p. 7; Anthony Howard, *RAB: The Life of R. A. Butler* (1988 ed), p. 81; Butler to Pickthorn, 24 October 1937, Butler MSS. H88/134.

17 Manuscript memoir, p. 3, Alport MSS.

18 A. Berriedale Keith, "The Empire", *Manchester Guardian*, 19 October 1937; E. H. Carr, "Problems of Empire", *The Times*, 10 October 1937; C. J. M. Alport, *Kingdoms in Partnership* (1937), p. 266; Edmund Burke, *Reflections on the Revolution in France* (1969 ed), p. 106.

19 Butler to Cub, 17 May 1938, Butler MSS, G9/23; manuscript memoir, p. 33, Alport MSS.

20 Manuscript memoir, pp. 32–33.

21 Butler to Cub, 12 October 1938, Butler MSS, H88/13; *National Faith*, pp. 54–5 and note.

22 *National Faith*, pp. 31, 61.

23 *National Faith*, pp. 20, 89–90. Sixty years later, Cub would point out a portrait in his house of a young man who had been killed in the First War, saying that his features showed the nobility typical of his generation.

24 *National Faith*, p. 68; *The Granta,* 7 February 1934.

25 *National Faith*, p. 89.

26 *Egyptian Gazette*, 24 January 1939.

27 *Cornish Times*, December 1938/January 1939 (no dates). Cub had already contributed three articles to the paper on "Europe after Munich", but these have not been traced.

28 Manuscript memoir, pp. 19–20, Alport MSS.

29 Cub to parents, 14[?] February 1940.

30 Robert Shepherd, *Enoch Powell* (1996), p. 42.

31 Cub to Rachel Bingham, 2 March 1941.

32 Manuscript memoir, p. 22, Alport MSS.

33 *Ibid.*

34 *Ibid.*, pp. 24–5.

35 *Ibid.*, p. 25.

36 Cub to Rachel Bingham, 28 December 1941.
37 Cub to Rachel Bingham, 19 April 1943.
38 R. A. Butler, *The Art of the Possible* (1982), p. 136; Cub to Rachel Bingham, 15 May 1943.
39 Manuscript memoir, p. 26, Alport MSS.
40 *Ibid.*
41 Cub to Butler, undated (received 10 April 1944), Butler MSS. 42. C. J. M. Alport, "Our England Today", *East African Command Fortnightly Review*, No. 5, 11 April 1944.

Chapter 3: "Love and War"

1 John Ramsden, *The Age of Churchill and Eden* (1995), p. 40.
2 Butler to Cub, 21 August 1942, Butler MSS. G14/68.
3 Butler to Cub, 21 August 1942, Butler MSS. G14/68-9.
4 *Ibid.*
5 Cub to Butler, 20 October 1942, Butler MSS. G14/73-4; Butler to Cub, 3 February 1943, Butler MSS. G14/75; Cub to Butler, 10 March 1943, Butler MSS. A163/1.
6 Cub to Butler, 10 March 1943, Butler MSS. A163/1; Cub to Butler, 17 November 1943, Butler MSS. G14/79; Cub to Butler, 30 December 1943, Butler MSS. G14/84; Butler to Cub, 25 October 1943, Butler MSS. G14/76.
7 Cub to Butler, 17 November 1943, Butler MSS. G14/79–81.
8 Cub to Butler, 30 December 1943, Butler MSS. G14/83–4.
9 Cub to Rachel Bingham, 26 July 1943.
10 Cub to Rachel Bingham, 22 November, 18 October, 26 September 1943.
11 Manuscript memoir, pp. 29–30, Alport MSS.
12 *Ibid.,* p. 30.
13 Rachel Bingham to Butler, March 1944 (no date), Butler MSS. G14/94; Butler to Treasurer of Middle Temple, 14 March 1944, regarding Cuthbert "Allport", Butler MSS. G14/96
14 Ramsden, *Churchill and Eden*, pp. 40–1; Cub to Butler, 10 March 1943, Butler MSS. A163/1.
15 A. Cecil Alport, *One Hour of Justice*, pp. 101–6.
16 *One Hour of Justice*, pp. 256, 38; Cub to Butler, 30 December 1943, Butler MSS. G14/84.
17 Cecil to Rachel Bingham, 24 May 1944; Cub to Rachel Bingham, 25 June 1944.
18 Cub to Rachel Bingham, 25 June 1944; Rachel Bingham to Cecil, 13 July 1944.
19 Hogg, and Cub's former Ashridge pupil Peter Thorneycroft, both won places in Churchill's 1945 caretaker cabinet.
20 Cub to parents, 19 October 1944; Ramsden, *Churchill and Eden*, pp. 44, 74; Cub to Butler, 11 June 1944, Butler MSS. A163/2.
21 Cub to Butler, 25 September 1944, Butler MSS. G14/105.
22 Cub to Butler, undated letter (arrived in London 10 April 1944), Butler MSS. G14/113; Cub to Rachel Bingham, 12 March 1945.
23 Angus Calder, *The People's War* (1969), p. 563; Cub to Rachel Bingham, 30 May 1945.
24 Manuscript memoir, p. 31, Alport MSS; Cub to Butler, 29 July 1945, Butler MSS. G7.
25 Cub to Rachel Bingham, 10 and 17 August 1945.
26 Cub to Rachel Bingham, 18 August 1945.
27 *Ibid.* Amazingly, in view of the life-long habit he shared with Cecil, Cub

claimed not to have smoked a single cigarette while writing this enormous letter: but then Rachel was not there to verify his words.

28   Cub to Rachel Bingham, undated letter (August 1945?).
29   Rachel Bingham to Cub, undated letter, September 1945.
30   Manuscript memoir, p. 31, Alport MSS.
31   Cub to Rachel Bingham, 23 August 1943.

Chapter 4: Reviving Conservatism

1   J. D. Hoffman, *The Conservative Party in Opposition, 1945–1951* (1964), pp. 43–6.
2   Marjorie Maxse to Stephen Pierssené, 22 November 1945, Conservative Party Archive, file on "Political Education", Bodleian Library; Ramsden, *Churchill and Eden*, pp. 73, 145; Howard, *RAB*, p. 152.
3   Butler, *Art of the Possible*, pp 136–37; ACPPE Minutes 1946–49, Conservative Party Archive, Bodleian Library.
4   Colm Brogan, *Our New Masters* (1947), p. 220; Cub quoted in Hoffman, *The Conservative Party in Opposition,* p. 73.
5   CPC, *Conservatism 1945-1950* (1950), pp. 7, 42.
6   *1948 Conservative Party Conference Report*, p. 18; Ramsden, *Churchill and Eden*, p. 118.
7   *Industrial Charter* (1947), pp. 16, 3.
8   *1947 Conservative Party Conference Report,* p. 16; Ralph Harris, *Politics without Prejudice* (1956), pp. 112–13; Hoffman, *Conservative Party in Opposition*, p. 159; R. A. Butler, "The Two-Way Flow of Ideas", *Observer*, 28 March 1947.
9   Butler, *Art of the Possible*, p. 137; Julian Critchley, "The Intellectuals", *Political Quarterly,* vol. 32, no. 3, July–September 1961, p. 268; Patrick Cosgrave, *R. A. Butler: An English Life* (1981), p. 94.
10 ACPPE, minutes, 13 May 1947, Conservative Party Archive.
11 "R. A. Butler talks with you about The Industrial Charter", CPC, 1947, pp. 2, 18.
12 Hoffman, *Conservative Party in Opposition*, p. 162; Ramsden, *Churchill and Eden*, p. 157.
13 Hoffman, *Conservative Party in Opposition*, p. 165; undated manuscript [1948?], Alport MSS, Box 6; Ramsden, *Churchill and Eden*, p. 158. Apart from Smithers and his ally Herbert Williams, the most prominent opponents of *The Industrial Charter* were Lord Hinchingbrooke, a founder-member of the supposedly "progressive" Tory Reform Committee, and the ubiquitous Kenneth Pickthorn.
14 Cub to Butler, 20 March 1947, Butler MSS. H92/30–1; undated manuscript [1948?], Alport MSS, Box 6.
15 *Conservative Agents' Journal*, May 1948; Ramsden, *Churchill and Eden*, p. 147.
16 Lord Woolton, *Memoirs* (1959), p. 331; Butler, *The Art of the Possible*, p. 149. Ironically, when Cub rejoined the Education Department Marjorie Maxse had noted that it had "worked in the closest co-operation with the Central Office before the war when Mr Butler was chairman and Colonel Alport Assistant Secretary": perhaps she might have guessed that their ambitions had grown since then. Marjorie Maxse to Stephen Piersenné, 22 November 1945, file on "Political Education", Conservative Party Archive.
17 Undated letter [March 1947], Butler MSS. H92/42–3. Woolton pressed for a delay in publication of about a month; in fact the *Charter* appeared twenty days after the original deadline.
18 Butler MSS, H92/31, H92/42; Hoffman, *Conservative Party in Opposition*, pp. 107–8.

19 Woolton, *Memoirs*, pp. 337–8.
20 Cub to Rachel Bingham, 18 August 1945; Woolton, *Memoirs*, p. 331; *1948 Conservative Party Conference Report*, p. 18.
21 Berkeley subsequently joined the Labour Party. Cub also helped to ensure that an even more celebrated maverick, Enoch Powell, joined the CRD. Having telephoned the Central Office on his return from wartime service, Powell turned up at the Wilton Street basement office in his Brigadier's uniform. Cub noticed that his boots seemed less than clean, but was impressed by his qualifications and sent him to David Clarke who immediately appointed him to the Parliamentary Secretariat ("The Red Notebook", p. 14, Alport MSS).
22 Interview with Lord Harris of High Cross, May 1998.
23 Given that the party claimed to have 1,200,000 members in December 1947, this figure shows how difficult it was to induce Conservatives to take an active interest in policy-making; see Robert T. McKenzie, *British Political Parties* (1964 ed.), p. 187, note. Ironically, when the Fabian Society celebrated its diamond jubilee at the Royal Albert Hall in October 1946 6000 members and "sympathisers" turned up; the overall membership was about 8000: John Callaghan, "The Fabian Society since 1945", in Michael Kandiah and Anthony Seldon (eds), *Ideas and Think Tanks in Contemporary Britain* (1996), pp. 38–9.
24 Ramsden, *Churchill and Eden*, p. 118.
25 J. A. Cross, *Lord Swinton* (1982), p. 262; Hoffman, *Conservative Party in Opposition*, p. 118.
26 C. J. M. Alport, *About Conservative Principles*, p. 23.
27 David Clarke, "The Conservative Faith in a Modern Age", in *Conservatism 1945–1950*, CPC, 1950, p. 7; Harris, *Politics without Prejudice*, p. 183.
28 Friedrich von Hayek, *The Road to Serfdom* (1962 ed.), p. 9, note.
29 Richard Cockett, *Thinking the Unthinkable: Think-Tanks and the Economic Counter-Revolution 1931–1983* (1994), p. 123.
30 Margaret Thatcher, *The Path to Power* (1995), p. 50.
31 Proof copy of *Imperial Affairs* in the possession of the Alport family; F. W. S. Craig, *Conference Decisions 1945–1981*, p. 14.
32 Ramsden, *Churchill and Eden*, p. 159; [C. J. M. Alport], *Imperial Policy* (1949), pp. 1, 5.
33 *Imperial Policy,* pp. 53-4, 46, 45.
34 Kenneth O. Morgan, *Labour in Power 1945-1951* (1984), pp. 224–25.
35 The conference was chaired by Lord Tweedsmuir, with Butler in attendance; unfortunately this seems to have convinced some of the journalists present that *Imperial Policy* was the work not of an individual but of a committee led by Tweedsmuir. In fact, although there had been such a committee, the only people who contributed to the writing of the pamphlet were Cub and Churchill.
36 *Daily Graphic, Daily Worker, News Chronicle*, 25 June 1949.
37 Ramsden, *Churchill and Eden*, pp. 160–61; *The Right Road for Britain*, pp. 5, 7–8. Significantly in a draft of one of Cub's speeches before the election Churchill's words on the need to avoid controversy were quoted – then scored out.
38 Maurice Maybury, *The Truth about the Inter-War Years: An Exposure of the Socialist Myth* (with a Foreword by R. A. Butler), (1949).
39 In fact, Cub was asked to maintain his connection with the CPC in an "honorary" capacity, but there is no eveidence that he took this role very seriously.

40 Cub to parents, 21 January 1947, Alport MSS.
41 Manuscript memoir, p. 48, Alport MSS. The "deselection" of Conservative candidates in the 1945–50 period was not unusual, although it was usually handled with tact; neither Powell nor Heath was the first choice of their respective constituencies.
42 Manuscript memoir, p. 49, Alport MSS; Cub to parents, 21 January 1947.
43 Manuscript memoir, p. 48, Alport MSS. In fact, Somerset de Chair, the former MP for South West Norfolk, was selected for South Paddington and won the seat with a fairly comfortable majority.
44 Ian Gilmour and Mark Garnett, *Whatever Happened to the Tories?* (1997), p. 39.
45 Manuscript memoir, p. 49, Alport MSS.
46 Cub to parents, 29 February 1948; Manuscript memoir, p. 49, Alport MSS.
47 Report on Colchester constituency, Conservative Party Archive, Bodleian Library, CCO/1/7/360.
48 *Essex County Standard*, March 1950.
49 Manuscript memoir, p. 50, Alport MSS.
50 Even so, there was some naughty behaviour; years later Lord Alport was told that some enthusiastic (female) Young Conservatives had changed Labour's "Smith Again" posters to "Smith Never Again". The ringleaders, Mary Fairhead and Joyce Brooks, both became Mayors of Colchester in later years.
51 At least Smith had been spared one humiliation: at the time of the election he was Parliamentary Private Secretary at the Colonial Office, but although Cub presumably was a lot better informed than Smith on colonial matters the subject hardly figured in the Colchester campaign. Years later Smith and Cub became good friends in the House of Lords.
52 It might even be said that he had Labour to thank for his victory, since recent changes in electoral law allowed postal votes for people moving house and this accounted for much of his support from absentee voters.

Chapter 5: "One Nation"

1 Manuscript, "The Red Notebook", Alport MSS.
2 Forty one of the new intake would become ministers, and 24 became Privy Councillors: Ramsden, *Churchill and Eden*, p. 219.
3 *Hansard*, vol. 472, col. 154, 7 March 1950.
4 Apparently Cub overlooked the fact that the same objection could be raised against the employment of European troops in tropical areas.
5 *Hansard*, vol. 472, cols. 1592–8, 1610, 1677, 20 March 1950.
6 *Hansard*, vol. 476, col. 175, 13 June 1950.
7 *Hansard*, vol. 476, cols. 145–51, 8 May 1950.
8 *Hansard*, vol. 483, col. 2145, 9 February 1951.
9 Quoted in Ramsden, *Churchill and Eden*, p. 220. In fact, the Labour Party maintained its record of never losing a by-election throughout its period in office.
10 Ramsden, *Churchill and Eden*, p. 219.
11 "The Red Notebook", p. 2, Alport MSS.
12 As with most aspects of "One Nation's" first months, Cub's story has been contested. Lord Carr, for example, believes that the offending speech was delivered by Osbert Peake, and after a careful sifting of the evidence Robert Shepherd plumped for Walter Elliot on 13 March. However, Cub's memory of the occasion is so vivid that his account must be followed here.

I am indebted to Lord Carr for discussing this matter with me. See also Robert Shepherd, *Iain Macleod* (1994), p. 62, and Edward Heath, *The Course of my Life* (1998), pp. 140–1.

13 "The Red Notebook", p. 2.

14 Other accounts (including his own) place Powell as the last of the nine, but this is an irrelevant detail; once Macleod was in, his old colleague from the Parliamentary Secretariat could not be far behind. See Shepherd, *Enoch Powell*, p. 83, and Enoch Powell "A Strange Choice of Hero", *Independent*, 27 March 1991. In the latter article Powell gave an inaccurate account of the genesis of the *One Nation* pamphlet.

15 Shepherd, *Iain Macleod*, p. 63.

16 Cub to Nigel Fisher, 12 August 1970; Shepherd, *Macleod*, p. 63; unidentified cutting of 25 August 1950, Alport MSS; Macleod to Butler, 9 August 1950, Butler MSS. H38/30–3.

17 C. J. M. Alport, "What the Tories Could Do", unidentified cutting, Alport MSS.

18 "The Red Notebook", pp. 3, 9, Alport MSS.

19 "One Nation" minutes, 23 January 1951, Alport MSS.

20 The plan for this attack was recorded in the "One Nation" minutes of 14 March 1951, Alport MSS.

21 *Hansard,* vol. 486, cols. 1596–1602, 1781–1992, 16 and 17 April 1951; "One Nation" minutes, 23 July 1951, Alport MSS.

22 "The Red Notebook", p. 5, Alport MSS.

23 "One Nation" minutes, 1 March, 28 June, 12 July, 15 November, 1951, Alport MSS. A year earlier Eden had visited a Conservative fête in Colchester Castle grounds; but Cub was still a loyal Rab supporter.

24 *Hansard*, vol. 474, col. 1392, 1 May 1950.

25 Peter Hennessy, *Never Again: Britain 1945–1951* (1992), p. 422.

26 *Essex County Standard*, 5 October 1951. Among the god-parents were Cub's friends Brian Harrison, Charles Fletcher Cooke, and Angus Maude who had asked Cub to stand as godfather to his own son earlier in the year.

27 In 1998 Cub celebrated a different outcome to a game between the same sides; a 1–0 victory for Colchester at Wembley, which secured them promotion to the Second Division.

28 Quoted in Ramsden, *Churchill and Eden*, p. 230.

29 Cub would later observe that Heath "had never contributed much either to the conviviality or the intellectual give and take of our meetings. There seemed to me to be a certain reserve and coldness about him and he was an obvious candidate for the Whips' Office". This was written many years later, when Cub and Heath were estranged, but judging from the group's minutes it seems a pretty accurate assessment; "The Red Notebook", p. 5, Alport MSS.

30 "One Nation" minutes, 7 April 1952, Alport MSS.

31 The success of Macleod's very rude speech shows the difference between baiting a major figure, as he had done, and Cub's mistake in losing his temper in the face of heckling. Macleod himself was attacked from the Labour benches, and the *Hansard* record suggests that he only just kept his nerve.

32 "One Nation" minutes, 24 July, 20 March, 1952, Alport MSS.

33 Gerald Nabarro, *Nab 1: Portrait of a Politician* (1969), pp. 6, 7.

34 C. J. M. Alport, *Hope in Africa* (1952), pp. 3, 7, 166.

35 *Ibid.*, p. 10.

36 Cub to Welensky, 22 October 1952; Welensky to Cub, 28 October 1952, Welenksy Papers.

37 See, for example, *Hansard,* vol. 497, cols. 311–12, 4 March 1952; vol. 499, cols. 1278–79, 29 April 1952; vol. 504, cols. 852–61, 24 July 1952; vol. 516, cols. 1222–35, 18 June 1953.

38 Sir Roy Welensky, *4000 Days* (1964), p. 63.

39 Undated cutting inside Lord Alport's copy of *Hope in Africa* (a review by Derek Marks). A similar criticism was levelled at Cub during the 1950 Conservative conference by Julian Amery, which led to a lasting breach.

40 *Evening Standard*, 9 October 1952. Mixed marriages were very topical at the time; in 1950 the Labour government had removed the Oxford-educated tribal chief, Seretse Khama, from Bechuanaland in response to protests about his marriage to an English woman.

41 *Evening News*, 15 January 1954.

42 The fact that the group had discussed fuel and power in the previous week might have been an attempt to square its own preoccupation with a known interest of Cub's; if so, it was a futile gesture.

43 "One Nation" minutes, 12 February 1953, Alport MSS.

44 "The Red Notebook", p. 7, Alport MSS; "One Nation" minutes, 19, 26 February 1953, Alport MSS.

45 "One Nation" minutes, 14 December 1954.

46 "One Nation" minutes, 9 November 1954, "The Red Notebook", p. 7.

47 Manuscript memoir, p. 11. Eden's visit to Colchester had been made in 1950; a photograph of the event was reproduced in Cub's 1955 election leaflet, without any acknowledgement that it was five years old.

48 "One Nation" minutes, 22 November 1955.

49 If Cub's historical memory had been better he might have been even more reluctant to take the job: Attlee had been Postmaster-General, and never held the post of Assistant.

50 "The Red Notebook", p. 8. At the meeting of 26 January 1956 the group resolved to produce a book on the commonwealth and empire despite the fact that the only interested member had departed.

Chapter 6: Early Postings

1 Manuscript Memoir, p. 8.

2 Cub to parents, 24 December 1955. Surprisingly he missed off his list the haunch of venison sent to ministers at Christmas from the royal estates; this traditional perk arrived within days of Cub's appointment, and fed the family for a fortnight (Manuscript memoir, p. 7).

3 Cub to parents, 24 December 1955. The speech in question is in *Hansard*, vol. 547, cols. 900–6, 12 December 1955.

4 This was the topic of Cub's first speech from the front-bench, in reply to an adjournment debate; *Hansard*, vol. 548, cols. 2763–68, 17 February 1956.

5 Charles Hill, *Both Sides of the Hill* (1964), p. 168. Hill was first elected to the House in 1950; ironically he had contested Kenneth Pickthorn's Cambridge University seat as an Independent candidate in 1945.

6 Manuscript memoir, p. 8.

7 Hill, *Both Sides of the Hill*, p. 168.

8 Manuscript memoir, p. 9.

9 Cub to Hill, 30 January 1956, Post Office archive 122/570.

10 Home Affairs Committee, minutes of meetings on 27 April and 4 May, 1956, PO Archive 122/570.

11 Eden to R. Martin, 18 June 1956, PRO, PREM 11/1537.

12 Howard, *RAB*, p. 221.

13 Hill, *Both Sides of the Hill*, p. 176.

14 *The Times*, 21 and 24 July 1956. The second letter showed Cub that the anonymity of junior rank could bring some benefits; it included a personal attack on Hill, who had been guiltless in the affair.

15 *Daily Telegraph*, 26 February 1953.

16 Julian Amery, "A Conservative View of the Commonwealth", *Political Quarterly*, vol. XXIV, no. 2, April–June 1953, p. 171.

17 *Hansard*, vol. 515, cols. 1123–27, 12 May 1953. Neither Powell nor Maude spoke in this debate. One obituarist has speculated that Cub's views on Suez encouraged Eden to find a way of "silencing" the unruly back-bencher; hence his promotion to Assistant Postmaster-General; see Andrew Roth, *Guardian*, 2 November 1998.

18 *Hansard*, vol. 483, cols. 928–31, 19 January 1951; vol. 501, col. 899, 23 May 1952.

19 Manuscript memoir, pp. 11–12.

20 Howard, *RAB*, p. 232.

21 Draft of speech, Alport MSS.

22 Butler to Cub, 11 January 1957, Alport MSS.

23 *The Economist*, 26 January 1957.

24 *The Commonwealth Relations Office List* (1959), p. 71.

25 The UK government retained the right to veto legislation which discrimi-nated against Africans, but this was never used.

26 Lord Alport, *The Sudden Assignment* (1965), p. 27; Lord Home, *The Way the Wind Blows* (1976), p. 128.

27 Unusually Cub had been chosen to open Prayers for two weeks running; in the previous week he had introduced a Bill to ensure that jobless people and the self-employed received state pensions on reaching retirement age. After being assured that the matter was already under review, Cub with-drew his motion: *Hansard,* vol. 525, cols. 1588–99, 26 March 1954.

28 *Hansard,* vol. 525, cols. 2403–12, 2 April 1954.

29 *Ibid.,* cols. 2472.

30 *Ibid.,* cols. 2413–98.

31 See minutes of cabinet discussion, 24 July 1962, PRO; *Hansard*, vol. 626, cols. 825–30, 7 July 1960.

32 Ironically Robert Carr, an old colleague from the "One Nation" group who failed to "remember the Empire", was for a time Minister of State at this short-lived department.

33 Barbara Castle, *Fighting all the Way* (1993), p. 344.

34 Hugh Thomas, *The Suez Affair* (1967 ed.), pp. 153–54; Morrison Halcrow, *Keith Joseph: A Single Mind* (1989), p. 15.

35 Halcrow, *Keith Joseph*, p. 19. Halcrow also claims that Cub was "a shade on the pompous side, and no great orator. Socialists saw him as a fuddy-duddy old Tory. His right-wing colleagues saw him as a boring liberal". According to Halcrow, Joseph often had to console Cub in the Smoking Room after being battered in debate: "It hadn't gone well, Alport would say. What did you think, Keith? Keith would reply bleakly. Not at all well". No sources are given in Halcrow's book; this imaginative account is among the more suspect of his passages. Cub had no recollection that any conversations of this kind ever took place.

36 I. M. R. Maclennan to Home, 25 May 1957, Alport MSS.

37 For Macmillan's comment, see PRO PREM 11/1925, scribbled on John Hunt's memo of 2 August 1957. Macmillan was responding to official concerns that Cub might resent a ruling that he could not take Rachel with him on the trip; the worries were misplaced, because Cub already appreciated the need to concentrate on business on this tricky visit. Cub's

itinerary had begun with a visit to Malaya, which was celebrating its independence.

38 David Scott, *Ambassador in Black and White: Thirty Years of Changing Africa* (1982), pp. 48–50.
39 Mary Benson, *Tshekedi Khama* (1960), p. 304; PRO DO35/7175.
40 For Maldives visit, see PRO DO35/10136. I am most grateful to Roger Barltrop for his help on this section.
41 Private information.
42 Robert Blake, *A History of Rhodesia* (1977), p. 281.
43 *Hansard*, vol. 578, cols. 866, 820–34, 808–20, 25 November 1957. Callaghan, however, recognised at this time that there was no constructive alternative to Federation, writing in this sense to Hastings Banda in October. Had Cub known of this letter Callaghan would not have enjoyed his debating triumph; see Kenneth O. Morgan, *Callaghan: A Life* (1997), p. 156.
44 *Hansard*, vol. 601, cols. 40–59, 2 March 1959; cols. 525–32, 4 March 1959.
45 *Hansard*, vol. 578, cols. 1251–52, 28 November 1957.
46 Lennox-Boyd to Macmillan, 7 March 1959; Macmillan to Lennox-Boyd, 15 March 1959, PRO PREM 11/3051.
47 Richard Lamb, *The Macmillan Years, 1957–1963: The Emerging Truth* (1995), pp. 234–35.
48 In July 1954 the equally blameless Sir Thomas Dugdale had been forced to resign over the Critchel Down affair.
49 Parts of the manuscript remain in the Alport MSS.
50 Manuscript memoir, p. 16.
51 D. A. J. Williamson, "Alport's Syndrome of Hereditary Nephritis", *The Lancet,* 16 December 1961.

Chapter 7: "Political Suicide"

1 Quoted in Alan Thompson, *The Day Before Yesterday* (1971), p. 180. At least this was a variation on the more familiar theme of Macleod's gambling tendencies.
2 Harold Macmillan, *Pointing the Way, 1959–61* (1972), p. 19.
3 See discussion at Chequers on 11 November 1960 in PRO PREM 11/3080.
4 Macmillan, *Pointing the Way*, pp. 140–43; Welensky, *4000 Days*, p. 167. In his memoirs Macmillan claimed that Shawcross's remarks "were taken somewhat out of context"; this would become a familiar refrain.
5 Lamb, *Macmillan Years*, pp. 242–44.
6 *Ibid.*, p. 244.
7 Lord Kilmuir, *Political Adventure* (1964), p. 315; Kenneth Young, *Sir Alec Douglas-Home* (1970), p. 114.
8 Cub to Home, 16 December 1959, Alport MSS.
9 Lamb, *Macmillan Years,* p. 245.
10 Cub to Home, 16 December 1959.
11 Welensky, *4000 Days*, p. 185; information on the Monckton Commission in letter from Sir David Scott to the author, August 1998. In April, Macleod denied that he intended to release the Kenyan nationalist leader Jomo Kenyatta, telling Macmillan that "There is no comparison between Nyasaland and the seven-year tragedy of Mau Mau". This might have been advanced as a reason for releasing Kenyatta and keeping Banda in detention. See Lamb, *Macmillan Years*, p. 226.
12 *Hansard,* vol. 619, col. 1176, 15 March 1960.
13 Macmillan to Cub, 22 March 1960, Alport MSS.

14 Nabarro, *NAB 1*, p. 7.
15 Macmillan to Cub, 13 May 1960.
16 Cub to Home, 19 July 1960, Alport MSS; Welensky, *4000 Days*, p. 271; Lamb, *Macmillan Years*, p. 252. Even in the face of clear evidence Macleod's friends insisted on praising Banda; Macleod's biographer Nigel Fisher claimed as late as 1973 that he "was a man of complete sincerity": Nigel Fisher, *Iain Macleod* (1973), p. 160.
17 Young, *Sir Alec Douglas-Home*, p. 116; Home, *The Way the Wind Blows*, p. 133.
18 J. R. T. Wood, *The Welensky Papers* (1983); PRO PREM 11/3080. In November Cub did go on one last trip as Minister of State, to Ceylon where he held talks with the Prime Minister, Mrs Bandaranaike.
19 Alport, *Sudden Assignment*, p. 24.
20 *Ibid.*, p. 17.
21 *Ibid.*, pp. 17–18: the passage is a clever subterfuge; he merely states that at the meeting "the proposal was first put forward . . . I did not take the proposal particularly seriously".
22 Minutes of meeting on 20 January 1961, PRO PREM 11/3485. The trend towards recruiting politicians to the diplomatic service continued in the following year, when (among others) Geoffrey de Freitas was appointed High Commissioner in Ghana.
23 *Sudden Assignment,* p. 21.
24 *Ibid.*, p. 26: " . . . a questioner had asked me at a public meeting in Tiptree, no doubt with the friendliest intentions, when I was going to the House of Lords. I had felt affronted and replied huffily to the effect that I hoped my parliamentary career had not been such a failure as that".
25 *Ibid.*, pp. 21–22.
26 *Ibid.*, pp. 22–23; minutes of meeting between Home, Cub and Greenfield, 29 January 1961, PRO PREM 11/3486.
27 It seems that Home made this light-hearted remark at the last cabinet meeting attended by Cub, on 7 February 1960.
28 *House of Lords Debates*, vol. 359, col. 946, 23 April 1975.
29 In the Gallup poll for February the Conservative lead over Labour was down to 1 per cent; four months earlier it had been 10.5 per cent. But Cub's seat was retained in the by-election by Sir Anthony Buck; an old friend and Essex neighbour, Bernard Braine, joined the CRO as an under-secretary. Cub would have preferred Dennis Walters to Buck as his successor in Colchester.
30 See Harold Macmillan, *At the End of the Day* (1973), pp. 314, 320.
31 *Daily Mail, Daily Express, Daily Herald*, 3 February 1960; Wood, *Welensky Papers*, p. 870.
32 *Essex County Standard*, 10 February 1960; *Colchester Gazette*, 7 February 1960. Among the gifts were two paintings of local Essex views, and an illustrated address which Cub described as "splendidly pompous, but that is what one wants one's descendants to read".
33 Lamb, *Macmillan Years*, p. 256.
34 *Sudden Assignment*, p. 21.
35 Lamb, *Macmillan Years*, pp. 257–58.
36 Shepherd, *Iain Macleod*, p. 224; PRO DO 158/63, minutes of CRO meeting 23 February 1961; Alistair Horne, *Macmillan: 1957–1986* (1989), p. 389. Julian Amery, then Minister for Air, later told Welensky that the British troops had been sent on Macleod's orders, and action had only been prevented when he intervened with Macmillan to stop it. Amery knew Welensky's feelings about Macleod and presumably chose his version of

the story to suit his audience. The operation, code-named "Kingfisher", was authorised by Macmillan: see PRO PREM 11/5041.

37   Welensky, *4000 Days*, pp. 304–5.

38   Shepherd, *Iain Macleod*, p. 225.

39   *Sudden Assignment*, p. 29; *Colchester Evening Gazette,* 17 October 1962; Shepherd, *Enoch Powell*, pp. 115–16.

40   *Sudden Assignment,* pp. 30–34. Of course in writing his memoir Cub was handicapped by the Official Secrets Act, but even so this must be regarded as the weakest part of the book, especially since he exploits the story to build an impression that Welensky was apt to make the most of every petty grievance.

41   *Ibid.*, pp. 30–34.

42   Lamb, *Macmillan Years*, p. 232. "The federal leaders under Welensky", Lamb declares, "were dedicated to preserving white supremacy, and there was no question of black and white partnership".

43   The notable exception is the historian J. R. T. Wood, whose massive study, *The Welensky Papers* erred in the opposite direction.

44   Lamb, *Macmillan Years,* p. 248; *Sudden Assignment*, pp. 35–43; Scott, *Ambassador in Black and White*, p. 92.

45   *Sudden Assignment,* pp. 45–6, 43.

46   Cub to Butler, 3 November 1961.

47   *Sudden Assignment,* pp. 59–60; *Central African Post*, 15 March 1961; Scott, *Ambassador in Black and White*, p. 93. Ironically, in describing the relationship he hoped to establish as Minister of Labour with both sides of industry in the late 1950s, Iain Macleod had used the phrase "parity of abuse"; see Macleod's review of Welensky's *4000 Days*, in the *Spectator*, 24 May 1964.

48   The proposed constitutional arrangements were more complicated than these figures suggest, but now that these controversies have been resolved the turgid details are thankfully unnecessary.

49   PRO, PREM 11/ 3492.

50   *Sudden Assignment*, pp. 61–2; Cub to Rab Butler, 14 June 1961, Alport MSS.

51   *Sudden Assignment*, pp 63–6; Rachel Alport's diary, 18 June 1961.

52   Harrison to Cub, 29 June 1961, Alport MSS.

53   Cub to Harrison, 6 July 1961, Alport MSS.

54   Welensky, *4000 Days*, pp. 307–8.

55   Shepherd, *Iain Macleod*, p. 249.

56   Horne, *Macmillan 1957–1986*, p. 397.

57   *Sudden Assignment*, pp. 89–93.

58   *Ibid.*, p. 110.

59   Cub to CRO, telegram of 14 September 1961, PRO PREM 11/3493.

60   Years later, when his daughter Carole bought a parrot it was named after Tshombe – rather a dubious compliment, since the bird was almost impossible to control.

61   *Sudden Assignment*, pp. 116–19.

62   *Ibid.*, pp. 122–32.

63   Brian Urquhart, *Hammarskjold* (1972), pp. 591–92.

64   Rupert Metcalf to Cub, 15 September 1961, PRO DO 158/60; *Sudden Assignment*, p. 152.

65   Cub to Butler, 14 August 1961; Butler to Cub, 14 September 1961, Alport MSS; Howard, *RAB*, pp. 284–85.

66   Shepherd, *Iain Macleod*, pp. 260–61; Brian Harrison to Cub, 17 and 25 October, 1961; Patrick Wall to Cub, 17 November 1961, Alport MSS.

67   Cub to Home, 12 October 1961, Alport MSS.

68 Cub to Butler, 3 October 1961, Alport MSS; *Sudden Assignment*, pp. 162–63.
69 Home to Cub, 4 January 1962; Amery to Cub, no date [early January 1962], Alport MSS.
70 Cub to Amery, 15 January 1962, Alport MSS.
71 Hastings Banda to Cub, 26 January 1962, Alport MSS.
72 Minutes of meeting with governors at Zomba, 10 January 1962, PRO, DO 158/60; Cub to Sandys, 19 January 1962, PRO, PREM 11/3492.
73 Lamb, *Macmillan Years*, p. 270; Howard, *RAB*, pp. 288–89; Tim Bligh to Rab, 19 January 1961; Rab to Bligh, 21 January 1961, PRO, PREM 11/3492.
74 *Sudden Assignment*, p. 164.
75 *Ibid.*, pp. 167–68.
76 *Ibid.*
77 Welensky, *4000 Days*, p. 321; *Sudden Assignment*, pp. 170–71.
78 Welensky, *4000 Days*, p. 327.

Chapter 8: "More Trouble with the Government, Daddy?"

1 Cub to Butler, 11 October 1961, Alport MSS.
2 J. C. Auret to Cub, 26 May 1961, Alport MSS.
3 *Sudden Assignment*, p. 56.
4 *Essex County Gazette*, 12 December 1961.
5 Cub to Deedes, 19 March 1962, Alport MSS.
6 Butler, *Art of the Possible*, p. 210; Howard, *RAB*, pp. 289, 395; Butler, *The Art of Memory* (1982), p. 140.
7 Cub to Sandys, 16 August 1961; note in file dated 19 October 1961; telegram from Macmillan to Welensky 13 March 1962, PRO, DO 158/77; Butler, *Art of Memory*, pp. 139–40.
8 *Sudden Assignment*, p. 175; telegrams of 14 and 15 March, 1962, PRO DO 158/77; *Tribune*, 23 March 1962.
9 Cub to *Essex County Standard*, 23 May 1961; *Daily Express*, 27 March 1962. The sweets were for Carole, who could not find any of her favourite brand in Africa.
10 *Sudden Assignment*, p. 176.
11 Scott, *Ambassador in Black and White*, p. 117; minutes of meetings between Butler, Cub and governors, PRO DO 183/129.
12 *Sudden Assignment*, p. 176.
13 Welensky, *4000 Days*, p. 335: c.f. Record of a discussion with the British High Commissioner held in the office of the Minister of Home Affairs, 13 April 1962, Welensky Papers.
14 The "Samson" idea originally came from Edgar Whitehead; Butler also adopted it in a letter to Macmillan, who spoiled the effect by reminding his colleague that "Samson has quite good cards, if he cares to play them"; Macmillan to Butler, 23 August 1962, PRO, PREM 11/4419.
15 *Sudden Assignment*, pp. 177–79.
16 Butler, *Art of the Possible*, pp. 211–16; Welensky, *4000 Days*, p. 362; Wood, *Welensky Papers*, p. 1045; Cub to Bill Deedes, 15 June 1962, Alport MSS.
17 Lamb, *Macmillan Years*, p. 275.
18 Cub to Butler, 12 June, 18 July, 1962; Butler to Cub, 19, 27 July 1962, Alport MSS.
19 Howard, *RAB*, p. 292.
20 Cub to Butler, 6 August 1962; Butler to Cub, 23 August 1962, Alport MSS; Butler, *Art of the Possible*, pp. 218–20.

21 Cub to Butler, 5 and 7 September 1962, Alport MSS.
22 Butler to Cub, 13 September 1963, Alport MSS.
23 Scott, *Ambassador in Black and White*, pp. 115–16; *Sudden Assignment*, pp. 206–7; Welensky, *4000 Days*, p. 350.
24 Welensky, *4000 Days*, pp. 351–52.
25 *Sudden Assignment*, p. 210; Memorandum by Cub, 9 November 1962, Alport MSS.
26 Butler to Welensky, 1 November 1962, Welensky Papers.
27 Record of meeting between Welensky and Cub held in the federal Assembly at 5.30 p.m, 7 November 1962, Welensky Papers.
28 *Sudden Assignment*, pp. 208–9; Cub to Butler, telegram of 9 November 1962; minutes of meeting at Admiralty House, 9 November 1962, PRO, PREM 11/4419; Cub to Sir John Maude, 12 November 1962, Alport MSS.
29 *Sudden Assignment*, p. 210.
30 *Ibid.*
31 Cub to Sir John Maude, 12 November 1962, Alport MSS; Scott, *Ambassador in Black and White*, p. 122; Cub to Butler, 10 November 1962, Alport MSS.
32 *Sudden Assignment*, p. 212; Butler to Cub, 13 November 1962, Alport MSS.
33 *Sudden Assignment*, p. 218; Welensky to Julian Greenfield, 24 November 1962, Welensky Papers.
34 *Sudden Assignment*, pp. 212–3, 220.
35 Cub continued to sound optimistic, although the High Commission's Southern Rhodesia specialist, Roger Barltrop, had reported on the basis of extensive research that the Rhodesian Front were likely to win.
36 Cub to Butler, 3 October 1962; Butler to Cub, 5 October 1962, Alport MSS. Significantly in Cub's reply of 6 October he suggested a visit to London for talks; perhaps he took Butler's refusal to help as a sign that they differed about the importance of this election, which implied that they had very different ideas about the best course of action over the federal break-up.
37 Cub to Butler, telegram of 14 December 1962, PRO, PREM 11/4418; *Sudden Assignment*, pp. 223, 230.
38 *Sudden Assignment*, p. 221.
39 Wood, *Welensky Papers*, p. 1120; *Sudden Assignment*, p. 224. Whatever his preferences Welensky had at least tried to make the Federation work.
40 *Sudden Assignment*, pp. 218, 232; Trend memorandum, 16 January 1963, PRO, PREM 11/4419.
41 Welensky to Julian Greenfield, 28 November 1962; Welensky to Lord Colyton, 24 December 1962; Lord Colyton to Welensky, 9 January 1963, Welensky Papers; Scott, *Ambassador in Black and White*, p. 122.
42 *Sudden Assignment*, p. 224.
43 *Ibid.*, pp. 224–26; Cub to Butler, 9 January 1963; Home to Cub 18 January 1963, Alport MSS.
44 Welensky to Lord Salisbury, 12 December 1962, 28 January 1963, Welensky Papers, pp. 664–5.
45 Butler, *Art of the Possible*, pp. 224–26; Welensky, *4000 Days*, p. 362.
46 Deedes to Cub, 3 March 1963; Butler to Cub, 15 February 1963; Butler to Cub, 7 May 1963, Alport MSS.
47 Butler to Cub, 21 February 1963; Cub to Butler, 25 February 1963; Butler to Cub, 1 March 1963, Alport MSS; Butler, *Art of the Possible*, p. 136.
48 *Sudden Assignment*, pp. 233–5.
49 *Ibid.*, p. 239.
50 For information on Cub's departure I am most grateful to Sir David Scott.

51 Butler had lost his nerve to the extent that he instructed Cub to tell Field that "there could be no question but that when the Federation is dissolved Southern Rhodesia will become independent. This will happen (legally or not). It is up to Southern Rhodesia to choose" (Rab to Cub, 12[?] May 1963, Alport MSS). Nothing would have been more calculated to prove Welensky's case that the British had simply washed their hands of a situation which they had caused themselves.

52 *Sudden Assignment*, p. 239; telegrams between Cub and Butler, 14, 15 May 1963, PRO, PREM 11/4421; Macmillan, *At the End of the Day,* p. 330.

53 Mysteriously, in his memoirs Butler chose to ascribe Field's capitulation to "pressures within his own territory": Butler, *Art of the Possible*, p. 228.

54 Wood, *Welensky Papers*, p. 1200.

Chapter 9: A Freelance Diplomat

1 Manuscript memoir, p. 52, Alport MSS; *Guardian*, 1 November 1962; Patrick Cosgrave in the *Independent*, 3 November 1998.

2 Manuscript memoir, p. 52; interview with Alan Brown, *Colchester Evening Gazette,* 11 October 1993.

3 Keith Joseph to Cub, 19 October 1961, Alport MSS.

4 *Sudden Assignment*, p. 15; Ian Smith, *The Great Betrayal* (1997), pp. 53–4. Smith's account has been contested, but Butler's correspondence with Cub in the run up to the conference had shown that he regarded independence as a formality, and was prepared to risk saying this.

5 Sandys to Cub, 29 October 1964, Alport MSS.

6 Butler to Cub, 5 and 9 November 1963, Alport MSS.

7 Butler to Sir Saville Garner, 5 November 1963, PRO, DO 183/190. Cub thought that *The Art of the Possible* was generous to both Welensky and himself; Welensky was amazed at how much of the story Butler had left out: Welensky to Cub, 3 August 1971, Alport MSS.

8 See correspondence in PRO, DO 183/190.

9 John Francis, "Doomed from the start", *Tribune*, 23 July 1965; Conor Cruise O'Brien, "Imperial Anachronism", *Observer* "Weekend Review", 20 June 1965.

10 John Connell, "The Breaking of a Loyal Heart", *Yorkshire Post*, 10 June 1965; Sir Saville Garner, memorandum on draft of *The Sudden Assignment*, 9 November 1964, PRO, DO 183/190.

11 Manuscript memoir, p. 53–4. I am very grateful to Charles Wilson for help on these matters.

12 Manuscript memoir, p. 55.

13 Cub to Carrington, 7 April 1965; Carrington to Cub, 14 April 1965, Alport MSS.

14 *House of Lords Debates*, vol. 254, cols 160–67, 17 December 1963.

15 *Colchester Evening Gazette,* 11 October 1993; Lord Alport, memorandum on events of January 1966, Alport MSS.

16 Memorandum, Alport MSS; record of meeting between Michael Stewart and Duncan Sandys, 21 January 1966, PRO PREM 11/1115.

17 Record of meeting between Wilson and Beadle, 19 January 1966; record of meeting between Michael Stewart and Duncan Sandys, 21 January 1966; record of meeting between Michael Stewart and Cub, 21 January 1966, PRO PREM 11/1115. Beadle later abandoned Gibbs and threw in his lot with Ian Smith.

18 Lord Alport, memorandum of 22 March 1966, Alport MSS.

19 Ben Pimlott, *Harold Wilson* (1992), pp. 450–52.

20 *House of Lords Debates*, vol. 277, Cols 1006–9, 10 November 1966; see PRO, PREM 13/1753.
21 Lord Alport, fragment of a diary, 18 April 1967, Alport MSS.
22 *Ibid.*, 20 April 1967.
23 *Ibid.,* 25 April 1967.
24 *Ibid.*, 28 and 30 April 1967; private information.
25 Cabinet minutes, 13 June 1967; Barbara Castle, *The Castle Diaries 1964–70* (1974), p. 266.
26 Lord Alport, note of a meeting with Hastings Banda on 13 June 1967, Alport MSS.
27 *Hansard*, vol. 748, cols. 305–9, 13 June 1967; *House of Lords Debates*, vol. 283, col. 1390, 21 June 1967; Cub to Wilson, 13 June 1967, PRO, PREM 13/1739.
28 *Sudden Assignment*, p. 230; *Daily Express*, 19 June 1967.
29 D. R. Thorpe, *Selwyn Lloyd* (1989), p. 400.
30 J. D. Hennings, telegram to Commonwealth Office, 14 June 1967; N. E. S. Simon to Cub, 23 June 1967; L. M. Lagis to Cub, 27 June 1967; H. Jessop to Cub, 28 June 1967, Alport MSS.
31 *Rhodesia Herald*, 28 June 1967; telegram to Commonwealth Office, 27 June 1967; "Lord Alport's personal notes for his report to the Prime Minister", Alport MSS.
32 Thorpe, *Selwyn Lloyd*, p. 401; "Lord Alport's report to the Prime Minister", Alport MSS.
33 John Bulloch, *Daily Telegraph*, 30 June 1967; *Rhodesia Herald*, 29 June 1967; J. D. Henning to CRO, 2 July 1967, PRO, PREM 13/1739.
34 Lord Alport's record of meetings with Wilson and Bowden, 17, 24 and 25 July, Alport MSS; Harold Wilson, *The Labour Government 1964–70* (1974 ed.) p. 542; cabinet minutes, 24 July 1967; *Castle Diaries*, p. 283; J. D. Hennings to Cub, 17 August 1967, Alport MSS.
35 Lord Alport's record of meetings with Wilson and Bowden, 17, 24 and 25 July, Alport MSS; Manuscript memoir, p. 36.
36 *Sunday Express*, 16 July 1967; Cub to Heath, 4 April 1967, Alport MSS.
37 *The Citizen*, 30 June 1967.
38 Pimlott, *Harold Wilson*, p. 450; Clive Ponting, *Breach of Promise: Labour in Power, 1964–70* (1989), p. 248.
39 *House of Lords Debates*, vol. 288, cols. 580–87, 25 January 1968; *The Times,* Editorial, 29 January 1968; anonymous letter of 16 June 1968; transcript of "The World and Rhodesia" programme, BBC Radio, 8 December 1967; Lord Alport, note of a meeting with Lord Shackleton, 7 October 1968, Alport MSS.
40 W. Knox (Rhodesian official) to Cub, 14 July 1970, Alport MSS; *Rhodesia Herald*, 10 October 1970; *Property & Finance*, October 1970; *Daily Telegraph*, 14 November 1970.
41 *House of Lords Debates*, vol. 265, cols. 719–27, 29 April 1965.
42 See PRO, PREM 13/1685. Cub wrote to Longford on 9 June 1966; on 15 June the House of Lords debated the idea of allowing in television cameras on a motion introduced by Lord Egremont. See also Cub to Lord Perth, 11 February 1972, Alport MSS.
43 Cub to Longford, 29 April 1965; Wayland Kennett to Longford, 14 June 1966; Longford to Wilson, 29 March 1967, PRO, PREM 13/1685; manuscript of article, "A New House of Lords", Alport MSS.
44 *House of Lords Debates*, vol. 275, cols. 854–60, 862, 872, 4 July 1966; Salisbury to Cub, 15 April 1965.
45 *The Times*, 4 July 1966; Ponting, *Breach of Promise*, p. 344; Janet Morgan, *The House of Lords and the Labour Government 1964–1970* (1975).

46 One of Cub's fellow-dissidents on this occasion was Lord Boothby, who responded to his speech with a note of warm appreciation; Boothy to Cub, 18 June 1968; c.f. Robert Rhodes James, *Bob Boothby* (1991), p. 443.
47 Morgan, *House of Lords and the Labour Government*, pp. 200–1.
48 Ponting, *Breach of Promise*, p. 347; Richard Crossman, *The Diary of a Cabinet Minister*, vol. III (1977), pp. 264, 440.
49 Lord Alport, fragment of a diary, 20 April 1967; Cub to Max Beloff, 9 January 1968, Alport MSS.
50 *House of Lords Debates*, vol. 286, col. 1002, 21 November 1967.
51 *House of Lords Debates*, vol. 286, cols. 998–1002, 21 November 1967.
52 *Ibid.,* col. 1001.
53 A slightly different and more recent example is the sudden enthusiasm for "Tiger Economies" evinced by Chris Patten while he was Governor of Hong Kong. The syndrome can also affect moral judgements; in 1903 the Viceroy of India, Lord Curzon, wrote on hearing of a scandal in high society "Good God, what is society coming to, rotten to the core". Yet Curzon himself had been somewhat dissipated while in England; his biographer attributes his "newly acquired disapproval" to his marriage, but to this can be added his distance from all the fun: David Gilmour, *Curzon* (1995 ed.), p. 224.
54 Cub to Butler, 24 April 1969, Alport MSS; Cub in *The Times*, 8 January 1968; Maudling to Cub, 24 March 1968; Cecil King, *Diary 1965–1970* (1972), pp. 192, 266.
55 Cecil King, *Diary*, p. 267.

Chapter 10: Gains and Losses

1 Cub to Heath, Carr, Thatcher, Butler and Powell, 23 June 1970; Powell to Cub, 11 July 1970, Alport MSS.
2 Manuscript memoir, p. 44; Hailsham to Cub, 1 March 1971; minutes of a meeting on House of Lords reform, 3 March 1971; Cub to Lord Perth, 11 February 1971, Alport MSS.
3 *House of Lords Debates*, vol. 326, cols. 396–403, 1 December 1972; vol. 334, cols. 687–93, 697, 4 August 1972; Thorpe, *Alec Douglas-Home*, p. 420–28.
4 *House of Lords Debates*, vol. 339, cols. 934–39, 5 March 1974.
5 Cub to Julian Ridsdale, 25 September 1973; Cub to Victor Rothschild, 19 November 1973, Alport MSS; see Rothschild's resignation letter reprinted in his *Meditations of a Broomstick* (1977), pp. 121–23.
6 Cub to Lord Coleraine, 7 February 1974, Alport MSS.
7 *The Times*, 4 March 1974.
8 Cub to Heath, 5 March 1974, Alport MSS.
9 Edward du Cann to Cub, 8 March 1974; Lord Coleraine to Cub, 15 Feburary 1974, Alport MSS.
10 Heath to Cub, 11 March 1974, Alport MSS; John Campbell, *Edward Heath* (1993), p. 637; Gilmour and Garnett, *Whatever Happened to the Tories?*, p. 294.
11 Correspondence between Cub and Keith Joseph, 23 and 24 April, 12 and 14 June, 5 August 1974, Alport MSS.
12 Lord Alport, "Draft manifesto for a National Government", *The Spectator*, 14 September 1974.
13 Wood to Cub, 8 November 1974; Cub to Wood, 6 December 1974, Alport MSS.
14 "Quiet Man in Race for Tory Leadership", *Sun*, 16 December 1974; Home to Cub, 24 December 1964, Alport MSS.

15 Cub to Heath, 12 October 1972, Alport MSS.
16 Thatcher, *The Path to Power*, pp. 261–81; *The Times*, 28 January 1975.
17 Charles Townsend, *Making the Peace: Public Order and Public Security in Modern Britain* (1993), p. 180.
18 Tony Benn, *Against the Tide: Diaries 1973–76* (1990 ed.), pp. 273–4; Cub to Wood, 6 December 1974, Alport MSS.
19 Manuscript memoir, pp. 57–8.
20 Jenkins to Cub, 1 April 1975; Cub to Jenkins, 4 April 1976, Alport MSS.
21 Letters from Cub to *The Times*, 14 June, 26 July, 1976; Thorpe to Cub, 6 June 1975, Alport MSS.
22 Cub to Margaret Thatcher, 2 and 13 May 1975; Margaret Thatcher to Cub, 5 May 1975; Cub to Anthony Wigram, 9 October 1975; Cub to Thorneycroft, 7 July 1977, Alport MSS.
23 Undated cutting (November 1965?) from *Rhodesia Herald*, with abusive message, Alport MSS.
24 Rachel's diary of 1977 African tour, Alport MSS; *Bulawayo Chronicle*, 17 November 1977.
25 Rachel's diary of 1977 tour; Cub to David Owen, 27 March 1979, Alport MSS; Ian Gilmour, *Dancing with Dogma* (1992), pp. 227–32. Given the problems that he and Welensky experienced over Katanga, Cub was amused in 1998 that Mugabe had interfered in the affairs of the Congo without arousing much international interest.
26 Cub to James Prior, 27 February 1980, 5 August 1981, Alport MSS; *House of Lords Debates*, vol. 426, cols. 1349–54; Cub to Heath, 3 July 1981; Heath to Cub, 20 July 1981, Alport MSS.
27 Howard, *RAB*, p. 362; Lord Alport, "The Memoir of a Friendship", *Pembroke College Annual Gazette*, No. 56, September 1982, pp. 6–10; Cub to Patricia Llewelyn-Davies, 19 February [1984], in the possession of the Alport family.
28 Crossman, *Diaries of a Cabinet Minister*, Vol. I (1975), p. 496; Scott, *Ambassador in Black and White*, p. 5.
29 *House of Lords Debates*, vol. 334, col. 723, 4 August 1972; note from Cub to Patricia, 8 November 1973, in the possession of the Alport family.
30 Undated note from Patricia to Cub, in the possession of the Alport family.
31 Lord Stanley of Alderley to Cub, 22 August 1984, Alport MSS.
32 *Hansard*, vol. 162, cols. 868–74, 30 November 1989. I am grateful to Roger Gale MP, for his help on this subject.
33 Manuscript memoir, p. 35; *House of Lords Debates*, vol. 457, cols. 234–41, 13 November 1984.
34 *House of Lords Debates*, vol. 457, cols. 266–68, 13 November 1984.
35 Lord Denham to Cub, 13 December 1984, Alport MSS; *House of Lords Debates*, vol. 458, cols. 300–2, 12 December 1984.
36 Ironically, Cub had made precisely this point in his reply to a circular letter sent by Denham in June 1981, which bemoaned the number of government defeats in the Lords and requested that "In view of the importance to the country of the government's strategy" Conservative peers should attend and vote more frequently.
37 Memorandum by Lord Alport on events of November 1984, Alport MSS; Cub to Lord Denham, 14 December 1984; Denham to Cub, 13 December 1984. I am most grateful to Lord Denham for his clarification of these events.
38 Cub had conceived a strong animosity towards Boyd-Carpenter, who had mutilated his Constitutional Referendum Bill of 1980. The letters which passed between them at that time (currently in the possession of the

author) would form the basis of an intetresting case-study of law-making in the House of Lords.

39 Letters from Hugh Dykes, Tim Yeo and Cyril Townsend to Cub, 19 December 1984, Alport MSS; Ian Gilmour to Cub, 30 December 1974, Alport MSS; Hugo Young in the *Guardian*, no date.

40 *Colchester Evening Gazette*, 17 April 1985; undated letter from Cub to Patricia, in the possession of the Alport family; letter from Lord Renton to author, 22 September 1998. Cub was very glad to hear about this tribute from an old friend a short time before his death.

41 Welensky to Cub, 21 August 1985, Alport MSS; Manuscript memoir, p. 37. When the present writer wrote to Lady Thatcher asking if she had any memories of Cub, she replied with a warm tribute.

42 *House of Lords Debates*, vol. 552, cols. 1053–55; vol. 572, col. 976; vol. 580, cols. 233–34; letter to *The Times*, 14 November 1995.

43 Letter to *The Times*, 19 October 1991; *The Times,* Editorial, 28 October 1991.

44 Through her close and lasting friendship with the Rothschilds Pat secured a minor walk-on part in British spy scandals; mention of this subject was one of the few things that could rouse Cub to indignation in his final months. See Peter Wright, *Spycatcher* (1987), p. 215. *Colchester Express*, 5 March 1995.

45 *Colchester Express*, 5 March 1992; *Evening Gazette*, 3 December 1992.

46 Interview with Lord Harris of High Cross, April 1998.

47 The extent to which the secret had leaked is difficult to gauge; certainly Lord Denham, who attended the service, had no idea of what had been going on for fourteen years (correspondence with the author, August 1998).

Bibliography

Primary Sources

Alport MSS, Arthur Sloman Library, University of Essex.
Butler MSS, Trinity College Library, Cambridge.
Conservative Party Archives (CPA), Bodleian Library, Oxford.
de Frietas Papers, Bodleian Library, Oxford.
Government Papers, Public Record Office (PRO), Kew.
Post Office Archive, Mount Pleasant, London.
Royle, John, unpublished diary of a visit to the United States, 1935–36.
Wall Papers, Hull University Library.
Welensky Papers, Rhodes House Library, Oxford.

Newspapers and Magazines
Colchester Evening Gazette, Essex County Standard, The Granta, The Guardian,
Property & Finance, Rhodesia Herald, The Spectator, The Sunday Express, The
Tonbridgian, Tribune

Secondary Sources

Alport, A. Cecil, *One Hour of Justice* (London: Dorothy Crisp & Co, no
   date)[1947].

Alport, A. Cecil, *The House of Curious* (London: Hutchinson, no date) [1938].
Alport, A. Cecil, *The Lighter Side of the War* (London: Hutchinson, no date) [1935].
"A Modern Conservative" [Alport, C. J. M.], *A National Faith* (London: Faber & Faber, 1938).
[Alport, C. J. M.], *The Imperial Charter* (London: Conservative Party, 1949).
Alport, C. J. M., *Hope in Africa* (London: Herbert Jenkins, 1952).
Alport, C. J. M., *Kingdoms in Partnership* (London: Lovat Dickson, 1937).
Alport, C. J. M., *The Sudden Assignment* (London: Hodder and Stoughton, 1965).
Alport, C. J. M., "The Tories and Rhodesia", *The Round Table*, July 1971, pp. 391–400.
Amery, Julian, "A Conservative View of the Commonwealth", in *Political Quarterly*, Vol. 24, No.2 (1953), pp. 167–180.
Benn, Tony, *Office without Power: Diaries 1968–72* (London: Hutchinson, 1989)
Birkenhead, Lord, *Walter Monckton: The Life of Viscount Monckton of Brenchley* (London: Weidenfeld & Nicolson, 1969).
Blake, Robert, *A History of Rhodesia* (London: Eyre Methuen, 1977).
Burke, Edmund, *Reflections on the Revolution in France* (Harmondsworth: Penguin, 1968).
Burridge, Trevor, *Attlee* (London: Jonathan Cape, 1985).
Butler, R. A., *The Art of Memory: Friends in Perspective* (London: Hamish Hamilton, 1982).
Butler, R. A., *The Art of the Possible: the Memoirs of the Late Lord Butler*, (London: Hamish Hamilton, 1982).
Calder, Angus, *The People's War: Britain 1939–1945* (London: Jonathan Cape, 1969).
Callaghan, John, "The Fabian Society since 1945", in Michael Kandiah and Anthony Seldon (eds), *Ideas and Think Tanks in Contemporary Britain*, Volume 2 (London: Frank Cass, 1996).
Campbell, John, *Edward Heath* (London: Jonathan Cape, 1993).
Castle, Barbara, *The Castle Diaries, 1964–1970* (London: Weidenfeld and Nicholson, 1984).
Castle, Barbara, *Fighting all the Way* (London: Macmillan, 1993).
Clarke, David, "The Conservative Faith in a Modern Age", in *Conservatism 1945–1950* (London: CPC, 1950).
Cockett, Richard, *Thinking the Unthinkable: Think Tanks and the Economic Counter-Revolution, 1931–1983* (London: HarperCollins, 1994).
Conservative Party, *Annual Conference Reports, 1957–1960.*
Conservative Party, *The Industrial Charter: A Statement of Conservative Industrial Policy*, (1947).
Cosgrave, Patrick, *R. A. Butler: An English Life* (London: Quartet, 1981).
Cradock, Percy (ed), *Recollections of the Cambridge Union, 1815–1939* (Cambridge: Bowes & Bowes, 1953).
Critchley, Julian, "The Intellectuals", in *Political Quarterly*, Vol. 32 (1961).
Cross, J. A., *Lord Swinton* (Oxford: Oxford University Press, 1982).
Crossman, Richard, *The Diaries of a Cabinet Minister, Volume One: Minister of Housing 1964–66* (London: Hamish Hamilton and Jonathan Cape, 1975).
Crossman, Richard, *The Diaries of a Cabinet Minister, Volume Three: Secretary of State for Social Services 1968–70* (London: Hamish Hamilton and Jonathan Cape, 1977).
Edwards, H. W. J., *Young England* (London: Hutchinson, no date) [1938].
Fisher, Nigel, *Iain Macleod* (London: Andre Deutsch, 1973).
Gilmour, David, *Curzon* (London: Papermac edition, 1995).

Gilmour, Ian, *Dancing with Dogma* (London: Simon & Schuster, 1992).

Gilmour, Ian, and Garnett, Mark, *Whatever Happened to the Tories?* (London: Fourth Estate, 1997).

Halcrow, Morrison, *Keith Joseph: A Single Mind* (London: Macmillan, 1989).

Harris, Ralph, *Politics without Prejudice* (London: Staples Press, 1956).

Heath, Edward, *Travels: People and Places in My Life* (London: Sidgwick & Jackson, 1977).

Heath, Edward, *The Course of my Life: My Autobiography* (London: Hodder & Stoughton, 1998).

Hennessy, Peter, *Never Again: Britain 1945–1951* (London: Jonathan Cape, 1992).

Hill, Charles, *Both Sides of the Hill* (London: Heinemann, 1964).

Hoffman, J. D., *The Conservative Party in Opposition 1945–51* (London: MacGibbon & Kee, 1964).

Hogg, Quintin, *The Case for Conservatism* (London: Penguin, 1947).

Home, Lord, *The Way the Wind Blows* (London: Collins, 1976).

Howard, Anthony, *RAB: The Life of R. A. Butler* (London: Jonathan Cape, 1987).

Kilmour, Earl of, *Political Adventure* (London: Weidenfeld and Nicolson, 1964).

King, Cecil, *The Cecil King Diary, 1965–70* (London: Jonathan Cape, 1972).

Lamb, Richard, *The Macmillan Years 1957–1963: The Emerging Truth* (London: John Murray, 1995).

Macmillan, Harold, *Memoirs, Vol. IV: Riding the Storm, 1956–1959* (London: Macmillan, 1971).

Macmillan, Harold, *Memoirs, Vol. V: Pointing the Way, 1959–1961* (London: Macmillan, 1972).

Macmillan, Harold, *Memoirs, Vol. VI: At the End of the Day, 1961–1963* (London: Macmillan, 1973).

Megahey, Alan, *Humphrey Gibbs: Beleagured Governor* (London: Macmillan, 1998).

Morgan, Janet, *The House of Lords and the Labour Government 1964–1970* (Oxford: Clarendon Press, 1975).

Morgan, Kenneth O., *Callaghan: A Life* (Oxford: Oxford University Press, 1997).

Nabarro, Gerald, *NAB 1: Portrait of a Politician* (London: Robert Maxwell, 1969).

Pimlott, Ben, *Harold Wilson* (London: HarperCollins, 1992).

Ponting, Clive, *Breach of Promise: Labour in Power 1964–1970* (London: Hamish Hamilton, 1989).

Ramsden, John, *The Making of Conservative Party Policy: the Conservative Research Department since 1929* (Harlow: Longman, 1980).

Ramsden, John, *The Age of Churchill and Eden* (Harlow: Longman, 1995).

Rhodes James, Robert, *Anthony Eden* (London: Weidenfeld and Nicolson, 1986).

Rhodes James, Robert, *Bob Boothby* (London: Headline edition, 1992).

Roth, Andrew, *Heath and the Heathmen* (London: Routledge & Kegan Paul, 1967).

Rothschild, Lord, *Meditations of a Broomstick* (London: Collins, 1977).

Scott, David, *Ambassador in Black and White: Thirty Years of Changing Africa* (London: Weidenfeld and Nicolson, 1981).

Shepherd, Robert, *Enoch Powell* (London: Hutchinson, 1996).

Shepherd, Robert, *Iain Macleod: A Biography* (London: Pimlico edition, 1995).

Skidelsky, Robert, *John Maynard Keynes: Volume Two, The Economist as Saviour, 1920–1937* (London: Macmillan, 1992).

Smith, Ian, *The Great Betrayal* (London: Blake Publishing, 1997).

Thatcher, Margaret, *The Path to Power* (London: HarperCollins, 1995).

Thompson, Alan, *The Day Before Yesterday* (London: Sidgwick & Jackson, 1971).

Thorpe, D. R., *Selwyn Lloyd* (London: Jonathan Cape, 1989).

Thorpe, D. R., *Alec Douglas-Home* (London: Sinclair-Stevenson, 1996).

Townshend, Charles, *Making the Peace: Public Order and Public Security in Modern*

Britain (Oxford: Oxford University Press, 1993).

Urquhart, Brian, *Hammarskjold* (London: Bodley Head, 1973).

Welensky, Roy, *Welensky's 4000 Days: The Life and Death of the Federation of Rhodesia and Nyasaland* (London: Collins, 1964).

Wilson, Harold, *The Labour Government 1964–70* (London: Pelican edition, 1974).

Wood, J. R. T., *The Welensky Papers* (Durban: Graham Publishing, 1983).

Woolton, Lord, *Memoirs* (London: Cassell, 1959).

Wright, Peter (with Paul Greengrass), *Spycatcher* (Richmond, Australia: Heinemann, 1987).

Young, Kenneth, *Sir Alec Douglas-Home* (London: Dent & Sons, 1970).

Index

293